The Mexican American

The Mexican American

Advisory Editor
Carlos E. Cortés

Editorial Board
Rodolfo Acuña
Juan Gómez-Quiñones
George Fred Rivera, Jr.

THE NEW MEXICAN HISPANO

ARNO PRESS
A New York Times Company
New York — 1974

Reprint Edition 1974 by Arno Press Inc.

We Fed Them Cactus is Copyright, 1954, by
  The University of New Mexico Press
We Fed Them Cactus is reprinted by permission of
  The University of New Mexico Press

Shadows of the Past was reprinted from a copy in
  The Albuquerque Public Library
Culture of a Contemporary Rural Community:
  El Cerrito and A Camera Report on El Cerrito
  were reprinted from copies in The University
  of Illinois Library

THE MEXICAN AMERICAN
ISBN for complete set: 0-405-05670-2
See last pages of this volume for titles.

Manufactured in the United States of America

Library of Congress Cataloging in Publication Data
Main entry under title:

The New Mexican Hispano.

  (The Mexican American)
  Reprint of Shadows of the past, by C. M. Jaramillo,
first published 1941 by Seton Village Press, Santa Fe;
of Culture of a contemporary rural community: El
Cerrito, New Mexico, by O. Leonard and G. P. Loomis,
first published 1941 in Washington, which was issued
as Rural life studies, 1 of the U. S. Bureau of
Agricultural Economics; of A camera report on El Cerrito,
by I. Rusinow, first published 1942, by U. S. Govt.
Print. Off., Washington, which was issued as no. 479
of Miscellaneous publications, U. S. Dept. of
Agriculture; and of We fed them cactus, by F. Cabeza
de Baca, first published 1954 by University of New
Mexico Press, Albuquerque.
  1. Mexican Americans—New Mexico. 2. New Mexico—
Social life and customs. 3. El Cerrito, N. M.
I. Series.
F805.M5N48   917.89'06'68   73-14210
ISBN 0-405-05684-2

CONTENTS

Cleofas M. Jaramillo
SHADOWS OF THE PAST. Santa Fe, 1941

Olen Leonard and G. P. Loomis
CULTURE OF A CONTEMPORARY RURAL
COMMUNITY: EL CERRITO, NEW MEXICO. (U. S.
Department of Agriculture, Bureau of Agricultural Economics,
Rural Life Studies: 1). Washington, D. C., 1941

Irving Rusinow
A CAMERA REPORT ON EL CERRITO: A Typical Spanish-
American Community in New Mexico. (U. S. Department of
Agriculture, Bureau of Agricultural Economics, Miscellaneous
Publications No. 479). Washington, D. C., 1942

Fabiola Cabeza de Baca
WE FED THEM CACTUS. Albuquerque, N. M., 1954

INTRODUCTION

Northern New Mexico has been the scene of a tenacious battle by Mexican Americans for cultural survival. With an intensity which reflects nearly four centuries of attachment to their land, these Hispanos (Spanish Americans, as they call themselves) have struggled with fierce pride to preserve their heritage and way of life. In nostalgic, analytical, and photographic terms, the selections in this anthology—*The New Mexican Hispano*—shed light on this unique region of Chicano society.

Nostalgia is provided by Cleofas M. Jaramillo's *Shadows of the Past* and Fabiola Cabeza de Baca's *We Fed Them Cactus*. Both authors are descendants of old Hispano elite ranching families. Both base their books on extensive interviews and sensitive personal observation. Both create verbal symphonies to the Hispano way of life—customs, traditions, songs, poetry, fiestas, food, artifacts, sports, and religious observances. Both suffuse their books with a deep love for the state's Hispano heritage and a deep sadness for the changes which time has wrought.

In contrast to the admitted romanticism of these two books stands *Culture of a Contemporary Rural Community* by Olen Leonard and G. P. Loomis. Prepared for the U.S. Department of Agriculture, this socio-economic analysis presents a detached, less empathetic view of Hispano life. Lacking the sensitivity of the two Hispano works, this somewhat ethnocentric study nonetheless reveals many of the problems faced by El Cerrito, a typical Hispano community battling for survival in a modernizing society.

Still a third perspective is found in Irving Rusinow's *A Camera Report on El Cerrito*. In this companion work to the Leonard-Loomis book, Rusinow presents a lengthy, affecting photographic essay on this small Hispano community. Taken together, the four books reveal both the special nature of the Hispano way of life and the cultural tragedy which technological change and the coming of the Anglo flood have brought to traditional Hispano society.

Dr. Carlos E. Cortes
University of California,
Riverside

SHADOWS OF THE PAST

New Mexico Penitentes

SHADOWS OF THE PAST

(SOMBRAS DEL PASADO)

by
Cleofas M. Jaramillo

*Illustrated
by the Author*

Ancient City Press

P.O. BOX 5401 SANTA FE, NEW MEXICO 87501

To the memory of my beloved daughter Angelina, whose interest in the old Spanish folklore encouraged me to attempt writing this book.

Printed in the United States of America
June, 1972

Contents

I.	Shadows Over Arroyo Hondo	11
II.	Spanish Pioneers	13
III.	Romance on the Chihuahua Trail	16
IV.	El Carroferril (The Iron Horse)	19
V.	Honeymoon Among Bandits	21
VI.	Memorias	24
VII.	Wedding, Baptism & Other Ceremonies	31
VIII.	Harvest Moons	37
IX.	The Indian Feast of San Geronimo	43
X.	La Funcion (Feast Day)	48
XI.	Games and Sports	54
XII.	Santos	60
XIII.	The Penitente Brotherhood	63
XIV.	Holy Week at Arroyo Hondo	67
XV.	Wakes	75
XVI.	Noche Buena and Religious Dramas	77
XVII.	Saints' Holy Days	85
XVIII.	La Villa Real, Its Beggars and Interesting Places	88
XIX.	Old Customs Vanish	96
XX.	A Bit of New Mexico Folklore	98

Introduction

As a descendant of the Spanish pioneers, 1 have watched with regret the passing of the old Spanish customs and the rapid adoption of the modern Anglo customs by the new generation.

In my desire to preserve some of the folklore of New Mexico, and in the interest of the rising generation—so few of whom now read the Spanish language—I started some years ago to write this book in English, although because of my Spanish descent my English is rather limited, for which I crave indulgence from those who could have done better.

With the same desire, five years ago I organized a Spanish Folklore Society, in hope that it will carry on the work of preserving the Spanish language and customs after I am gone. On account of familiarity with the old customs, we had not awakened to the fact that they were worth preserving, until in recent years, and have turned our effort to revive them.

My pioneer forefathers, searching through rugged mountains and hills, over almost impassable trails, found the beautiful hidden little valley of the Rio Hondo, in the northern part of New Mexico. In this isolated nook, rich in verdure and scenery, my ancestors built strongwalled houses, fought the Indians and shed their blood to protect their families, and here they left a most interesting folklore, the history of which fills the pages of this book, dating back to my grandmother's time, as far as I can remember.

For some of the Spanish names and phrases I have not found an equivalent. Also in the translation of songs and verses, the simple meaning is given without any attempt at rhyme, which would change the meaning.

For the drawing on the cover I am indebted to my friend, Miss Roberta Martin.

CLEOFAS M. JARAMILLO

I. SHADOWS OVER ARROYO HONDO

> "My heart is in the village,
> In dwellings of the past;
> Sweet memories are enshrined,
> In ruins that still last."

The valley of Arroyo Hondo is a fertile, green refuge hidden in the flat sameness of the gray and yellow plain stretching a hundred miles or more westward and southward from New Mexico's Taos Mountains.

The unique formation of the valley is difficult to describe. It's a bowl scooped out between two canyons, bounded on the north and south by a double ridge of high hills. The basin wider in the center narrows gradually towards the east and west ends, where the canyon gates close it.

Through the rocky gateway of the canyon on the east the Rio Hondo emerges clear as crystal bubbling over its rocky bed. Its source is high up in the mountains—so high that by means of open troughs laid up the sides of the ridges some of its water is conveyed over two hundred feet up to the green patches tucked in the folds of the Atalaya hills.

A two mile ride down the stream, which courses through the center of the basin, brings one to the stupendous gate, where the Rio Hondo empties into the Rio Grande. Here with a dashing noise the Hondo mingles its crystal waters with the musky, green depths of the Rio Grande.

In the deep chasm of shimmering water, now green, now blue, is reflected the figures of fishermen swishing their silken cords into the calm waters of the Rio Grande, and then into the clear rocky pools of the Rio Hondo, which sends irresistible siren calls to passing fishermen.

The road crosses the Hondo river, continues to the toll bridge across the Rio Grande and ascends one of the most spectacular steep roads in America, winding amid pillars of dark rock that rise in places like giant sentinels, in other places laid in layers overhung with wild bushes. It reaches the top where a magnificent panorama spreads out over a vast expanse of about a hundred miles. To the east is the high pyramided Taos range, changing its colors of blue, green, gold and purple with every mood. It might well be taken for a section of the Alps. To the west the immense, sage-covered plain merges with the horizon, and the gigantic, black serpentine canyon twists its way through the center, catching the waters from all the tributaries on its long march to the south.

Here lies the spell that urges one to search through purple mountains, tumbling streams, and rolling plains—on and on, over country trails of New Mexico.

Back at the fertile little valley of the Arroyo Hondo, emerald meadows, green fields, crystal streams and sleepy adobe villages lie under scorching suns and brooding shadows—shadows of the past. For through the old mingles the new. Still the memory of former times seems almost as strong as the reality of the present. In the place of a modern automobile speeding by on new highways, one can almost see the caravans of covered wagons toiling slowly down the rocky hills, bringing silks and other luxuries imported from the old world to Mexico's markets.

Shrouding the peace of the hidden valley is the memory of landmarks and battles fought during the days when bandit bands and hostile Indian tribes terrorized the land, and hovering over the simple beauty of the villages is mystery, for who knows but that the spirits of the old witches still creep into the bodies of black cats, when the moon is full? Religious feasts vividly recall old holy days, when the Flagellants, members of the *penitentes* brotherhood, wound in masked, bloody procession from the church to the hills above, the sound of their whips cutting streams of blood in their bare flesh, and the weird flute, sending chills down the spine of those who heard and watched them.

Present feast days also bring back brighter memories of days when the people, dressed in their best clothes, carried statues of the saints about the towns, and were not too proud to kneel on the ground in prayerful supplications.

The music of the fiddle and guitar accompanying the folk dances which closed the feasts, and the laughter of children playing in sunny *patios,* still half fills the air. The joy of past Springs revives in the farmer as he plants his seed (still by hand, in the old way), and the peace and beauty of bygone, busy harvests come with the first touch of autumn's ripening, coloring brush.

The main village, still little touched by modern styles, nestles against the north ridge, its sun baked adobe houses forming a double square almost indistinguishable from the ground. The upper village was formerly the main town. The ancient church with its massive walls stood in venerable dignity in the center of the square. Its cemetery in front was full of wooden crosses marking grave mounds, which left open only a narrow path to the church door. At each end of the valley stood the other two villages. The tall, green *Lemitas* bushes formed a hedge along the lower ridge. The green berries furnished an acid drink, and the hard gum boiled in water made a nice flavored chewing gum. In those days nature supplied all the simple wants of the people.

II. SPANISH PIONEERS

Situated on top of a low mesa was the Indian Pueblo of Abiquiu, which some years ago became extinct. The few Indians who remained in the village mixed in with the white people and today all types are found from blond descendants of Catalonia to the dark Indian type.

About eight miles north of the Pueblo are the crumbling church and ruined houses of an old Spanish settlement. Here in the early eighteenth century lived my father's grandfather, Don Jose Manuel Martinez, with his eight sons and two daughters. But having been molested by the Abiquiu Indians, who made big raids on his stock, he realized that he could never make much progress in that place. In 1832, he therefore sent a written request to the "Excelentisima Deputacion Provincial," the most Excellent Provincial Deputation, at Mexico City, that they present his petition to cede some lands up the Chama river to him, his eight sons, and those neighbors who might wish to accompany him, in the name of the "Soberania de la Nacion Mejicana," to whom they had the honor to belong. He explained that although in the present jurisdiction of Abiquiu he enjoyed the possession of some lands, this territory was old, demerited and exhausted, and even the most careful attention and rigorous labor were not enough to raise the needed provisions for his large family and big herds of stock.

The government heard his petition and ceded to the Martinez family the Tierra Amarilla grant of over three hundred thousand acres, the richest grant in timber, water and pasture in northern New Mexico.

Four of Don Manuel's sons, inheriting the spirit of colonization from their ancestors, took their families, sheep, cattle and shepherds, and moved up the Chama river. Here they founded a settlement at Tierra Amarilla. One of the girls married into the Chavez family at Abiquiu, the other into the Lucero family at Los Luceros. The other four boys moved to Taos county, two of them settled at Ranchitos, one started a farm at San Cristobal and my grandfather, Don Vicente, bought part of the Arroyo Hondo grant and built for his family a big seventeen room house, on the *cordillera* which connected the two main villages and ran along the edge of the lower ridge, flanked on the south side by the mansions of the *haciendados*, land and sheep owners.

The house was built in the old Spanish style, with rows of rooms enclosing a square court-yard, surrounded by porches on both the inside and outside. Thick round posts, carved lintels, and scroll-cut corbels supported the round beams and ceilings of the porches.

On the west wing, opening into the high-walled corral were the two store-rooms, pelt and *piñon* rooms, stacked high with pelts and *piñon* bags, the carpenter shed and *fragua*, blacksmith shops. Houses like this were a combination of family domicile, handicraft center, factory, and work shop for all the necessities of life.

Across the garden, on the east side, stood the private chapel built by my grandfather, Don Vicente, in thanksgiving for the safe delivery of the family on several occasions from the attacks of the Indians, who once in a while raided the village. In the back yard of the house the chapel bell was cast. The devout brought their gold and silver jewels as offerings, and cast them into the boiling caldron of melting metals.

When the cry, "Indians," spread through the village, striking terror into the people's hearts, this chapel bell would ring out, calling all the villagers to gather in the chapel and inside court. The hand-hewn, paneled doors of the arched front *saguan*, and the massive, double doors of the back one, were then locked with huge keys and barred inside. The few outside windows were packed with wool pillows and mattresses to keep out the Indian shots.

From the roof tops the men shot at the Indians through the water trough holes. During one of these battles, my father's youngest brother was killed by an arrow-shot which pierced his head as he was climbing a ladder, carrying ammunition to the fighting men above. The women, accustomed to crying aloud when a member of their family died, had to smother their cries, for if the savages knew that some one had been killed, they doubled with fury their attack.

Don Vicente, with the aid of the stock that his father had given him, soon became one of the big sheep and land owners. He served his people as *alcalde mayor* and judge and was elected to the legislature as representative from Taos county. In their troubles the villagers always found in him a ready helper, and he was greatly esteemed and respected by all of them.

Thus did this family come to the hidden valley of the Arroyo Hondo—another family to help, by means of bloody battle and peaceful law, to bring civilization to wilderness—another family to help adapt the old customs of Spain to a new land, adding something to the heritage of the Spanish Conquistadores who came before them.

III. ROMANCE ON THE CHIHUAHUA TRAIL

The caravans of white covered wagons which left Arroyo Hondo, El Cerro, Taos and other northern towns, and wound their way southward into Mexico were surrounded by an air of romance, both by those who watched them go slowly on their way, and the ones who braved the perils of the journey. One of these *conductas* held romance of a different sort, for it was during one of these trips that young Jesus Maria Lucero, one of the family into which my great-aunt had married, met his bride, my maternal grandmother.

Jesus Maria and his elder brother, Don Jose Nemecio, fell in line at Los Luceros, with their white-hooded wagons and pack mules loaded high with woolen blankets, red and green chile strings, jerked meat, tanned buffalo and deer hides, and other New Mexico products. They reached La Villa de Santa Fe in time to join the caravan that left there once a year. At La Villa Don Nemecio left, leaving his wagons and *peones* in charge of his brother-in-law, Don Gaspar Ortiz (The Piñon King). Don Gaspar added his own wagons piled with piñon nut bags, bolts of calico, and unbleached muslin, as well as fine coaches, purchased in the states and brought laboriously over the Santa Fe Trail. All these goods were to be exchanged in Chihuahua and Durango for Mexican products, imported European luxuries and jewels. Among Don Gaspar's purchases were rich silk dresses, rare Saltio Serapes, so closely woven that they held a pail of water, and three-hundred dollar silk-embroidered shawls, one for each of his three daughters.

Late in the month of November the long caravan wended its way down the trail through the Rio Abajo. Every large town on the way added a few heavily loaded wagons or pack mules. People gathered to view the dusty march of the cavalcade or to give the *fleteros* more goods for the Mexican trade. For several weeks the wagon rolled over the desert plain, La Jornada del Muerto.

Upon reaching Chihuahua, Don Gaspar camped his wagons near an hacienda on the outskirts of the town. At sunset a Spanish *señorita,* accompanied by a maid, came to the well to fill a jar with fresh water. One look at the young girl—her fair face, large blue eyes, and ebony curls—and young Lucero lost his heart. On the return trip he insisted that his brother-in-law accompany him to the *señorita's* home to ask for her in marriage. The well-known

Don Gaspar did not have a difficult time in getting his tall, handsome brother's proposal accepted. However, the mother only consented after she had obtained permission to accompany her daughter to New Mexico.

A few days later the wedding took place in the imposing Chihuahua cathedral, noted for its beautifully sculptured front, showing two tiers of stone-carved statues of the twelve apostles.

Then the caravan continued its journey northward, escorting a coach carrying the newlyweds, the mother, and the Indian maid. The lonely trail marked by many crude graves of massacred victims of murderous wild Indian tribes did not offer a very pleasant honeymoon journey to a timid young bride. During the day they passed through wild and uncivilized land; at night she heard the men around the camp-fire tell of previous trips, when roving Indian bands raided their camp, carrying away provisions and teams. But on this occasion fortune favored them, and the weary travelers reached Santa Fe in safety.

Leaving his bride, her mother, and the maid at Santa Fe, Grandpa Lucero proceeded to his home at Los Luceros and from there to Taos to dispose of his load of Mexican wares.

Passing north through Arroyo Hondo, he stopped at the home of Don Vicente, his brother-in-law. He found the place so attractive that he bought a farm on the cordillera and contracted to have a double house built for the two families. It was to have two courts, one opening to the east which the mother would occupy, and the other to the west, with a high wall enclosing the two on the south side.

When the house was finished and furnished, a big dance was given as a house-warming. Relatives from Tierra Amarilla, El Rito, Rio Arriba and Taos were invited. They came, and were all charmed with the new bride, declaring she outshone the five Gallegos girls from Abiquiu, who up to that time had been famed for their beauty. And through the years she has maintained the reputation and fame of being the most beautiful and charming woman of Spanish descent who came to New Mexico in those early days.

* * * * *

Years passed, and in time a son and three daughters had come to bless the new home. The boy—tall, fair-skinned, with golden-brown, wavy hair—resembled his father. The three girls were as picturesque as they were different. Soledad, the oldest—tall and graceful, with abundant brown hair reaching down to her knees, and a sweet smile lurking on her dainty lips—emphasized a beauty which captivated. Marina, who was destined to be my mother, was a pale, delicate blond. She took life seriously and quietly, kept at her mother's side to help her in her numerous duties. Petra, the youngest—delightfully plump and rosy-cheeked, with a merry laugh and a sparkle in her eyes—inherited much of her mother's beauty. Robust and lively, she was fond of riding and out-door games; her mother could not tame her to take an interest in the domestic arts of which my mother was so fond.

The fame of the Lucero girls' beauty spread over northern New Mexico, and many wooers came to ask for them in marriage. My father, Julian, second son of Don Vicente Martinez, sought the hand of the second daughter and was accepted. There was a quiet wedding, for Don Julian's father had died only a year before and at that time mourning was continued for two or three years.

My father and his young brother divided the large double house with the two saguans separating it. Father chose the east side of twelve rooms. It was here that he raised his family of five boys and two girls.

IV. EL CARROFERRIL (THE IRON HORSE)

A generation after my grandfather met his bride while journeying with the caravan, the "iron horse" brought romance to his daughter, the beautiful Soledad. In the year 1871, when the Santa Fe railroad was being laid through Denver, Colorado, the owners of teams and wagons from the northern part of New Mexico sent their peones and teams, in charge of their grown sons, to Denver to haul ties for building the tracks.

There was in camp a crowd of young men of the best Spanish families. In the evenings they gathered around the camp fire to compose songs and tell tales of adventure and love.

Háy viene el carroferril,	There comes the railroad
Con dirección a Durango;	In the direction of Durango;
El qué se embarca en el,	The one who embarks on it,
Díos nomas sabe hasta cuando.	God only knows until when.
Allí viene el carroferril,	There comes the railroad,
Vamos a ver donde está,	Let's go and see where it is;
Há, qué gusto nos dará;	How happy we will be
Cuando ló veamos venír.	When we see it coming.
Háy viene el carroferril,	Here comes the railroad,
Viene cargado dé indíanas;	It comes loaded with calicos;
Viene quebrando los precíos	Breaking up the prices
A las tiendas Mejicánas.	For the Mexican stores.

Young Chavez who admired my aunt Soledad, confidentially told Manuel Chacon that in Arroyo Hondo lived the best-looking young lady he had ever met; he intended one day to ask her hand in marriage. Chacon listened attentively, and secretly he made up his mind to propose to the girl himself. Others besides Chacon had heard about Señorita Soledad, however. La Branch, a handsome gentleman, half French and half Spanish, had received a letter from his sister in Taos some time before, telling him that she had picked out a fine girl for him. She gave him such an attractive description of my aunt that the young man made up his mind at once to become acquainted with this charming young lady at the first opportunity.

Chacon lost no time. He was the first to leave camp, and upon arriving home he requested his father to go with him to ask for the hand of Soledad. Since the young man's family was one of the influential and well-known of Conejos, Colorado, he was considered a good match. A few weeks later his father received a favorable reply, and Chacon hastened the wedding.

When La Branch left Denver, he met on the way a girl walking by the side of a man, driving a team. They had descended from their buggy, on reaching the steep hill of La Garrapata, because it was safer to climb on foot. The young woman wore a green veil thrown back over her hat, affording La Branch a glimpse of her fair face as he passed. Charmed by her loveliness his heart beast faster, but he continued on his way, arriving that evening at my grandfather's house. He asked if he might see the daughter Soledad, but was told that she had that morning left on her wedding trip to Denver. It occurred to La Branch at once that the girl he had met climbing the hill was the one he had travelled so far to woo, and remembering her beautiful face, he lamented aloud his loss. My mother and her young sister listening in the next room had a good laugh on hearing him.

Jose Chavez who had told Chacon of Soledad, returned a few weeks later, and he was also disappointed to find the girl of his dreams already married.

V. HONEYMOON AMONG BANDITS

In the days when aunt Soledad and her husband were bride and groom, New Mexico was a much more civilized and peaceful land then when Grandfather Lucero brought his wife from Mexico in the caravan. Still the peace was frequently disturbed, not by Indian raids but by outlaws that roamed the countryside.

Three days after their marriage, my aunt and uncle reached La Trinchera, in Colorado, on their wedding trip. There they heard that the Montoyitas, two brother bandits, had been especially active, robbing and kidnaping travelers passing through the mountains. Frightened for the safety of his bride, Chacon went straight on to Fort Garland without stopping.

On reaching the fort, they heard of the capture of Doña Mariana, (nicknamed "La Fuerte"—the strong), by these bandits. She was a strongly-built, masculine-looking woman, who could knock down a man with a blow of her fist. Doña Mariana travelled a great deal on horseback; from her home at Arroyo Seco, she travelled alone all over the country. She had decided to make a trip to Denver, but as she was passing through the Canon del Rito de la Sangre de Cristo, she was caught by the bandits, who hid her in their cave in the mountains. The Governor of Colorado offered a reward for the capture of these outlaws. Thomas Tobin was one of the volunteers; and while the two bandits were sitting on a log before their cave one evening, eating their supper, Tobin, who was a sure shot, killed the two men and rescued the woman.

* * * * *

After the newlyweds returned home, Chacon, who was very proud of his young wife, wanted to introduce her to his relatives at Abiquiu and El Rito. My mother accompanied them on this trip.

Late one evening they reached Ojo Caliente. Before going into the town, they stopped in the hills to plan where to stay for the night. La gavilla de Miguel Maes, a band of bandits under Maes, lived there. Chacon thought it wiser to stop at the leader's home, because if they chose another place the bandits would steal his horses that night. The bride and my mother were very much afraid, but they finally agreed to let Chacon carry out his plan. By night they were at Don Miguel's house at Gavilan, on the Ojo Caliente river. Don Miguel, the chief, a tall, good-looking man, and his wife received the party with great hospitality, placing his house and servants at their disposal. A *peon* came in with a *tarima,* a long bench, set it in the middle of the room, and went back for the dishes, which he set on the bench. Then the cook brought in the food, and the guests were invited to move their seats close to this improvised table and partake of the supper, after which the *tarima* was removed to the kitchen.

While they were sitting and talking, they heard two horsemen at the door. One of the men stood at the door, while the other—a short, dark man wearing his hat pulled down over his eyes—walked straight to Don Miguel's side, rattling heavy spurs. He bent and whispered something in Don Miguel's ear. Don Miguel looked up with a frown on his face and answered in a commanding voice, "Con caballeros, se trata de caballeros y a los que no se les da su lugar." (When you deal with gentlemen, you treat them as gentlemen. Others, you give them their place.) The man turned with a scowl on his face, and the two of them left without further ado.

Don Miguel brought out a deck of Mexican playing cards and said, "Don Manuel, tiraremos la suerte, haber a quien le toca." Chacon, frightened lest he should draw the unlucky card, for he did not quite understand Don Miguel's meaning, drew a card from the deck. Then Don Miguel drew. Having drawn the lucky high card, Chacon sat at ease. Too, by this time, he knew that they were simply to play a game of poker.

The game ended, Don Miguel rose, removed three guns that lay across the bed and called a servant woman to fix the beds for the guests. The young bride and my mother, who were watching every move of Don Miguel's and had seen him take the guns into the next room, spent a wakeful night of fear. They had called in Salvador, their driver, to sleep by the door, but the night passed quietly. Early the next morning, the party was on its way again.

* * * * *

At Arroyo Seco, in Taos County, Don Miguel's brother, Francisco, operated another band. Having heard of Chacon's visit at his brother's house, he took two of his men and rode to Arroyo Hondo one dark night. Boy Ramon, the sheepherder, was walking home, when he heard horsemen approaching. He ran into an old barn by the road and hid behind a pile of straw. The horsemen stopped at the door, dismounted, and went into the next room.

"Fidel, you are a good friend of Chacon. You ask him to let you in, and after that, leave him to me," said Maes.

The sheepherder did not wait to hear more, but jumped out of the window and ran to tell his master to be on the lookout for Maes.

Close to midnight, there was a knock at the door of uncle Manuel's house.

Chacon asked from within, *"Quien?"* ("Who is it?").

"Your friend, Fidel."

"What brings you here so late?" asked Chacon.

"We sat playing cards without noticing the time. Will you give us a bed for the rest of the night?"

"No," answered Chacon. "But I will give you a few shots if you don't leave my door at once."

The men outside mumbled something in angry voices, mounted their horses and rode away. Some time passed. Then one evening, Ramon failed to come home with the herd of sheep. Chacon rode up the hills in search of him. There in *la Cañada* a grim sight met his eyes. Hanging from a pine tree was Ramon, his body stiff in death. With the rope he always wore around his waist, serving the double purpose of holding up his trousers and lassoing a sheep, he had been hung. He had paid with his life for saving that of his master!

Miguel Maes and his brother Francisco operated closely with the *Cuates*, who belonged to the band of forty bandits under the command of Vicente Silva. In 1892 Silva's band terrorized San Miguel county, stealing, murdering, and committing all kinds of horrible crimes. And for their operations, *Los Cuates* (the twins) were assigned the northern section of the state, composed of Mora, Taos and Colfax counties.

Before this time, "Los Gorras Blancas," an organization which also sprang up at Las Vegas, was formed in protest against the fencing of free government lands, which the people were acquiring as homesteads from the government.

Los Gorras Blancas met at night in their secret gathering places. Wearing white caps which partly concealed their faces, they formed long processions and went along cutting wires and tearing down fences. The homesteaders, unable to cope with such formidable force, were forced to abandon their lands and let the Gorras Blancas have the use of the pasture lands, which the people had been using free.

With the passing of time peace was again established.

VI. MEMORIAS

The memory of my grandfather and grandmother and many of my aunts is also the memory of old-time customs and ways of living. Aunt Dolores especially adhered strictly to the Spanish customs and was one of the outstanding examples of the dignified lady of the past.

She arrived one evening in her old fashioned cart, with her Indian maid sitting in the back on the old, low trunk. This was a marvel of antiquity, made of tanned hide woven into squares and diamonds, the open spaces filled in with red flannel. Aunt Dolores had lost her husband, and left alone with her maid she sold her farm and home at Ocate and came to live with us.

On meeting the family, she gave each member the semblance of an embrace by stiffly placing the tips of her dainty, jeweled fingers on the shoulder. She was at once accepted as one of the family.

Aunt Dolores' veneration for the old religious customs played a great part in her life. She would awaken the family early in the morning with her *Canto del Alba* (hymn at dawn).

Coro: Cantémos él álba
Yá viene él día.
Darémos gracías,
    Áve María!
	Let's sing the dawn,
	The light is coming;
	Let's give thanks,
	    Ave Maria!

Lós cínco Señores, Dél cielo nós valgan; Hó, Jauquin, humáno! Cuída nuestras álmas.	The five saints, In heaven help us. Ho, Jauquin human! Take care of our souls.
Náce él álba, María Y él Áve tras élla; Desterrando lá nóche Y nuestras penas.	Born is the dawn, Maria, And the Ave comes after her; Vanishing the night And our troubles.

And this was her morning prayer, said after the hymn:

Én este nuévo día,
Gracías té tributámos
Hó, Díos omnipotente!
Dueño dé todo ló criado.
Vuestra divina cleméncia,
Sé há dignádo sacarnos
Dé lá nóche obscura
á lá lúz dél sól claro.
Leno está de tu gloria
Todo el vasto teatro.

On this new day,
Thanks we attribute Thee,
O, God Omnipotent,
Master of all created;
Thy divine clemency
Has deigned to bring me
Out of the obscure night,
Into the light of the clear sun.
Full of Thy glory
Is the vast theatre,

En el mundo cuanto existe,	That in the world exists.
Es óbra de tu máno.	It's the work of Thy hand.
Por vós nacen las flores,	By Thee the flowers bloom,
Reverdes en los campos,	The fields grow green,
Los árboles dan su frut,	The trees bear their fruit,
El sól da sus rayos,	The sun gives out its rays,
El agua sus péces	The water its fish,
Los pájaros cantan	The birds sing Thy holy,
Tú nombre sánto, sánto.	holy name.
Dirigue Díos immenso	Direct, powerful God,
Y guia nuestros pásos.	And guide our footsteps,
Para qué eternamente,	So that eternally
Tú santa léy sigámos.	Thy law we may follow.

Aunt Dolores' salutations were always given in the name of God: "Buenos dias les de Dios" and "buenas tardes les de Dios" were answered in the same manner: "God give you a good day." People although strangers, never passed each other without saluting this way.

In my grandfather's time the family gathered in the chapel for evening prayers; now the family knelt before aunt Dolores' little altar. At the end of prayers the children and servants, one by one, knelt before the great aunt and my mother, to receive their blessing and kiss their hand, in sign of respect.

This blessing was always asked from parents and elders by the young before retiring and before starting on a journey.

Profound respect was always paid aunt Dolores. Whenever she asked one of the servants or children to hand her her silver tobacco box and beaded *ojero,* they stood before her with folded arms, until she handed back the article to be put away. She often called out "Ave Maria" to a relative or friend she saw approaching. If the guest happened to be a man, he immediately removed his hat and stood with folded arms reciting the Ave Maria, to himself, and asked her to offer it.

This compact of the Ave Maria and the one of *valerse a la comadre* lasted through life time, even when made in early youth. Those who compacted the "Ave Maria," locking their little finger with their friend's little finger, said:

"Cuantas hóras tiene el día,	All the hours the day has,
Tiene el Áve María."	The Ave Maria has.

The ones who made the "comadre" compact repeated the following verses:

"Chiquiguitito de flóres no té derrames,	"Little flower basket, don't spill over,
Qué en esta vída y én la otra,	For in this life, and in the next,
Siempre serémos comádres."	We will always be *comadres.*"
"Redondito, redondon,	"Round and rounded,
La que se vále a la comádre,	The ones that become *comadres,*
Se lé parte él corazón."	Their hearts split in two."

Prayer entered into every action or undertaking. Even in cooking, when starting to mix bread or any food, if you wanted it to come out specially good, the name of the Holy Trinity was invoked. A cross was marked on the bread dough before setting it away to rise.

When someone said or did something shocking, the one shocked pointed at him a cross formed by placing the thumb over the index finger, saying: *"pongote la cruz."*

Among aunt Dolores' heirlooms was her album bound in red plush, filled with quaint tin-type photographs of her relatives and friends, some of them wearing long curls and hoop skirts, their hands on their hips, every finger outspread to show the gold rings. Her most favored treasures were: her gold locket with a raised flower design in which was enclosed a ringlet curl of her mother's hair; a pair of gold *coquetas*, earrings with gold dangles like a fringe; a long gold *bejuco* caught together with a *centro*, ornamented with pearls set in black enamel, from which dangled a goldfish made of minute hinged scales that twisted as though it were alive; a necklace of round gold beads with a large bow-knot in the center, a long emerald pendant hanging from it; and the hand-hammered silver water pitcher and goblet which always stood on her table. Mela, her maid, kept this pitcher filled with fresh water, which she brought up from the spring at the foot of the hill. At the same time she used to bring up a *tinaja* full of water, carried on her head and never a drop spilled.

In the *trastero*, built in the wall and closed with hand-carved doors, was kept Aunt Dolores' set of fine china, little *posillos* (mugs), and her copper *jarra* imported from Mexico. These were brought out on special occasions, especially when serving the spicy, foamy Mexican chocolate to some distinguished guest, such as the Bishops and other high dignitaries.

Ours was the home of priests, friends, and even mere acquaintances passing through to some other town. As old man Manuel once explained when he dropped in, in the midst of a big dinner for invited guests, leaving his muddy footprints on our varnished floor, "Jaramillo, I saw you had such a nice hay stack, I thought my horse would surely have a good feed here, not saying anything about myself."

Our city guests could not understand how anyone could drop in without an invitation, but this was almost an everyday occurrence. The cooks always had to be prepared for such emergencies.

Aunt Dolores especially went out of her way to entertain the religious guests. With great pride, she showed them her motto hanging over the door, "God Bless the Home," embroidered on *canavé* with delicately-shaded silk floss; her crucifix, *de Marfil*, a gift from *"Sú Señoria él Obispo Lamy."*

When not entertaining guests, she busied herself knitting, embroidering, and supervising the making of her *mistela,* spiced wine, cosmetics, wax and tallow candles, and vegetable dyes. *Mistela* was made by adding sugar and spices to fine brandy and simmering the mixture for a whole day in an earthen pot, the top sealed tightly with a piece of dough. Green *chimaja* leaves boiled in a sugar syrup and strained were added to brandy for another kind of *mistela.*

Ground wild-rose leaves and romero were added to strained, melted beef marrow for homemade hair pomade.

Homemade hard soap was cooled, the top skimmed off into another pot and boiled with water until there was no lye left. The soap was cooled, cut up into shavings and put into a bag; the bag was put into a pail of water covered with corn husks and left to soak for three days, the water being changed every day. Then the bag was drained out of the water, the soap mixed with melon seeds, romero, wild rose leaves, and home-made bran starch; the whole mixture was ground into a paste and formed into little cakes, which were set out in the sun to dry. These *javonsillos* were used as face soap only and were kept as something very precious.

It was interesting to watch the making of tallow candles for use in the kitchen and of wax ones for the chapel altar. Long, cotton strings were dipped into melted tallow or wax and hung on a string to cool. Starting at the other end, with the ones that were already cool, the candles were dipped again and again until they were of the desired thickness.

Mela sat on her bed, which was rolled on the floor against the wall by the window, spinning her *malacate* inside an Indian *escudilla,* twisting the fine wool carded from the finest sheep skins which had been laid aside. The spun wool was then tied into skeins and boiled in the vegetable dyes of fadeless colors. Bunches of *brazil* sticks, *añil,* and a purple powder were imported from Mexico for this purpose. The *brazil* sticks cut up into shavings and boiled with the wool dyed it a rich brick red. The *añil* colored it indigo; yellow *chicoria* flowers, a pretty yellow, and the powder. *azul presado,* a bluish purple. Yellow dyed wool dipped into the blue *añil* turned it green. The wool from black and brown sheep were used in their natural color.

These fine wools were used to make hand-knitted hose and for embroidering *colchas,* bed covers. From coarser wool were woven blankets and long strips of black and white and brown plaid *jergas* to cover floors.

When Grandmother Refugio came to visit the family, she always brought her work basket. Needlework was her pastime: she embroidered dainty scallops and eyelets on chemise yokes and attached the long loose part with shirring and dainty *panalito*. The servants trimmed theirs with pointed *piquitos*. Embroidery and shirring adorned her sons' shirt fronts; and fine drawnwork, the table napkins and cloths.

Chaquira, bead work, was Grandmother's specialty. With the finest needles and beads she worked hand bags, *ojeros,* little cases to hold the corn cigarette leaves, and tiny hearts used to join together the pink coral rosaries which she sent to *novios* for their engagements. These were used instead of rings.

These dames of old had their *desayuno* of *mistela* or chocolate with sweet cookies or fried *sopaipas* brought to their beds every morning. At four o'clock in the afternoon, after the *siesta,* they partook of the same drinks, varied with curlicued *biscochos, empanaditas,* or *puchas* and *marquezotes.* The recipe for puchas calls for twenty-four yolks.

The imported Mexican chocolate came already spiced and sweetened, but the most fastidious bought their own cocoa beans, pecan nuts, stick cinnamon, and maple sugar, and had them ground at home on a heated *metate* stone. The heat of the stone melted the nuts, formed the mixture into a paste. Out of it little round cakes were made, dried, and kept for future use.

The preparation of Spanish dishes requires much time and labor. However, with the aid of modern conveniences the work is now made much lighter than in olden times when the ingredients were ground by hand. But one is amply repaid for the labor by the appetizing flavor and attractive coloring of the dishes, for nothing quickens the appetite more than a stack of blue corn tortillas spread with pink onion and yellow cheese, red chile poured over this and a shredded, green lettuce garnish on top.

Recipes for the genuine New Mexico Spanish dishes will be found in my book of recipes; also a list of some of the herb remedies Grandmother used to prescribe for all ills, her medicated baths, smokes, fortifying plasters and massages.

* * * * *

Aunt Dolores was greatly missed when she passed away to the happy land she saw in her visions, while she fondled her rosary repeating her favorite "Ave Maria."

Mother brought out her black taffeta silk *mantona* to wear for the funeral. This silk cape was made with three lace flounces trimming the circular bottom, and the black lace veil fastened at the collar dropped over the head.

The *mantonas* were worn in mourning and at the church services during lent and Holy Week. On other occasions colorful, long silk *rebosos* were worn wrapped around the head or shoulders, tied in front with the two fringed ends thrown back over the shoulders. Elderly ladies wore the fine, black *stambre,* jersy, shawls, wrapped over their heads, the long silk-fringed end thrown gracefully over the left shoulder. The length of the silk fringe denoted the wealth of the wearer. For dressy occasions the silk embroidered shawl was worn, and in the summer time, the long, scarf-like, lace *mantilla de castilla* or the triangular lace *pañueleta*. In the passing of these colorful wraps New Mexico has lost one of its attractive, typical customs.

* * * * *

Grandfather Lucero loved to see his grand-children around him, and to tell us about old times and his school days. Each pupil he said had to bring his own seat to school, and every morning an arm full of wood to heat the room.

Tobias, his teacher, strictly observed the old Spanish rules. He held no school on Saturdays, but his pupils went to the school house on that day at the usual hour.

Knocking at the door, each pupil called out: *"Jesus, Jose, Ave Maria."* The teacher asked from within *"quien toca la puerta de esta mision?"* (Who knocks at this mission's door?) The pupil answered *"Yo buscando mi salvacion, penitencia, penitencia."* (I, seeking my salvation.)

Here the teacher opened the door, and the pupil presented to him the *Pan del Sabado,* the Sabath bread (bread, biscuits, or whatever he had to offer).

After all the pupils were assembled the teacher stood them in line, and the two pupils having the highest marks in their class were given a little stick. With this stick they went down the line hitting the hands that had not been washed and the heads that were uncombed.

An hour of religious instruction followed.

* * * * *

Grandfather's old-maid sister was quite amusing. She was very stately, tall and fair, with a delicate skin, for the sun or wind never touched it. She wore her long silver braids like a crown around her shapely head, which was always covered with a silk skull cap to protect it from the air. She ground roots and herbs, rubbing them on her temples and back of her head, to cure her continuous headaches, which she said were caused by *aire en la cabeza,* air in the head.

At night she pushed her bed into the farthest corner, away from doors and windows, placed two chairs on the side, and spread the bed cover over them, to screen off the air, which she said made whirls in the corners. When not occupied with her remedies or knitting, aunt Cencionita made thin, long-necked, long-waisted, rag dolls for her nieces. When we begged her for thread to sew our doll dresses with, she would give us a long strip of muslin and show us how to pull out some strands and twist them into thread.

Tiodora, our nurse went home to get married. After a few years of mother's good training, our maids usually won a marriage certificate and were soon selected as fine house-keepers.

Mela, aunt Dolores' maid, was now promoted to the rank of nurse. She was not as patient as Tiodora. When the children refused to be quiet and go to sleep at night, she at once called to her aid the *"Vieja Ganchos"* or the *"Orejas de Burro."* The *Vieja Ganchos* would appear crouching at the door with a long iron hook. Or the Orejas de Burro would stick in his long donkey ears, through a crack in the door. Immediately there was dead silence. But oh! those awful dreams during the night! I saw myself being carried out to the mountains hanging from the *Vieja Ganchos'* long hook, and would wake up stiff with fright, my heart thumping so hard that I could hear its beats.

I believe now that this fear of the *abuelos* and Lupe's ghost and witch stories, and the sore example put before us of bad children like the *mal hijo* made our lives exceedingly timid. I was very young when the *mal hijo* passed through our village, but he impressed me for life. Mounted on a burro, he went from town to town preaching to the young; showing them his clenched hand and the scar on his wrist where the knife turned and stuck when he raised it to strike his father. The earth had opened beneath him and swallowed him up to his waist. His mother ran for the priest, the priest came, and after many prayers and sprinkling with holy water the earth released him. Repentant of his sin, he promised to travel over the world, advising the young to respect and obey their parents.

Other strange characters passing through the village broke the quiet monotony. Turks and Arab gypsies, dressed in their picturesque garb, came peddling trinkets. They told the natives that they came from the Holy Land, and that the rosaries and medals they were selling had been blessed in one of the Blessed Virgin's trays. This the poor people, in their simple faith, believed; took them in, fed them and bought their trinkets.

VII. WEDDING, BAPTISM & OTHER CEREMONIES

Weddings were always big events in New Mexico—occasions for joy and feasting. Of course not every girl's marriage had the romance attached to it that the weddings I have mentioned in my family had. It was unusual for a lover to come from afar to claim his bride. Generally, since there were so few pure Spanish families in the small villages and so few opportunities of becoming acquainted with outsiders, there was a great deal of intermarriage between first and second cousins, in order to keep the Spanish blood from mixing. This happened a great deal among my own family. But even if a girl had grown up with her husband a next door neighbor, knowing him as well as her own brother, still her marriage was, then as now, the most dramatic event of her life.

Marriages were arranged by the parents. If the family connection was advantageous and the boy came from good stock, the proposal was accepted, sometimes without the bride knowing anything about it until preparations began for the engagement. The groom's father, accompanied by the boy's godfather or most intimate friend, called on the father of the girl and addressed him with a formal speech; sometimes the formal proposal letter. A few weeks later, the girl's father made a formal answer, either of acceptance or refusal.

A wedding which impressed me greatly was that of my cousin Biatriz, which occurred when I was eight years old. She was the only daughter of my father's brother, who lived in the west wing of our twenty-room house. Both sides of the house were redecorated for the great event.

A month after the acceptance of the proposal and three days before the wedding, the groom arrived at the home of the bride, accompanied by his parents and sisters. Behind their carriage rode the chef in a wagon loaded with a big trunk and boxes full of chickens, eggs, flour, and other provisions for the wedding feast.

The betrothal, or *prendorio,* took place as soon as the groom arrived. All the bride's relatives had been invited to meet the groom. Both families assembled in the long living room. The father presented the bride to the groom's father, saying: *"aqui tiene la prenda que usted busca."* The groom's father then introduced her to his family, and introduced the groom to the bride's family.

In my grandmother's time, after the introductions, the sweethearts knelt before the bride's oldest uncle or godfather (*tatita,* as he was affectionately called) and he slipped a coral or pearl rosary first over the boy's head then over the girl's. That ceremony made them *prendados,* the rosary being used instead of an engagement ring.

At my cousin's engagement the big trunk was then brought in and presented to her. In it was the wedding trousseau, always bought by the groom, consisting of the long-trained, white satin gown, with all its accessories, veil, wax orange flower wreath (which was afterwards kept in a frame), white shoes, gloves, a set of combs, other silk dresses, and silk patterns with buttons and trimmings to match, a set of jewels, including the wedding ring. This wide gold band was decorated with two locked hearts in a raised design. The other rings had clusters of grapes and leaves, the grapes and leaves tinted a faint purplish rose and light green.

There were also a pair of long pearl earrings and a round brooch to match. Then came the presentation of gifts to the bride by the groom's relatives, followed by refreshments served by the bride's parents.

Preparations were then begun immediately for the wedding. The *padrinos* were invited; they served as best man and matron of honor and had charge of the couple until after the wedding. The *madrina* saw that the gowns were altered if necessary, and both accompanied the couple to make arrangements with the priest for the marriage. The banns had to be announced in church for three successive Sundays before the marriage.

Wedding invitations, printed in the name of both parents and distributed by messengers, respectfully requested the recipient's presence and that of his family at the wedding and at the reception in the home afterwards.

It was customary for marriages to be celebrated in church at Mass, but my cousin's groom, influenced by modern ideas, planned the wedding for the evening at home. However, at the first opportunity, the newly-married had to be *velados*—that is, they must kneel with the *padrinos* before the sanctuary rail, holding lighted candles, from the Gospel to the end of the Mass services, in order to receive the nuptial blessing.

The bride's house was placed at the disposal of the groom's parents, for they took charge of the wedding feast and other preparations. While the cooks heated the mud oven in the back yard and baked the bread, cookies, cakes, and roasted the chickens stuffed with a dressing made of ground meat, raisins, *piñon* nuts, and flavored with wine and spices, the men of the family sprinkled, rolled and packed the court-yard ground and prepared it for the dance. Lanterns were hung on each porch post, decorated with evergreen branches. On one corner of the proch an altar was fixed by covering a table with lace curtains and decorating it with candles and flowers.

Before this improvised altar the wedding took place at seven o'clock in the evening. My brother and I carried the bride's train. Behind us marched the best man and matron of honor, *damas*, parents and relatives. After the ceremony the fiddlers, playing a march, led the bridal procession to the long *sala*, where the dinner was served. The big table was filled several times with different groups of guests. At the end of the dinner, the bridal couple led the grand march around the enclosed court. When the march turned into a round waltz, my brother, thinking we should still follow the bride, kept whirling me around so fast that I soon was so dizzy my head hung back limp. My mother caught sight of my undignified position, grasped brother by the arm, stopping his fun and the great merriment the guests were having at my expense. During the dance, a few guests at a time were invited to partake of the refreshments, which had been placed on the table, after it had been cleared of the dinner dishes.

Before midnight the bridesmaid helped the bride change her white gown to a colored one. Sometimes the gowns were changed two or three times during the dance, thus giving the bride an opportunity to display the finest dresses in her trousseau. My mother told me that once when a poor man brought his bride only one extra dress, she came out, after her second change, wearing a new, bright red, fancy petticoat that came in her trousseau.

I was sent to bed quite embarrassed after mother stopped my dancing. Next morning I was told of the *entriega*, which took place in the wee hours of the morning after the dance was over. The musicians again led the bridal party, relatives, and friends into the *sala*. Here the singer gave improvised verses; some were long verses of advice or complimentary songs to the newly-weds; others were parting songs to father and mother, which brought tears to the eyes of those present. In verse the parents were told to bless their children, and the bride and groom, kneeling before them, received their blessing.

The *padrinos* now turned the couple over to their parents, as told in the following verses of the *entriega*, which has in all about twelve verses. The singer sometimes received as much as a five dollar tip for this ceremony.

Señores, estas criaturas,	Gentlemen, this couple
Fue decretado de Díos,	Was destined by God,
De recibír el sacramento	To receive the sacrament
Y ponerse en estado de gracia.	And come into a state of grace.
Él padrino y la madrina	The padrino and the madrina
Se echaron la obligacion;	Undertook this obligation,
De entregar a sus hijados	To return to the parents their godchildren

Y darles su benedicion.	And give them their blessing.
Al padrino y la madrina, Al esposado y la esposa; Díos guarde larga vida, Por el estado que gozan.	To the godparent and godmother, The spoused and her consort, May God grant them a long life, In the new state they enjoy.
Padres, reciban sus híjos, Con gusto y con alegría, Y que cumplan con su estado Como San José y María.	Parents, receive thy children With joy and happiness. May they comply with their duties As did Joseph and Mary.
Padres, reciban sus híjos, Y échenles la benedición; Se van sus híjos queridos, Nacidos del corazón.	Parents, receive your children And give them your blessing. They are parting from you, Thy loving children, born from your heart.

BAPTISM. The arrival of a new baby was always announced to the relatives and friends by word sent by a messenger saying: "Mr. and Mrs. So and So announce *que ya tienen un criado, o criada mas a quien mandar*—that you have one more servant at your command."

It was during the month of August that my cousin, bringing her new baby, came to visit her parents. The next day she invited my father and mother to act as *padrinos* (godparents) at her baby's christening. Mother dressed the baby in a long, starched, white linen dress trimmed with shirring, tucks and fine embroidery ruffles, that hung almost to the floor. The baby was given a long litany of names, as each member of the family added his favorite saint's name.

When the *padrinos* returned to the house after the baptism, the godmother handed the baby over to his mother saying:

"Recíba esta prenda amada, Que da lá iglesia salío; Con lós sántos sacramentos Y él água que recibío."	"Receive this loving jewel, Who from the church comes With the holy sacraments And holy water received.

The mother, as she took the baby, answered with the same verse, changing only the first line to, "I receive thee, loving jewel."

Refreshments were served to the godparents and intimate friends invited to the feast. *La pastilla* was asked of the *padrinos* in fun by the grownups, but the children received nickels and dimes, and the baby was given a five or ten-dollar gold piece, according to the means of the godparents. At the christening the *padrinos* promised to assume the responsibility of looking after the child in case he lost his parents or if the parents neglected to provide a Christian education.

Parents were so scrupulous about having their babies baptized a few days after its birth that once my father, then a boy fifteen years old, carried a tiny, week-old baby on horse-back twelve miles to and from Taos to be baptized. This trip was thought necessary, because the priest would not visit the parish for two weeks, and the parents could not keep the baby a heretic so long, in danger of dying without receiving baptismal water.

After being christened a baby must be confirmed to mark his full membership into the church.

The Bishop visited the Arroyo Hondo parish about every four years. It was during the school vacation that Bishop Chapell came to administer confirmation in our private chapel. Other Bishops always administered the sacrament in the main church of the upper town.

On the afternoon before the Confirmation day, all the people of the valley as far as San Cristobal rode two and three miles to meet *Su Señoria,* the Bishop. They alighted from their carriages, reverently kissed the Bishop's ring, and then escorted him under decorated arches erected along the street to the chapel, where the Bishop gave a short talk and his kindly blessing to the people.

The next morning after the Mass there was great consternation and wailing amongst the children who filled the chapel when they were handed over to their godparents and beheld the Bishop, who gave them a soft blow on the cheek after confirming them, to remind them that they must be ready to suffer everything for their religion. The godparents who stood for the child in baptism, confirmation and matrimony were addressed as *compadres* by the parents, and the child was considered their spiritual son. The *compadres* held each other in great esteem. It was considered almost a sacrilege to quarrel with a *compadre* or to break his spiritual relationship. This attitude, I believe, accounted for the harmony and peace in which the village people lived side by side.

* * * * *

During my early childhood, an epidemic of diphtheria swept through the village and took little brother Tomásito. He was dressed in a long lace-trimmed dress and laid on the black round table that stood in the corner of the livingroom. A wreath of white artificial flowers crowning his fair forehead and a smaller one held his little clasped hands together. Jose Manuel, the carpenter, made the small board casket; and my aunts covered it with pink muslin, trimming it with white lace inside and outside. The family and relatives gathered in the *sala* early in the evening to sing the rosary and hymns. Even the "Our Father," "Hail Mary," and "Glory Patri" were transposed into hymns and song, for no sad *alabados* were sung at *angelitos* (little angels') wakes.

The next morning, Tiodora, our nurse, gathered the children in the play room. I recall her putting me up in the window, so that I could see the silent line of carriages forming the funeral procession. Then she let us out into the sun-filled patio to play.

I was then the baby of the family. So Tiodora, feeling her arms empty that night, picked me up and rocked me to sleep, singing softly the sweet lullaby that she was accustomed to singing to little brother:

Señora Santa Ana,	Blessed Saint Ann,
Señor San Jauquín,	Blessed Saint Jauquin,
Arulla este niño	Rock this baby,
Sé quiere dormir.	He wants to go to sleep.
A la rrú chiquíto,	A la rru, little one,
A la rrú Señor,	A la rru, baby;
Yó te doy de cuna,	I give you my heart
Mi corazón.	For a cradle.
Éste niño quiere,	This baby wants me to sing,
Qué le cante yó;	Let his mother sing to him,
Cántele su madre, pues ella lo crío.	For she is the one who nursed him.
El niño llorába	The baby cried,
San Juan lo mecía,	Saint John rocked him;
Sopitas le daba,	Soup he gave him,
Y no las quiría.	But the child did not want it.
Duérmete niñito,	Go to sleep baby,
Qué tengo qué hacer,	For I have to make
Una camisíta, qué te has de poner,	A little gown for you to wear,
El día de tu Santo, Señor San José.	On your feast day, Saint Joseph's day.

Tiodora also entertained the baby with little nursery rhymes, like these:

La zorríta, zorríta,	The little fox, little fox,
Se fué pa la loma;	Went to the hills;
Por andar en buréos, buréos,	On account of roaming around,
Víno pelóna, pelóna.	She came back baldheaded, baldheaded.

Jumping the baby on her knees she would sing:

Bríncan y saltan lós enenítos,	The little dwarfs jump and skip,
Bríncan y saltan de sus cerrítos.	Skip and jump down their little hills.
Ya los enános se enojáron,	Now the dwarfs are angry,
Porque a la enána la pelliscáron.	Because their wife was pinched.

When one of the children came to her crying, because of a cut or bruised finger, she rubbed it gently saying:

Sána, sána,	
Colíta de rana,	Heal, heal, little frog tail,
Si no sanas hoy,	If you don't heal today,
Sanarás mañana.	You will heal tomorrow.

Many little songs she sang, The Tecolotito, Decima del Niño; riddles she told. Mother would sometimes tell us lovely stories, of which I have written a Childrens' Story Book, translated into the English.

VIII. HARVEST MOONS

Autumn turned warm harvest sunlight into Indian summer, imparting its ripening richness to the poor farmer's crops.

These were the happiest days. I loved the hustle and bustle of this busiest of all seasons, the loud yells, "gid-up," and the cracking of the long leather whip, by the men keeping the herd of goats or wild horses running around the stacks of golden wheat and oats, stacked high on round, earthen *eras* (threshing grounds) until trampled to the ground. The herd was turned out and the men winnowed the grain in the wind, with their wooden forks, much the same as the Israelites used to do. The women, with their shawls wound tightly around their heads and tied in a knot in the back, came in with their gray sage brooms, swept a clean space on one end of the *era,* where two men stood holding between them a *criba*. The women poured into it the straw-mixed grain from their baskets, and the men rocking the *criba* back and forth sifted the grain. Sometimes this work went on until late at night, by the light of a bonfire and a lantern, hung on a post. Then came the rumble of heavy wagon wheels:

"In the bright gold of the harvest moon they came,
Bearing the richness of the field and vine."

They filled mud *torjas* to the ceiling with rich grain, for these great, big houses were built for abundance and to be self-sustaining. In those years Taos county had become the granary of New Mexico. The wheat that was not shipped out was washed, dried and carried to the flour mill, to be ground into flour.

EL MOLINO. The *molino* or flour mill, a twelve-foot square log room, stood in the meadow. The *acequia,* banked on both sides with willows and lovely wild flowers, carried the water which turned the large wooden wheel under the mill. The water dropped eight feet on the other side, forming a foaming pool in which the boys bathed.

Inside the low door frame stood the *molinero,* with bent shoulders, covered from head to foot with white dust. The miller patiently smoked his long corncob pipe while he watched the grain drop down from the cone-shaped, bull-hide hopper, hanging from the ceiling. The grain dropped into the hole of the upper round stone and was mashed by this stone revolving over the lower one, eighteen inches thick, which was fastened to the floor.

The flour which fell into the box built around the stones was poured into sacks with a gourd dipper and carried up to the house. Two women sitting on their heels with a white canvas spread before them sifted the flour by running up and down, on a smooth rod, a high wooden swiss-covered sieve filled with the meal. One sifting prepared the *semita* for whole-wheat bread; a second sifting, through a thicker sieve, was given the flour to be used for cakes and other dainties.

THE MIELERO. A great attraction for the village children in the fall of the year was the *mielero*. This mud stove was built against the outside wall of a house in the same style as the *braseros* in the old Mexico kitchens. It was made of plastered adobes in the shape of a narrow, long table, with six round holes on the top, where earthen pots were set to boil.

This primitive hand factory seemed to belong to the community. Each family brought sugar canes to make its supply of cane syrup. Large bonfires were kept burning in the yard to give the necessary light and heat. There was a great deal of hustle and bustle around the *mielero*. In the yard men sat before long logs, pounding the cane with wooden mallets. This pulp was put into a large barrel, and a round press was placed over it. Across the press the *viga prensa* (a long beam) was placed. The boys fought and scrambled for a ride on the *viga*. Two boys sat on each end, see-sawing. This motion lifted and let down the press, squeezing the juice out of the pulp. The juice thus extracted ran out through a hole in the side of the barrel into a wooden trough. The women poured the liquid with a gourd dipper into the *ollas,* strained it, and boiled it until the juice was a clear red. Then it was poured into jugs. A *jumate* filled with the boiled syrup was passed around to the friends to sample the *miel,* which in flavor surpassed the store syrups of today.

From the pile of yellow pumpkins on the back porch, the smallest ones were selected, peeled, cut in half, and hung on the orchard posts to dry and sweeten in the sun for *tasajos*. They were to be used for *empanaditas* and pie fillings mixed with raisins and piñon nuts. These *tasajos* were also made from melons cut in strips and dried. Tender, young green squashes were cut into round *ruaditas* and spread on cloths on top of the roof. Wild plums also were dried in the same way. Green chile was roasted, peeled, strung, and hung to dry.

Beeves and hogs were butchered, the beef cut into thin *sesinas* and hung on long strips in the sun to dry. Some of the pork was cut in narrow strips and put to soak in *adobo,* a thick liquid made of red chile highly seasoned with garlic and salt. The fat cut in little squares was fried in large copper kettles. These crisp *chicharones* left from the residue of the fried pork fat, were kept to be used instead of bacon, and were also given to the poor when their children were sent to beg for a soup bone to boil with their beans. The soup bone was sometimes passed from house to house to their neighbors, as lard was a luxury possessed only by the rich.

* * * * *

A three or four-day break came in the harvest, to afford the people an opportunity to attend the San Geronimo Indian feast on the thirtieth of September, and the San Fernando de Taos festivities.

After the gayeties of the fiestas, the *peones* took a two or three-day *siesta,* to make up for sleep lost during the celebrations. It mattered not that the *patron* (master) waited a week, with part of his harvest still out in the fields.

"Why hurry?" they said. "*Mientras vida dure tiempo sobra.* (While life lasts there is time left)."

I always compared this axiom with my mother's common admonition: "*Tiempo perdido los santos lo lloran.* (Over lost time the saints cry)."

About this time, Lupe, our Indian cook, would wash and drain in a basket clusters of native grapes bought at San Geronimo and hang them on the storeroom *vigas* to dry for raisins.

When the *peones* went back to work, the corn was hauled in and stacked in the backyard; and in the warm, moonlit evenings of the Indian summer the servants and children sat around the corn pile to husk the corn. Erineo, the Indian servant raised in the family, chopped off the corn stem with a hatchet. This loosened the husks, so that they were easily removed, even by the children, who were told that if they finished the pile quickly they could eat, before going to bed, the watermelon that was hidden under the pile. Sometimes, after working hard, the children were disappointed to find a pumpkin instead of the coveted melon.

The blue and white corn was thrown into separate heaps, afterwards to be brought in and peeled: first, three or four rows of grain up and down the *helote* were peeled with a pointed rod; then one ear was rubbed against the other, knocking the grain off. Two or three *almures* of the blue and white corn were roasted in the mud oven and sent to the mill to be ground—the white meal to be used for mush, and the blue for atole, the hot gruel served with salted boiled milk, the poor man's supper.

Some of the white corn was made into *nixtamal,* boiled in lime water until the skin peeled off, then washed and dried for *posole;* the remainder was ground on the *metate* (a long black pumice stone). This dough was used for making the *tamales.* The blue corn was treated in the same way for making *tortillas.* The wide corn husks were saved for wrapping the *tamales,* and the narrow ones for cigarettes.

The few tender ears of white corn found, were left with a few leaves on, and roasted in the oven for *chicos.* When dry, the grain was peeled off the cob, broken on the metate and tossed up and down in a basket, to allow the air to blow away the skin. *Cilantro, aniz,* and other seeds used for flavoring foods were cleaned in the same manner.

The extra female help needed was never hired. The fathers or husbands considered it an insult to be asked to hire out their wives or daughters. The mistress of the house could ask her neighbors to help, and they would remain with her as long as she needed them, giving them *lo que le nacia* (anything she pleased); but no wages were accepted.

Work on the farms was slow, and the hours were long. The workers started at sunrise and sometimes continued until after sunset. Nevertheless the *peones* worked happily, taking great interest in doing their best for the *patron,* whom they held in great esteem and respect.

The harvest was over, with the threshing of the dry, ripe beans and peas, and the *peones,* leading two or three ox teams to a wagon, were sent to Las Salinas to haul the salt which supplied northern New Mexico and the state of Colorado, as far north as Pueblo. In preparation for cooking purposes, the salt was washed in a large kettle, the water drained, and the top salt skimmed off and spread to dry—the sand and pebbles settling at the bottom of the kettle. To refine the salt for table use, it was boiled until dissolved; when all the water was evaporated it was spread on cloths to dry.

Passing through Bernalillo, the freighters would pick up a few jugs of native wine to bring north. This was the only soft drink then known. The making of this wine was a long process. The grapes were washed, cleaned, and put into a rawhide bag.

The bag was then tied and hung out in the sun to allow the grapes to ferment. After a while it was brought down and tramped on to crush the grapes; then the juice was strained and poured into earthen jugs.

Late in the fall came a richer crop.

Half the village's population would go to the thickly-wooded forests between Arroyo Hondo, San Cristobal and Cerro to gather the brown *piñon* nuts. The forests rang with gay talk and laughter, for this God-sent gift meant not only a prosperous winter for the *pobres* but a vacation of a one or two weeks' camping trip as well. Periodically, every three or six years a full crop was yielded.

Flocks of bluejays added their cries of *"pi-ñon-es"* to those of gleeful children making a lucky find of a *ratonera,* a rat or squirrel hole packed full of *piñones.*

Red flames and blue smoke leaped up through the trees as the fires were started for supper. Later the people visited their neighbors' camps and sang and danced in the silver moonlight. When tired, they stopped to sit around the camp fires and hear the stories of the elders; the children always listened attentively.

At grandpa Vicente's house there was work even during the bleak winter months. In November, word was sent to Don Jose Maria Baca, the tailor from Abiquiu, to come to outfit the family. And Vivian, the shoemaker, was called from Taos to make *el calsado* (shoes). For months these two men roomed and boarded at the house, for they were slow workers. The tailor had to make suits for the entire family, including the servants. The thread for this sewing came in small skeins and was rubbed with a wax candle before used. With a piece of hard soap the lines were marked on the cloth for cutting. *Cordován* (cordovan morocco or Spanish leather), imported from Mexico, was used for the shoe tops. The servants made their own *teguas* from raw-hide.

This work finished, Grandma put the tailor to work, making fancy tin sconces adorned with little mirrors, surrounded by bits of colored glasses. He also made lovely tin frames for Grandma's collection of *santos,* donated to her by the bishop and priests who stopped at the house during the year.

There wasn't space left for another frame on the sanctuary wall of the *capilla,* so thickly was it covered with frames of all sizes. And when Bishop Chapelle came to administer confirmation, he told our parish priest that there were too many *santos.* The Indian maids wove and embroidered altar cloths and made rugs to be laid before the altar. Grandma made *los ramilletes* (paper roses), dipping them in melted wax and arranging them into stiff sprays. These same flowers were still adorning the altar in my young days.

About the first of December, the Ciboleros loaded up their

wagons with bedding and *biscocho,* beans, corn meal and other provisions, and started on their two or three month buffalo hunt. Coming back in early spring in time to start their farming.

Before they had time to unload their big canvas sacks filled with dried buffalo and deer meat, they were met by the villagers with music and feasting.

These loads of meat and salted broiled soup bones, supplied the people's food through the hard working spring and summer.

* * * * *

Early in May, Erineo was sent to the sheep camp to help with the lambing. With two leather bags filled with lunch, tied behind the saddle of the black mule, his roll of brown wool (*sarapes*) tied over it, the *cantina* filled with fresh spring water and hung from the head of the saddle, he was off. After the shearing, he returned, bringing Mother a roll of long-haired, fine silky goat skins. After the pelts were washed and dried, cooked sheep brains were spread on the wrong side. Then they were set out in the sun until the brains melted and soaked into the skins. The skins were rubbed until soft, then rubbed again with a damp soap. The soap suds were then wiped off, and the goat skin was as white and soft as a chamois. Some of the *saleas* were dyed in bright colors and spread before the fireplaces to keep our feet warm. Little, curly lambskins were used on the baby's bed, instead of rubber sheets. These were softened after each washing by the same process as that used on the goat skins.

IX. THE INDIAN FEAST OF SAN GERONIMO

For two weeks before San Geronimo's feast, fierce-looking, filthy Utes trekked slowly over rocky mountain trails from southern Colorado. From their country came the artistocratic Navajos, riding better steeds; and the tamed Apaches arrived, seemingly peaceful but with the wild spirit still smouldering in their hearts. The friendly Picuris, Santa Clara, San Juan, Tesuque, and other Pueblo tribes came from the South. Then followed squeaky wagons, buggies and horsemen, over lofty mesas, down deep arroyos—forming an almost continuous procession descending the Arroyo Hondo hill.

Some took advantage of friendly hospitality and stopped in the village to visit friends and relatives and to rest after their two or three days' rough journey; others went on to Taos.

On the eve of the feast, wagon after wagon camped overnight under the wild plum trees by the Rio del Pueblo. The glow of their supper campfires mingled with that of the fires before the Indian tepees. The Pueblo *coyes* (houses) were filled with visitors from other Pueblos. Indian women bearing great water jars on their heads climbed steep ladders with grace and poise, and glided softly into their neatly white-washed rooms. Indian men, resembling oriental Arabs and Egyptians, shrouded in white cotton mantle, stood on the high roofs—white sentinels etched against the blue vault of heaven. Even their call was strikingly oriental.

These original Americans were building these four-story Pueblos, weaving textiles and decorating their simple utensils long before the Spanish colonists discovered this continent. With the dark blue pyramid mountain as background, this Pueblo exceeds all others in beauty and setting and architectural grandeur.

Beyond La Glorieta, the picnic grounds of the Taos people, the Indians forbade white people to enter the river canyon. Stories were told about the Indians having an enchanted gold mine in the mountains; others about the Indians having a *biboron* (monster rattlesnake), to which they fed infant babies on certain feast days, and this was the reason for the non-increase of the Pueblo's population.

During the Indian and Spanish uprising against the American occupation, and while the United States soldiers were bombarding the pueblo church, where the natives had fixed their stronghold, the *biboron* was being moved to safety from the north Pueblo to the south side across the river, on a hand-cart covered with blankets. The Indian who braved the shower of missiles, in order to save the idol, dropped wounded, as he reached the mouth of the kiva; he dragged the monster wrapped in blankets down the ladder, only to drop dead at the bottom of the kiva.

* * * * *

By six o'clock in the morning on the thirtieth of September, a line of rattling wagons loaded with people had passed by. Buggies washed and shined followed on the twelve-mile ride to Taos, over the sage covered plain, to the Arroyo Seco hill. Below the Taos valley spread in a broad sweep before the eye, like a checker-board in green and gold. Wandering south and west, winding streams and irrigation ditches cut their way like shimmering silver ribbons through ripened fields. Next, they crossed El Rio Lucero, named after the morning star because of its crystalline waters. In another hour's ride they had reached El Prado. Attention was drawn to a high round tower, built against the corner of the large Spanish style house, owned by Don Isidro Valdez. From the inside of this *Torreones,* the people in early days fought the Indians, shooting at them through the loopholes at the top of the tower.

By now the whole valley was astir. Over all the roads leading to the Pueblo were seen all kinds of conveyances and men on horseback raising great clouds of dust. At the north entrance of the Pueblo, etched against the purple mountain and unspotted blue sky, stood part of the front wall and high tower of the ruins of the old Pueblo church destroyed during the Indian revolution in 1847. Crumbling adobes and broken roof beams lay in heaps, as on the day of the battle.

The carriages drove on and parked on both sides of the race track. And from the covered wagons camped under the shade of the cottonwood trees by the river came the fruit vendors, carrying in their arms willow baskets piled high with luscious black grapes, rosy peaches and pears, and yellow melons brought from the warm lowlands of El Rio Abajo. It did not take long to dispose of their loads among the assembled country people. Children greedily devoured the fruit, for this treat came to them only once a year. They paid little heed to the ringing of the chapel bell and to the procession which moved from the church to a shrine of tree branches on top of a *tapeiste*.

The Inditas, carrying the statue of San Geronimo, the patron saint, climbed the ladder and placed the statue in the shrine. Below, in front of the shrine, stood a semi-circle of young Indian men swaying, their nude bodies painted in patches of green, yellow and white, with red *almagra* (ochre) around their eyes and on their temples. Yucca was tied to their ankles for speed, and colored feathers were stuck in their hair.

Then the relay race, the big event of the day. Two of the young Indians, one from each pueblo, started down the track; and two others ran from the opposite end of the quarter-mile course. Along the race course—about four hundred yards in length—stood old Indian chiefs wrapped in bright-colored blankets; others were dressed in beaded chamois, strings of bright feathers circling their heads and hanging down to their heels. Becoming excited when their runners fell a lap or two behind the opponents, these old men would yell excitedly "ha-ma-pah, pu-lu-lu" and hit the heels of the racers with aspen branches as they sped by.

After the races, the chiefs and drum men encircled the runners. Then, singing, dancing, and rustling golden aspen tree branches to the beat of the drum, they slowly moved to the victor's pueblo, where Indian squaws, dressed in gorgeous colored silks and flowered shawls, came out on the terraced roofs with baskets full of *tortillas* and biscuits, which they dropped down to the victors, a gesture significant of the abundance of the harvest. In every house there was a feast spread for visiting tribes and friends. The fields were turned into free pasture, and the sweet, wild plums were gathered freely.

For color, this feast is unrivaled in New Mexico. The north side Pueblo, resting at the foot of the mountain, at this time of the year is gorgeous in Alpine autumn colors. The pueblo fields covered with yellow sunflowers, green and yellow pumpkins, wild plum trees decorated with bright red and yellow fruit, the terraced pueblo roofs a solid mass of people and Indians, in bright silk and satin dresses, the golden aspen tree branches carried by the Indians and decorating the shrine, the vendors' fruit baskets—all mingle in a riot of color.

* * * * *

In a cloud of dust the crowd of people left the pueblo and poured into the sleepy town of Don Fernando, which suddenly awoke to make ready every available room in hotel and home to house the arriving throng. The ancient town, made famous in New Mexico's history by the names of Governor Bent and Kit Carson, famous scout, still preserved the appearance of the old dwellings of the days of the *conquistadores*. It was a bit of old Spain mingled with a touch of Anglo and French, left there by the American troops and Canadian trappers. The Pueblo Indian always in the plaza added another touch to the romantic background of this interesting place.

In the afternoon the crowd flocked back to the Pueblo to see the *chifonetes* perform their clownish stunts. Out of the kivas came the clowns, their nude bodies and faces grotesquely painted.

They clambered over walls and into wagons, frightening children and playing tricks on the women and girls. After they had amused the crowd for a time, they discovered the smooth-shaved, greased pole standing in the yard. With miniature bows and arrows they tried to bring down the fat lamb, watermelon and bundle of biscuits tied at the top of the pole. Then they decided to climb the pole and get them. After many unsuccessful attempts, two or three of them formed a line on the pole, each pushing the foremost one with his head. The top of the pole, in this manner, was reached without difficulty. A rope was tossed to the topmost clown, and by that means the sheep and bundles were lowered, to be divided among the clan.

After witnessing this fun-making, the crowd went back to the plaza of San Fernando de Taos, where the Spanish part of the fiesta was in full swing. In three or four *salas* a *fandango* was going on. Musicians had come from other towns, rivaling each other in displaying their talents; and the dancers visited one hall after another, the largest and best crowd finally settling in the one that had the best music. The dances continued for three nights, until on the third of October the crowd moved over to Ranchos, to celebrate vespers on the eve of the feast of San Francisco.

This feast started the round of fiestas throughout the valley. Los Cordovas, Rio Chiquito, La Loma, each in turn celebrated its patron saint's feast. La Loma celebrated the feast of Saint Anthony on the third of November, although this saint's feast day came on June 13. But in the spring the people had no time for feasting and their store of supplies was at an end, so the fiestas were always held in the fall of the year.

At El Llano, near Ranchos, the old play of Los Comanches, which is a New Mexico drama, was given frequently. The *llano* (flat) was chosen for the play. Here the saint of the day was placed in a tent made of sheets attached to poles. Near it sat a woman guarding two children, representing the two who had just been rescued from the Comanches by the Spaniards. The town men from Ranchos and Llano took the parts of the Spaniards and Indians. Dressed in costume, they rode out to the plain. After a series of speeches or recitations, word was given for the fight to begin. A rescue of the children was made and the Spaniards gave chase to the Comanches, racing for miles. The side that had the better horses was able to race longer and brought the larger number of captives to the shrine; the dejected vanquished returned, bending over their saddles.

Another historical drama given at the fiestas was *"Los Moros."* From the action and the nations represented, I judge that this play dates back to the Crusaders, or to the time when Christian

Spain fought with the infidel Moors and restored the sacred shrines to the Church.

"Los Moros" was also given on a level plain. A cross was placed on a table, beside which sat a watchman. A cavalcade of men dressed in Moorish costume rode up to the watchman and demanded the holy cross. He refused to surrender it. The Moors then rode away, but returned later. This time, finding the watchman asleep, they took possession of the cross and carried it away. A cavalcade of Spanish knights rode out to the plains in pursuit of the Moors. There they met, and the Spanish chief demanded the return of the cross, which the Moors refused to surrender. The two lines of horsemen turned and rode off, clashing their swords as they passed each opponent. Several times the two double lines met, and in each encounter the two chiefs recited a long argument in flowery Spanish.

The Spaniards rode away to the Moorish temple, where the cross was kept; and finding the Moorish guard, who had drained the wine jug laying empty at his side, asleep, the Spaniards seized the cross and returned it to the shrine.

On the second of November, the Indians observed All Souls' Day. They had a Mass offered for the repose of those souls who had departed during the year. On this day they paid the priest the *diesmo* (ten percent. duty), which used to be paid annually to the Church. Not a grain of their crops was sold until after the choicest ears of corn had been selected and each color strung separately in long strings. These strings of corn were stacked in the corners of the Church by the door. In the center two tables were placed by the Indians, one filled with sweet cookies and candies, the other with bread and biscuits. After the Mass, the priest was invited to make a selection from the tables. All that was left was distributed among the people attending the services, as a reward for their prayers. The corn, in two or three wagonloads, was taken to the priest's home.

Before leaving, the priest was asked to go to the graveyard to bless the graves. On each grave had been placed a pretty dish filled with cookies and biscuits. After the priest blessed them, the Indians broke the dish and buried the food and broken pieces in the earth of the grave, so that their dead also might partake of the feast.

X. LA FUNCION (FEAST DAY)

"Often, happy feasts brighten the day,
When, toil forgetting, the village
people turned to play;
Led up to ancient sports,
That pleased in peaceful sorts."

The people, with their mud *trojas* now filled to the brim with precious grain, ripe pumpkins, dried fruits, and vegetables, now turned to play and feasting.

The *mayordomo,* who had been named at the previous feast day took charge of naming the people who were to help clean the church. The statues were brought down from their niches, dusted, dressed in new tunics and set back in their places. Not only the church was cleaned but every house in the village was white-washed inside, and smoothly plastered outside.

At my house a wagonload of home-woven, wool carpets and blankets was hauled down to the river to be washed. Early in the morning the water was heated in a large copper kettle. Erineo cut and pounded the *amole* roots and threw them into the *tablon* —a long log trough; bare-footed women knelt around the trough and with bare arms beat the warm water until the foamy *amole* suds filled the *tablon*. Into the suds the blankets and carpets were dipped, beaten and squeezed, until the fadeless colors were again bright. The *amole* water wrung out, the various articles were dipped into the river to rinse; then they were spread on the meadow grass to dry. The merry chatter of the working *peonas* frightened the meadowlarks and black birds, and they flew out of their nests with a swish of their wings and a snap of their beaks in remonstration for being disturbed.

After the inside cleaning was finished, the porch walls were white-washed. The floors were given first a thick coat of brown mud mixed with fine straw; then they were covered with a fine *alis* (a thin plaster of *tierra ballita*), fine black earth mixed with fine sand. This was rubbed on and smoothed with the bare palms until it was as even as a cement walk. The finishing touch was given to the walls with a piece of woolly sheepskin dipped in the golden *tierra amarilla* dissolved in water. A *regla* or wainscoting, about two feet high, was painted around the base of the walls: no ruler was used to make this straight line. Red *almagre* and *tierra ballita* was mixed to paint the *guarda polvo* in the kitchen and storerooms, in order to protect the white-washed walls.

When everything was in readiness, down to colorful silk

dresses, people from the neighboring villages rode and walked into town to take part in the *fiesta,* which started on the eve with the usual religious ceremony of vespers.

Bonfires lit the path for the procession that came out of the Church and moved around the *plaza* in the twilight. The men standing around the bonfire poured gunpowder on an old anvil, placed a heavy rock on top, and with the red-hot point of an iron rod touched the powder. This resounding salute to the patron saint added a staccato to the beat of the drum and the gay ringing of the bell, which a man, ascending to the roof by a ladder, struck with a rock in each hand.

The next day, after the morning services, the choir and friends were invited to bountiful feasts by the *mayordomo,* who stood at the door as the people poured out of the church.

Before an organ was bought for the church, the priest brought "al Frances, el cantor," the French singer, from Taos; and Don Miguel de Herrera, the fiddler, furnished the music. The two stood by the rail inside the sanctuary. Between each Latin hymn of the Mass, el cantador paused, and Don Miguel came in with a twirling tune on his fiddle. One of the Spanish priests had taught Don Rafael an ancient Mass; and when Don Rafael died, Don Miguel picked up the theme by ear and added this gay twirling tune.

There were no seats in the old church; the maid walked behind the *patrona* and spread on the mud floor, wherever her mistress chose to kneel, the fancy *sarape* she carried rolled under her arm.

In the afternoon different sports were held. The *Matachines* dance was given sometimes in the open *plaza* square; starting from there the dancers went up the *cordillera* dancing in the *patios* at different homes. I faintly remember the *Matachines* I saw dancing in the *patio* at my home. Whether the dancers were invited to come by my father or whether they came expecting a treat at our store, which was a combination dry goods, grocery and drug store, I do not know, but they were treated, and so was the family.

I remember the dancers' fantastic costumes: purple shirts trimmed in pink, green ones in yellow—all in bright, contrasting colors. Bunches of bright-colored ribbons hung down their backs from the fancy, bishop-like caps; jewels, laces, and fringes half-covered their faces. Gay silk handkerchiefs floated from their shoulders and waists. This costume made a wave of color as each dancer took his turn, and with a stamping step to the tune of the one fiddle danced in and out around the single file of dancers, facing forward in two lines. Each participant held stiffly in one hand a fan-like wooden *palma* made of gayly-painted sticks. Each dancer went through different *danzas, la corrida, la palma* and other figures. *El Monarca* and the *Malinche* (a girl dressed in white, with her hair hanging loosely down her back) also took part. Then came the *abuelo,* a man dressed in shabby clothes, carrying a long whip; he acted as a clown—hitting the dancers on their heels with his whip or mimicking their dancing. At the end, the *abuelo* fought and killed the *toro* (wild bull), represented by a man wearing a bull's head. The dancers made their exit dragging out the dead bull.

This aboriginal dance was brought from Mexico. Some say that it is an Aztec dance; others believe it to be of Spanish and Moorish origin. My mother told me that it was the dance danced by the Aztecs when they went to meet Montezuma on his visits to the different Pueblos. The writer finds the Spanish and Aztec blend most likely, as evidenced by the names *Malinche* and *Monarca*. The name *Matachines* has been traced back to an Arabic word, meaning "maskers," suggesting that the dance drama was brought from across the seas.

The villages, usually dark and quiet at night, were now lighted and lively, for the *mayordomo* was giving a dance, the closing event of the *fiesta*. The women, using the high, deep window sills as dressing tables, placed their oil lamps or candles in the sills and rested their mirrors against it while they applied the red *carmin* to their cheeks and the white *albayalde Mejicano* to their faces and necks with the finger tips. Dusted over the dark skin, this preparation had an ashen hue, although these *trigueñas* had gone through a week's bleaching by wearing a mask of wild raspberry juice or white "cascara" made from finely ground egg shells dried in the oven and mixed with soaked rice and the nuts of melon seeds. This cosmetic was made also from deer or elk horns burned until they were white and soaked with corncobs for several days, changing the water often. The bones were then ground finely, and a little *Romero,* which is good *para el aire,* and melon seed nuts were added to keep away wrinkles. The whole combination was sifted through a fine, swiss cloth. The sifted powder was moistened into a paste and formed into little round cakes, dried and applied as a powder or wet as a bleaching mask. *Talvina* was another face-bleaching mask made of bran and the crushed red spikes of the Algeria plant or wild raspberries. With hair dressed high on top of their heads, with a few flat ringlet curls pasted on the forehead with wet sugar, the high-bustled dresses donned—the *doñas* and *señoritas* were ready to be escorted or chaperoned to the *baile*.

The *sala,* where the dance was given, was illuminated by candles placed on *arañas,* two crossed sticks hanging from the ceiling. Between dances, the mud floor was sprinkled with water to keep the dust down. At Abiquiu the mud floor was covered with wheat straw to keep the dust from flying.

The musicians, a fiddler and a guitar player, sat on chairs placed on top of a table at the head of the hall. Against the two side walls sat the chaperons and the *abuelitas* cuddling sleeping babies under their black shawls and puffing at their cigarettes. The whole family, from the grandparents to the wee baby, attended the dance.

A *bastonero* was chosen, whose duty it was to call out the dances and to pick from the crowd standing at the door the men who were to take part in each dance; by this means, he avoided crowding. The chosen men walked to the middle of the hall where they stood in a line the length of the room. Each man invited a lady partner; and taking her by the arm led her to the center, to stand in line with the other women, opposite the men. This was the rule for the *cuna, valse de cadena,* and *indita.* For the *valse redondo,* polka, schottische, and the graceful *varsoviana,* the couples promenaded around the hall, while the musicians tuned their instruments, took a *tragito* and started the music.

As no introduction was needed, the visiting girls—if at all good-looking—were the most popular and were invited for every dance, to the envy of the village girls, who sometimes were passed by for the better looking strangers.

Any open gayety on the part of the women or girls was met with disapproval by the husbands and fathers, but the gallant *pretendientes* were never slow to take advantage of the improvised songs to convey meaning glances or to apply their implication by a tight squeeze of the hand. Aided by the easy rhyme of the Spanish language, the natives had a natural talent for improvisation, and the guitarist interposed through the waltzes and other dances with improvised verses. If the gallant *caballero* and comely *señora* were pleased with the verse sung to them, the *caballero* went up to the singer and tipped him a *peseta* (silver coin).

The amusing verses were usually addressed to the men, the complimentary to the women. When the singer made a ready hit, it caused great merriment and loud *"que viva! que viva! Don"* —here mentioning the name of the person to whom the verse had been addressed.

Some favorite verses:

"Por la luna doy un peso,
Por el lucero un toston;
Por los ojos de esta joven,
Mi vida y mi corazón."

"For the moon I give a dollar,
For the morning star a silver coin;
For this maiden's eyes I would give,
My life and my heart."

"Eres Rosa de Castilla,
Eres clavo de comer;
Eres la mas linda que
Que en el mundo puede haber."

"You are a rose from Castile,
You are a fragrant clove,
You are the most beautiful
That in the world can be found."

"Una manzana verde,
Le dice a una colorada,
Que manzana tan bonita,
Y yo tan achicharada."

"A green apple
Says to a red one,
What a pretty apple,
And I so shriveled up."

Three different kinds of steps went into the make up of these dances, the waltz step, the polka and the Jarabe step, with perhaps a little mingling of Indian steps in some of them, as in the Indita. In the Indita, the singer sang the verses of the Indita song while it was danced.

Indíta, Indíta, Indíta,
Indíta dé Cochití,
Qué le hace qué sea indíta,
Si alcabo no sóy para tí.

Indíta mia sí nó mé quíeres,
Indíta mía ten compación,
Mira que este hómbre qué té idolatra,
Sé siente herído en el corazón.

Porqué me miras indita mía,
Porqué me miras mí bien haci?
Cual es él crimen que hé cometido,
Pór haverte amádo nomás a tí?

El valse Despacio (chain waltz) was danced by two couples joining hands and waltzing around in a ring. They separated and waltzed around each other and proceeded to chain with the next couple coming from the opposite direction.

El valse de las Mascadas (Handkerchief waltz) was danced by a man and two ladies. The man held in each hand a large silk handkerchief, the two ladies holding the handkerchiefs by the other end, crossing back and forth under the man's arms. The women wore these gay colored *mascadas* hanging from their waists.

El Chiquiado waltz was danced by a few who had the gift of verse. The dancers waltzed around the hall until the leading couple came opposite the chair placed in the middle of the floor. The man placed his lady partner on the chair, sang or recited a verse to her and walked to the crowd of men standing by the door. He chose two men and brought them back, one on each arm, and presented them to his lady. If the verse each one recited to her did not please her she disdainfully turned her face away. Her partner went back for another two, until he found one whose verse pleased her. She then arose and finished the waltz with him.

La Polka Suelta was danced by the boldest couple, who did not mind the gaze of the whole crowd. Standing a few feet apart, with their hands on their hips, they polkad back and forth and to the sides until tired out.

La Cuna (Cradle Dance) was a great favorite, and there were several tunes to it.

El Pso Doble, El Fandangito, El Talian, El Vaquero, La Raspa, and quadrilles, were also favorite dances.

El Espinado was danced like the *Indita*—with a hop step, lifting back first one foot then the other, pretending to be picking thorns from their heels. First with one hand then with the other, they twisted gracefully from one side to the other singing at the same time.

Sometimes a tall six-footer coaxed out a bashful little girl, eight or ten years old, whirling her around the hall to the merriment of the whole crowd. The women and girls bedecked her with silk handkerchiefs and gay ribbons, for always on her first dance a girl was *prendida*. The man perched her on his shoulder, carrying her around the hall, while the musicians, who had descended from their seats on top of the table, followed them, playing a march. The parents of the little girl gave a dance or feast afterwards to reciprocate.

Besides the common songs and improvised verse, *coplas* and *corridos,* which were considered part of every gathering and social pastime, there were also a great variety of *decimas*. This eight-syllable line ballad which was the modern version of the Colonial-day ballad, was the accepted form of poetry in New Mexico. The hero's achievements were extolled, parted friends were mourned, the history of tragedies told. The charm of a *simpatica señorita* was set to music by a gallant *trovador*. Sheepherding, buffalo hunts, caravans, brought new *decimas,* written under prairie moons and open skies. *Decimas de lo divino,* taken from the Bible, were sung. Riddle decimas were amusing; a prize was won by the first guesser. My mother once won a cake with this one:

Yó soy como Díos mé crió,	I am as God created me,
Un hombre tan alto y grueso,	A man, tall and fat,
Sin sangre, carne, ní hueso.	Without flesh, blood or bone.
El qué sé halláze sujeto,	Whoever finds himself capable,
Hábleme con claridad;	Answer me with clarity;
Soy viéjo y de tíerna edad,	I am old and of tender age.
Yo no se ni quien me crío,	I don't even know who created me.
Cuando el mundo sé inventó,	When the world was invented,
Yó ví formar lá luna,	I saw the moon formed,
Y sín vanidad ninguna,	And without any vanity,
Yo soy como Díos me crió.	I am as God created me.
Yó ví formar él sól,	I saw the sun formed,
Pero diré dé qué suerte,	But I'll say by what luck,
Fuí padríno dé lá muerte	I was godfather to death,
Y lá lleve a buatizar;	I took her to be baptized;
Ella mé quíso matar,	She tried to kill me,
Pero nó mé halló el pescuezo,	But could not find my neck,
Y por eso mé quedé,	And that is why I remained,
Un hombre tán alto y grueso.	A man tall and fat.
Respuesta—el sueño.	Answer—Sleep.

In some of the old *decimas* the lines do not conform with the eight syllable rule, either through a mistake of the composer or because of some change of wording in transmission, as these *decimas* were orally transmitted from generation to generation. In some, lines were no doubt forgotten, and the four-line introductory verse lost.

XI. GAMES AND SPORTS

The season of repose had come; and while the land rested under a blanket of snow, the farmers sought diversion in sports and games.

After the gay young men left on their buffalo hunt and others in caravans, the village settled down into dormancy.

White bearded men with hard-lined faces sat on their haunches, resting their tired backs against the sunny walls, fully occupied with cracking *piñon* nuts and quietly discussing the last county election or *fiesta*.

On a large level field across the river, on bright Sunday afternoons, the more active men played *El Juego de Pelota*. When the upper town men played against the lower town team, the ball was brought down through the fields, a distance of two miles. A hot struggle carried the ball back and forth until one of the sides succeeded in hitting the fence marked as the winning goal. The losers paid by giving a dance.

Horse races took place out on the level *Llanito*. The men bet money, the women *sudarios* and *rosarios*.

In sunny *placitas* men gathered to witness cock fights. For weeks before the fight, the roosters were fed and given special care. Heavy wagers made the sport exciting.

When not engaged in sports or exciting games, the men played *el hoyo* and moved with the sun to snow-cleared patios. Two small, round holes were dug in the ground about thirty feet apart. Each player, standing by one of the holes, took two turns at throwing his *tejas* (a flat, round stone about three inches in diameter), into the opposite hole. Three points were won with each *teja* that fell inside the hole, one or two points by the ones that fell on the edge or touched the hole. Sometimes the next player knocked his opponent's *teja* into the hole, counting three points for him. Twelve points won the game.

Through the long, winter evening, neighbors gathered before warm fireplaces to play *cañute,* card games, and to tell interesting stories. *La Casina, El Briscan, El Porrazo, El Cuncan, El Entripado,* and *El Monte* were all popular games.

For *El Briscan* the *descarte* (eights, nines and tens) were removed from the deck of cards. After discarding, four cards two at a time were dealt to each of the two players; one card turned up for trumps was slipped half-way under the deck placed in the center of the table. The *briscas* were the aces and deuces; the aces counted twelve points each, the deuces ten, the kings four, the queens three, and the jacks two; the ace and the deuce of trumps were the highest trumps. The dealer played last. The first player tried to lead a small trump if he had a face card to play on his next turn, or a large trump if he had a *brisca*. He played twice, the one who took the trick leading. He took two cards, one at a time from the deck, to complete four cards in his hand. This process continued until all the cards were played.

The game of *Porrazo,* played by four players, calls for the dealing of all cards. A small pile of unshelled *piñons* or beans were placed in the center of the table for the *troja*. Each player took twelve *piñons*. The person next to the dealer led. If the next player happened to have the same card as the one led, he gave it a *porazzo* (bang) with his card and won four points, if the card were a king; three, if it were a queen; two for a jack; and one for any other card. The one who made the most points won five *piñons* from each player. When the twelve piñons were used, each player took twelve more from the *troja*.

The dealer in the *Monte* game was called *El Montero*. He discarded the eights, nines and tens, shuffled the rest of the cards; and holding the deck face down on his hand, he drew out two cards—one at a time—from the bottom of the deck. He laid the two cards lengthwise on the table. The first player chose one of the two cards, turned it across and placed his bet beside it, leaving the other card for the *Montero*. For example, if the cards laid on the table were a three of spades and a six of hearts, and the bidder bet on the three of spades, he would place the amount of his bet beside the three. *El Montero* then drew a card from the bottom of the deck. If he happened to get a three, it was called *salio a puerta* (it came at the door) and the bettor won only half of his bet. If the three were turned up after several cards had been drawn, but before the six, then he would win all his bet. If the six came first, the *Montero* won. There were several ways of betting in this game, as when playing at *mata*. If the three of hearts were out and the player threw a card over the three of spades, lying on the table, he would call, "*Mata tres de oros.* (Kill three of diamonds.)" If the three of diamonds came at *puerta*, the bettor won all his bet. If the three of clubs came first, the *Montero* won.

In *Vieja,* the bidder placed all his money on the card he bid, laying half the money on the card and partially covering it with the rest. If the same card in a different color came first, *a puerta,* he won *vieja,* only half of his bet. If the same number and the same color were turned up first, he won the whole of his bet. If the opposite colored card came first, the *Montero* won.

In *Alza,* a bet larger than those previously indicated is made usually after two or three of the other bids have been made. The bidder placed his money on one corner of the card on which he was betting; and if his card came at *puerta* he won all his bet. If a different card came first, the *Montero* won. The card on which the bet was made was taken off the table, and another one drawn out of the deck and paired with the one left on the table. In this way several pairs lay on the table and several players made their bets at the same time.

Card Game Song

Pequé mi Jesus, pequé,
Si fue por jugar el As,
Mas a quíen he ofendido mas?
Pequé mi Jesus, pequé.

I sinned, my Jesus, I sinned,
If it was for playing the Ace.
But who did I offend the most,
If I sinned, my Jesus, I sinned.

El dos es mi meca mia,
Tantas veces lo jugaba;
Y yo por jugar travieso,
Perdi hasta el ultimo peso.
Bien me puedes condenar,
Pero no tratemos de eso.

The deuce is my mecca.
So many times I played it,
And in playing for pleasure,
Lost even my last dollar.
You may well condemn me,
But let us not treat of that now.

Aquí me tiene esta sota,
Como el heno en el trigo;
Yo quisierva verla rota,
Pero todavia no me fatigo.

Here this Jack holds me,
Like hay in the wheat;
I would like to tear it up,
But I am not discouraged yet.

A mí mé dío una coz,
La reina de Virjan;
Todo me habian ganado,
Hasta el caliz de San Juan.

It gave me such a kick
To play the Queen of Virjan,
For they were beating me out of everything,
Even the chalice of St. John.

Lós reyes té adoráron,
Metido entre lá paja,
A mi los de la barája
Ni las pajas me han dejádo;
Pues yo por jugar travíeso,
Perdí hasta el ultimo peso.

The Kings, they adored Thee,
While Thou lay amongst the straw;
Those belonging to these cards,
Not even a straw have they left me.

* * * * *

Hearing the singing as he passed Doña Casimira's house, Pablino, who had lost all his money at the gambling place, peeped through the window. And seeing a circle of men sitting in front of the fireplace playing *Monte,* he went in and joined the players. The dishes from which the players had just enjoyed a midnight supper were still spread on the mud floor before them.

"Lend me ten dollars," said Pablino to Casimira, but she shook her head in refusal.

"Lend me just five," said Pablino.

Casimira handed him the five, and Pablino gambled until he had won forty dollars; then he stopped playing. Noticing a little white bundle by Casimira's side, he reached around her back and took it. There was something hard inside the knotted handkerchief. He put it into his pocket and left the house. On reaching home, Pablino took the little bundle out of his pocket to show to his wife. Untying the knot, he found a small, hard mud figure, its head encased in cactus, and a small round stone with something that looked like fur growing all over it.

The wife said to Pablino, "You better not touch those things. They mean that Casimira *'le tiene echo mal a su esposo'* (has her husband bewitched). Throw them into the fire."

The minute the mud figure and cactus touched the fire, they began jumping into the air. Pablino's wife made the sign of the cross over them and prayed. Immediately the little figure and cactus settled down, crackled in the fire, and burned.

In the meantime, Casimira's *Monte* game had ended, and she looked around for her handkerchief; not finding it, she lost her mind. This was the punishment suffered by the owner of the magnetic "Piedra Iman" who lost it. Her husband, however, became cured of his terrible headaches which had troubled him for so many years.

La Chuza was played with three little balls, which the manager rolled around inside a wooden bowl in which were rows of numbers. This game proved attractive to women, who staked heavy wagers on the different numbers.

El Cañute Game. The beat of a drum sometimes broke the dead silence on clear, moonlit winter nights. The leader of a crowd of people passed through the street, beating a drum as an invitation to those who were interested in joining the crowd on their way to a private *sala* to play the game of *Cañute*. Two sand piles were placed equally distant from the corners at each end of the room. A tallow candle was placed on top of each pile, to light the room. The winning side of the last game chose its sand pile first and started the game. The men held up their *sarapes*, which they had worn as coats, to form a screen around the sand pile, while one of the players hid the little metal rod in one of the four hollow wooden tubes (the *cañutes*), used to play the game. Then he hid or buried the tubes in the sand, leaving the closed side exposed. The opposite side chose its best guesser, and he was given three chances to guess and draw out the tube that had the rod in it. If he guessed correctly, his side took the *cañutes* and hid them in their pile. If he failed, the same one hid them again. Grains of corn or beans were used to keep count of the points made by each side.

The game was made more interesting by the singer who improvised verses about the players and the *cañutes*. Each tube had a name according to the design stencilled or singed upon it. One was called *cinchado* (girthed); the dark one was *El Mulato;*

then there was *El Uno* (The One) and *El Dos* (The Two).

Luisa dressed in men's clothes was one of the famous gamblers, as well as the clown, at these games. The following verse was composed about her and added to the *cañute* song:

Voy a la otra banda,	I am going across the river,
A traer vara de carrízo,	To bring a reed-grass rod,
Y a decírle a Pedro Serna,	And to tell Pedro Serna
Qué ponga a sú Luisa en juicio.	To make his Luisa behave.

Some of the other verses were:

Tengo de ír a la tienda,	I must go to the store,
A traer liston colorado,	To bring some red ribbon
Para decorar al Muláto,	To decorate the Mulato,
Por lo bíen que me ha pagado.	For the good luck it brought me.
El Cincháado y el Muláto,	The Singed and the Mulato,
Tienen un pleito agarrado,	Have a fight on,
El Dós es juez de distrito,	The Two is district judge,
Y el Uno es su apoderado.	And the One is his attorney.
El camino de Santa Fé,	The road from Santa Fe,
Tiene mil altos y bajos,	Has many ups and downs;
Los primeros cañuteros,	The first canute players,
Entraron del Rio Abajo.	Came through from the Rio Abajo.
Allí vienen los cañuteros,	There come the canute players,
Con atropeo por la cañada,	Tramping through the dale,
Dicen que se llevan palo,	They say they will take the sticks
Pero no se llevan nada.	But they will take nothing.

The winners took the canutes to their village, and for the next game the losers had to go to the winner's village.

Los Titeres (The Marionettes.) A Mexican who had been held captive by the Indians and had learned their dances came into the village one November day. He came out in the *convite* (parade), dressed as an Indian chief and carrying a lance and *chimal,* and went through the streets dancing Indian steps. All of a sudden he would make a dash and poke his lance at a timid child peeping over an adobe wall, frightening the children. That night in one of the *salas* the man gave the performance of *los Titeres*. The people in the audience sat on the mud floor in front of the table which served as a stage for the puppets. A kerosene lamp set in a niche in the wall dimly lit the room. Another lamp behind the black curtain threw the light on the *titeres*. The three most amusing acts were *El Padre Tequesquite, Juan Panadero,* and *La Vieja de los Tamales.*

* * * * *

The children also had their games and toys. During leisure hours, Erineo taught my four young brothers how to make their play tools. From green willow sticks he made bows and arrows with flint points. *Chuecos* (crooks used in the ball game of *pelota*) were made from green scrub-oak sticks. Several deep rings were cut on the handle end to keep the stick from slipping. The other end was heated in the coals of the fireplace and bent into a curb. This curbed end was slipped around a fence post, tied and left to dry in the sun. The balls were made of calf hide, stuffed with rags until they were hard.

Play violins were cut out of grocery box boards, a tin can tied on the back for a sounding board. When Erineo killed a sheep, he cleaned a long piece of the intestines, turned it wrong side out with a little willow stick, and scraped it until it was thin and transparent; then he stretched it between two wooden pegs. When dry it was cut into violin strings.

Maromeros (little acrobat figures) and mouth harps were also made from thin boards.

Manufactured toys and games being very scarce, the games were played on the fingers and hands sitting around in a circle, or around a table. In summer evenings the more active games were played out in the court-yard which was the center of life and activity.

The nurse or older brother took the lead in teaching the younger children. We girls were seldom allowed to play outdoors and then only under our mother's or nurse's watchful eye. We were entertained indoors with quiet games and stories such as I have written in my children's story book, "Spanish Fairy Tales."

XII. SANTOS

We find many objects of great artistic merit in the field of New Mexico medieval arts and crafts: artistically carved chests, *armarios* and *estantes,* lovely embroidered *colchas* and linens, woven *sarapes,* tin frames and niches, fine filigree jewelry. These things may find their counterpart in other countries, but the *santo,* this crude, primitive, wooden sculpture, is New Mexico's unique artistry. Some of the *retablos, reredos,* and statues still found are of real artistic merit, and have a dignity which inspires respect, for they were carved and modeled with great love and reverence. Others are so out of proportion, it must have taken a very simple faith to be inspired with devotion by them.

A special power has been attributed to each saint. The great favorite, San Antonio, is implored to find things lost. He might even find a good husband and money, as the verse suggests:

Sán António bendíto,	Blessed Saint Anthony,
Tres cosas té pído,	Three things do I ask,
Salúd, dinéro,	Health, wealth,
Y ún buen marído.	And a good husband.

Sometimes when a saint turns a deaf ear, after prayers and *novenas,* he is punished by having his picture or statue turned face to the wall, or locked in a trunk, until the request is granted.

San Isidro was invoked by farmers, to send rain in time of drought and to protect crops from pests and storms. An invocation addressed to him says:

Sán Isídro labrador,	Saint Isador, land tiller,
Liberta nuestros sembrádos,	Protect our crops
Dé langostas y temblóres.	From pests and storms.
Sán Isídro bárbas de oro,	Saint Isador, golden whiskered
Ruega a Díos,	Pray to God,
Que llueva a chorros.	To send us rain in torrents.

This saint was so faithful in attending Mass every morning that God rewarded him by sending an angel to plow his field while the saint was at Church.

Santa Barbara was called upon for protection against storms. On many occasions when a dark cloud or lightning storm approached, Lupe, our Indian cook, would step out on the back porch and throw a handful of salt in the form of a cross up to the clouds, saying:

Santa Barbara doncella,	Maiden Saint Barbara,
Libranos Señora del rayo,	Protect us Lady,
Y de la centella.	From storm and lightning.

Each family in this country had its favorite *santo*—an individual, as it were—which was treated as part of the family, sharing the family's joys and sorrows, and appealed to in all troubles. So attached were the old colonial descendants to their saint statues that when the French priests took charge of the New Mexico parishes, they had as much trouble removing the wooden statues from the church as they had exterminating the *penitente* brotherhood.

In the old church at Arroyo Hondo, the penitentes had such a gruesome array of four wooden *Sangre de Cristos* (crucifixions) on either side of the altar, depicting so vividly the Santero's conception of the divine anguish of Christ, that they inspired more awe to us children than devotion.

Under the altar lay *El Santo Entierro,* Christ in the Holy Sepulchre, in a long box with open grating in front. On Holy Friday, when the statue was brought out at three o'clock, the jaws on the statue which were set with a spring, were made to open and shut, simulating a person in his last agony. As the people became accustomed to the new, manufactured statues brought in, the old ones were gradually removed.

At El Rito, the priest finally persuaded the members of the upper *morada* to come to the Church for the Lenten ceremonies, instead of going out to the hills to scourge themselves. But they persisted in bringing in procession to the Church their life-sized, red robed, wooden statue of *Jesus de Nazareno*. Once, while the procession carrying the statue was passing through the town, some Anglo-Saxon traveling men standing in front of the store made ugly remarks, which were overheard by the store owner. As the *hermanos* were returning from the Church, he called them in and told them that if they promised to keep the statue in their *morada,* he would give them a new one. The men agreed to this, and the new statue was ordered. It came in lovely cream robes, but the old statue continued to occupy the principal place in the *morada* and in the hearts of the *penitentes,* who said jokingly that the manufactured statues were not so miraculous, because these *santos Americanos* did not understand the Spanish language.

Don Miguel, *el santero,* who had modeled the sad-looking statue of *Nuestra Señora de la Soledad,* after Aunt Soledad, now came and asked grandmother to let my mother pose for the statue of *Nuestra Señora del Rosario,* the pretty little statue of Our Lady of the Rosary, carried out with Saint John on his feast day.

This reminds me of a little story about Saint John:

A woman, who had made a votive promise to hold a wake in honor of San Juan, lived in a remote mountain village many miles away from the church. She was having great difficulty in finding a statue of the saint. She told her husband, "I guess the only thing for me to do is to hold the *velorio* (wake) using my statue of Saint Anthony."

She fixed up an altar table with Saint Anthony's statue and invited her neighbors to the wake. While they were all devoutly kneeling in prayer, in walked a *borachito* quite tipsy. Kneeling before the statue, he exclaimed, *"San Antonio bendito onde a ti siendo santo te hacen Juan, pues que no haran conmigo!"* ("Blessed Saint Anthony, if you that are a saint they fool and make of you a 'Juan,' what will they not do with me?")

In their distress and troubles people resorted to many religious devotions, and their simple faith was many times rewarded by faith cures, for saints are good friends through whose intercessions one may obtain help. On the feast of *San Blas,* his protection was implored against diseases of the throat. Strands of colored yarn were twisted into *medidtas de San Blas* and taken to Church to be blessed by the priest. After being blessed, these strings were tied around the children's throats.

When their children were ill, the mothers made votive promises. If the child were cured through the intercession of a certain saint, the mother would have *el habito* (the habit of the saint) put on the child. An intimate *comadre* was invited as godmother. She sewed the red habit del *Santo Nino* or the blue or brown ones of Saint Anthony or Saint Joseph, had them blessed, and with a prayer, holding a lighted candle, she slipped the *habito* on the child. He wore it under his clothes until the habit wore out.

XIII. THE PENITENTE BROTHERHOOD

In my youth, *La Hermandad de los Penitentes* (the penitentes' brotherhood) was still active.

Some years ago, I wrote to Mr. Jose Maria Chavez of Abiquiu, who was very well read in history, asking him to give me the origin of the penitentes. I quote his answer, translated as closely as possible from his original Spanish.

"As to the origin of the marked association *Los Penitentes,* it is a well-established fact in history. Born in the Holy Land, the same throng who demonstrated their joy by singing "Hosanna" while they spread their garments on the ground before Jesus, as he entered Jerusalem, afterwards cried out, "Crucify Him," which brought his death. On hearing of His resurrection, some of them tried to choke themselves by tying handkerchiefs around their throats. Others covered their heads and ran distracted. A few gashed their flesh and let their blood flow, trying in this manner to atone for the Innocent's bloodshed.

"Here you have the *penitentes;* later on, the *flagellantes,* their actions modified but not in the form of penance. From Egypt the practice spread to Germany, from there to Spain, and from Spain to New Spain. There is nothing wrong in its object, but it seems rather barbarous and scandalous before modern society."

However, the beginning of the sect is lost to history and different opinions exist as to its origin. St. Justin says that it first appeared in Perugia, and soon spread through Italy, across the Alps, into Switzerland and Germany.

During the sixteenth century, the *flagellantes* were found in Spain and all southern Europe. Some opinion prevails that there is a connection between the New Mexico *Penitentes* and the European *flagellantes*. Others believe that they are a survival of the Third Order of St. Francis and that the sect was brought here from Old Mexico by the Franciscan monks, gradually spreading through New Mexico and southern Colorado.

The first Christian to flog himself voluntarily seems to have been St. Pardulf, a Benedictine monk. The sect spread even among Protestants. In 1535, there was a group called Anabaptists, who whipped themselves.

Among the rules of the Order, most of which still hold good today, is one which states that associates must be members of the Catholic Church and of good repute. The *Hermano Mayor* is the elected head. Newly-initiated members are branded by three gashes cut lengthwise on their backs with a sharp *pedernal* (flint). Members must renounce all evil practices and abandon all feuds with their neighbors. Ill-gotten goods must be restored or atoned for by penance. They believe that pain and penance endured here on earth lessens suffering in the hereafter.

Due credit is given to the English writers who come to New Mexico and write such interesting books from second-hand information, but I wish here to contradict some of their statements.

One author starts his article on the *penitentes*: "Are they lunatics or murderers?" They are neither. The members that live according to the brotherhood's rules are the best, most sincere religious people.

My parents, who lived in Taos and Rio Arriba counties, two strongholds of the *Hermandad* penitente brotherhood, never heard of a penitente being crucified alive and left on the cross to die. In some of the most remote places, like Penasco, Mora and Las Truchas, penitentes have been tied to the cross, and there may have been an instance where a *penitente* died on the cross from exhaustion, from the long fast, loss or blood, or from the flogging which he had been practicing.

As to the statement that some of them have been buried alive, in punishment for the betrayal of secrets of the order, this is another exaggeration. I have heard of their being punished in various ways. One penitente was made to walk with chains, tying his feet together, while he carried a cross on each shoulder. Another was forced to walk blindfolded, his arms extended, holding in each hand a sword with its points resting on his loins. It was alleged that this brother met his death, when he stumbled and fell, the two swords crossing through his sides. A few days later, his clothes, tied in a bundle, were sent to his family, with word that the boy had left for the Holy Land.

One form of punishment was the criss-cross gashing of their backs, laying them on the floor and switching them with a knotted rope until they fainted.

A penitente sometimes requested, before his death, that he be buried bare-foot or without a coffin, as a penance. His request was always carried out.

The *desciplinas* (palm whips) were usually dipped in Romero decoction, to soothe the cuts and to keep them from becoming inflamed with the cold, and not to add more sting, as some writers say.

Penitentes never walked into a church or chapel carrying their crosses. They slipped from under them covered with their blanket, and each pair left their two crosses standing outside, interlocked in some way.

The Catholic Church has condemned the Order for years, excommunicating the members of the *moradas* who insisted upon going out and scourging themselves. This strict order of the Church, together with the weight of opinion among the younger members who are becoming educated, will in a few years put an end to the sect.

Penitente Morada

XIV. HOLY WEEK AT ARROYO HONDO

In this hidden nook, isolated from the outside world and still untouched by modern progress, people were contented to live their simple lives. Still holding to ceremonies carried on from the medieval age of faith and religious traditions, during Lent every year they reenacted with sincere religious fervor the Sorrows of the Passion Play. The *penitente* brotherhood took charge of the religious ceremonies, inasmuch as there was no resident priest in the town in my time.

On Monday and Tuesday of Holy Week the conical adobe ovens were seen smoking throughout the three villages, while the week's supply of bread and *panocha* was being baked. The mud ovens must be blessed before using them, or they won't bake the bread right; it will come out heavy and soggy. To bless the oven, a cross is laid on the floor of the oven, salt is sprinkled on the cross and prayers recited.

At the *penitentes' morado* where half the male population congregated on Wednesday, one *mayordomo* (sometimes two) was chosen for each day to supply the food for the brothers who fasted each day from Wednesday morning until Saturday noon, when the *mayordomos* vied with each other in treating the *hermanos* to the nicest repast. Four or five of the *accompanadores* (brethren of light) were seen coming out of the *mayordomo's* house carrying four copper kettles hanging on a stick. These kettles contained *torrejas con chile* (egg fritters in chile sauce), *rueditas* (fried dried squash), and *sopa de fideos* (home-made spaghetti). They carried in an earthen bowl bread pudding, with cheese and raisins. All meat was forbidden during the four Holy days. Recipes for these lenten dishes will be found in my cook book of Spanish recipes.

There was a great deal of exchanging done of *charolitas*—dishes—at noon on both Holy Thursday and Good Friday. Neighbors and friends were seen carrying back and forth small bowls filled with *panocha, capirotada, torejas,* or whatever other nice dish they had prepared. This exchange of special dishes went on in every small village during Holy Week.

The *morada* stood across the river a few yards below the town. On each side of the door, resting against the wall, was a pile of century-old crosses, which were kept inside the secret room from year to year.

With a field glass my family had a very good view of the *penitentes* as they came out of the *morada*. The members were told that with this field glass we could distinguish their faces through the black masks. After this, for fear of being detected, the brethren of light stood in line outside the front of the door, holding up outspread blankets, thus screening the *penitentes* while they came out. They took up their crosses, over which a blanket was thrown, leaving only their heads and feet exposed. Followed by the *hermanos de déciplina* (flagellantes), they dragged their heavy crosses around to the back of the *morada* and proceeded on their painful way up the rocky trail to *el calvario* (Calvary Cross on the hill).

* * * * *

On *Viernes de Dolores,* the Friday before Good Friday, my grandmother carried out her votive promise of giving an alm and a dinner to the poorest family in the village.

She had brought from Old Mexico her favorite painting of *Nuestra Señora de Los Dolores* (Our Lady of Sorrows). The beautiful madonna face, with a tear like a pearl rolling down her pink cheek—her white hands clasping tightly the handle of the sword piercing her breast under her blue mantle—was tinted in soft shades on a tin sheet and framed in a fancy tin frame. Throughout the year every dime or nickel that the grandchildren could save was pasted around the picture inside the glass covering it.

The daughters and their children were invited also to the dinner. At the end of the meal, the tin frame with the painting was brought down; the nickels and dimes were taken off and together with a crown made from coffee cake dough baked very nice and brown, the hollow center filled with *melcochas*—candies, was given to the poor family as the promised alm.

The *Tenebrae*. On Wednesday evening, *Las Tinieblas* were held at the *morada*. The name *Tinieblas* was given this office because towards its close all the lights were extinguished to represent the darkness that shrouded the face of the earth at the time Christ expired on the cross, as well as to express the profound mourning of the Church at that time.

Fifteen candles were placed on a triangular wooden stand. Those at the sides were snuffed out successively, beginning with the lowest one, at the end of each of the eleven Penitential Psalms, representing the flight of the eleven apostles; the other three candles represented the three Marys.

When the central light, representing Christ, was the only one left, it was removed by the *resador* to the back of the altar, where they continued their chant. Between chants, one of the *resadors* stepped out to the front of the altar, and striking a match he whirled it around saying, *"Salgan vivos y difuntos, que qui estamos todos juntos."* The flash of light from the match represented the lightning. In the dim light the bent, huddled figures of the *penitentes,* their bodies bare to the waist, filed in through the low door. With their masked faces and long white trousers they looked ghostly. The air in the small oratorio room, already packed with men and women kneeling on the floor, became stifling. Above the roar of the wooden *matraca,* the rumbling of chains, the wail of the reed *pito,* groans and prayers, was heard the thud-thud of the *penitentes'* blood-matted whips.

The removal of the central light and its sudden reappearance represented Christ's death and resurrection.

At the close of the ceremony, all but one of the *penitentes* filed out to their secret room across the hall. The one who remained stretched himself across the floor at the door, and the brethren of light who accompanied him told the people that the brother requested in the name of God that every one step on him on their way out. I heard of a cruel woman who more than complied with the request by grinding her heel into the flesh of the *penitente's* bare back. Another one, more kind-hearted, begged the *hermano* to excuse her from complying with his request.

Moved by curiosity to see the inside of the *morada,* I once asked a *penitente's* wife, who was going to pay a votive debt to the *santos* at the *morada,* if I might accompany her. We climbed the hill on which the *morada* stood in the upper town and were admitted to the chapel. On the wall of the hall dividing the chapel from the secret room hung a row of whips. The woman crawled on her knees from one statue to another, placing lighted candles before each. I was left kneeling before the statue of the Crucifixion. Paralyzed with fear, I could not move, for there before me on the mud altar table stood the statue of *La Muerte,* Death, staring at me with one glass eye, the other eye shut, aiming at me with her drawn bow and arrow. Behind me I heard the *hermanos* going in and out of the room. I did not dare turn around for fear of seeing a *penitente* standing in back of me. This visit satisfied my curiosity.

For a couple of years during Holy Week a flagellant *penitente* with his *acompañador* came to our private chapel and asked permission to go in and make a visit. While the brother of light recited the prayers, the brother lay prostrated with arms extended on the floor before the altar. He got up and stood by the door while flogging himself, leaving the bloody marks of his *disciplina* on the white-washed walls. Then he left, still flogging himself as he passed in front of our store on the way back to the *morada.* My family persisted in believing that this was the man who had helped himself to one of the fat lambs from our corral and had come to atone for it. The oft-repeated verse of *"Penitente pecador, porque te andas azotando? Porqué mé comí un carnero gordo y ahora ló hando desquitando,"* applied in this case.

On one occasion, hearing the doleful notes of the penitentes' flute, I ran out to the front porch in time to see three *penitentes de madero* passing on their way to visit the lower town *morada*. My uncle, sitting on the porch step, teasingly grabbed me by both hands and swung me out towards them. My breath caught with fright as I thought that one of them had stretched out his hand from under his blanket to grab my feet.

Anyone wishing to see a *penitente* now must stay up quite late at night, and then he may get only a glimpse, as they come out only one or two at a time and are very carefully guarded and screened-in by the *acompañadores*.

HOLY WEEK. On Maundy Thursday at two o'clock in the afternoon, the *Emprendimiento* (Seizure of Christ) took place. The men carrying the statue of *Nuestro Padre Jesus,* a life-sized statue of Jesus of Nazareth, crowned with thorns and dressed in a long red tunic, led the procession out of the Church. The *resador*, reading the seizure and trial of Christ, walked behind the statue, followed by the throng of women.

From *la morado* on the opposite side of the town two files of brethren of light, representing the Jews, started out. These men had red handkerchiefs tied over their heads with a knot on top representing a helmet. They were preceded by a man dressed like a centurion. The Jews carried long, iron chains and *mattracas,* or rattlers. On meeting the procession coming from the Church, they stopped before the statue and asked "Who art Thou?" The men carrying the statue answered, *"Jesus de Nacareno.* (Jesus of Nazareth.") The Jews then seized the statue, tied the statue's hands with a white cord, while their leader read the arrest sentence. The other Jews stood, loudly clanging the chains and rattling the *matracas*. They led the procession back to the *morada*, carrying with them the statue.

El Incuentro. The next morning—Good Friday—the same two groups took part in the ceremony. This time the group that left the Church carried the statue of *Nuestra Señora de la Soledad* (The Sorrowful Mary), dressed in black; a black mantle covering her head, over which a silver halo shone. The procession of men representing the Jews came from the *morada* carrying the statue of Christ. The two groups met half way around the town, representing the meeting of Christ and His Mother. One of the women took a white cloth from her head, and approaching on her knees wiped the face of the statue, while the grieving Marys wept real tears aloud. The *resador* read the passage of the meeting of Christ and His Mother as the procession walked back to the Church.

About half an hour later, *La Procesion de Sangre* (The bloody procession) of all the *penitentes* combined, in the long double file of flagellants, was seen winding its way up the rocky trail to the *calvario,* then back again to the *morada.* Special self-imposed penances were practiced between one and three o'clock in the afternoon. A lone penitente sometimes staggered up the trail surrounded by brethren of light. He dragged his feet tied with a heavy iron chain. On his back a bunch of sharp cactus needles pricked his flesh at every step.

Good Friday. *Las Tres Caidas* (Three Falls). The largest and heaviest cross was picked out and laid upon the shoulder of the *hermano* who chose to represent the crucified Christ. A crown of thorns was placed on his head, and a bunch of prickly cactus was hung on his back. Laboriously, the *penitente* dragged the scraping cross up the rocky trail. Two brethren of light walked on each side of him, one reading the three falls in the Stations of the Cross from an open book in his hand. The other, acting the part of Simon Cyrene, helped the *hermano* lift the weighty cross when he stumbled and fell under its weight. A group of brethren of light had already dug a pit and gathered a pile of rocks by Calvary Cross. They stood around the *calvario,* awaiting the arrival of the *Cristo* brother, who on reaching the hill was stretched upon his cross and tied with ropes. The cross was raised and placed in the pit surrounded by the pile of rocks to hold it upright.

The *hermanos* knelt with bowed heads around the cross, praying and reciting the Seven Last Words of the crucified Savior. The voice of the man upon the cross grew more and more faint, as he repeated the words, until his body hung limp, and he was taken down and carried on a blanket, too weak to carry his cross back to the *morada.*

Las Estaciones. At three o'clock the people gathered at the Church for the Stations of the Cross. The procession of *penitentes,* some carrying crosses and others switching their lacerated backs, came first. Between the two files walked a masked *penitente* pulling a small cart in which stood the statue of Death. "Comadre Sebastiana" death was called. The *acompañador,* walking behind the cart, now and then picked up a large stone and dropped it into the cart to make it heavier to pull. The men carrying the statue of *Nuestro Padre Jesus,* another man with a crucifix, and the reader walked in the center of the procession. As the *resador* read each Station of the Cross, the people knelt on the ground, then arose and walked singing a verse of the *alabado de las columnas.*

Én una columna atádo,	Onto a pillar,
Estaba El Réy del Cíelo.	The King of Heaven was tied.

Chorus

Herído y ensangrentádo	Wounded and bloody,
Y arratrádo por los suélos.	He was dragged on the ground.

A few days after the close of Holy Week, some of the young men would appear at the store looking pale and haggard. My brother, curious to find out if a certain young man were a *penitente*, gave him a friendly slap on the back. Taken unawares, the man betrayed his secret by a painful shrug and expression of agony on his face.

Sabado de Gloria closed the Holy Week with joy and cheer, for Lent ended at noon on Holy Saturday, and a big baile was given that night.

In most of the old Spanish mansions a *sala* (long living room) was always included. In this room the private invitation dances were given. To these dances only the exclusive Spanish society was invited. For the private dances of *carestrolendas,* egg shells filled with confetti or cologne water, were taken to the dance. These were playfully broken on the heads of the dancers, providing much merriment. Refreshments of wine, *biscochitos,* cakes and candies were passed to all the guests. This custom was attacked by the towns' parish priests in their sermons, but in the remote villages, which the priest visited only once a month, the people followed their own rules and customs.

* * * * *

On the first of August, the *penitentes* celebrated the wake of *La Porsiuncula,* the most important event, excepting Holy Week. The two *moradas* combined for this wake. The gloomy interior of the old church was illuminated by tallow candles placed on tin sconces hung on the side walls and stuck on the mud floor before the statues of *La Sangre de Cristo* (Christ on the Cross) and *Nuestra Señora de Los Angeles* (Our Lady of the Angels), which were brought down from their niches and set before the sanctuary steps.

The weird strains of the flute announced the approach of the *penitente* procession which stopped outside. The women and men kneeling on the mud floor moved to the sides, men to the left, women to the right, opening an aisle for the penitente chief and the brethren of light, who passed in, chanting hymns accompanied by the lonesome notes of the flute.

With arms crossed, they knelt in prayer before the statues, while the *mayordomo del velorio,* chief of the wake, distributed to each person a lantern. The lantern was made from a beer bottle, the bottom of which had been taken off by tying a string saturated in kerosene around it, and then burning off the string. Through the open bottom, candles were set in the neck of the bottle and lighted.

"Comadre Sebastiana" (Statue of Death)

The penitentes, numbering about thirty, led the procession. First, walked the flagellantes, their bare backs streaming with blood. In unison, their whips were raised first over one shoulder and then over the other. They took two or three steps, paused, and then swung the palm whips over their shoulders again. Following the flagellants were those carrying crosses, each guarded by an *acompañador,* walking by his side. The brethren of light and the men carrying burning pitch-wood torches came next. In the middle of the procession walked the men with the statues; behind them came the *resador* and the singer, Hemerejildo, reciting with great fervor the rosary on large blue and white glass beads hung around his neck. The women followed. The two lines of candle light circled the town, and the outline of the square could be seen from the top of the hill.

Each decade of the rosary was offered in song:

Jesús mí dulce dueño,	Tódo cristíano procura,
Desagraviarte queremos,	Llorar ún paso tán tíerno,
Recíbe Padre amoroso,	Libra Vírgen del infierno
Las flores dé este mistério.	Quíen resara sú rosario.

The lonesome lament of the flute and the wailful chant, punctuated by the painful slap of the palm whip, lingered in the echo of the hill after the procession had gone back into the *morada.*

XV. WAKES

The wailing of the unearthly *pito* or the doleful cadence of the *alabados* were heard no more except at the *velorios*, or wakes, which were held in different houses and at the Church throughout the year, paying votive promises to the saints or for the dead. When a *velorio* was given in honor of a saint, the statue was brought from the Church to the house or borrowed from a neighbor and placed on an improvised altar, surrounded with tallow candles and stiff sprays of waxed paper flowers. The whole town turned out to attend the *velorio*. The people knelt or sat on the mud floor around the altar, while the *resador* recited the rosary and other prayers. Then the men and boys took turns singing *alabados*, hymns of praise to the saints. About midnight supper was served to all the people, some of whom remained until early morning, when they returned the statues, singing on their way.

When a wake was held for a deceased person, it sometimes lasted two nights, according to the wealth of the deceased or of the relatives. The next morning a home-made pine coffin, containing the remains, was carried in a wagon to the cemetery. The women mourners stayed at the house, lamenting. The *resador*, the singers, and the crowd of bareheaded people followed the wagon chanting the *alabados* in mournful voices. I have read that this custom of singing while burying the dead was observed in early times in the old country.

En route to the *campo santo* or to the Church cemetery, where the exclusive were buried, in graves two and three deep, a stop or two was made. At each stop a wooden cross was afterwards propped up with a mound of stones to remind the passer-by to pray for the repose of the soul of the dead, whose funeral procession stopped at that place for rest.

When the deceased belonged to a family whose members belonged to the *penitente* brotherhood, groups of flagellants visited the remains from midnight on, after most of the people had left the wake. Early in the evening the remains, shrouded in a long black *mortaja* were placed on a stretcher and carried out in procession, while the people recited the rosary. In the summer the wake was held in the open yard, candles and lanterns lighting the procession and the yard. Under the silent spell of the night rose the mournful chants instilling their sad cadence into one's soul. For weeks after the funeral people called to offer sympathy to the bereaved. Women and even young girls must call, dressed in black and wearing black shawls.

A week after black-bordered cards were sent to relatives and friends announcing the *misa de ocho dias,* and at the end of the year for the anniversary mass.

When a sick person was in his last agony, the *resador* whose profession it was to recite prayers at religious gatherings was called in to *gritarle Jesus,* call out the name of Jesus three times as the person was expiring.

XVI. NOCHE BUENA AND RELIGIOUS DRAMAS

>"Let the luminarias leap high
>As the night grows long,
>And the shadows dance
>To the caroler's song."

On the twenty-fourth of December the snow lay heavily on the deep valley, half burying the silent little villages nestling among the while hills. As the last rays of the setting sun turned the highest snow-capped peaks into gold and rose, the men and boys of the three villages busied themselves clearing the snow from the front yards in every house. They were preparing the ground for the *luminarias,* which later in the evening they built of *ocote*—pitch wood sticks, placed by fours in log cabin fashion. Rows of these *luminarias* outlined the towns and *cordilleras.*

As the deepening shadows of night spread over the valley, the brown adobe houses were brightened with the red glow of their fire, which warméd the groups of men and boys standing around them. The fires built in front of my house were kept burning brightly until midnight by an occasional addition of an empty kerosene barrel, which had been saved in the store for that purpose.

Inside the house there was great activity in the kitchen. The children warmed the *piñones* and shelled them by rubbing them between two boards. These nuts were used in the mince meat for the *empanaditas* (little fried pies). An extra hired woman beat the white corn dough until it was so light that a small piece dropped into a cup of water floated on top. It was then ready for the *tamales,* which were made and steamed, to be served with hot coffee after the midnight chapel services. Lupe and her helpers were kept busy until almost midnight, frying the *empanaditas* and *buñuelos* for the *Oremus* boys, who came to the door singing:

Orémos, Orémos,	Oration, Oration,
Del cíelo venímos,	From heaven we come,
Angelitos somos,	Angels we are,
Sí nó nós dán Orémos,	If you won't give us gifts,
Ya no volverémos.	Alas, we won't return.
A lás señoras caséras,	From the housekeepers,
Aguínaldos pedímos,	New Year's gifts we ask.
Con mucha alegría,	With great joy,
Con mucho conténto,	With great contentment,
Vamos celebrándo,	Let's celebrate this birth.
Este nacimiento.	Give us here, if you will give,
Dénos aquí, si nos han de dar,	For the night is long,
La noche es larga,	And we have lots to walk.
Y hay mucho qué andar.	

A large pan of fried dainties was passed to these *Oremos* boys at the kitchen door, and they ate them, sitting around the bonfires.

Santa Claus was still unknown in those days. The *abuelo* (bug-a-boo man) took his place, although he was a stern old man dreaded by the children. Dressed in an old, shabby, patched suit and shabby hat, the *abuelo* went around the *luminarias* cracking his long whip, sending the boys home on the run. He followed some of them into their homes and made them kneel down and say their prayers. If they did not know their prayers, he gave them a good scolding and told them to stay home and learn them, but no sooner was the *abuelo* out of sight than the boys were out again, hopping, running and jumping over the bonfires, for the Spirit of the Christ Child filled their innocent hearts and fear could not remain long in them.

Down in the village the group that was to take part in the performance of the play of *Los Pastores* was going from house to house making *Las Posadas*. They represented Mary and Joseph going through the streets of Bethlehem seeking shelter for the night.

In earlier times, for nine days before Christmas groups of children led by a couple representing Mary and Joseph went through the village to nine houses. The group was refused entrance until they came to the ninth house, where they were admitted and refreshments passed to them. Here the hermit held up his cross at the door, trying to prevent *el diablo* from entering, but the shrewd evil one watched his chance and entered while the hermit was busy eating the refreshments spread before them. Satan played his pranks, helped himself to anything he liked, rattled his long nails, wrote in his book the names of the girls and women who smiled at him when he asked them if they wanted to come with him.

At the end of the village the group came to the chapel where the wake of *el Santo Niño* was taking place. Here the group gave the play of *Los Pastores,* the religious drama of the shepherds.

When making *Las Posadas,* Joseph knocked at the door of each house singing:

Quién le da posada
A estos peregrinos,
Que vienen cansados
De andar los caminos?

Who will give lodging
To these travelers
Who come weary
From traveling long roads?

A voice from within answered:

Quién da golpes a la puerta,
Que de imprudente hace alárde,
Sin reflejar que ya es tarde
Y a los de cása despierta?

Who bangs at the door?
The imprudent makes a commotion,
Without noticing that it's late,
And the household he awakes.

Joseph:

Señor os implóro,	O Lord, I implore Thee,
Que en vuestra caridad,	That in Thy mercy
Le des posáda a ésta dáma.	Thou wilt give shelter to this damsel.

Voice from within:

Para él qué tiene dinéro	For him who has money,
Mí casa está lista,	My house is ready,
Para él qué no tiene,	For him who has nothing,
Díos lo asista.	May God assist him.

Into a stable door they retired, where an ox and a mule were their only companions.

A BRIEF SYNOPSIS OF THE DRAMA "LOS PASTORES." There were twelve shepherds in the original play of *Los Pastores,* but at the time of which I write only six took part:

Characters

Shepherds—Tubal	Gila
Belicio	San Miguel
Lipido	El Ermitaño
Bato	La Estrella Oriental
Lizardo	Bartolo
Tebano	El Diablo

In earlier reproductions of this play, there was another female character—Dora, wife of Barto, one of the shepherds.

A shrine had been arranged with white sheets and a table at the head of the *oratorio* chapel. A double row of pine trees formed an aisle from the shrine to the middle of the room, through which the shepherds marched in double file, carrying flowery staffs with dingling little bells. A bundle slung over one shoulder suggested the bedding of the shepherds.

Ahead of them walked Hila, a serious-looking little girl, dressed in white, wearing over the veil on her head a tinfoil covered crown. She carried a small baby statue in a basket filled with snow.

Bartolo, the lazy shepherd, walked behind the other shepherds, carrying a sheepskin, which he spread under a tree and then lay upon.

The shepherds tramped up and down the aisle singing verses about the heavy snow and their flocks sleeping down in the valley.

Shepherd Song

Cielos soberános,	Sovereign heavens,
Tenednos piedad	Have pity on us
Que ya no sufrímos,	For we cannot longer endure
La Nieve qué cae.	The snow that falls.
Suspénde tus íras	Suspend Thy rage
Y tanto quebránto,	So many damages,
Qué ya están poblados,	For the valleys
De Nieve lós cámpos.	Are already covered with snow.

Las estréllas bríllan,	The stars shine brightly,
Y luego se apágan	Then get dim
Absortas se quédan	Amazed to see
De ver tal neváda.	Such a heavy snow.
Que cópas de níeve,	What large snow flakes
Caen sobré el ganádo,	Fall over the flock,
Aunque entre el monte	Although resting
Está reclínado.	Under the forest.

Belicio suggested stopping a while, to let the flocks rest, saying:

Pues hermanos míos,	Well, my brethren,
Ya que el cielo nos ha permitido,	Since heaven has permitted
Traernos con grán dicha,	Bringing us with great happiness
A estos valles dé Egipto,	To this valley of Egypt,
Si les pareciere bien,	If it seems right to you,
Parémos aquí un poquíto,	Let's stop here a while
Que descansen los ganádos.	To rest the flocks.

The rest of this drama will be found in my book of translated Spanish dramas.

EL DIA DE LOS INOCENTES (Holy Innocents Day). I do not know why this day was celebrated on the twenty-eighth of December instead of after the Kings' visit to the Manger, for it commemorates the day on which King Herod put the children of Judea to death by the sword. On this day one had to be very careful about lending things; and if you loaned something, you must not forget to say, *"Se la empresto, pero no por inocente."* Anyone who forgot to say this had to pay a penalty.

On one occasion my aunt, who lived close by, sent her maid to ask my mother to let her have my baby brother for a little while. My mother, forgetting the day, let the girl take the baby. A few minutes later the maid returned with a tiny broom made of a few straws tied with red floss and wrapped in a little note with the words, *"Barrete la inocencia paga la pena."* Mother at once set to work baking a cake which she sent to my aunt to *desempeñar* (redeem) the baby; he was sent back with the same cake bearer.

DIA DE ANO NUEVO (New Year's Day). Instead of the birthday, the Spanish celebrate the Saint's name day. New Year's day is the day of los Manueles, and the women and men called by this name were serenaded on this day.

One year my brother, who was visiting at my home during the holidays, thought he would play a joke on my husband. He slipped quietly out of the house at four o'clock in the morning and rounded up the musicians who were going around the town *dando los dias a los Manueles* (serenading).

We awakened with the sound of music and singing at our front door; my husband in bathrobe and bedroom slippers opened the door and was greeted by the usual verse:

"Por aqui caigo, por aqui levanto,
A darle los buenos dias,
Pues hoy es dia de su santo."

He politely invited the serenaders to enter; and they made themselves at home, while he ransacked my pantry for refreshments. My brother sat among them, with a broad smile, quite pleased with the success of his joke.

My husband's grandmother's name was Manuelita; and not wishing to disturb her so early in the morning, my brother had them come to our house to give the serenade in her honor.

* * * * *

Gifts were exchanged on the sixth of January, celebrating the arrival of the Three Kings at the Manger in Bethlehem to offer their gifts to the newborn Babe.

On New Year's day Grandma Melita started counting *"Las Cabañuelas"* for twelve days. Each day of the month represented one of the months of the year, and as the weather showed on each day so would the month be fair, stormy or cold. If January the second was fair and mild, so would the month of February be. The third was counted as March, and so on through each succeeding month. On the thirteenth, *Las Cabañuelas* were reversed and counted backwards, beginning with the month of December. This count was said to come out more true. The definition given for the word *"cabañuelas"* is *"Festival of the Jews of Toledo,"* so this custom must be originally from Spain.

This marked the end of the Christmas ceremonies.

RELIGIOUS DRAMAS. As the dramatization of Bible stories was an old Spanish type of entertainment, it has been assumed that the Spanish *conquistadores* brought the religious drama to Mexico, and that from there the Spanish missionaries introduced it into New Mexico in their efforts to convert the Indians to Christianity. There are four Christmas plays that come in a cycle—in this order: *El Coloquio de San José; El Auto del Niño Dios*, or *Pastorela*, now called *Los Pastores* with several versions; *Los Reyes Magos*; and *El Auto del Niño Perdido*.

El Coloquio de San José begins with a summons from Simeon to all the males to appear at the temple with a reed in hand, for the purpose of choosing a husband for Mary, one of the Virgins in the Temple.

When Feliciano, the herald, comes to Joseph, he voices the wishes of his master, saying:

Vós patriarca escuchad.	Patriarch, thou listen.
Pues ya sabeis que Simeón,	Well thou knowest that Simeon,
Cabéza de éstas comárcas,	Head of this territory,
Manda púes qué los patríarcas	Commands that all the patriarchs
En sú real generación,	In his royal generation,

Hoy al templo soberano	Today at the sacred temple
Sean obligados a llevar,	Are obliged to appear
Una vara en sú máno	With a reed in their hand,
Y de parte de Simeón	And I, for Simeon,
He venido a tí avisar.	Have come to inform you.

Joseph, because of his poverty, is reluctant to go into the temple, and he sits in the portico. Suddenly his reed sprouts forth a lily, and he is chosen to espouse Mary.

After the Annunciation, several months elapse; and Joseph and Mary are on their way to Bethlehem. On reaching the town, they go from house to house seeking lodging for the night. This part of the action is represented by *Los Posadas,* which is an introduction to the play of *El Niño Dios,* or *Los Pastores,* the second drama of the cycle.

Then comes the third drama, *Los Reyes Magos.* The three kings, noticing the new star in the East, decide to go to Bethlehem and offer gifts to the Christ Child. They stop at the palace of King Herod, who gives them welcome and asks them to stop again on their return. The kings reach the manger and present their gifts. After they leave, an angel appears and bids Joseph to take Mary and the Infant and flee into Egypt. On the way the Holy Family meets a number of shepherds, who recognize them.

The fourth drama of the series is called *El Niño Perdido.* Christ, being separated from His parents comes, in his wanderings, to a rich man's palace. The rich man is seated at a banquet table when the Child arrives. He tries to confuse the Child with his questions, but is given wise answers. At the end, the Child arrives at the temple, and the Doctors of the temple gather around to question Him, while Mary and Joseph are looking for Him. The script of this play is given in my book of Spanish dramas.

* * * * *

Besides the Christmas cycle, there is an earlier one of more simple folk plays, some of which are still enacted in remote mountain villages. This cycle is composed of three plays: *Adam y Eva, Cain y Abel* or *El Primer Pecado,* and *Lucifer y San Miguel.* It is claimed that "Adam and Eve" is the oldest play written. It opens with a song by Adam and Eve, as they are sitting on a bed of boughs underneath the Tree of Knowledge:

Song

Guerra és lá vída del hómbre
En la estación de sú império,
Dé morir en la campaña, irrevocable el decréto.

Lucifer calls all his helpers to dethrone man from the position to which God has elevated him. "Appetite" volunteers to tempt Eve, in the form of a serpent. Eve snatches an apple from the forbidden tree, and passes it to Adam, who is eating it when

God, in a thundering voice, reproves them for their disobedience. Shamefacedly, they try to cover their nudity with branches of leaves. God orders them out of the garden. "Mercy" intercedes and begs that the penalty be waived. God promises man redemption through the birth of Christ. Eve laments their fall in a long recitation. The angels then foretell the coming of Christ, and the play ends with the song:

| Glória a Díos en las altúras, | Glory to God in the highest, |
| Y páz al hombre en la tíerra. | And peace to man on earth. |

The first drama presented in New Mexico, was The Moors and The Christians, given at San Juan de los Caballeros, during the dedication of the first church built by the Oñate expedition. When first enacted these darmas were held out in the open; afterwards they were given in *salas* (dance halls).

During the past thirty years the Spanish religious dramas have been discontinued. A few years ago a new legend of Our Lady of Lourdes was presented at Chamita, and in recent years Los Pastores have been revived, and the legend of Our Lady of Guadalupe, but these few presentations given, are not acted with the same vim, nor in the natural setting and costumes, and they have lost much of their attractiveness.

The legend of Our Lady of Guadalupe, which originated in Mexico over four hundred years ago, tells the story of a shepherd:

Juan Diego, the Indian shepherd, while tending his sheep on the hills near the city of Mexico, sees a vision. The Virgin, surrounded by a radiant light, appears to him, saying: "Juan, go to the Bishop and tell him to build a shrine in my honor here on this spot." Juan delivers the message, but the Bishop refuses to believe his story, until after the fourth apparition, when he brings a proof in the form of fresh roses which the Virgin commands him to pick on top of the mountain and to take to the Bishop. This is taken as a miracle, being in the month of November when the country was barren of flowers.

Upon being admitted, Juan kneels before his superior and relates the episode of the roses. As he opens his blanket, the fragrant roses tumble out at the Bishop's feet. On the blanket was stamped the image of the radiant Lady, just as the Indian boy had seen her in the apparitions on the hill. In robes of blue and rose, rays of light surrounding her, she was poised on a crescent moon, born up by a cherub's wings. The astonished Bishop is now convinced and orders the shrine of Our Lady of Guadalupe built on Tepeyac hill. The miraculous blanket was hung in a gold frame over the altar.

A new shrine, noted for its riches, now stands at the foot of the hill. The rail enclosing the sanctuary and the stairways leading to it contain many tons of solid silver. Twelve massive, solid silver candelabras hang from the ceiling, and a dozen silver candlesticks adorn the altar.

I visited the *santuario* during the holidays, which start a week before the celebration of the feast of Our Lady of Guadalupe.

Crowds of pilgrims visited the church. Some of them holding lighted candles crawled on their knees from the door to the rail before the altar. Others sat in the yard eating their lunch, or at the booths where hot lunches were being served. Many climbed the hill to the spring, on the site of the old shrine, and filled bottles with the miraculous water to carry home. Faith still gives it the power to perform miracles and to cure.

XVII. SAINTS' HOLY DAYS

DIA DE SAN JUAN (St. John's Day). Icy winter glided into spring. April showers gave life to the gray valley and turned meadows and fields into verdant seas. In warm, sunny May, rivers and arroyos filled with water that came from the mountain's melting snow. The overflowing *acequias* wound their way through freshly ploughed and planted fields.

School closed late in June, and on the twenty-third my father awaited me in the convent parlor. After bidding goodbye to my teachers and to Sr. Rosana, the principal, who was one of the pioneer sisters brought by Bishop Lamy, I joined him and climbed in the high seat of our buggy, of a make now forgotten. We rode along, inhaling the delicious fragrance of the newly-awakened sage and gray-green rabbit brush, which later in the summer would be covered with yellow blossoms. The desert plain seemed a fairyland. Here and there the road dropped into a verdant little valley, the sparkling river fringed with fresh green trees and drooping willows. From the edge of the highest ridge one looked down into the Arroyo Hondo, sunken valley, which in its rich verdure seemed to lie asleep, the deep silence enveloping the valley—broken only by the rattling of our buggy wheels or the distant barking of a dog.

I arrived home in time for the feast of the beloved disciple St. John. The women of the village were up early on the twenty-fourth of June. At six o'clock they were bathing in the river or in the *acequias*. Later in the morning the small children were seen also in the river and ditches, splashing cold water at each other, for on this day the waters in the streams were believed to be holy. Better health awaited those who rose early to bathe at least their faces and feet in the holy water. For was it not St. John who baptized Jesus in the river Jordan and blessed the waters?

The day was kept at Arroyo Hondo as a Rogation Day. By eight o'clock in the morning a procession started from the Church in the upper town. Standing on a wooden platform, the statue of *Nuestra Señora del Rosario*, dressed in a gala blue silk dress, and the statue of *San Juan*, carried in the arms of one of his devotees, were taken on a tour through the fields, along the foot of the second ridge of hills to the lower village—a distance of three miles. On arriving at the village, the procession visited each house. A boy beating a drum went ahead announcing the approach of the procession, which halted about ten feet from the door of the house. The lady of the house came out to meet the *santos,* with a *scudilla* full of live coals, over which aromatic incense had been sprinkled. She incensed the statues and helped carry them into the *sala,* where they were placed on an improvised altar decorated with wild flowers and tree branches.

Around the altar the crowd of people knelt while the lady of the house recited prayers, sang a hymn, and pinned a flower or jewel on Our Lady's veil or dress. Then the people arose and proceeded to the next house. Having visited every house in the lower village, the procession walked to the middle town, then up the *cordillera* to the upper town, reaching the Church at dusk, where a wake in honor of the saints was held. Sometimes the wake was held at the house in which the procession stopped just before dusk.

* * * * *

On the Fourth of May was celebrated *El Dia de La Santa Cruz* (Feast of the Holy Cross). At the chapel or at the home of a devotee an altar was erected in tiers. On the top tier a wooden, decorated cross was placed. From here it was brought down and rested on each step, while a prayer or hymn was sung or recited. Then the cross was taken out in procession to the next village, where a wake was held in honor of the Holy Cross.

* * * * *

DIA DE SANTIAGO. The feast of *Santiago,* the national patron saint of Spain, was and still is celebrated in some of the northern towns, on the twenty-fifth of July. After the morning services at the Church, the statue of Saint James, the patron saint of *los caballeros* (horsemen), was carried in procession through the town. Two files of gallant horsemen, *socios de Santiago,* with their horses' bridles decorated with flowers and flags, rode ahead of the procession. A few yards from the procession they halted, turned, and rode back through the center of the procession in pairs to meet the statue. The two files crossed and galloped ahead. Again they whirled and galloped back to the statue, repeating this during the whole procession.

The *gallo* race, held years ago, has been replaced by horse races and modern sports. The rooster race of old was similar to the rooster race the Indians have at San Juan Pueblo, except that the Mexicans, instead of hanging the rooster as the Indians do, bury it in the ground, leaving its head exposed.

At Arroyo Hondo a group of *galleros* gathered at one end of the street, about fifty feet from the buried cock. One by one, they raced past the rooster, back and forth at full speed, leaning over the side of their saddles to grapple at the fowl, until one of them succeeded in grabbing its head and unearthing it. Swinging it by the legs over his head, with a triumphant shout he spurred his horse and raced ahead, the whole pack of horsemen yelling and racing after him. Up the *cordillera* they chased to the upper town. When finally one of the *galleros* overtook him, he turned and hit the man with the rooster. The challenged horseman grabbed away the trophy and raced on ahead, hotly pursued by the others. The rooster changed hands in this way several times during the race. Back they came like an avalanche, lashing their horses, yelling and racing down the hill to the lower town, where they crowded around the leader. A hot skirmish ensued. The *gallero* defended himself by striking in all directions with the rooster, until the cock was torn to pieces.

After several roosters met this fate, the crowd scattered, and a wagon was hitched, in which the *convite* for the *baile* started out. A fiddler, a guitarist, and a singer climbed into the wagon and rode around the three towns, playing and singing, finally coming back to the hall where the dance was to be held. This was the public invitation to the dance.

Early in the evening the hall was packed. Gray-haired *abuelitas* cuddling the *nietos* lined the back row around the hall. The young women who took part in the dances sat in front. All classes mingled in these public dances, from the silk-gowned *patrona* to the calico-dressed Indian maid. The elite left the dance early, before the men became too gay with drink. Sometimes a drunkard forced his way into the hall, causing great excitement when the *bastonero* tried to push him out.

Jealous husbands and lovers sometimes took advantage of the commotion to get even with their rivals, and a fist fight took place in the middle of the hall. The women—screaming and jumping over seats, dragging by the hand children that were half asleep—pushed their way out. When finally the *bastonero,* with the aid of the sheriff or sober men, restored order, the dance went on.

Through the clouds of smoke from the home-grown *punche* tobacco cigarettes, the bent heads and crouching shoulders of the *musicos* were seen. There was languor and softness in the wire strings, then recklessness and madness, as the dance wore on and *tragitos* from the musicians' pocket flasks went to their heads.

DIA DE SANTA ÁNA. The next day was *Santa Ána's* day. Every woman fortunate enough to own a riding horse and side saddle brought them out. And with a white sheet thrown over the saddle and tied underneath to keep the long flowing skirts from soiling, she rode off, dressed in all her finery, to join the other lady riders. When tired of riding, they dismounted at the dance, which continued through the hot afternoon into the night.

These Holy days were always gala occasions eagerly awaited and long remembered.

XVIII. LA VILLA REAL, ITS BEGGARS AND INTERESTING PLACES

Preparations were made for my entrance at the Loretto Academy, at La Villa Real de La Santa Fe de San Francisco de Assise. Autumn's coloring brush had already touched the little valley, turning its summer greenery into bright fall shades. Flocks of wild ducks flew overhead on their journey to the south. Meadow larks sang their morning song, robins chirped on tree tops, and all nature smiled out of doors, this bright sunny morning, as if trying to cheer my sad heart at parting with my loving family. My father and I started on our one seated buggy on our two and a half days trip to La Villa. A stop for the first night's rest was made at Los Luceros, where my father's uncles, Don Nemecio and Lucas Lucero lived, in the big double house built by their father, Don Diego. The house stood on top of a high hill commanding a beautiful view of the Chama and Rio del Norte valleys.

This was the region of the explorer Oñate. Here with his courageous colonizers and pious friars, Oñate built the first Spanish settlement and church near San Juan de Los Caballeros, and started a culture of arts and science in the New Spain, before the Atlantic seaboard was settled. The industry of weaving started here and the first drama of Los Moros was given during the dedication of the church.

From Taos we traveled over the old road which connected Fort Garland with Fort Marcy in Santa Fe, called *El Camino Militar* (the military road). The building of the new road, running through the box of the Rio Grande river, was done later, through an appropriation obtained by Mr. Antonio Joseph, when he was a delegate to Congress.

Another day's ride brought us to Tesuque. Fresh horses were secured, and the last pull up the Tesuque hill was made, just as the last rays of the fading sun painted in bloody hues the mighty Sangre de Cristo Range, rising majestically behind the round towers of the *Catedral de San Francisco*. The silvery notes of the cathedral bells chiming *Las Aves Marias* floated through the air. Pausing and raising our eyes to *La Estrella de la Oracion*, we fervently repeated an Ave Maria with each three even strokes of the bell. These strokes were divided by a pause, followed by a long ring for the *Oremos* prayer. Descending the hill, we entered the *plaza,* settled then into quiet evening peace and deserted except for a few men standing in front of the dimly oil-lamp-lit saloons.

My father's aunt, Mrs. Caspar Ortiz, welcomed us to her home on the corner of El Rio Chiquito, on the site of the present Montezuma hotel. From a two-story building with white *portales,* the house gradually sloped into a one-story building on the corner of San Francisco street. In the large room on this corner was *El Numero Cuatro,* the only large grocery store in town.

Walking down Rio Chiquito then was like walking through old Juarez town. Ancient-looking houses and Mexican shops lined the narrow street. The most popular place was *El Parian de Doña Chata.* Here were found all kinds of *remedios,* medicinal and flavoring herbs, *pilonsillo, tortas de pan, bollitos,* baked into all shapes in adobe ovens, and blue and white cornmeal for *atole* and *tortillas.* At the end of *El Rio Chiquito* we came to *La Sala de San Francisco,* built by the *Socios de San Francisco. Los Pastores* and other Spanish plays were performed in this hall.

* * * * *

Further up the street was the two-story mansion built by Don Perfecto Irrisarre for his first wife, Magdalena Lopez. Don Perfecto was a descendant of two of the wealthiest New Mexican families, the Armijos of Albuquerque and the Irrisarris. He married into the wealthy Lopez family of Santa Fe, and thus came into possession of a great fortune, which he lavished on his wife and home. Magdalena Irrisarre wore the finest diamonds and jewels; her table service was of solid hand-hammered silver. One's foot sank into her soft, thick, floor carpets. But Magdalena enjoyed these luxuries only a short period.

After she passed away, her parents—not willing to let this immense wealth pass out of the family—tactfully hinted to Don Perfecto that Pablita, the second daughter, was then of marriageable age. *"La China Lopez"* (Pablita's nickname, because of her auburn curls) told her mother that she objected to the marriage, but her father's word was law; and when Don Perfecto made the formal proposal, her mother stood beside the girl, giving her timely pinches until she answered "Yes." A second elaborate wedding took place, but La China, although surrounded by luxuries and servants, was not happy, for there was no love in her heart for her husband. Sometime later, she eloped with a doctor, who deserted her after a few years.

Then Don Mariano Larragoite, still remembered as the flowery orator in New Mexico legislatures, succumbed to the irresistible alluring charms of La China's beautiful eyes, peach complexion and tumble of auburn hair. La China embarked on her third matrimonial adventure, becoming the wife of Don Mariano. He lost his fortune and took his wife to live on his farm at

Chamita. She then had to be her own maid and was seen even doing her washing in the *acequia* (stream); but this time La China had married for love, and she did not mind the hardships. She was happy. Later, believing that luck would favor them more kindly in California, they moved to the "Sunny State." But fate was against La China, and her romantic life ended there in an automobile accident.

Don Mariano's father, Don Benito Larragoite, called *"El Gachupin,"* (as the Spaniards born in Spain were then called) always rode on horseback. In his long full cape and flat-crowned, black hat, he was a real, dashing *Caballero*. There were a few more of these *"Gaupos Caballeros"* seen leisurely strolling through the streets of La Villa, with the right end of their full capes thrown over the left shoulder. They gracefully swung their gold or silver-handled walking canes with an air of importance as they swept off their fine black hats when they met with the friendly greeting of, *"Caballero! como esta?"* There was a great contrast between the pious Don Felipito, coming from Church every morning dangling his silver-medaled rosary, and the dudish *abogadito* twisting his long, curling mustache. This Spanish dude held the record for the greatest number of marriage contracts. He ordered his wives through the "Police Gazette," and they left him in less than a year. When he finally succeeded in keeping the last one for more than a year, he was host at a noisy celebration of the anniversary.

On Sunday afternoon, when *La Banda de Don Pancho* played, the plaza was crowded with people. Dignified, stout Doñas promenaded up and down the old Palace porch. Boys and girls filled the park, circling around in quiet decorum—the girls chaperoned by their Indian maids.

But the most picturesque sight in *La Villa* and not seen in our northern towns was the *carretas* and trains of burros loaded with wood. The *leñadores* guided the animals with a stick, while they bargained their wood around the town. In my village burros were a rare sight, seen only when the fruit vendors from Rio Arriba came with their willow crates filled with yellow apricots, melons and the sweet, little Mexican apples.

El Callejon del Burro, which has now vanished into memories before the march of modern progress, was then a picturesque alley, with its ancient adobe houses, dusty show windows and trains of burros placidly asleep in sunny corrals behind Gold's and Candelario's curio stores.

Carmelita, who impressed me as a second Tules Barcelo, although in a different way, occupied perhaps, in this alley, the same *sala*—saloon, in which the notorious Doña Gertrudes, queen of the gambling den and her companion, Francisca, held sway over governors, generals and other high officials.

A glimpse of the arched opening, underneath which artists have pictured Spanish Troubadors, and the view of the distant blue mountains seen through the crack in the tumbling wall in the rear of the *patio,* stopped me at her door.

On a cot in the open *saguan* sat the *medica*. Beside her sat her servant, old Rumaldo, tired of walking the streets selling honey, on a broken chair behind the door, resting his chin on his hands, clasping his walking stick. His twenty-pound tin can was at his feet.

Both were listening attentively to the story Carmelita was telling them. She paused when she saw me, but I asked her to continue her story of the Four Wise Councels. Her facial expression and hand gestures gave life to her narrative. A black cat jumped upon the cot and curled up on her lap. She gently stroked its fur, then picked up the gray one pitifully meowing at her feet, jealous of the attention his mistress was giving its rival. The magpie sitting quietly perched on its stick with its head cocked to one side, seemed to be listening too.

"Beware of the *medica*," people whispered. "Witches keep magpies and black cats. These are people she has bewitched."

Carmelita with the smattering of medicine, which she had acquired from her American husband and her knowledge of herbs, followed the humble calling of *medica* (doctor). She was known for her generosity, not that she ever went around scattering gold coins like the famous gambler, but she dispensed her chile, beans and tortillas with equal generosity to Anglo, Mexican and Indian, and her table seldom lacked a guest.

At night passers-by heard the click of wine glasses and squeaky phonograph music mingled with the gay revelry inside. "My magpie likes music," explained Carmelita when she bought the phonograph, as an excuse for an old women like her having such lively noise in her house.

* * * * *

"Our town is full of history, which our ancestors helped to make," said my cousin Lolita, who was showing me the town. "Look down the list of names of the Spanish governors in the old Palace, and you will find several Martinez: Francisco Martinez de Montoya, second acting governor after Oñate, Cap. Gen. Governor Felix Martinez, the last one who served under Spain's rule, and from whom your family descends, down to Mariano Martinez, who according to Governor Prince's history was the most energetic man that ever occupied the executive chair."

"I must show you San Miguel's chapel," said Lolita. "It's the oldest church in the United States. Built about the year 1621, it was destroyed in the Indian rebellion of 1680 and rebuilt by De Vargas in 1692."

I felt quite privileged, when the good Brother handed me the clapper and my gentle tap on the treasured old bell rang out in silvery tones through the silent chapel, as once its sweet tones echoed through the peaceful Andulucian hills of Spain, before it was brought to this country. The Spanish crown formed the handle from which the bell hung in the old tower.

The Brother pointed out the historic beam under the choir loft, placed there by the Marques de la Peñuela, and showed us where the remains of General Diego De Vargas were buried.

"Here men who bore the arms of Spain
Once had the faith to kneel,
Before a greater King, whose
Might is not conquered by steel.

"And we who pass this shrine today,
No matter what our creed,
We see this citadel of Faith
Still serving human need."

The quiet Palace Hotel had now taken the place of La Fonda, the popular Inn at the end of the trail. La Fonda had been famous for its fine wines and high life, in the wild days of the "Wooly West."

* * * * *

At the Cathedral of Saint Francis, Lolita led me through the sacristy, which was part of the old church. The two chapels on the *cruseros* on each side of the main altar were also part of the old building. Through a very low door in the back of the altar we entered the sacristy museum, where old wooden *santos* and *retablos* taken from the old church were housed. Against the wall rested the carved stone *reredo,* bearing the inscription that it was donated by Governor Antonio Maria del Valle and his wife, who ordered it made for *La Castrensa,* the old military chapel on the south side of the *Plaza.*

The Castrensa had not been used for several years for religious services, and it was sold and the *reredo* moved to the church. The high stone altar carved by Spanish craftsmen is one of the finest examples of Spanish Colonial and religious New Mexico art, which has been preserved for more than two hundred years. A new Cristo Rey Church has now been built to house this bit of marvelous art.

* * * * *

After viewing the painting of Christ in Gethsemane, painted by Pascual Veri in 1710, which hung over Saint Joseph's altar, and another of the same painter's works that hung over the Virgin's altar, we left the Cathedral to join my uncle, who awaited us in his fine *coache,* brought several years before from Saint Louis by his father-in-law, Don Gaspar. The driver took us up the road to *La Garita* and Fort Marcy. *La Garita* had been the Spanish prison during the Spanish occupation, but was at this time owned by Mrs. Gaspar Ortiz. While I was on a visit to her home, Governor Prince called and asked Mrs. Ortiz if she would donate *La Garita* to the Historical Society. They wanted to use it as a museum, and would place her statue and that of her husband in it. But Mrs. Ortiz had suffered great losses in properties and found it necessary to realize some cash from the sale of *La Garita.* The building which Adolph Gusdorf had leased from her for his dry-goods store on San Francisco street had burned to the ground. *El Polaco* had skipped the country, leaving Don Gaspar with a nine thousand dollar note; which Don Gaspar had signed as security for *El Polaco;* and Don Gaspar paid the note in full. Her sons, brought up in luxury and riches, had learned only to spend money; and her properties, once extending from the river to San Francisco street, were disappearing rapidly, because of heavy mortgages and taxes. Before his death, Don Gaspar had donated the land running through his corn *milpas* for the street now bearing his name.

The devout General De Vargas also built the Rosario Chapel, when he returned to find the works of devout Franciscan labor destroyed. He had made a vow that if the Virgin of the Rosary, whose image he carried on the expedition, would help him conquer the savage Indians, he would erect a temple in her honor. After a bloody, all-day battle, he and his men won the victory, and a new title of *"La Conquistadora"* was added to the long list of the Little Lady's titles. De Vargas kept his vow and built the chapel on the ground where his little army camped on his first expedition for the re-conquest of New Mexico.

In *La Cuidad Real de la Santa Fe de San Francisco de Assisi,* the faithful live up to the teachings of their faith and practice the old religious ceremonies. They are especially loyal in keeping De Vargas' promise. Every year in the spring, the partly-patriotic, wholly-religious procession takes place. On a Sunday afternoon, after vespers, the beautiful little statue dressed in lovely blue, wide-skirted dress and white lace, her flowing black hair reaching almost to the hem of her dress, is carried perched on a platform supported by four young girls belonging to the Association of the Children of Mary. They walk between two lines of little girls, dressed in white and carrying flowers. Brilliantly-dressed women and sober, black-dressed nuns and priests follow.

The procession emerges out of the *Arroyo de Los Mascaras,* and the little *Conquistadora* is carried triumphantly into the dim Rosario Chapel. Candles flicker, monks chant, and the faithful kneel on the floor. They leave the Chapel glad in their hearts that they have honored *Nuestra Señora del Rosario* and kept their hero's vow. Every morning before six o'clock the Chapel is crowded with the faithful, who flock there for the nine-day novena of Masses. On the last day, the statue is again carried reverently in procession back to the Cathedral.

Besides its many religious feasts, the old Villa has its patriotic *Fiesta,* held in compliance with the proclamation made by the Illustrious *Cabildo* on September 16, 1712, in which it was ordained that a fiesta season be annually observed in honor of the redemption of the ancient capital from the possession of the Indians. Each year, in the month of September, the city gives itself up for three days to the celebration. The first night the fiesta opens with the grand ball of the *Conquistadores,* which everyone attends in Spanish costume, on Sunday the religious part of the proclamation is completed by the church services and candle-light procession to the cross of the martyrs. On Monday everyone joins in the *Pasatiempo,* dancing in colorful Spanish costumes. Old-time frocks, folk dances, dramas, and shows vivify the visitors' illusions of dwelling in the past. The *gente,* who have come from the surrounding farms and villages go back to their humble mud houses with their hearts full of happy thoughts of the *fiesta.*

The day after our arrival in the city was Saturday, the day on which the village beggars called for alms. Early in the morning, Higinio, the cook—a cute, little elf-like man with pointed chin, hooked nose and bent shoulders, was seen on his way to the *Numero Cuatro* market, carrying a large basket on his arm. He returned with the basket piled with candles, soap, coffee, bread and other articles, which were divided and wrapped into smaller packages.

At nine o'clock in the morning, the beggars began to come. The blind, led by a small boy, called at the door, *"Ave Maria Purisima!"* They continued to pray while Irene, the maid, handed them their bundle. On receiving them, they repeated a *"Deo Gracias"* and a long blessing on the home and family.

Mendicity apparently has always had a lure for certain beings. We read about a Moore-Carew, Malone Compote, and other chronic mumpers who even in our present times have amassed fortunes through fraudulent begging.

In New Mexico our beggars have always been worthy cases and there are but few now left.

El Mum-ma-ma was a pitiful sight. With a wooden block held in one hand, he pushed his half-paralyzed body, dragging on the ground. He stretched out his active hand for an alm, mumbling *"mum-ma-ma."* Nurses told the children that he was an example of God's punishment sent upon children that disobeyed their parents, that Macedonio had sworn at and cursed his mother and that God had struck him dumb and decreed that he should murmur, *"Mum-ma-ma"* the rest of his life. The real story, however, is that Macedonio was a dancer in a Mexico show house down on San Francisco street. A mud table with a hollow center filled with red coals served as his stage. After one of his daring dances on the coals he suffered a stroke which maimed him for life.

Biatriz, the young woman who was half-witted, had a hobby of collecting trinkets of all kinds and slipped them into her four large pockets which she wore tied around her waist, until her dress skirt stood out like a hoop skirt.

The most notorious character about the streets of La Villa was *El Rey.* As an insignia of his royalty, he wore a shiny tin star or a cross pinned on the front of his stiff derby hat.

Leaving the crowd after church services, I was warned to look out for *Tio Pellizco,* the pinching man, who with his arms crossed, looking very devout, from under his arms would give the girls and women uncomfortably hard pinches.

Two old women sat in the old Palace porch all day long begging alms, *"una limosna por amor de Dios."*

There were many more interesting sights in La Villa Real, that we now miss.

XIX. OLD CUSTOMS VANISH

Times were changing since Oñate unfurled the flag of Spain over the old Palace in the capital of Santa Fé. In August, 1846 General Kearney unfurled the stars and stripes over the same building and took possession of the Territory of New Mexico, in the name of the United States.

American immigration began to pour into the territory. The rich Spanish Dons, up to this time owners of the land for which their fathers had fought and bled, now found themselves against something they could not cope with. Transferred to a new sovereign of alien language and divers political views, the Spanish population, sensitive, proud, constantly fought to maintain its political and social equality.

Accustomed to a slow, leisurely life, they could not compete in business with this quick, business-like race. The rich began sending their sons to eastern schools to be educated in the English language. The sons returning from Notre Dame and Georgetown Universities with a fair knowledge of the English, could have taken up their father's business, but they had not been taught to work. Time hanging heavy on their hands, they took to saloons for amusement, learned to gamble and drink the Anglo's hard liquor, until then unknown to them, and soon squandered their parents fortunes. Land grants and business properties passed into the hands of the stranger for minimum sums. In their sad, humbled state, the families of the *Dons* retired into the background, holding to the small possessions they had left.

Race issues between the two races began kindling. The continuance of the harmonious relations, and political tolerance and respect became a problem. Young Ven. Jaramillo saw no other remedy but to enter politics, run for the legislature, and see that good laws were enacted, to protect his people. He made the run for representative of his county and won.

In January when the legislature convened, the Democrats lacked three members in the House of Representatives to have a majority. Having succeeded in unseating two Republican members, the hot fight turned against the Rio Arriba county Representative. They had found out that young Jaramillo was not yet twenty-one years old and was illegal to vote. His friends, members of the famous Rough Riders, Captain Maximiliano Luna, and Llewellyn, Charles Spiess (the San Miguel County "Black Eagle"), and others rose to his aid. Time must be made. They brought out their most eloquent, long speeches in his favor. At last the 28th of February arrived, and as the young representative walked triumphantly into the House, his friends rose from their seats with extended hands to congratulate him. His twenty-first birthday had arrived and saved the situation.

After our marriage my husband went more strongly into politics. He was elected senator on the next two elections. He won for his home town the state Spanish American School, worked hard for its growth and improvement and today this school has become a great institution, of great benefit to his people.

When next elected as member of the Constitutional Convention, which formed the laws of New Mexico, when the territory was admitted into statehood, his ambitions were realized. New laws were passed and the native population have since enjoyed better recognition, and greater understanding and harmony exists.

But the old customs have vanished. The young generation finding the strangers' customs new and attractive, began to adopt them and to forget their own. The colorful *rebosos* and *tapolos* vanished. Modern music, songs and dances, have replaced the soft, musical melodies and graceful folk dances. The quiet reserve and respect has gone, which was so great that even after the sons and daughters were grown up and married, they knelt before their parents to receive their blessing and kiss their hand, and would sooner burn their hand, than to be seen by any of their elders with a cigarette in their hand. I heard my mother's aunt once tell her: "That's one thing my sons have never done to me, is to smoke my gray hairs." The old Spanish courtesy and hospitality has also changed, to the regret of the elders, who have found it hard to get accustomed to the new ways.

The land of *Poco Tiempo* has become the land of haste and hurry.

XX. A BIT OF NEW MEXICO FOLKLORE

There is great interest found in the study of folklore, of old ballads, music, beliefs and customs of peoples, who, isolated in their mountain sheltered villages, kept their customs unchanged by modern culture.

A few years ago a vast treasure of Spanish folklore that originated in Spain was still found in New Mexico. It was said to be the same folklore that was found among other primitive nations in Europe. The belief in witchcraft was the most widespread, which still survived a few years ago among a great part of the native population, and still survives among a few of the elders.

The *ambularias* were graduates in witchcraft and held schools where the beginners were taught how to bewitch and how to transform themselves into different things and animals. The *ambularias* that came into the possession of a *Piedra Iman,* were still more powerful; they knew everything and could transform themselves into any shape. The *Piedra Iman* was a fury stone which was fed needles and water, and if the stone was lost or stolen from its owner, the owner immediately lost her mind or dried up into a skeleton.

Four miles north of our village of Arroyo Hondo was the remote little hamlet of San Cristobal, consisting of a few scattered houses hidden in the bleak wilderness of the wooded hills. On a low hill cleared of pine trees and shrubbery stood the house of Don Benerito, the *medico* famous for curing people *malificiada* (bewitched). A peculiar malady especially prevalent among women attacked the people of this place. After attending a large gathering, such as a *velorio* or dance, where she had been offered a *cigarrito* or refreshments, the person the next day would lose her mind. As it was an act of courtesy for the women to pass their tobacco pouches and beaded *ojeros* to those sitting near them at these large gatherings, my family concluded that the secret was this: a woman jealous or having a grudge against another would grind some *pellote* (loco berry) found on some of the trees and mix it in the tobacco or drop a pinch of the powder into her food. Although some of the persons cured by the *medico* declared afterwards that they had only drunk water from the same glass that another woman had used, I often wondered if the *medico* himself did not have something to do with the distribution of the loco powder, for he was in great demand at this place.

When called to cure ill persons, the *medico* told them that someone *"les tenia echo mal,"* and that the remedy sometimes was in their own home, which meant that a member of their own family was harming them and that he could not cure them until that person was removed. He said this when he failed to cure them. A few he cured permanently, but most of his patients lapsed into the same malady every few weeks or months. The doctor was called in again and again, thus making a lucrative living for himself.

* * * * *

Old women who lived alone were usually suspected of being witches. La Chon was one of these women in our village. She was usually found sitting on a sheepskin in the corner of her fireplace, smoking a *cigarrito* and poking the fire with a stick to keep her pot of beans boiling. A low door, always kept covered with a ragged patch quilt, led into her storeroom. No one was allowed to enter this secret room, where bunches of dried herbs hung from the rafters of the ceiling and a pile of ripe pumpkins stood in a corner. From the pumpkin rinds, Chon made the *guejas,* into which she crawled and sailed through the air to places she wanted to visit. Once La Chon was met walking through the park in Santa Fe by a lady who knew her well. The lady asked Chon if she would take a package to her mother who lived in the same village. La Chon called for the package and delivered it to the lady's mother the next morning. In those days it took three days to make the trip from Arroyo Hondo to Santa Fe, and her neighbors could never find out who had brought the old woman to town. Many stories were told of how she was met at night in the form of a dog, cat, or some other animal.

One night the husband of a woman who was always ailing and was supposed to be *malificiada* (bewitched) met a dog coming out of his yard. Picking up a stick, he gave the dog a good licking. The next day the old woman was found sick in bed with black and blue bruises over all her body. Others said that they had seen her running around town in the form of a black cat. One night a crowd of mischievous boys caught the black cat, sewed its eyes with a strong piece of thread, tied its legs together and hung it on a ladder. The next morning the boys went to see the cat and found it had gone. The old woman went to her neighbor's house early in the morning to beg for a live coal to start her fire. The neighbor, noticing the old woman's eyes red and swollen, asked her what was the matter. "I went to stir my pot of *atole* and the boiling gruel spurted into my eyes, burning them terribly," said the old woman. But the boys had their suspicions, and after that they kept away from the black cat.

The wife of the foreman at our ranch told my mother another story; and when Mother looked incredulous, Andrea was ready to swear that it was the truth: Andrea and a girl friend, who lived near Chon's house, went into see the old woman one evening. Not finding her in her room, or in her usual corner by the kitchen fireplace, they tiptoed softly into the secret storeroom. There in a corner on a pumpkin sat Chon, holding her two eyes on a little cushion in her lap. Her dark eye sockets frightened the girls, and they ran out to tell their mothers.

A horseman who often rode into town on dark nights was bothered at times by different objects appearing in the middle of the road. Sometimes a black sheep fleece rolled and rolled before his horse for miles, then it would turn into a bright spark of fire, skipping before him. One night a dark shadow kept leaping at his horse's head, frightening the animal. The faster he raced, the faster moved the shadow. The man suddenly leaned over his horse's head and grabbed at the black object. When he opened his hand, he found he held only a piece of a black shawl; and the black shadow had disappeared. When he entered the town, he saw the black shadow against the old woman's house. Dismounting, he went up to it and found it to be the old woman Chon, panting for breath and tired out. She cried out to him not to hurt her, promising never to bother him again.

* * * * *

Don Pedro had taken his son Carpio to several doctors and no one had been able to find out what caused his strange ailments. Whenever the boy was left alone in the house, his mother would come back to find him crouching in a corner. He would tell his mother that some women wrapped in black shawls came in and pricked him with long cactus needles, and after sucking his blood, they threw him in a corner and disappeared. As a last resort, he decided to try Librada, the *ambularia*. She was a smart witch.

"I can cure your son," said Librada, "but I must be very careful that the witches don't catch me, because they will give me a good licking. Leave your son here and come back for him in three days."

She asked Don Pedro to bring her a new copper kettle and the largest sun flower he could find. He brought all that Librada asked and left his son with her.

Librada reached up to the shelf, scooped out in the wall, and brought down a bunch of dried herbs. She threw a handful of the herbs into the copper pot with the sun flower, poured water into it, and set it to boil in the fireplace. Before going to bed, she locked and barred the door, covered the window, gave the boy a cup of the herb potion, swept the coals and ashes out of the fireplace, and stood the *bulto* statue of San Cirilo inside the hearth, who is the saint invoked for protection against witchery and all black arts.

Late in the night the boy heard noises at the door and window, as if someone were trying to enter: then he heard hooting and flapping of wings on the chimney top. A loud downpour of water came through the chimney. Carpio sat up, lighted a candle, and looked into the fireplace. The statue stood undisturbed inside the fireplace and everything was quiet, so he went back to bed. The same thing happened the second night, but the witches could not get in, for San Cirilo was guarding the only opening. On the third day Don Pedro took his son home cured.

* * * * *

People were most superstitious about the owl. If an owl were heard hooting on the chimney top at night, the people of the house were struck with terror. A witch! Some evil was about to visit the home. One of the brave occupants of the house would go out and say to the owl, "*Mañana vendras por sal.*" ("Tomorrow you come for salt.") The first person who came to the house the next morning to ask for something was believed to be the witch who, as an owl, had hooted on the chimney top the night before. One way to find out if he were really the witch was to make a cross out of two broom straws and place it on the door-sill. The supposed witch would make several attempts to leave the house but would always turn back from the door with some excuse. Not until the cross was removed would she pass through. A needle was sometimes placed on the door sill. If the eye was turned down, the witch would not leave, but if it was turned up she escaped through the eye of the needle.

One evening, hearing an owl hooting on a tree top, Marcos took his gun and shot at it. Seeing it drop to the ground, he ran to pick it up and was surprised to find Candelaria, a woman neighbor, sitting against the tree. The woman rose, limping on one foot, and said that she had hurt her leg. She went home and Marcos looked around the tree for the owl, but it was gone. Candelaria owned a herd of goats and made very delicious goat cheese. Marco's brother insisted on going to buy a cheese from her, but his mother knowing that Candelaria had alienated her husband from her was afraid to eat the cheese. When she cut the cheese at the table, she quietly slipped the first slice into her apron pocket, because she had heard that the evil spell was always in the first slice. Unobserved, she threw the piece of cheese to the dog. A few days later the dog grew thin and sick. When the boys investigated, they found the dog swarming with worms.

"You see," said the boy's mother, "I suspected that witch Candelaria was trying to get rid of me."

* * * * *

Rosalia felt worried. For months she had not heard from her son, sheepherding out on the wide Wyoming plains. She went to Honsha, the *abularia,* told her her trouble, and asked for help.

"I will take you to see your son, if you let me blindfold you," said Honsha.

She tied a large red handkerchief over Rosalia's eyes. Rosalia heard her go into the store-room, and then come out and busy herself at the fireplace. Immediately the odor of burning herbs assailed her nostrils, and she felt herself being lifted. After sailing through the air, she landed on top of a high tree. Below her she saw her son eating his lunch by a camp fire. She started to speak to him, but he vanished from her sight, and she found herself back in her own house. A week later her son returned home. He told her that one day while eating his lunch he had had a strange feeling. An owl had stood on top of the tree, under which he was sitting, and when he aimed to shoot at it, it disappeared. From that day on he longed to get home. The date and hour corresponded with the day the *abularia* had taken Rosalia to see her son.

* * * * *

This witch story was told to me by Matias, father's sheep caporal:

"One night I was riding to Arroyo Seco. After climbing the last ridge, I came in sight of an old vacant house almost in ruins. As I approached the house, I saw a light in the *sala,* and through the broken window I saw people dancing. So I rode around to the front of the house, dismounted, and went to look in through the window. The *sala* was dark and quiet. I had a strange feeling, as I mounted my horse and rode away. A few yards distant I looked back and saw again the bright lights and gay dancing going on in the old house.

"Arriving at the village of Arroyo Seco, I stopped for the night at Doña Librada's house. She pulled down a mattress from the *tarima* and fixed me a bed. I had not been asleep long when a strange noise awakened me. I saw big sparks flying from the fireplace that dimly lit the room. Then there was a scraping sound in the chimney, and out of the fireplace flew a large pumpkin (*gueja*). Another and yet another one came through the chimney. Out of the *guejas* crawled women dressed in their best clothes. They stood around the table, rouging and powdering their faces and admiring themselves in small pieces of broken mirrors. Librada walked in softly and asked them where they were going.

"To the dance at the old *sala,*" they answered.

"And they crawled back into their *guejas* and flew out of the chimney.

"After the women had gone, Librada took her eyes out, placed them on a saucer on top of the fireplace, and went back to her room. After a while, I got up quietly, picked up the saucer and took it into the kitchen, and threw the eyes into a pot simmering on the fireplace. I went back to sleep. Early the next morning I softly opened the kitchen door. Librada quickly covered her face with her arm, while she picked up from the table a pair of eyes and pushed them into her empty eye sockets. Then she turned and asked me what I wanted. I told her that I was leaving. She offered me a cup of coffee; but I was afraid to take it. I thanked her and went out. By the door crouched a blind dog. I felt its eyelids; there were no eyeballs under them. Librada must have pushed into her eye sockets the dog's eyes, in place of her own which I had thrown into the boiling pot. I mounted my horse and rode away.

"And the witches were holding a dance in the old *sala*."

* * * * *

El Llano above Ranchos de Taos was the witches' rendezvous. Every evening the people at Cordova and Ranchitos, across the river, sat on their doorsteps and watched the flight of the witches. Sparks of fire flew out of the houses and landed bouncing on the *llano*. Men named *Juan* had a special power of catching witches. One evening, two Juans went to *El Llano*. They stood opposite each other, each holding a stick; and as each spark dropped, one of the men marked a circle with his stick on the ground around the spark. The sparks went out, and in their places women sat on the ground begging the two Juans to let them go, but the men kept on drawing circles until they had caught a dozen witches and had seen who they were. Then they set them free.

The general belief among the natives was that complete transformation took place at will among the witches.

* * * * *

Of all the stories told by Nurse, the one about the *duendes* (dwarfs) interested me most. Some persons give the following as the origin of the dwarfs. When Lucifer was cast out of heaven, so many of the angels followed him that God, fearing there would be none left, said, "Enough," and the gates of heaven were closed, leaving multitudes of angels in the air. These spirits were the *duendes*. They became mischievous little spirits who inhabited old, vacant houses and threw pebbles from the tops at the passing people. Sometimes they took possession of newly-built houses, annoying the inhabitants at night with all kinds of pranks and queer noises. The noises sounded as if the furniture were moving about the house. Next morning, things were found out of their places. When something could not be found, it was always said that the dwarfs must have taken it.

* * * * *

There was a myth of *La Llorona,* the weeping woman. She was believed to be the soul of a woman who went from house to house weeping at night to atone for her sins. Each village seemed to have a different version of *La Llorona.* Nurse told me that the weeping woman lived in a big, black rock that stood in the meadow in back of our house. At night she came out wrapped in a white mist. She grew taller and taller, finally vanishing from sight, and only her moans and cries were heard throughout the village. Whenever we passed by the black rock I hung closely to Nurse's side, until we were at a safe distance.

* * * * *

One of the most common superstitions that formerly existed was the belief in *El Ojo,* the evil eye. About six years ago I stood as god-mother for my baby niece. A black-shawled woman, holding a six-day-old baby stood beside me, awaiting her turn to have her tiny baby baptized. The woman was very much attracted to my baby, who being three months old was very wide awake and observed everything that was passing, with her big blue eyes. She wobbled her head disapprovingly when the priest poured the cold water over it. The ceremony over, I sat down to tie on the baby's cap. The woman smiling came to my side and placed the tips of her fingers on my baby's forehead. She said, "Díos te guarde tan linda." ("God keep you, pretty baby.") Often I had heard these words in my young days, spoken by persons admiring a pretty child. These words were believed to break up the spell of the evil eye. A little jet heart or a coral bead string was tied around a child's throat to protect it from *El Ojo.*

When a baby became suddenly ill, the person who had admired it or spoken to it last was at once suspected of having made it sick with the evil eye. If a Friday were allowed to pass, without calling in the person to cure it, the child would die. The person must be sent for before Friday. In order to cure it, she had to give the child a drink, and get in bed cuddling the baby close to her until the baby perspired. This sometimes cured the child if it happened to be ailing from a cold. Another cure was to break an egg in a saucer and hold the saucer over the sick child. If an eye appeared in the yolk, the baby would soon be well. If the baby died, the mother felt a resentment toward the person who had killed her baby with the evil eye. They made *el ojo* sometimes on plants they admired, and the flower wilted and died, unless cured by spitting it with salt water. Flowers planted together also became jealous of their colors; the white geranium sometimes stole the rose or red of its neighbor, and the rose-colored flower faded and wilted.

As Josefa was passing Ignacias house, she saw in the window a lovely plant covered with flowers. She went into the house and said to Ignacia: "You better give me a slip of your plant because I am terrible about making *el ojo,* and I don't want to kill your plant." Ignacia very carefully broke a slip of her plant and gave it to Josefa. Next day she noticed her flower droopy and wilting. She at once took some salt water in her mouth and spitted the plant with it, and watered it with luke warm water. The plant kept on wilting and by night it was dead. Ignacia pulled up the plant and found the root black as coal. Even after applying all the cures for *"el ojo"* on plants, she had not been able to break up Josefa's strong evil eye and save her plant.

* * * * *

If a person had a cut or sore he must stay away from outsiders. If the sore became inflamed after he had attended some gathering of people or someone had come into the room where the sick person was, the person was blamed for having infected the sore.

The sick must be especially careful of a woman carrying a baby for a woman in this condition was believed to be most *"inconosa."* The woman was perfectly innocent of having caused any harm; it was just some unconscious, uncontrollable, malignant power in her, as in the ones who caused the evil eye.

These women were also credited with being *"muy antojadas"* and people were always careful to offer them a taste of any appetizing food they were cooking or eating, if the prospective mother chanced to come in and see the food. It was believed that she would miscarry her baby, if she wished for the food and did not get to taste it. Other persons suffering with a painful pimple on their tongue were asked "What did you see and were not given a taste of?"

An expectant mother was cautioned not to sleep near a window where the moonlight would shine on her, for her baby would be born with a hand, foot or some other important member of its body missing, eaten up by the moon.

The moon had a great effect on many things. If the hair were cut at the new moon it would grow long and thick. But never cut the nails at this time for they will grow too fast and have to be trimmed too often.

Plants that must make a good growth above ground were planted at the new moon; those that must grow a large root, at the decrease of the moon, otherwise they would go to leaves and have no root.

The people watched strictly the changes of the moon as a weather bureau. If the old moon ended dry and the new moon set in dry there was no hope of rain during the whole month, but if the new moon appeared with *"los cuernos colgados"* (its horns turned down) the whole month would be rainy. Woe to the farmers if the moon turned up its horns. They would say *"ya bramo la luna"* (the moon has roared). A long drought would follow until lady moon would deign to turn her horns down again and let the water out.

The position of the stars marked the seasons of the year. *"Los tres reyes y las tres Marias,"* the three kings and the three Marys, were seen in the east at the beginning of the winter and found in the west by summer time. *"El carrito del cielo," "los ojitos de Santa Lucia,"* the pair of tiny stars so evenly matched, *"las cabrillas,"* the group of small stars bunched together like a herd of goats, *"el Lucero,"* the morning star, *"la strella de la oracion,"* the evening star, the traveling of all these stars across the sky was watched with the same great interest as the moon.

If the ashes in the fireplace whirled around on a very quiet day the weather would turn bad.

Loud cracking of the ceiling beams indicated that an intimate friend or relative had just passed away and that his spirit had come to *"despedirse,"* bid you farewell.

Some people were found to be *muy sangre pesado* (heavy-blooded); and no matter how much servants tried to do things for them, nothing came out right. Everyone found it easy to work for people who were *sangre liviana* or light-blooded. The cook's bread rose quickly and baked light and fluffy especially if the cook *tenia buena mano* (was light handed). All work was done in a short time and with good results for the *sangre liviana* and by the ones who had *bueno mano*.

Children and even pet animals, having become greatly attached to a person who went away and left them, became *melarchicos* (melancholy) and refused to eat. Babies became sick, and a red ribbon was tied on their wrist as a cure. Birds also refused to eat or sing, and died, when they became *melarchicos*.

People often became *empachados* from eating fresh, hot bread. The *sobador* (masseur) in order to locate the *empacho*, rolled the yolk of an egg over the abdomen, with the tips of his fingers. The yolk stopped, adhered and turned black, when it touched the spot where the *empacho* was attached to inside. Here the egg yolk was broken, massaged over the spot and left on until the *empacho* loosened and was expelled.

When medicinal baths were taken, or herb teas, the rule was to take them for three days in succession in the name of the Holy Trinity. If more had to be taken, they must be taken in odd numbers.

When a baby was born the first thing the midwife attended

to was to *subirle las varias de la nariz,* raise the rods on the baby's nose by pressing with her thumb the roof of the palate, so the baby would not grow up *chato,* flat nosed.

A few drops of Asafran tea were administered, to throw out of its system the *chincual,* which came out sometimes in a red rash. Then a little Alusema was chewed, tied in a little muslin rag and put in the baby's mouth, to prevent colic. The baby's navel was kept to bring him good luck in his love affairs after he grew up.

My working girl became very fond of my fine black and white kitty. When I went away for the winter I gave her the cat. On my return, I asked her about the cat. "It died some weeks ago," said the girl. "My mother has always told us it's well to raise some pet animal, because God sometimes revokes the sentence or punishment coming to one, by letting it fall on the pet. I had suffered so badly from sinus for so many years, until I thought I would lose my nose. That cat's nose rotted; it could not eat, so it passed out and I am almost well of my sinus."

Some people would not grow a white geranium in their home, because when it bloomed someone in the family would die.

"Never wash the sugar bowl when I am cleaning house," said our maid, to Lupe our cook, "because company is sure to come."

"If you scrape cooking pots, it will rain on your wedding day," Lupe would tell us.

* * * * *

SAINT LEGENDS. Many saints legends are told. One morning a mule came down the mountain at Chimayo and stood for hours before the door of the fabled church until someone called the sacristan's attention to it. The man came out to investigate and found that the mule carried across its saddle a long coffin-like box.

On opening the box, they found inside it a small statue of a saint nailed on a cross. The sacristan took the statue and placed it in the Church, giving it the name of *Nuestro Señor de Esquipula.* Soon the news spread that a miraculous statue had appeared. People from over all the state visited the statue to pay votive promises; some devotees holding lighted candles crawled on their knees to the statue.

For many years, before Don Bernardo Abeyta built the attractive church, wonderful cures had been performed by a strange virtue of the soil taken from a hole in the mud floor. People deformed or suffering with a malady beyond the curative power of physicians flocked to the *Santuario,* inspired with faith that the Divine Providence, through the supernatural remedial power manifested in the soil and in the miraculous statue, would alleviate their suffering or restore their health. The pilgrims who came from a distance took back with them some of the earth and used it to abate violent storms by throwing a few grains of the earth into a blazing fire. When the smoke reached the top of the chimney, it calmed the storm and changed the course of the lightning.

* * * * *

The statue of the *Santa Niño de Atocha*, near this interesting shrine, also attracted many devotees. In a few years its long, full cape was covered with tiny votive offerings. Tiny silver or gold legs, arms, eyes or crutches were pinned on by grateful devotees whose prayers had been answered with a cure. So numerous were the errands of mercy performed by this *Santo Niño* that he wore out his shoes, and tiny new pairs were brought to him ever so often.

A prominent Spanish family, who owned a private chapel in the Tesuque valley, had a precious little *Santo Niño,* about eight inches high, jointed like a doll. Decked in silk garments he sat on a little silver chair. On his head rested a round, silver hat adorned with two long, silver filigree plumes. The square-toed shoes were of silver; and white silk-brocaded capes and habits, made from the owner's wedding gown, were included in the statue's wardrobe, which filled a little chest.

Little Juanita and Lucia, when their mother was seriously ill, fell on their knees before the *Santo Niño* and promised to donate the most precious gift they possessed if their mother recovered. Their gift was two little silver baskets filled with silver fruits, which a friend had brought them from Mexico City. The mother recovered, and Juanita and Lucia each hung her little basket on the little statue's hand. The mother never removed them, for they were the offerings of her children.

A mother whose two-year-old son was stolen by the Indians during a raid on her town had for years hunted and prayed to find him, but unsuccessfully. Hearing of the miraculous *Santo Niño,* she promised a novena in honor of the Holy Child. She poured out her grief in her prayers. The last day of the novena came, and she had not heard of her child. Frantic with grief, the mother strolled out of the house and followed a road leading to the hills through an arroyo. She had not gone far when she tumbled on an object in the road. Stooping down she picked up the object—a little hat carved out of stone, round-brimmed, with two carved ostrich plumes across the high top.

"A *Santo Niño's* hat," she was thinking, as she walked along, examining the little article. She heard a wagon approaching, and looked up. She saw a man driving, and sitting beside him was a four-year-old boy. Recognizing him as her son, the distracted mother ran up to the wagon, signalling the man to stop.

"My son!" cried the mother, as the child jumped down into her arms. When the happy mother turned to thank the man, both he and the wagon had disappeared. No trace of them could be seen on the road.

* * * * *

La Gran Quivira, in New Mexico, like El Dorado in South America, was the subject of fabulous legends and myths. The golden phantom, which lured the Coronado expedition north and was so important in the making of New Mexico's history, incited many private expeditions to search for the lost mines and treasures left buried by the Spaniards. An old map found tucked under a rock in the hills by a sheepherder was the means of squeezing a good sum of money from a prominent man in Las Vegas. My husband was also tricked several years later by the lure of this fabulous buried treasure.

Tucked away in the fastness of the mountains between Vallesito and Taos lies the remote village of La Petaca. Scattered here and there among the pinon-wooded hills are seen the rustic houses of the *rancheros,* the farmers. From one of these isolated ranches a *ranchero* came into our town one bright summer day, carrying a letter to his uncle, Don Alcadio Velasquez, a man well-read in New Mexico history. The man said that the letter had been brought to him by a hermit who lived in the Petaca hills. He described the hermit as being tall and fair, with long, white hair and a snowy beard that reached his waistline. He was dressed in a coyote skin and wore sandals of the same hide. The hermit had come to his hut one night and had left his two tame lions outside to guard the door while he went in to talk to the *ranchero.* He had told him the story of a Spanish expedition of which he was the only survivor.

The Spaniards on their way to Taos had found a rich gold mine in those hills. Before the assault of the Indians, they had hastily buried the gold and mine machinery in three holes at the foot of the hill and covered up the mine. He said that all the Spaniards had been killed and that his own mother had died of fright. He still had her body preserved in his cave by a secret process known only to himself.

Mr. Velasquez took the *Petaqueño* and the letter to the parish priest. The second time the *ranchero* came with a letter, the priest and Don Alcadio brought him to my husband, who did not at first put much faith in the story. But when the farmer continued to come every week with new, interesting stories and letters, and then with an old manuscript and map, he marveled how a simple, uneducated rancher could make up such wonderful stories and repeat them exactly every time he came.

The letters, written in an old-fashioned handwriting, worded in fine Spanish and bearing no date, since the hermit knew not the month nor year, told of the hidden mine and vast gold buried treasure. They were signed, *"El Ermitaño."* The curiosity of my husband and the priest was aroused, and they decided to go to Petaca and search for the gold.

Early one morning they had one of our *peones* load a wagon with bedding and provisions and they sent him ahead with the rancher. The priest and my husband followed them later, after having packed their guns and cartridges under the buggy seat. I was taken into the secret. And being just a young bride, I was very much elated over the prospects of such a vast wealth coming into our possession. The priest promised that if the treasure were found, he would build a new church. My husband and I promised to build a fine school for our poor people.

The men reached the Petaca hills that evening and sat in front of the fireplace in the *ranchero's* hut, studying the map by candlelight until far into the night. The next morning they were out early measuring the ground. They found the three stones with their markings corresponding exactly with those shown on the map. And so many paces *para donde el sol sale* (to where the sun rises) from a large, black rock marked with a cross they dug the first hole, but found nothing. The second hole was dug, five paces in the direction pointed to by the arrow-head carved on the rock. Here they found pieces of iron from broken tools and charcoal. They started to dig the third hole, hoping that here they would strike the treasure. The men dug and dug, searching the hills for two days, but the treasure remained buried somewhere in the Petaca hills.

Among the many legends told were those of the Pojuaque Giant, the Hermit of El Porvenir, the buried treasure in Cañon de la Soledad, and the enchanted mine in the Taos mountains.

* * * * *

Cañon de las Brujas, called by Americans, "Ghost Canyon," is situated near Abiquiu. Various stories are told about this red cliff *cañada.* One was about the *Vaqueros* and *borregeros,* who were always in dispute over the grazing land around the canyon. One day the cowboys and sheepherders clashed, and several men were wounded and killed. Thereafter the canyon became infested with ghosts, especially at night. White ghosts were seen climbing the cliffs and terrible agonizing moans were heard throughout the canyon. *Vaqueros* and *borregeros* abandoned the place, the quarrels ceased and no one wanted to come near.

Don Miguel Gonzales, who owned a small farm and house at the entrance of the canyon and who did not believe in ghosts, sent his cowherder to graze his cattle on the farm.

"If you are afraid to stay in the house, build a hut outside," Don Miguel told his *vaquero*.

"No, I am not afraid," he said. But two weeks later when Don Miguel went to inspect his cattle, he found his man living in a tent pitched under a tree.

"Why are you living out here?" asked Don Miguel.

"Oh, Patron, I could not stand the noises in the house. All night I would hear a man and woman quarreling; then they would cry and moan. People tell me that a man and woman lived in the house all alone. They quarreled a great deal, and one day the woman disappeared. The man went away and has never been heard from since."

Don Miguel sold the farm and house. While the new owners were fixing over a room, the skeleten of a woman was dug out from under a wall; it was removed and buried outside. The noises ceased, and the house is now an attractive summer resort.

* * * * *

THE PADRE'S BURIED TREASURE. Father Antonio Jose Martinez was born at Abiquiu. Here he learned how to read and write from the parish priest. After his parents moved to Taos, he married my grandfather's sister. She died a year later, and the baby girl she had soon followed the mother.

Left a widower Don Antonio Jose decided to study for the priesthood, and he started on horseback for Durango, Mexico, to enter a seminary.

Six years later he returned as an ordained priest, well versed in the Latin and Spanish languages. He took charge of the parish at Tome. Later he moved to Taos, where he was not only priest but also educator. Sixteen of the young men he educated became priests. Becoming active in politics, he foresaw the change of government coming and undertook to prepare his pupils for a different life. He told the young men that now they must fit themselves for lawyers and legislators instead of the priesthood, for the American government was very progressive. The change of government he foresaw did come, and he was elected president of the first Council held in Santa Fe, under the United States Government.

On a second visit to Durango, Mexico, the Padre bought a printing press. On this press, which took several months to make its way here, the first newspaper in New Mexico, "El Crepusculo," was printed in Taos.

His friend, Padre Lucero, at that time had charge of the parish at Arroyo Hondo, then two flourishing villages before the advent of the railroad and gold strike in Colorado, which lured away about one-third of the sunken valley's population. By thrifty living the Padre managed to become rich. At this time, the Spanish priests throughout New Mexico, being such a great distance from their Bishop's jurisdiction, became careless in keeping the laws of the Church and established their own rules, abrogating the celibacy of the priesthood.

Father Martinez had been in charge of the ancient parish at Taos for thirty years, when Reverend Bishop Jean Baptist Lamy came to take charge of the New Mexico diocese. He visited the Taos parish and from there rode to Arroyo Hondo to administer confirmation. While stopping at my grandfather's house, the Bishop sent for Padre Lucero and had a long talk with him, but found him as obstinate as Padre Martinez in recognizing his authority. He refused to give up his old way of living, saying that they were under the jurisdiction of the Bishop of Durango, not having received any different orders from the Mexican Bishop.

Bishop Lamy decided to let things stand as they were until he could find a priest strong enough to handle the situation. With this object in mind, on his second visit to Rome he brought back with him Father Taladrid, who was at once sent to Taos. At the Bishop's request, Padre Martinez resigned the parish, but continued to administer the Sacraments in a Chapel he built for himself and to dictate the lives of his people, the majority of whom were on his side. Having educated most of the young men of the prominent families in that section, he had great influence with the people.

Soon Father Taladrid and Father Martinez were at war and the Bishop sent Father Valiant with a letter of excommunication for the Padres Martinez and Lucero. This letter was read by the priest at the Church in Taos and at Arroyo Hondo. The two padres conferred and schemed to hold the people. At Arroyo Hondo a mystic man sprang up in the person of Eduardo Gallegos (called 'Luardo' for short). He made the people believe that he had vision in which God told him that the Padre's Church was the true church and the people must continue to obey the Padre.

On a certain day during Lent Luardo promised to perform a miracle, a *madero* (cross) he said, would appear on top of *El Cerro del Utah*—such a heavy cross that no one would be able to move it from its place. Every evening processions of people carrying lights and led by Luardo were seen ascending and descending the mountain. They tried to move the cross but no one could lift it from its place. On another day he was going to bring a church bell down from the Cerro. On the way he would give three rings, the last one at the top of the north ridge. As he approached the village at this last ring, the dead would rise from their graves in Padre Lucero's cemetery on the hill. A large throng of people from Taos, Arroyo Seco and San Antonio lined the road from the south ridge to the north, all expecting to see the miracle. My father's brother wrapped in a sarape borrowed from one of his *peones,* and his wife, wearing a skirt and *reboso* belonging to one of her *criadas,* went to see the crowd, thinking that Luardo would not recognize them in that garb. But Luardo spied them, and made the excuse that he could not perform the miracle because there were some unbelievers among them.

Another time he was about to perform a miracle. While a large crowd waited outside the Padre's Chapel, Luardo stretched Juan Vernal before the altar and knelt praying and making signs over him. Then in a fit of fanatic zeal he stabbed the man in the heart with his knife. Failing to revive him by prayers and signs, he dragged him out and showed him to the people. He told them, "Here, I have killed the *Antecristo* and set you free."

Juan's brothers, who did not belong to *Los Luardos* became enraged at this act and called for help from a detachment of government cavalry men, who were passing to the north. The brothers led the soldiers to Luardo's hiding place. Luardo came out brandishing his knife and started running, but the soldiers overtook him and gave him a good beating with their muskets. Then they left him.

A song was composed to Luardo. I have been able to collect only two of the verses:

Los Cuandos de Luardo

Cuando sé llegaran lós cuandos,
Qué lós cismaticos vean,
De Luardo sú nueva estrella
Qué el está profetizando.

En él Cerro de Lá Utá
Endónde Luardo se divierte,
Con sú maldíta songita
A toda la génte divierte.

One dark night Padre Lucero had an encounter with two robbers who, knocking at his door, asked him if he would hear the confession of a dying man. As the Padre opened the door, two men sprang at him, beating him with sticks. The Padre quickly drew out his knife and stabbed one of the men in the throat; the man staggered back, and they both disappeared in the darkness. The commotion aroused the servants who came running to the priest's assistance. The next morning the wounded man was found dead by the river where his companion had left him. The dying man had tried to stop the hemorrhage by stuffing green grass in the wound.

Doña Mela, the priest's wife, had passed away a few months before this encounter. When she became seriously ill, she asked Carmelita, her confidential Indian servant, to call my father to write her last will; but the Padre, fearing that she might reveal his secrets, told her that my father had sent word that he was busy and could not come. Doña Mela died leaving only her own lands to her relatives. She had gone around almost in rags, while the favorite Indian servant wore the jewels and silk dresses that the Padre bought her.

Father Taladrid often visited the Arroyo Hondo parish to instruct the people; and the people soon lost faith in the Padre and Luardo and joined Father Taladrid's ranks. My grandfather had asked the Bishop for a priest, and Father Tomas de Aquino was sent to officiate in my grandfather's private chapel, where every morning he held services for the family. Father Tomas was a very charitable man; all the *diesmo* that he received from the people he again distributed among the poor. When he left my grandfather's house, they had to give him money for his trip, for he had not saved a cent for himself.

Padre Lucero, feeling that he was losing his hold on the people and because of his failing health, moved to Ranchitos de Taos. He lived his last years in apparent poverty, saving even the blood from th sheep and beef he had butchered for food. (A *morcia*—sausage—was made from hog's blood fried with piñon nuts and raisins.) When the priest died, he left several herds of sheep and cattle to his relatives, and the old house at Arroyo Hondo he left to his favorite, Carmelita, the Indian girl. No mention of money was made in his last will, so people thought that the report of his wealth was false.

In the course of time, Carmelita married Jose Chacon. She told Jose of her suspicions that the Padre had left some money buried in the old home at Arroyo Hondo. The husband was afraid to search for the treasure alone, so he took into his confidence a man named Labarta, a Spaniard, who was roaming around the country.

Late one night my mother's uncle, who lived near the Padre's old house, heard horses racing past his home. Getting up, he looked out of the window and saw two horsemen ride into the patio of the priest's vacant house; and he became curious to know what was going on. He dressed in a hurry and went out. Seeing a light in the old storeroom of the Padre's house, he climbed upon the roof and listened through the chimney of the fireplace. He heard men digging and talking inside. After a while, two men came out, each with a bundle, and mounted their horses—their guns across their saddles—and rode away.

Under the trees by the river, the two men hid their bundles and went to the saloon to play a game of poker. Pedro, whose turn it was to irrigate that night, came along with his hoe on his shoulder to turn the water off his corn patch. Stumbling on something heavy, he stooped down to feel around. "Ah, money . . . . and the thieves must be around here watching it," he thought, as he quickly got away from the place.

The men left the saloon and everything was quiet. Chacon

and Labarta went for their bundles and took them to Chacon's house. Uncle Nieves went back to bed. Early the next morning he went to see what had happened in the old storeroom. Two holes dug out in the mud seat built along the wall and two empty earthen pots told the tale. The Padre's buried treasure had been unearthed and carried away in the secrecy of the night.

The shrewd Spaniard, who was a learned man, told Chacon and his Indian wife that it was not safe for them to keep such a large sum of money in their house, and that he would deposit the money in the bank. He went away with the greater portion of the treasure and was never seen again.

Chacon consoled himself by composing comic verses to tease his old mother and wife, for no loss could kill his wit.

Los Fleteros, by Chacon

Háy vienen ya los fletéros	There come the freighters,
Que reme como és costumbre,	Paddling as is their custom;
El carro dé adelante	The driver in front
Llega hacíendo lúmbre.	Arrives starting the fire.
Allí vienen yá los carréros	There come the wagoners,
Bajando por el cañon,	Coming down the canyon.
Le traen a mí madre Maéstas	They bring Mother Maestas
Zapato rechinador.	Creaking new shoes.
Alli vienen ya los carreros	There come the wagoners,
Bajando por la ladera,	Down the hill they are coming,
Le traen a mi madre Maestas	Bringing Mother Maestas
Un buen tapalo de seda.	A nice silk shawl.
Aquí viene ya los carreros	Here come the wagoners,
Saliendo el callejón	Coming out of the alley,
Le traen a mí madre Maéstas	Bringing Mother Maestas
Una rosa de listón.	A pretty ribbon bow.

Jose Chacon's Pants

Asómense a esa ventána,	Look in through that window,
Enderesen ésa verjíta	Straighten that window grate,
Y verán a José Chacón	And you will see Manual Chacon
Junto con la Carmelíta.	With his Carmelita.
Asomense a esa ventána	Peep in through that window,
Y veran lo que se está rifándo,	And you will see them raffling
Los calzones de José Chacon,	Jose Chacon's pants
Echos ún vivo remiendo.	All full of patches.

* * * * *

Several years later, one afternoon, Tiodora went to see her parents who now lived in the Padre's house and took me to show me the loop hole in the old sala wall through which the Padre kept watch on his buried treasure. We were resting in the sala when the loud bleating and the tingling of bells of a herd of goats coming home from pasture on the hills approached the house. "It is milking time," said Tiodora rising and taking me by the hand. She led me across the back orchard to the goat corral. I watched Matias, father's sheep *caporal,* milk the goats, through the cracks in the closely standing cedar posts. Soon he came out carrying in each hand a pail of foamy milk. As we walked back to the house, the fragrant smoke of burning cedar and piñon wood rose from every hearth; and the air rang with the echo of the ax.

In the kitchen, Tiodora set a pot of the strained milk to boil in the roomy hearth of the *fogon de campana,* its wide hood extending out over the posts set on iron *tinamastes* on the coals. She took from the coals the pot of blue *atole* gruel, set it on the door sill and sat by it, cooling it by letting the hot gruel drop in the air from a gourd *jumate,* which she dipped and raised with a quick, deft twist of her hand. Each cup was filled half full with the salted boiled milk and the rest with the gruel, and the family sat in a semi-circle in front of the fireplace, with a stack of nicely-browned *tortillas* and a pot of mutton stew before them. Supper finished, Matias wiped his long mustach with his big red handkerchief, leaned back against the wall while he packed his pipe with home grown tobacco and lit it with a burning rag set on fire by a spark struck with a flint and steel.

This was a very peaceful scene compared with that of the old Padre worried about hoarding his money under the wall in this same house.

THE END

CULTURE OF A CONTEMPORARY RURAL COMMUNITY

El Cerrito, New Mexico

by *Olen Leonard and G. P. Loomis*

RURAL LIFE STUDIES: 1
November 1941

U. S. DEPARTMENT OF AGRICULTURE
BUREAU OF AGRICULTURAL ECONOMICS

CONTENTS

	Page
El Cerrito People, Land, and Culture	1
History and Background of the Settlement	10
The Background of Present Population	14
Cultural: Ethnic and Nationality Origins	14
Patterns of Social Behavior	15
Dominant Values and Sanctions	17
The People on the Land	21
Land Use: Patterns of Ownership	21
Techniques of Agriculture	24
Commercialization and Self-Sufficiency	28
The Farm Business	30
The Role of Hired Farm Labor	31
Transportation and Communication	31
Government Programs	32
Attitudes and Value Systems Related to Land Use, Commercialization, Self-Sufficiency, and Governmental Programs	34
The Community	37
Spatial Distribution	37
Patterns of Informal Association	37
Recreation	49
Patterns of Formal Association	50
The School	51
The Church	54
Farm Organizations and Cooperatives	56
Local Politics	56
Leadership and Class Structure	57
Youth as the Critical Age-Group of the Community	60
Value System and Its Supporting Sanctions and Attitudes	61
Integration and Conflict	62
The Farmer's Expanding World	66
Communication and Transportation	68
Value Systems and Attitudes Toward Wider Economic and Political Problems	69
Integration and Disintegration in Community and Individual Life	70

LIST OF ILLUSTRATIONS

Fig. No.		Page
1	The brush and rock dam raises the water to the mouths of the lateral above the village now as it has for many generations.	3
2	A village deprived of its grazing lands does not repair adobe stables and storage spaces	5
3	The age and condition of this revered crucifix reveal the age of the culture and the poverty of the people	9
4	Without irrigation there would be few beans and tortillas	11
5	The songs of "Old Spain" are still remembered	16
6	"A man's home is his castle." The patriarch of the village	18
7	A "larger family at mealtime	18
8	"We are stockmen, not farmers." the people will tell you	23
9	Bread is still baked outside – a survival of many generations	27
10	In kitchens such as this the traditional diet is prepared – a diet balanced by generations of experience	27
11	Months items produced on farm or in garden were used by the family, El Cerrito. New Mexico 1940	29
12	Location of houses and buildings El Cerrito. New Mexico. 1940	38
13	Visiting of families El Cerrito New Mexico, 1940	40
14	Visiting of parents showing frequency El Cerrito New Mexico, 1940	42
15	Families taking meals together El Cerrito, New Mexico 1940	43
16	Visiting of children and other individuals, El Cerrito. New Mexico, 1940	45
17	Families loaning farm implements, El Cerrito, New Mexico 1940	47
18	Families exchanging work, El Cerrito, New Mexico, 1940	48
19	English is spoken only in the school	53
20	At worship – all villagers are devout Catholics	55

FOREWORD

This is a report on one of six communities which were studied contemporaneously by six different participant observers or field workers during the year 1939. Each study was sufficiently independent of the other five to warrant, in fact make desirable, separate treatment and publication. The reader, however, will gain full understanding of the findings only when he has read the six studies as a group.

The six communities selected for study - El Cerrito, New Mexico; Sublette, Kansas; Irwin, Iowa; Lancaster, Pennsylvania; Landaff, New Hampshire; and Harmony, Georgia - were not selected in an attempt to obtain a geographic sampling of contemporary rural American communities, but as samples of, or points on, a continuum from high community stability to great instability. At one end of the continuum, an Amish community, Lancaster, Pennsylvania, was selected. At the other end of the continuum, a "Dust Bowl" community in Kansas was selected. The other four communities, for one reason or another, range themselves between these extremes. El Cerrito is a stable community culturally, in fact almost a cultural island. It has, however, suffered severely because it has lost a large portion of the land which supported it and because it is poorly equipped with technologies to meet the competition of other producing areas.

Something approaching commonalty of observations was attempted by all field observers in that a basic manual of instructions was available to, and used by, all of them. Each observer, however, had wide latitude in making his observations and pretty free rein in writing up his findings.

A seventh report in this series will present the complete methodology used in the six studies and a body of generalizations which grows out of the combined observations of all who participated in the studies.

Olen Leonard lived 5 months, and Charles Loomis 3 months, in the village of El Cerrito. Both of these observers speak Spanish, and to a considerable extent became members of the community during the period of the study.

Carl C. Taylor,

EL CERRITO PEOPLE, LAND, AND CULTURE

Many villages in San Miguel County, N. Mex. seldom see an Anglo. When one does appear, it is generally taken for granted that the visitor is representing some relief agency from the city. Such visits do not seriously interrupt the placid routine of everyday life. Investigators are anticipated, and so are the questions and answers that accompany the interrogation. But when a strange Anglo arrives asking for board and room, that is quite another matter. When he offers a more definite and tangible purpose for being there than to write something in the nature of a local history, the results are downright confusing.

Gaining entrance into such a situation was not easy. It was with noticeable reluctance that a family finally consented to house the stranger although the money he offered for this service was obviously an inducement. It was difficult for them to believe that an Anglo could be interested in their village, as such, or in their culture. Experience and repeated stories had conditioned them to fear that acceptance of the "Americano" was likely to result in loss and deprivation.

So, during the first month of the investigator s stay in the village, he was a constant subject for conversation and speculation. Some accused him of being a detective and others of working as an agent for big stock companies. It was only the most trusting that voiced opinions that he was not there for some purpose detrimental to the interests of the group.

After a month of carefully guarded speech and action, the consensus of opinion slowly began to change. Some became willing, and often eager, informants, especially about the more objective aspects of the village. It was only as a result of patiently cultivated friendships that they came to talk at all frankly of their more personal affairs.

It was not difficult to get these people to talk of their history and conquest of the land. They are proud of their heritage of forefathers who dared an unfriendly environment and hostile Indians to establish themselves on the land. The old-timers still live in the past and are always willing to oblige an interested listener with tales of large herds of stock owned or tended and of daring freighting trips to the East. It is more difficult to persuade them to carry the story on into contemporary life, for the second half of the story is an account of sure and steady loss against new and encroaching conditions. It entails admission of defeat in a new struggle - that of defending early gains against a new people and a new culture, usually recognized as superior in its ability to accumulate, absorb, and expand.

In selecting a village in San Miguel County for intensive study an attempt was made to find one typical of as large an area as possible and one that had, in a measure, retained its individuality in the face of the changing conditions that confront them all. Three distinct types were available one of the scattered villages of the mountains; a dry-land farming village and the more common type, one located along the river. After a brief reconnaissance of the area and numerous discussions with persons working over the county the latter type was finally selected, although either of the other types would probably have been equally acceptable. The same problems and characteristics are found in all. Actually the native villages of San Miguel County are strikingly similar. Inclination and topography have combined to distribute the people into scattered groups that, because of resulting isolation, have become highly integrated socially. Living so completely within themselves, these groups have acted as safety vaults for the preservation of old customs and traditions. Change has come slowly where entry by an outside force is so reluctantly allowed.

The physical structure of these villages varies little. Houses are grouped closely together around a church, a school, and perhaps a store. None are farther separated than the distance across the plaza. Many are joined in long rows stretching along the sides of the plaza square. Away from the cluster no more houses appear until the next village is reached.

The village of El Cerrito is 30 miles southwest of the town of Las Vegas. Sixteen of these miles are over first class pavement, three over a semi improved surface with the remainder only a very rough and often changed entrance to the village itself. It is well hidden from the outside world. Only one familiar with the area or equipped with detailed instructions would be able to find it without patient searching or striking good fortune. One comes upon the village suddenly. Driving over the high mesa covered with juniper and scrub pine, the road abruptly rises, turns sharply to the right, and a panoramic view of the entire village and valley land lies ahead. Still over a mile beyond and below, the houses stand out in quiet relief against the far side of the valley wall. The little fields stretch out in rectangular pattern clearly bounded by rock or the more modern barbed wire fence. Approached in winter the village seems as quiet and lifeless as the little cemetery just above it.

The exotic appearance of the village strikes one with singular force. Here is a bit of rural life far removed from the modern everyday world. Intuitively one sees that there is little here of the material goods that are designed to make living less arduous.

As one approaches still closer to the cluster of houses, almost the full length of the little irrigation ditch that brings the water from the river to the homes and numerous fields can be seen. This ditch is an engineering feat done without the aid or benefit of modern science. Its style of construction and the height of the banks built by annual cleanings give ample testimony of its age. For it was probably first constructed by the Indians, predecessors of the present inhabitants of the village, who taught the bearded white men much of what they still know and practice regarding earning a living in the New World. Modern machinery and the science of agricultural production have little influence here. It is rather a combination of indigenous and Old World folklore modified by the wits and ingenuity of the people.

1. *The brush and rock dam raises the water to the mouths of the lateral above the village now t has for many generations.*

El Cerrito is on the Pecos River in one of the many land pockets formed at irregular intervals where the valley widens out sufficiently to allow space for a few houses and a little bottom land. The valley land has never been sufficient in extent to allow full-time farming, but has constituted an indispensable basis of operations for the more extensive enterprises of dry-land farming and stock raising. Usually the individual family owned a tract large enough to grow a garden and enough feed crops to maintain a horse or two, a cow, and perhaps a pig. The principal source of income was livestock, which with few restrictions, roamed the surrounding mesa. It provided profits, even riches, for the owners and labor for those who had only their services.

Today, in northwest central New Mexico, these same people and their descendants have lost practically all their once vast holdings. Almost all that remain are the small, inadequate, irrigated holdings that were never sufficient in size and capacity to support a family. The outlying mesa, which actually supported the livestock industry, has been transferred to other hands. Huge tracts of land that were granted to them by the Spanish and Mexican Governments have been sold to pay delinquent taxes or squandered by ruthless grant trustees. Also, courts frequently failed to recognize the validity of claims to these grant lands. El Cerrito is a part of an early Spanish Grant that contained over 400,000 acres. In 1901 the Court of Private Land Claims denied all but a little more than 5,000 acres. Not only did the people lose their land in this case but also much of their tangible property went for lawyers' fees to plead their case. Another local case, and one more typical of the area, is the Anton Chico Grant which borders the village of El Cerrito and to which an El Cerrito family once had rights. The history of this grant, according to the records of the Soil Conservation Service is as follows:

"The Anton Chico Grant was originally made to a community of 36 persons by the Mexican Government in 1822. As confirmed by the United States Government in 1860 it contained 278,000 acres. At the present time there are 700 descendants and heirs of the original grantees. The grant is owned in community by the heirs and is administered by a Grant Board of 5 persons elected by them. Land contained within the grant is subject to the regular property taxes of the State of New Mexico. At a very early date delinquency in payment of taxes became very serious.

"In 1926 the tax laws of the State of New Mexico were revised, making land subject to foreclosure by the State after taxes were delinquent 3 years. Starting in that year, sections of the grant were sold to outsiders in large tracts to pay the delinquent taxes, with the result that at the present time (1939) only 85,000 of the original 278,000 acres remain in community ownership. Of the 85,000 acres, 22,000 are leased to outside commercial livestock operators under 5-year leases at 8 cents per acre. Thus only 63,000 acres are now actually available for community use. At this date the Grant Board is considering sale of 3,000 acres more to secure enough money to pay currently delinquent taxes."

The cases cited are amazingly similar to many others over the entire State. In the words of one of the natives: "The people here are worse off than they ever have been in their lives. There is no wage work for them any more and the farms have become too small to earn a living from. People here could still earn a living if they had more grazing land. Farming is out of the question here as this land (mesa) is good for grazing only. I can remember when almost all the people here had flocks of sheep and a few cattle. My father and all my uncles had flocks of sheep, big ones. There was plenty of land then, free land, to graze them on. It's pretty bad. I don't know what we are going to do."

Although the process of losing this land began several decades ago, the disastrous consequences that finally resulted have been recent. Large tracts of land were being bought and leased during, and before, the 1880's but the people were little concerned. The railroads were building their tracks over the mountains and paying wages far higher than those offered by local sheepmen and cattlemen. Ties upon which the steel rails were laid were in demand at a good price. A man could earn more money cutting and selling ties to the railroad companies in a week than he could earn herding sheep for several months. Nor did the era of prosperity cease when the tracks were completed. Big farmers and labor scouts from the North came into New Mexico soliciting workers for the beet fields and metal works. Old timers say that they were able to choose their work and within certain limits, to name the price.

FIG. 2. *A village deprived of its grazing lands does not repair adobe stables and storage space.*

The era of prosperity lasted well into the 1920's. Not until 1928 did conditions become so grave that people began to doubt that better times would soon return. By this time large numbers were without work and the reserves from better days had long been liquidated. After 1930 little hope remained of obtaining outside labor and a wholesale retreat began back to the villages and their land. Although it was generally realized that the small tracts of land remaining in their possession were inadequate these tracts afforded a house and garden spot that would help cushion the shock from the collapse of practically all demand for their labor.

It was not until the families were again more dependent on their land that full realization came as to what had happened when day wages were better. All free or grazing land was gone. Large concerns had bought, fenced, and posted huge areas from which it was forbidden that the people should remove even wood for fuel. Land that had not been bought or leased had been homesteaded in such a crazy-quilt fashion that its use had practically been destroyed. A man might own a section of land only 2 or 3 miles away by the most direct route but because of new fences it would be necessary to travel 10 miles to reach it. Homesteads that were more accessible were apt to be useless because of lack of water The new concerns had been thorough in taking over water sources which, in turn, meant control of the surrounding area. In total, the natives realized that they had allowed themselves to be led into a situation from which there was no retreat. There was no longer any alternative but work or aid from the outside.

The Federal Emergency Relief Program provided the first straw at which these people could grasp. Shortly after its initiation the new county offices were filled with destitute villagers asking for work, clothing, and food, and San Miguel County became one of the most heavily subsidized in the State.

After 7 years of such subsidy the basic conditions in the rural villages of San Miguel County remain largely unchanged. Although new agencies have been set up to deal with the problem and the functions of the old ones have been broadened, they are yet doing essentially what the early relief agencies began, namely, passing out the little extra in the form of work or material goods that enables the people to keep body and soul together. Agricultural programs now existing were not designed to meet the peculiar problems that exist here. Farm programs proposed to rehabilitate farmers on their present units are likely to do more harm than good under local conditions. No self liquidating loan is feasible for a tract of land one-half acre in extent. The only alternative for the existing agencies seems to be to stretch the functions of their programs as far as possible toward meeting the problem. Essentially, this has meant grants or outright contributions of funds.

Among the people of this area today is found a growing feeling of futility a general sense of inability to cope with circumstances as they exist. Although a few of the families are trying to farm outlying tracts of dry land, these ventures are meeting with scant success All too often a promising crop in the early part of the season is killed by subsequent drought and literally blown from the field. If they are fortunate enough to obtain adequate moisture there is the constant threat of hailstorms. Frequently, natural forces may completely destroy in a single afternoon a season's patient labor. So it is always with doubt and misgiving that the people speak of dry farming. It is a deep conviction of all that farming the mesa land will never be successful unless some means is devised to provide irrigation water. This would be a task of herculean proportions even if the rough and thin mesa soil would justify it. Although the people often speak of this as a possible project it is without enthusiasm. It is obviously a thought conceived in desperation and nurtured as a last hope in the face of ever increasing frustration.

Under such conditions why have so many remained in the village? Why is it that within the last 15 years only two families have moved away with little thought of returning? Of the large proportion of the men who have traveled over surrounding States working and searching for work, why have so few failed to return? These answers do not lie in the direction of security and availability of employment. Practically all of the men admit that financially they would have been better off had they remained away. The answers lie much deeper. They must be sought among such subtle factors as the attitudes and values of the people, the importance of community and religion, the integration and solidarity of the family, and the place of the individual in it all.

In the search for answers to these questions the first clue comes from the composition of the people themselves. They are a distinct racial group speaking their own language and tenaciously clinging to old custom and tradition. They are ill at ease with the Anglo, who has never held an exalted opinion of a culture differing from his own. Because of antipathy toward them they are driven closely into their own group for appreciation and self expression. When one of the men is away from the village working he is usually among Anglos who regard him as a stranger and he thinks of himself as being among a strange people. He is willing to live and work away from the village mainly because of the thought that in a few weeks, a few months, or at most a year or two he will again be able to return to his home.

The desire and the expectation to return to the village have been the principal reasons why the families have tenaciously held on to their meager possessions in the village. Such possessions represent a home to which they may always return when the harvest or spring planting has been done. Families are willing to endure great sacrifice and deprivation that their village holdings may be retained. A mortgage or lien is seldom found on one of these tracts of irrigated land. A villager may mortgage or sell patented land on the mesa, but only the most pressing needs will force a family to chance losing its home and holdings in the valley. The irrigated land is usually located near the house and is definitely a part of what the family thinks of as home. It was originally grant land and has been handed down for three or four generations. It is land that the father feels obligated to bequeath to sons and daughters always divided equally, for here there is no knowledge or practice of primogeniture. Age and sex inherit alike, although it is generally recognized that the male members of the family may buy their sisters' shares if they are financially able to do so.

This practice of subdivision has naturally been greatly abused in an area where original units were much too small. Today, most of the holdings are no longer easy to express in such broad terms as acres, but in yards measured along the river. This practice of measuring along the bank of the river has resulted in long and narrow fields often no more than a few yards in width.

The irrigated land is held almost entirely by residents of the village. The absentee landowners are largely women who have left after marrying into one of the neighboring villages. Such land is usually tended by some member of the family with little thought or arrangement for the payment of rent. None of the irrigated land is owned by Anglos. It is not unusual for a tract of valley land to be handed down with the stipulation that it shall never be sold or transferred except to a member of the immediate family. This is not true of the dry land which may be, and often is, sold to outsiders.

The physical structure of the community is also a significant factor in the integration and stability of the village. The houses are compactly located to form the perimeter of a circle, with barns and corrals in the rear. Although such an arrangement interferes with efficient farming it greatly facilitates living. The house is farther from fields and pastures but is closer to school, church, and neighbors. Such proximity of living has developed a sociability and an integration of group life that would be difficult, if not impossible, to duplicate in any other type of arrangement. Seldom does a day pass when a farmer does not converse with a number of his neighbors. Children are seen playing together, after the chores are done, both night and morning. Childhood associations are almost as close between playmates as between members of the same family. They grow up to know each other almost as well as if they had been reared under the same roof.

The sense of community is strong with these people. Individuals are identified as much by the community in which they live as by family name. To be born into a community is to inherit an identification with it that is never forgotten. The few families from El Cerrito who are living away always refer to the village as their home. The reputation of the home village fixes to a certain extent the general status of a resident. The esteem for an individual is measured largely by the general opinion of the village as a whole. Loyalties to the community and to its people amount almost to a passion. It is not uncommon to hear someone speak in derogatory terms of a neighboring community or its people, but seldom does he dare breathe criticism of his own community or of its residents.

Few families in El Cerrito cannot claim at least a third cousin relationship to every other family. Thus the community is bound together not only by bonds of community relationships, but by blood ties as well. Marriage within the village has been common. It is only within recent years that close degrees of kinship have become so general that young people are forced to go outside their settlement for a mate. Existing statutes prohibit marriage between couples related as closely as second cousins. Although the church may sanction and thus bring about such a marriage, these cases are becoming comparatively rare. Many of the rural priests make it a point in their educational program to teach the undesirability, physically and morally, of close intermarriage.

The influence of religion and the church on these people is profound. All are devout Catholics. Evidence of this is found in their thinking, in their attitudes and values, and in their day-to-day activities. Services are attended regularly and in a humble spirit. Fees are paid promptly and special contributions are made periodically if meagerly. Although little money may be available for food and clothing, a way is always found to obtain candles to be burned for special occasions or a new costume for a child's first communion. The women are especially devout. It is they who carry the major burden in conducting services. When special services are held in the church some of the men are likely to remain away, but seldom a woman. Only in case of severe illness or similar misfortune will her conscience permit failure to attend.

The church is by far the best kept building in the village. Willing hands are always available should it need repairs or a new coat of whitewash. Despite the fact that the priest, who lives in a neighboring village, is able to visit the church only once each month, services are held regularly each week and innumerable other times during the year. There are 3 months during which services are held from one to three times each day.

Holy days are rigidly observed and Ascension Week receives special consideration and compliance. No work is done on these days because of the general knowledge that serious punishment would surely be meted out to the offender. The stories that tell of violations and subsequent retributions are many. All are familiar with the experience of a local farmer who, a number of years ago, plowed his corn on a Holy Day, only to have it destroyed by hail the next day. That the punishment was special was proven by the fact that adjoining fields were unharmed.

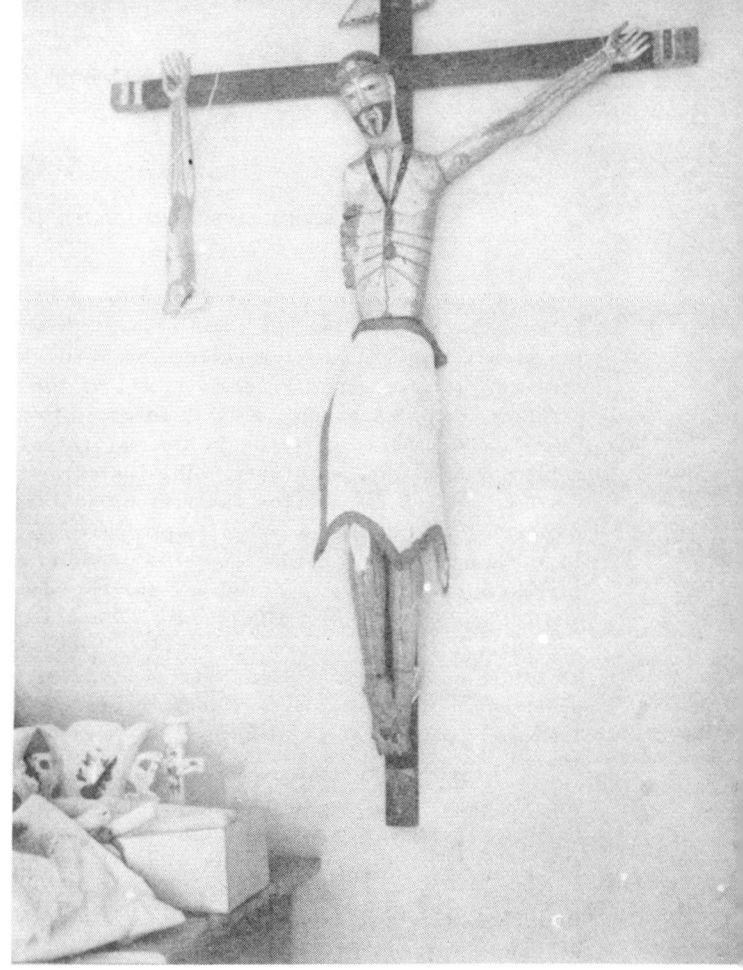

FIG. 3. *The age and condition of this revered crucifix reveal the age of the culture and the poverty of the people.*

Training of children in the knowledge and practices of the church is begun at an early age. The first reading is often done from books on the catechism. Teachers in rural schools are especially esteemed by the parents if they are willing to help teach the catechism to the children. When a child has arrived at the age of 10 he is expected to know the church rituals and to be familiar with the teachings and practices of a good Catholic.

By way of recapitulation, it may be said that the village of El Cerrito, when compared with more modern rural communities of the country has its own characteristic features. It is peculiar in its age - a community that has existed in its own way and with little physical change for many decades. Until very recently it has existed with little concern or dependence upon the outside world, except for the meager material substance that enabled its people to live. Until absolute necessity deprived them of choice, the villagers were able to resist change and adjustment. Their resources and opportunities have now reached so low a point that the people are becoming convinced that radical change must be made in their way of life. Some are of the opinion that necessary adaptation will mean abandonment of many values and customs that have been the support of these people and, in large measure, the very purpose for which they live.

HISTORY AND BACKGROUND OF THE SETTLEMENT

The date of the present occupancy of El Cerrito goes back well over a century. It is shown as a village on a map of New Mexico compiled as far back as 1844. One of the oldest residents of the village was born here and says that his grandfather came here when he was young. Practically all of the families are descendants of the pioneer settlers who moved to the locality in order to be closer to their grazing lands. They came from neighboring villages, the majority from San Miguel which is only about 12 miles north on the same river. This parent settlement is one of the oldest in New Mexico. Two of the settler families owned large flocks of sheep. Most of the other families followed this source of employment. A few of the families most closely related to the stockmen soon had small herds of their own. More land was available than the current stock could cover and any entrepreneur, with a little capital and courage, might begin a business of his own. These new businesses were begun mainly on the initiative of the entrepreneur himself, because the stockmen realized the possibility of future competition. Thus, letting herds on a sharecropping basis was not a popular practice in the early days. Stockmen preferred to pay wages, even though these were frequently paid in terms of goods.

In such a situation people naturally developed a deep sense of dependence upon the stockmen and came to depend upon their employers for advice as well as employment. Fortunately such men accepted this responsibility and eventually came to dominate all the affairs of the village. Dependents and incapacitated persons came under their protection. Under a well-regulated and organized system, available work was distributed in accordance with need to those not regularly on the "Patron's" payroll. The only independent economic pursuit of all laborers was the cultivation of their small irrigated land holdings. As the local irrigated land was grant land and as all families were descendants of the original grantees each family was entitled to a small holding.

These early settlers in El Cerrito found the area especially adaptable to stock raising. Though it was poor farming land, the mesa had a good covering of bunch grass. It was this abundant pasture land that induced the settlers to move. Part of the area had been in use by the people from San Miguel previously, but distance from the village had prevented their making full use of it.

Farming on land which could not be irrigated has never offered a great deal of inducement in this area. A rigorous climate and scant rainfall are serious handicaps to such an enterprise. Rainfall is not only meager but extremely uncertain. Although the annual precipitation for this area ranges from 15 to 18 inches, half of this may come within a few days' time with no more for a period of weeks. There is usually sufficient moisture for planting of crops in May, but June is likely to be extremely dry, with rain again in July and August. This is the expectation pattern under which the local farmers operate.

The altitude in this area is between 6 and 7 thousand feet. The winters are long and the growing season short. Crops are limited to those which will mature quickly. There can be little waiting for rain, and only a brief postponement incurs the risk of death to the crop from an early frost before it has had a chance to mature.

Soils of the high mesa land are not suitable for agriculture. Generally of a rough, stony variety, they are shallow and unsuitable for proper cultivation. Their absorptive power is usually low, rendering them subject to both water and wind erosion. Once the grass cover has been removed, rain and wind quickly take their toll. Even close grazing seriously weakens the resistance of the soil. The effects of the destruction of this cover are not limited to the area affected. Reports of studies completed and others in progress on the Pecos Watershed repeatedly point out that the depletion of the grass cover has added tremendously to the flood damage along the Pecos River during the last two or three decades.

FIG. 4. *Without irrigation there would be few beans and tortillas.*

Despite the odds against such an enterprise, many of the new settlers undertook part-time farming on the mesa lands. Corn and wheat were the principal crops cultivated, and for a time the new soil and favorable seasons combined to make such enterprises partially successful. But within a brief period of time the majority of the families abandoned the practice in favor of the more certain jobs with local stockmen. Those who did continue farming the mesa did so on a substantially reduced scale.

Because of these peculiar environmental factors, dry farming did not become a profitable and certain enterprise. Only the irrigated land of the local valley has ever assured a bountiful harvest. This land was fertile and water from the Pecos River was always available. Hence the people became more and more dependent upon their small irrigated holdings as a supplement to their livelihood. Money and goods earned at wage work, plus the subsistence products grown at home enabled these families to survive in a satisfactory way. Both sources were of tremendous importance. The failure of either to contribute heavily meant deprivation if not near destitution.

The early economy of San Miguel County was one of abundance. Land was available and could be had for either the asking or the taking. Temporary depletion of the grass resource invoked little more hardship than moving livestock to another proximate area or spreading it over a wider base. Little thought was given to the fact that some day the soil might be impoverished or exhausted. On the other hand, some effort was made to preserve the valley soil. The practice of spreading barnyard manure on the soil seems to go back well into the history of the village of El Cerrito. During the last few decades the necessity for this practice has been increasingly realized.

Each of the two classes of land cultivated, dry and irrigated, had its own special crops that were planted year after year. The dry-farming land was devoted to wheat and some corn, the irrigated land to corn, alfalfa, and garden products. There was little diversification. The same piece of land might be planted to the same crop year after year.

The general pattern for agriculture is little changed in present-day El Cerrito. Little attempt is made to experiment with new crops. The fairly recent shift to beans as a staple crop to substitute for wheat has been the only significant change. The value of this change is questioned by many of the people. Only a few are convinced that any appreciable benefit has accrued because of the substitution. Beans are grown for food as was wheat. Instead of the old process of selling wheat and buying beans the reverse now prevails.

The changes that have come about during the last half century in the economic resources of these people have brought about a realization of the need for adjustment. These changes are vividly outlined in the life history of one of the oldest men in the village. It is given below as he unfolded it.

> I was born in El Cerrito and have lived here all of my life except 2 or 3 years. These years were spent in other parts of New Mexico while I was working for the railroad and as a freighter. I owned a little property in El Cerrito all this time and thought of it (El Cerrito) as my home.
>
> My father was a very strong and healthy man. I remember him very well as he lived to be 55 years old. He was born in Santa Fe He used to tell us many stories of life in Santa Fe when he was a boy. The place was very tough then and there was always danger from the Indians. He used to fight the Indians and was a very good fighter too.
>
> When he was very young he came to Pecos (town in San Miguel County) and worked there for a long time He then moved to San Miguel and it was there he met my mother and they were married. When they were married he bought some land in El Cerrito and moved there. I was born here in 1862.
>
> My father worked very hard and was a good business man. Soon after he came to El Cerrito he bought more land (in another village some 10 miles from El Cerrito) but most of his money went for cattle. He was very well off financially, had lots of money always. In a few years he had several hundred head of cattle. He used to keep money around the house in jars.
>
> My father believed in working hard and he made us work hard too. He used to get up very early in the morning, while it was still dark. There were horses to feed and water to bring. A boy of 8 years then was expected to be able to work all day. We worked much harder than the boys do now. Oh, much harder. The girls worked, too, but it was for the man. The women had plenty to do around the house. There was wool to card and spin. There were clothes to make, too. We made most all of our clothes then. It was so much better than now when one has to buy everything. Money wasn't important then. Everything was made at home and not bought at a store.
>
> Although we worked hard in those times, we used to find time for play. We could play on bad days, on Saturday afternoons, and Sunday after Rosary. We

couldn't play before Rosary on Sunday. There were several games which we played. We used to take a ball and toss it to one another. Used to play a game something like golf. The balls were made by hand and so were the sticks.

My father didn't mind our playing as long as we did our work well. He would never join in with us but would often stand and watch us play for long periods of time.

When I was a boy many people would die and get killed. There was much danger during those days. When a person died the custom was for all of the man's friends and relatives to visit the dead man's family. I didn't mind going to those places. There was always plenty of food to eat. However, I didn't like the burials. I used to get scared when they began to throw dirt on the body.

When I was a boy the Indians would come to the village at night. They would steal meat and lard from the houses. The people here always had meat and lard made from the buffalo. The Indians used to steal tortillas too. They would bring long pointed stocks and spear the tortillas from the windows.

One time the Indians came while my father was taking an ox to water. They took the ox away from him and ran up into the mountains. When father came back to the village he ran to a huge drum in the village, used for warning the people against the Indians, and began beating on it. When the people heard the noise they came and went after the Indians. They finally found the ox but there was nothing left but the bones. The Indians had killed the ox, cut off the meat, wrapped it in a serape and gone away.

I went to school very little when I was a boy. The school term was short and we were taught in Spanish. Nothing more than the catechism and the letters were taught then. About all the teachers knew then was how to say A, B, C, etc.

I can remember those teachers very well. They were all men and were very mean to the children. They believed in using the whip freely. They used to make us cross our fingers then they would tie the fingers together and whip us. They used small leather quirts. Sometimes they would make us take off our clothes before they began whipping us. I think everyone was too afraid of the teacher then to learn anything.

I can remember when the church sponsored lots of fiestas and dances. Those were good times when everyone had lots of fun. Sometimes the fiestas would last for several days. People would bring food and eat together.

When I was small a woman who was very rich lived here. She made a lot of money from sheep and cattle. (A member of the rival family in the village.) She had several peons and was very mean to them. Used to have them lashed when they disobeyed her. She didn't get along very well with the people here. She would cheat them and pay them very little when they worked for her. I remember a foreman that used to work for her. He was a very mean but a very funny fellow. He was always playing jokes. He used to milk cows for her. I remember one time he milked a pail full from a cow and then sat in it. That was very funny.

Times were good then and everyone had some money. No one lacked food and there was always work. There was a system here then that has died out. The people in El Cerrito used to elect a conservator each year. He acted as a sort of governor of the village. The people had to do what he told them to. In those times the people would work together in planting and harvest time. The conservator would call the men to work and could determine which work should be done first. When someone wanted to hire a man he had to come to the conservator. He could determine who could have the job. Always he would select the family that needed the work most. In that way the needy were usually provided for. In case they were not he could ask the people for money or grain to give the pobres. I don't think he ever had much trouble with the people, everyone did as he told them.

My family was very large. There were eight children, four girls and four boys. When my father died we were all living at home. He left the property to mother but the boys managed everything. We did this dividing the profits equally. This continued until my mother died four years later. Then the property was divided into eight equal parts.

A few years after my mother died a man by the name of R. came to Las Vegas. He had some money and quite a few sheep. He talked three of us boys into taking some of his sheep on a share basis. We did this and gave him a mortgage on a part of our cattle. For a few years we did pretty well then came a number of very dry years in succession. We lost so many sheep that we had to give R. some of our cattle. I lost so many sheep that it took all of my cattle to pay R. I lost everything that I had. I paid him though, every penny of the debt, I paid him.

> After this misfortune I began to work as a freighter. Used to travel between the towns of Las Vegas, Tucumcari, Santa Rosa, and Lincoln. I did this work for about 10 years. During this time I saved enough money to buy about 3 acres of the irrigated land in El Cerrito. There was no need to try to buy cattle or sheep again. The land around El Cerrito was taken up. I guess good times are gone from El Cerrito for good.

The area of land owned by villagers was somewhat increased in 1916 by the opening of surrounding land for homesteading. Many of the El Cerrito families took advantage of this opportunity and filed upon tracts of land varying from 40 to 640 acres. Unfortunately, many of these homesteads were poor or so inaccessible from the village that little material benefit has ever been derived from them. Only two of the local families are seriously undertaking to make these homesteads support them. These two families are cultivating some 30 or 40 acres and devoting the remainder to chickens and livestock. One of the men is singularly optimistic about his enterprise, stating that last year he managed to live with no aid from outside sources. However, he admits the necessity of having some source of cash income in addition to his present resources in order to enable him to live for the next few years. Once firmly established, he expects to earn his entire living from his farm.

THE BACKGROUND OF PRESENT POPULATION

Cultural Ethnic and Nationality Origins.

The entire population of El Cerrito is of native or Spanish-American stock, descendants of Conquistadores who mixed their blood with that of the indigenous population. They are a segment of a larger whole that has blended blood, knowledge, and techniques of old Spain with that of a new world. The Indian heritage was leaned upon heavily for local knowledge of terrain, the elements, and the means of combating them. Agricultural techniques were of special significance, for many of the early Spanish Colonists were not farmers. Evidence of knowledge gained from the indigenous peoples can be seen today in the mud houses, the crops and foods, the methods and tools of farming used by the natives. The process was one of borrowing rather than assimilation. Today the native still speaks the language, enjoys the customs, and is endowed with the superstitions of Andalusian Spain. Nor is there any conflict in the combination. Time and struggle have compounded these elements into a singular product - the native or Spanish-American people.

The native people of San Miguel County, N. Mex. have never been a landless proletariat. Most of the families have been able to establish enough relationship with an original land grantee to become eligible for a home site on some Spanish or Mexican grant. Each family in El Cerrito either owns a tract of land or is in line for inheritance. These tracts have been handed down from the beneficiaries of the original San Miguel del Bado Grant, and the families have clung to them tenaciously. Only a very limited number of present inhabitants of this grant own more than a few acres of grant land, and most of that has been inherited. Stockmen have established themselves on the surrounding mesa. The grant land is limited in the concentration of its use as well as in its ownership. Few families are interested in doing full-time farming even if the local holdings could be gathered together into a paying-sized farm.

The pattern of ownership of the mesa land has changed during the last 40 years. Before 1900, or even 1916, there was little large-scale local ownership of the mesa land.

Families had deeds for their irrigated holdings but the mesa land was either leased or used free. The greatest change took place immediately after 1916, when land in the area was opened to homesteading. Some of the stockmen in the area placed families upon desirable tracts of land, buying them out as soon as their claims had been lived up and recorded. Other claims were bought from bona fide settlers who had come into the area for land. Extensive tracts were still leased, however, from the State and Federal Governments and from homesteaders who did not continue to live on the homesteads after they were proved up. Lease rates were, and still are, reasonable, varying from 3 to 8 cents an acre depending upon the condition of the grass, whether there is a fence, and the availability of a water supply. The latter factor is the more important. A well-built ground tank or spring on the land will easily double its value to the stockman.

During the last decade, the marked lull in the demand for the services of these people has resulted in increased dependence upon individual holdings. Despite this trend, apparently attitudes toward conserving this land have undergone only slight modification. The concensus is that little could be accomplished by better and more intensive use of the small acreage that most of them have. Attention is predominantly centered upon the possibility of finding labor on the outside. As a result of this attitude, little concern is shown for the possibilities of complete use of owned resources. The home garden may be neglected, even abandoned, to follow the merest chance of obtaining a job outside. Sometimes the family may continue to care for the garden and subsistence crop during the husband's absence in search of work, but unless there are boys large enough to take the place of the husband, total loss of the home production may result.

Patterns of Social Behavior

The colonists to New Spain brought with them a highly integrated pattern of social life, built around two principal institutions, the family and the church. Each of these institutions aided and supported the other. The church was the final authority for and initiator of all forms of formal social participation. Church festivals, fiestas, horse races, games, dances, and serenades which formed the basis for all social life were usually under the sponsorship and direction of the local priests. Even the activities of daily life, conduct, and functions of the family were tremendously influenced by the authoritarian church. The integration, loyalty, and discipline of the family is still vitally tied in with the role and function of the church.

Although the family is still a highly integrated unit among the native people of New Mexico, it was even more so in the early history of the State. The structure and functions of this unit were definite. The authority of the father was never questioned. The oldest male in the group occupied a position that was never lost or relinquished until his death. His authority was felt in every function of village life. It was he who could fix the group opinion about any current problem or event. It was for him to say when the corn should be planted, how the family property should be managed and divided, what the share of each individual should be. As long as he lived none of the heirs might have exclusive right or use of a particular part of the family estate unless it was his particular will that this should be so. In many cases the family members pooled their efforts in running the estate and the profits were divided among them. If the head of this hierarchy lived to a ripe old age it might be that sons and grandsons would occupy a community of ownership between them. In such a case the head of the family group might have retired from active participation, contributing no more than his knowledge to the operation of the property.

FIG. 5. *The songs of "Old Spain" are still remembered.*

Often such a family, or group of families, lived in adjoining houses, in definite section of the village. They were segregated and frequently alined against another and similar group in the village. Such a situation led to friction, which was sometimes intense. Differences between individuals were likely to get the separate groups involved, often leading to open fights between the groups. Once begun, these group differences or conflicts were likely to continue and gain in intensity with the passing of time. Some of these begun decades ago still persist, although the loca situations may have undergone radical change. Many of these group conflicts exist where the knowledge of the cause has been forgotten for one or more generations.

Although changes have been far-reaching in the economic situation of El Cerrito during the last half-century or more, the old pattern of living of the early colonization days still persists in many ways. The practice of cooperation and mutual aid are still dominant traits of their culture. Efforts are still pooled in any endeavor that necessitates it. This pattern of behavior involves the entire village of El Cerrito although it is obviously stronger among the more closely related families. The pattern in former communal ownership can still be discerned in the attitudes of the people toward borrowing and lending. Tools and equipment are exchanged freely with little thought of their belonging to any particular member. The local Farm Security Administration supervisor says that such a background makes it easy to conduct cooperative enterprises among the native people, if the different groups are recognized and properly taken into account.

Dominant Values and Sanctions

Every group has its dominant mores and customs, with sanctions and taboos for human conduct, to which the individual is expected to conform. The values attached to the expected modes of behavior play a tremendous role in the life and conduct of both groups and the individuals that compose them. To understand these dominant sanctions and taboos, and the values attached thereto, is to go far toward understanding a people and its culture.

Among the native people the values attached to such practices as thrift and hard work as ends in and of themselves have never attained the importance they have with other groups of people. These natives are able to see neither sin nor moral corruption in idleness and leisure time. They see neither virtue nor common sense in keeping busy for the sake of occupying the hands and the mind. Work is simply a means to an end - a means of accomplishing that which is valued or desired, and as such these people realize its importance. Children are taught at an early age the necessity of labor and are given ample opportunity to put it into practice. But the necessity of work lies in what it will bring in a material way - money, land, and independence. It is not believed that it adds to the moral fiber of the individual. Furthermore, the mere accumulation of material goods adds little to the popular esteem for an individual. The prestige of the man depends in no small measure upon his contribution to the fiestas or his activities in the political life and interests of the group.

Contacts with the Anglo-American in recent decades have somewhat affected the attitude of the natives toward hard work and thrift, especially their regard for the latter. Contacts with this new element have convinced them that the emphasis placed upon thrift and hard work by the Anglo has substantially accelerated his progress in New Mexico. It has brought about a general recognition of the need for a greater emphasis upon these practices in order to meet competition successfully.

But these new contacts have failed to alter materially the social contexture of the village life of these natives. Any apparent changes are superficial, scarcely touching the deeper convictions of the people. The real alterations in attitude apparently come from the realization of the need for adaptations in order to compete more successfully in a struggle that to date has been almost disastrous.

FIG. 6. *"A man's home is his castle."* The patriarch of the village.

FIG. 7. A *"larger family"* at mealtime.

The role of the woman has always been a subordinate one in the Spanish culture. Her role is definite, and despite its subordinate nature is one of extreme importance in the stability and integration of the group. It is a much more restricted one than that of the man. A woman is expected to be faithful to the teachings and practices of the church. In doing this she may make up for some of the negligence of the husband. Her principal function is to produce children. Her interests are centered in the family and the home. She receives neither encouragement nor appreciation for participation outside this limited sphere. If she follows these rules of conduct she will have been successful in her role in the village. Failing in any one she will have incurred the serious displeasure of the group. It is rarely that she dares risk stepping out of the role prescribed for her. To do so might mean ostracism from the social life of the womenfolk. This is no easy punishment to bear when visiting and conversation with other women offer the only release from the drab routine of housework and child care.

The role of the man is much less restricted. Although he is expected to attend church, public opinion censors him much less severely than it censors the woman in case of failure to do so. His role and obligations are much more closely interwoven into the function and interests of the group. He is expected to be loyal to his family and assume the material responsibility of supporting his wife and children. But failure to live up to his obligations and responsibilities to the group are met with much greater disfavor. He is soon forgiven for a clandestine affair with a woman other than his wife but refusal to lend his farming tools to a neighbor is long remembered. He is seldom criticized for intoxication, but should he fail to report for duty at the annual cleaning of the community irrigation ditch the ire of the group would be strongly aroused.

A strict code of honesty and fairness within the group is found. Thievery or plundering seldom occurs in the village. Such an act would be entirely foreign to the thinking of a member of one of these closely integrated villages. The present Justice of the Peace claims never to have had such a case before him. The residents unanimously state that such things seldom happen in the rural native villages. An act of this kind would bring such extreme displeasure from the group that an individual could scarcely bring himself to do it even if the desire were present.

The people remember two cases of criminal conviction in the history of the village. One case happened during Prohibition when a local man was apprehended and convicted for making and selling liquor. The local people did not seriously disapprove of his act and had they disapproved it is unlikely that it would have been committed. The other incident happened several years ago when a local man was assaulted and severely beaten by a rival, in an affair involving the use of certain pasture lands.

It seems unlikely that a family could seriously violate the social codes of the native villages and remain for long. Group approval means too much.

In many respects the village of El Cerrito has changed little in the last hundred years. The most obvious change, as mentioned above, has been the dwindling material resources of the people. Economic retrogression has been from ample resources to a situation where the people are literally stranded in their village homes. It is doubtful if the resources of El Cerrito could adequately care for more than one-fourth its present population. The reasons for the extreme tenacity with which the people have clung to their village and their meager possessions must be found in other than the economic.

The ties that bind these people to their land and village are many and strong. They have a strong sense of belonging to the village and feel strange elsewhere. The situation into which the local residents are born ill fits them for living in any other place. The local organizations, amusements, means of recreation, even ideas and superstitions, belong to sixteenth-century Spain much more than to the modern world. Once these things are given proper consideration it is not difficult to see why the people cling to their native habitat at great material cost.

It is only a few of the younger people, those who have been away to school or to one of the recently established Government camps, who express a preference for life outside the village. A majority would prefer living full time in the village if only they were able to earn the means that would enable them to do so. It is with extreme reluctance that some of the people are coming to admit the lack of any choice between obtaining greater resources in their village and moving away to where such resources may be found.

THE PEOPLE ON THE LAND

Land Use: Patterns of Ownership

Each family in El Cerrito either owns or is in line to inherit some land. Unfortunately, only a few have holdings sufficiently large to justify full-time farming or stock raising. The largest landholder owns 2,000 acres of dry mesa land. Although this land is poorly stocked the annual income from it is usually sufficient to maintain the resident family at a mediocre level of living. The smallest tract in the settlement is one-fourth acre of irrigated land. This holding furnishes the family a home site and a small garden. The husband, wife, and seven children depend for their livelihood upon the wages earned at irregular intervals by the husband.

The majority of these families own and operate from 10 to 40 acres of dry-farming land plus 1 to 4 acres of irrigated land. Little of this is used or regarded as a source of cash income. In especially good years there may be a few extra sacks of beans for sale, but little more. It is expected that this land will furnish little more than a good portion of the food for the family table and enough forage for the small number of livestock possessed.

The smaller landholders have never owned more than tiny tracts of land. They have depended upon the local patrons or outside sources to furnish them with labor. Only a few have ever bought land. Those who own more than the small strips of grant land homesteaded it, either during or subsequent to 1916. Little of this patented land has been sold. The strips are so scattered or otherwise so undesirable that a buyer is difficult to find.

Few of these families have advanced from the status of laborer to a position where resources owned would allow self-sustenance. The two families in the village owning and leasing sufficient land to be independent are descendants of the one-time big stockman of the settlement. Their holdings were inherited, in large part, although the owners have shown above-average ability in clinging to them. Other members of one of these families have long ago lost or disposed of their shares until they are definitely back on a level with families which at one time worked for them.

The people of El Cerrito think in terms of their immediate problems. There is little thought or planning with a view to accumulating property and advancing toward a status that would enable them to live from their own resources. Much more concern is shown toward being certified for WPA work or the possibility of securing some sort of seasonal labor on the outside. The one exception is a resident, who during the last 10 years, has traded for and bought enough land to merit some hope of becoming self sustaining on his own farm. With the help of a son and a daughter employed in the CCC and NYA camps, respectively, and with his own earnings from various governmental agencies, he has been able to add approximately 20 acres to his original 10. Another 10 acres will support his family at a comfortable level of living. This additional acreage he hopes to buy within the next few years, providing his present sources of income are not further curtailed.

The abuses inherent in the local pattern of land inheritance are slowly being recognized by these people. Subdividing tracts that were already too small for efficient operation has almost reached a limit. Many of the holdings have become so small that it is difficult for the owners to know exactly where the boundaries lie. Fences are often impracticable as they remove a certain amount of land from cultivation and interfere with proper plowing and cultivation.

During recent years the custom of equal inheritance has been further abused by the inability of a few members of the family to buy the shares of the others. It is generally recognized that the male members of the family have the right to buy the shares of their sisters if they are financially able to do so. Because of recent limitation in outside employment and consequent reduction in income few have found this possible.

The staple crops in El Cerrito are corn, beans, and alfalfa. Beans and corn are grown for family consumption. Alfalfa is grown as feed for the livestock, and is well adapted to the valley soil. More feed is produced per acre from this crop than from any other. Largely for this reason, more than half the irrigated land is continuously devoted to this one crop.

Several different varieties of corn are grown, the most common being native blue corn. This variety was grown by the Indians, who taught the Spanish colonists how to plant and cultivate it. A great variety of dishes are prepared from it. All of the local people agree that it is far superior to any other variety in taste and nutritive content. Although the other varieties may be fed to livestock, the blue corn is seldom so used. It is too important and necessary as food for the people.

Limited numbers of livestock are found in the village. Those owning cows and horses are handicapped by lack of space in which to keep them. Chickens are common, although the number in a flock is usually limited to 10 or 15. These are kept for the eggs they produce, as they are considered much too valuable to eat. Only the most fortunate families ever feel justified in killing one for meat.

Most of the families have from one to three horses, and a few keep milk cows. The milk cows are more than family concern. A cow produces milk and butter, not only for the immediate family, but also for sons, daughters, and possibly a neighbor. Milk and butter are not common elements in the local diet. Only the small children get milk to drink. An adult is considered fortunate if he has enough for his coffee.

Only four of the families keep hogs. Others say that buying lard is more economical than producing it. Meat is not considered an essential part of the diet, and it is only during the winter months that meat is bought, and then in very small quantities. Lard is deemed much more important. Hogs that are butchered for home use are killed chiefly for the lard they will render. When a family butchers a hog some o

FIG. 8. "We are stockmen, not farmers," the people will tell you.

the meat is given away to relatives and less fortunate neighbors but very little lard is given away, as it is considered far too valuable. This butchering is one of the rare occasions on which each family in the village has meat. There is very little waste in the process. Even the blood is saved to be used in preparing a special pudding. The butchers are particularly careful to preserve any parts of the hog that will render lard. All cuts of meat are closely trimmed to remove each bit of fat. While the butchering is in process children of the various families come by for an expected bit of the kill. Each is given something, though it be only a foot or a morsel from the head.

Although many reasons may account for the woeful shortage of livestock in the village, a few are dominant. One is the lack of available pasture. Only a few of the families have access to range that does not necessitate long drives. Farming land is too limited and too valuable to produce food for a cow throughout the entire year. To corral-feed a cow during the summer months means use of the feed crop that will be sorely needed during the winter. And to the physical situation must be added a certain inertia. Years and even decades of living without the benefits that may be derived from domestic livestock has conditioned these people to make little effort to obtain them. It seems likely that many are not even conscious of the full benefits that might be obtained from making these products available to themselves and to their children.

One of the most important byproducts of agriculture in this part of New Mexico is fruit. A large percentage of the families in El Cerrito have orchards that range in size from a few trees to half an acre in extent. When the rather uncertain season allows a good fruit crop the source of food is not only extended but many families have several dollars worth of peaches and apricots to sell. Fruit grown in the valley has the reputation of being unusually good and brings an excellent price in the market. The surplus is disposed of without difficulty.

In addition to fruit sold and that eaten in season, a large volume of fruit is preserved and canned for the winter months. Certain housewives claim to store enough fruit to meet the needs of their families until it is again in season. Most of this fruit is stored in glass jars, but some apricots and peaches are dried.

Unfortunately, these orchards are not receiving adequate care and attention. Few of the trees are pruned, and the older and less productive ones are seldom replaced. Insects that destroy the apple crop year after year are allowed to continue their ravages. But despite the heavy losses by insects and frequent late frosts, the growing of fruit still remains one of the most valuable enterprises of the valley.

Another infrequent source of income is the gathering of wild piñon nuts that grow on the mesa near the village. These nuts are comparatively easy to gather, are free for the taking, and command a good price on the market. Some local families claim to have made more than $200 in a season gathering and selling piñons. This crop is too seldom productive, however, to be depended upon. It is claimed that good crops are produced only once in every 6 or 7 years.

Techniques of Agriculture

Agricultural practices in this region have not changed greatly. Sons have truly followed in the footsteps of the fathers, and their sons, in turn, have followed after them. An early colonist returning to El Cerrito today would find little change in crops grown or in methods of cultivating and harvesting. Beans, corn, and alfalfa are planted year after year, with infrequent rotation. The one pronounced crop change has been the substitution of beans for wheat. Older residents claim that much more wheat was grown in the past when rainfall was heavier and wheat flour more difficult to buy. Only two local families are still growing wheat. All other families regard bean crops as more important. They are more likely to produce with scant rainfall and add more to the family diet. It is more economical and desirable to be without flour than to be without beans.

The type of livestock kept is far below standard. Hogs, cows, and horses are of a scrubby, yet hardy breed, usually poor and carelessly tended. Few attempts have been made to improve the native breeds. The villagers prefer what they have and can find reasons for justifying this preference. Little education as to the advantages of better stock has been available to them, and any such attempt would likely meet with some resistance. One of the local stockmen was persuaded to try improving his herd of cattle several years ago but met with little success. He claims that the cows he bought and moved to his ranch were not adapted to local conditions and that half of them died in less than a year. He summed up the situation as follows: "In certain areas of New Mexico a high grade of cattle is profitable, but not here. If one is lucky enough to have a good year and plenty of grass there is more profit in high-grade stuff but if a dry year happens along this type of cattle is not able to rustle like the native stock, and may starve. Over a long period of time I much prefer our native stock."

It is true that better livestock would not receive proper care and attention. Proper shelter is not available, even during the severe parts of the winter. No one would consider calling a veterinary if a cow becomes sick or injured. The distance to town would be too great and the cost prohibitive. Even the proper medicine would not be available. Native stock is treated with home remedies that require only the simplest of ingredients such as lard, salt, and a few native plants and herbs.

The farm equipment and machinery used in this area are of the simplest sort. Large machinery is neither used nor appreciated. A horse, a turning plow, and a few hoes and forks make up the standard equipment in common use. The turning plow is used to turn the soil, plant the crop, and cultivate it. Wheat and beans are threshed by hand. If the crop is large enough to justify it horses or goats may aid in the threshing. A corral is built with a good hard floor, and the horses or goats are driven around on top of the harvest until the grain has been separated out. The grain is cleaned by means of winnowing. Women and children often lend aid in doing this.

Alfalfa is the sole crop that is not harvested by hand tools. Two of the families have horse-drawn mowing machines which cut most of the alfalfa in the valley. The owners of the machines are given a portion of the alfalfa or its equivalent in labor as payment for cutting it. Cash is never involved in the exchange.

Plowing and planting operations begin in late May or the early part of June. The date may vary from 2 to 3 weeks, depending upon the mildness of the season or the quantity of moisture in the ground. The two operations are usually carried out simultaneously. As the soil is being turned the seeds are dropped into each third furrow.

The village has only one planting machine. It is a walking device, pulled by one horse and capable of planting one row at a time. The owner is regarded as the most modern farmer in the village, although he received some criticism for his investments in more efficient farm tools. People feel that time and labor saving devices are of minor importance. Efficiency and saving of time mean little where already man power is far in excess of the work to be done.

Intensive cultivation of the crops begins in the latter part of June. Beans and corn are plowed from three to five times, depending upon the rainfall and the number of times the land is irrigated. The crops are weeded and thinned when, according to local standards, these operations are deemed necessary. These tasks fall to the boys, aided at intervals by the father. Alfalfa, which besides harvesting requires about three irrigations in spring and summer, entails less labor than any crop grown on the irrigated land. It requires reseeding only once in each 5 to 7 years. Most of the farmers agree that reseeding is best at each 5 year period but that many wait longer because of the cost involved in buying new seed.

The system of irrigation in use by the many villages along the Pecos river in New Mexico is an old one. No one remembers when it was installed in El Cerrito. There is considerable evidence that it may have been built originally by the Indians who once inhabited this area. The present course of the ditch has been unchanged for many years. Evidence of this is found in the many feet of bank that have been built up by annual cleanings. Even in places where construction of the ditch would have necessitated removal of only a few feet of dirt, the height of the lower bank has risen to 10 feet or more. The Madre acequia or main ditch is slightly less than 2 miles long. It begins at a bottle-neck part of the river, where a makeshift dam has been built. This dam was constructed by means of laying a line of stone across the river and stacking brush and long poles behind it. Thus the bed of the river, above the dam, has been raised a height of approximately 6 feet. This added elevation enables the water to flow out into the main ditch and on to the valley below.

The construction of the dam is such that there is little assurance of its permanency. Any big flood or unusual flow of water might destroy the entire structure. No provision is made for diversion, hence the dam must carry the weight and pressure of any quantity of water that happens to come over it. If the pressure is too great the dam is destroyed, as are the crops below which are dependent upon it. Before it can be restored lack of water has probably killed the crops in the valley.

From the dam the main ditch runs along the river, but the ditch's fall is less than that of the river, and it carries its water many feet above the surface of the river at the entrance to the valley. This main ditch and its smaller tributaries are maintained and repaired communally by the users of the water. The organization for carrying out these tasks is one of the most highly integrated and efficient in the community. Its chief functions are carried on by a mayordomo or ditch boss who supervise all work on the irrigation system, and a committee which is responsible for all rules governing the use of the water. All of these are elected annually. There is seldom an occasion for interference or supervision of the use of the water. It is available for anyone needing it, with never a longer wait than 2 or 3 days.

There are no intense and extended seasons of farm labor in El Cerrito. Although such tasks as planting, cultivating, and harvesting require a few days of intense effort they are soon over and the farmer is again able to distribute his time and labor over a wide variety of tasks. A full day's labor during the busiest season is interspersed with periods for relaxation. Although the worker may rise early and go about feeding

FIG. 9. *Bread is still baked outside — a survival of many generations.*

10. *In kitchens such as this the traditional diet is prepared — a diet balanced by ations of experience.*

and caring for his domestic livestock there is no hurry at breakfast time. After breakfast and a brief planning of the day's work, he is off for the field until 11 or 11:30. The noon meal consumes a good half hour, followed by 1 or 2 hours of siesta. The afternoon's work in the field assumes the same tempo. The farmer is usually back home when the sun is an hour or more high, for supper and to do the evening chores around the house. He attends to the horses and the cow, if there is one, after the evening meal is over. Throughout the day he has had time for brief chats and frequent exchanges of advice with passing friends or relatives. In brief, there is little rushing brought about by time or season. Caring for the average farm unit necessitates little haste. One is able to choose here between a slow tempo and a more complete use of time and greater haste which would result in larger blocks of leisure time or idleness. Custom and habit usually favor the moderate work tempo.

Commercialization and Self-Sufficiency

Little of what could be designated as commercial farming is found in El Cerrito. The sale of a few beans and, during productive years, a few dollars worth of peaches constitutes the sole income from cash crops. With the exception of the two families owning sheep and cattle almost all cash is earned from labor on the outside. The most extensive dry-land farmer in El Cerrito sold only $80 worth of products last year. The range was from this sum to zero. Few families sold more than 10 or 15 dollars worth

The emphasis in El Cerrito is upon subsistence farming. An effort is made by all families to produce as much of their food as possible. Beans and corn, which form such a substantial portion of the local diet, are grown in sufficient quantities to last the family for the major portion of the year. During the summer months well-kept gardens support the family table, with the exception of flour and the few smaller items that must be bought. One of the residents estimated that the cash needs for food of his family was no more than $2 a week during the months when his garden was producing. When the gardens are at their peak of production the families are able to use no more than a small percentage of what it produces. Unfortunately, there is little storing or canning of these perishable foods. None of the knowledge or equipment necessary for canning vegetables is available. Food experts claim that canning fresh vegetables requires a very high temperature in order to make them safe for keeping and consumption. In the high altitude here this would necessitate pressure cookers. These people have neither money to buy them nor knowledge of how to operate them. Fruit canned in glass jars is almost the sole product preserved. Only one family had canned or dried vegetables other than chili for more than 3 months of 1940. Four other families reported some canned or dried home-produced vegetables.(fig. 11). Home-produced lard, potatoes, flour, chili, meal, fuel, dried corn (chicos), and soap are available to most of the families during most of the year. Products such as chili and lard must also be bought.

Although the term "commercialization" would mean little to these people, they have definite concepts about how machinery, coupled with large-scale farming, has affected them. They feel that this combination has been highly influential in making it more difficult to find work. One often hears the expression that machinery is now doing much of the labor that used to require men. Some of them know large farms in other States that at one time employed large numbers of men, but now use only tractors

It is highly doubtful if commercialized farming is resented as such. It is the technological changes that commercialized farming has brought about to which they object

Fig. 11

MONTHS IN WHICH PRODUCED FOOD AND FUEL ITEMS WERE NOT AVAILABLE TO FAMILIES, EL CERRITO, NEW MEXICO, 1940

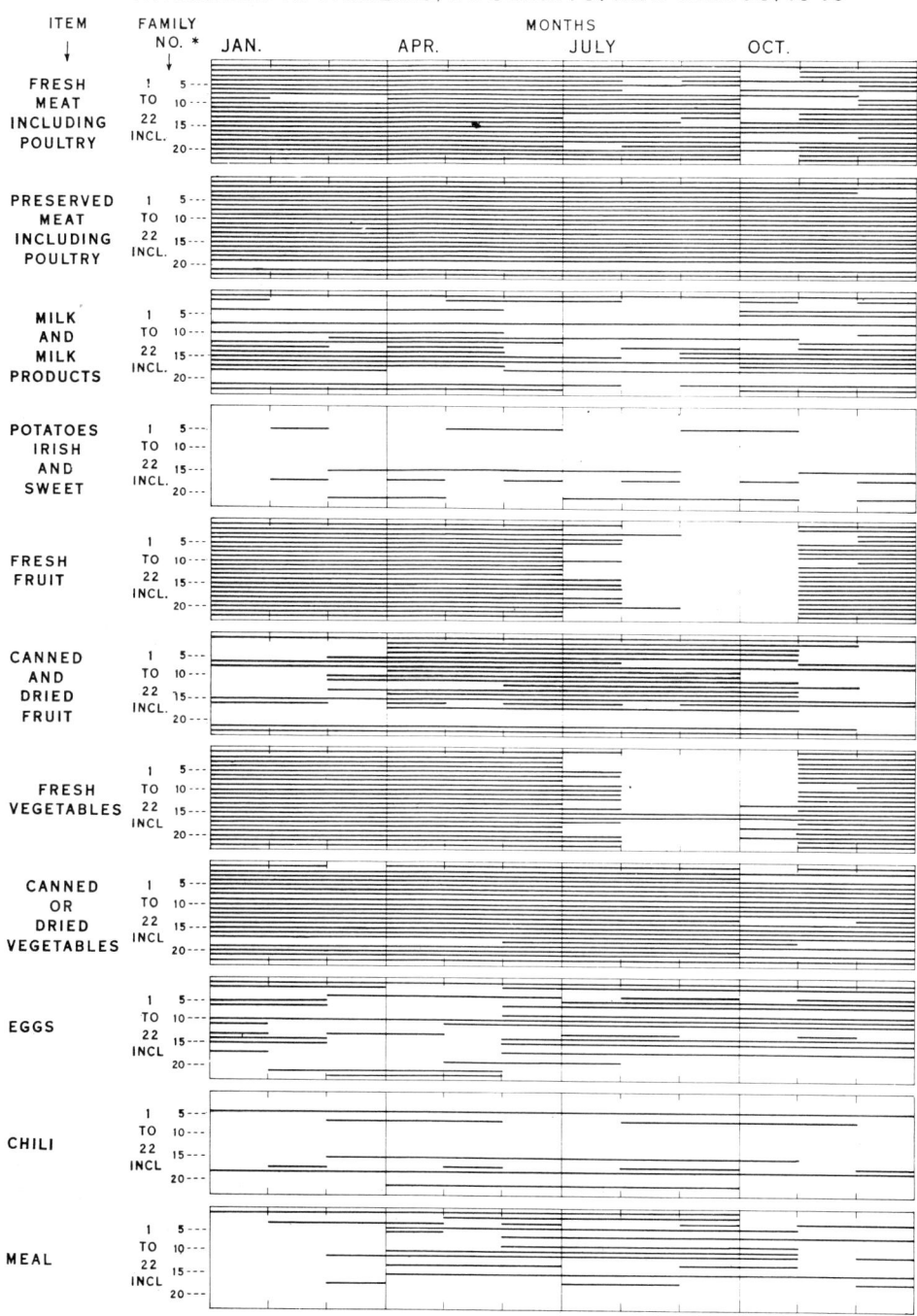

SOME LARD, FUEL, AND SOAP AVAILABLE ALL MONTHS FOR ALL FAMILIES.
*FAMILY NO. 7 NOT INCLUDED, DATA NOT AVAILABLE.

U. S. DEPARTMENT OF AGRICULTURE   NEG. 39458   BUREAU OF AGRICULTURAL ECONOMICS

If it could be felt that the benefits of commercialized farming were distributed in accordance with some standard of equality it would fit well into their philosophy of living. Apparently nothing in their standard of values would make taboo any technique or device for making life easier or richer.

The Farm Business

The total cash family income from farming operations varied from 0 to $3,000 in 1939. The incomes of the two largest farmers, from the sale of farm products, were greater than all others combined. None of the farmers could give accurate figures on their incomes and expenditures. Records of the farm business are not kept.

Little money is borrowed outside the village. To borrow money one must give security. The sole security these families have to offer is their land or livestock. But they usually refuse to mortgage the irrigated land, and credit based on the average farm operation would be practically worthless, as there is little cash income by which such a loan could be repaid.

Several years ago some of the people learned by painful experience the danger of offering their land as security for a loan that was expected to be repaid from outside sources. All know of families that lost their land when outside employment became so scarce that the loans could not be repaid. These losses have had their effect in El Cerrito. Today one seldom finds a mortgage or lien on the small irrigated holdings. These terms have become synonymous with loss and even eviction. Signing papers has come to be such a duel that Governmental agencies operating in this area are often refused cooperation because of the fear that giving adequate security might jeopardize land holdings. Any program that necessitates security or obligation meets with distrust.

An experience of one of the villagers with the Farm Security Administration illustrates the prevailing attitude. He borrowed a little less than $200 and gave his property in the village as security. Failing to produce enough on his land to pay the loan, or even interest on the loan, the following year he was threatened with foreclosure. After some time elapsed he was able to arrange to repay the loan from his WP job at the rate of $2 a month. His brother remarked that this experience had taught him the danger of risking his property as security for loans. He said, "I would never risk losing my property in that way. That is the reason I want nothing to do with any Government program that operates by making loans. If I can't get the money without any strings tied to it, then I won't take it." One of the most appealing features of the works projects program is that participation entails no obligation on the part of the people.

These people have little interest in outside trade agreements and the current prices of farm products. No attempt is made to keep abreast of the fluctuations in the outside markets except the one big sheepman whose sole interest is in the current price of wool. Not a single farm journal or periodical comes into the village. Only a few bulletins dealing with farm products or farm practices are ever received and read. The people are not aware of the sources from which they might obtain them and few could read and understand them. The majority are printed in English, a language that only few can read with any appreciable degree of understanding.

The County Agent is a stranger to the local people. It is doubtful if a single villager knows his name. No more than three of the families have ever attempted to us his services. The majority would not know what he has to offer or how to go about getting his cooperation. The general opinion is that he exists only for the bigger farmers and stockmen, that he has neither the time nor the interest to help them with their problems.

The Role of Hired Farm Labor

Only three men in El Cerrito occupy the position of full-time laborer. They are employed by the one big sheepman. Others furnish labor during the busier part of the spring season but usually earn far more money working at other occupations. These farm laborer families live in the village and form an integral part of it. They are in no way discriminated against, in fact they are all in some way related to the man who employs them. All have their small land holdings in the valley and are descendants of early settlers in the village. Two of the full time farm laborers are sons of former sheepherders who worked for the father of their present employer.

It seems fairly certain that most of the early differences that separated the large operator from the laborer have been destroyed. There is no longer the immense difference in worldly possessions that once separated the wealthy don from the lowly peon. The dependence upon the large operators for wages and maintenance has been shifted to other sources, as such operators have gradually lost their once vast holdings. Although still occupying a somewhat different role, both are now struggling for essentially the same thing; to prevent further retreat in the fight for survival. Often there is actually little difference in their real status. Although the former patron may still have his large flocks of sheep, they are being kept on a share basis or mortgaged at their full worth. There is little pretense about the situation. Laborer and operator alike are fully aware of what they have to face.

Transportation and Communication

The people of El Cerrito have limited means for contacts with the outside world. Roads are extremely poor, often impassible during inclement weather. There are no telephones and only two radios that function when the owners can afford batteries to run them. Two antiquated automobiles and two trucks of the same era transport the residents when they need to go into Las Vegas. Once in a great while a family will travel to town in a wagon. This involves almost a full day's travel over the 30 miles and another day to return not only a long and difficult trip but a dangerous one as well. Sixteen of the miles must be driven over a much traveled highway that is hazardous because of passing automobiles on the many curves and turns through the hills.

A satisfactory system has been worked out with the available means of transportation to take the people to town as needs arise. The two important motives for going to town are to make purchases and to inquire about possibilities of employment. Passengers desiring a trip for pleasure or some equally unimportant purpose are given second preference by the owners of the automobiles. A set fee is charged for such transportation. If the owner of the automobile initiates the trip he is paid little more than the cost of gas and oil. If the trip is a special one the set charge is $3.00. There is seldom less than a capacity load of passengers. If the passenger list is not filled with those actually needing to go, others are willing to make up the deficit. It is not uncommon for these passengers to be charged less than the others. None ride free however. All are expected to contribute something.

Government Programs

The functions of all Governmental programs that directly affect the local people are common knowledge in El Cerrito. Despite its physical isolation from the outside world, knowledge of these programs quickly filters in. If a new Government project is initiated that might give work to additional men, the people of El Cerrito know of it almost as quickly as those living in town. This seems surprising when the poor means of communication, the limited transportation facilities, and the limited amount of English spoken and understood are considered. The explanation is puzzling unless the lines of communication between village and town are understood.

Knowledge of a new program comes first to the attention of relatives of villagers living in Las Vegas. These relatives learn of the programs and pass the news on to the people of El Cerrito when they come to town. In this manner the news quickly spreads to all who might benefit.

Knowledge of and interest in programs are limited to those from which the people may benefit. Any program designed for another purpose, or one that operates in a way which they do not approve, is soon forgotten. Such programs are never mentioned or discussed. Interest and discussion are centered solely upon those from which they may expect to gain some material benefit.

The Governmental programs of most common knowledge are the Works Projects Administration, the National Youth Administration, the Civilian Conservation Corps, the Farm Security Administration (Rehabilitation), and the Agricultural Conservation Program. Any adult in El Cerrito would know something of the purpose of such programs, who is eligible, and the procedure of being certified. He would also be able to name any person in the village who is participating in the program and the benefits to the person. The participation of a family in a program is discussed freely and furnishes one of the most frequent topics for everyday conversation.

The benefits of the WPA program are the better known and most sought after of all the Governmental programs. Even the smaller children have a fair acquaintance with this program and are able to give their preference of projects to work on when they grow up. The regular procedure, as well as many unethical means of gaining certification on a project, is common knowledge to all. Knowledge of how best to gain admittance to the investigator is pooled and passed on to the beginner or the family head who is unemployed. The means are important only as they contribute to quick certification to work.

The popularity of this program rests upon two general principles. Probably the most important is that it pays a livable wage. It enables a family to return somewhat to the old pattern of living on a level that requires some cash. The second principle and one only slightly less important, is that it entails no obligation on the part of the laborer. It offers money for labor done with no threat to personal or family possessions. Although such work is sometimes handed out in a condescending way the recipient is doing something to pay for it by exchanging his skill and labor.

Very few of the families would recognize the title of the Farm Security Administration but all are familiar with the term "rehabilitation." They know that the Rehabilitation Division makes loans to qualified farmers, asking a chattel mortgage a security. In fact, all know the local farmers who have borrowed money for seed and equipment on such a basis. Such cases have become well-known examples of what not to do.

These people also know that the Rehabilitation Division will make direct grants to needy families trying to live at home. This last feature is the attractive one. The first is now taboo. Any man in El Cerrito will quickly point out the impracticability of borrowing money on the average local farm business. Those who did borrow on such a basis in 1936 claim to have done so under the impression that such loans were not to be repaid. All recognize the fact that their small holdings are subsistence units only and are convinced that, under any type of practice or management, they could not be so operated as to repay a loan. In the words of one of the men:

"The FSA gave me a loan about 3 years ago. That was a big mistake for me. The agent (county supervisor) didn't explain it to me very well. I thought that the program was to help me but they wrote me later that it was a loan and that I would have to pay it all back or lose my land. Sure gave me a scare. I thought I was lost and so did everyone else. I was getting ready to leave to look for a job to pay it back when the agent came out and told me it wasn't as bad as I thought. Said that I could have several years to pay it back. Don't know how I can do it. I have paid a little of it back but don't know when it will all be paid back. They won't get me to sign any more Rehabilitation papers. I won't sign any more notes."

The NYA and CCC programs are well liked. In certain respects they are regarded as serving the same purpose for the young people as the WPA program does for the adults. The difference lies largely in the educational possibilities such programs offer. One of the most important functions such programs serve, however, is to add to the family income. In many instances the income from these sources alone has enabled the family to live while the father was unemployed. If a family is fortunate enough to have both a girl and a boy in these camps simultaneously, the combined incomes are enough to afford the family a comfortable living. One of the local families was able to buy a small tract of land while the son and daughter were thus employed.

The sole objection to these programs is a general opinion that living in the camps for a year or more is likely to wean the young people away from their home village. They become accustomed to better living conditions and to having a certain amount of cash to spend for their own benefit and pleasure. After a year or two of this they are less satisfied to return to the village, where amusement and recreation is local and where cash to spend is almost impossible to earn. Many of the young people admit this. One of the young men who spent 3 years in a CCC camp said that he would never be satisfied again in El Cerrito. He plans to leave permanently as soon as he has an offer of a job on the outside.

These programs are very popular with the young people who are not yet old enough to apply. Brothers and sisters of those who are away in these camps readily state their desire to go as soon as they reach the proper age. They have heard of experiences in the camps and now are anxious to see and live through them. Another road has been opened to them. They may now expect to go to camp and then to a WPA project.

All the farmers that are eligible have participated in the ACP program. The two biggest farmers have built water reservoirs on their land and a few of the others have built smaller tanks or have been reimbursed for construction of rip-rap along the river to prevent further washing away of the land touching its banks. This is another program that meets with local approval. It entails no obligation and offers a little remuneration to the men for doing what they realize should be done anyway. The smaller farmers feel that they have been discriminated against somewhat by this program but all have hope that next year, or the next, it may be altered so that it will reach them.

Questions about any Government program, other than those mentioned, bring a quick denial of any knowledge concerning it. Unless these programs in some way actually touch these people themselves, they have no interest whatsoever in them. Their concern deals solely with everyday life and what directly affects it.

Attitudes and Value-Systems Related to Land Use,
Commercialization, Self-Sufficiency, and Governmental Programs.

Individual ownership of land has come to mean much more to the native of New Mexico than it did to his forefathers. Beneficiaries of early grants seldom attempted to get personal ownership or control over any large part of the land. They were satisfied with the right to use it.

This underemphasis on the importance of landownership undoubtedly played an important part in the rate at which the grant land of New Mexico has been lost. Sections of the grant land have been sold without the vendors realizing that use of the land was sold also. Huge tracts of surrounding public land have been transferred to private ownership with little realization on the part of the natives of what was happening until their livestock had been crowded back on remaining inadequate land.

The results of the rapid loss of this land have been to instill a grim determination on the part of the people to cling desperately to what still remains of the better land. Few would sell their irrigated holdings at anything like a reasonable price. All realize that any further decrease in their holdings would impel readjustment to an entirely new way of life.

Until recently, the term conservation has had little meaning for these people. Ample land or abundant work on the outside have always been available. Curtailment in both of these is bringing about a desire for and appreciation of better and more efficient use of the land that still remains in their possession. More of the land is being brought under cultivation. Some of the men are considering terracing to prevent further erosion. They realize definitely the need for scientific advice in combating insects and crop disease, and are anxious for advice and suggestions for improving crops and methods of cultivation. All are welcoming the efforts of the new agricultural agencies to improve and safeguard their land from which such a large proportion of their living comes.

Among all groups in El Cerrito there is marked regret that changes have been wrought in the old way of life, and an almost unanimous agreement that people were better satisfied and life more complete under the old conditions. Men who left the village during the 1920's for the high wages being paid for labor feel that they should have remained at home and made an effort to gain control of some of the outside land that sold for less than a dollar per acre. All feel that the families which homesteaded tracts on the surrounding mesa were the most fortunate and that if all the men in the village had done this they would not now have the problems that large stockmen and commercialized farming have brought them.

But surprisingly little resentment toward these new forces is found. The general opinion of the people is that the fault lies with themselves. There is little talk or thought of getting their former possessions back. Nevertheless, the more farsighted among them are looking toward a solution that will begin with their present economic foundation and will, by some means, add enough to it to allow them to live at a level that will provide the essentials of food, clothing, and shelter for their families.

The statement is heard frequently in this part of the southwest that "the native people are perfectly satisfied with a WPA job. They are making more money than they have ever made in their lives." Such a statement is far from fact in El Cerrito. The people of El Cerrito are fully cognizant of what the WPA program is doing. They understand its good features and its bad ones. It is true that the monthly wage on a WPA project is greater than that which can be earned herding sheep. However, wages earned in a sheep camp are clear profit. A sheepherder is furnished his meals and lodging. There is no house rent to pay as in town, no coal to buy, and no transportation charges to and from work. His family lives at home where a garden and a small crop may be planted to supplement his wages. This is seldom possible if the wage earner is employed on a WPA project where he is almost forced to live in town.

If wages are computed on an annual basis the results show that the WPA laborer earns less, as a rule, than he formerly did on the outside. When work on the outside was plentiful and wages fairly good a man would probably earn considerably more working for farmers or for private industry. Providing a man had one or two sons to help him it was nothing unusual to earn 5 or 6 hundred dollars a year doing farm work. On the WPA he seldom earns more than 3 hundred. Frequent lay-offs and a maximum wage of approximately $45 a month may aggregate even less. One of the men states his own case as follows:

"The new government agencies aren't meeting the problems here very well. About all a fellow can do here is apply for a WPA job. These jobs just let you live. I have been working for the WPA, off and on, for a long time. During that time I have been able to work about 3 months at a time and then I would be turned off for a while. Lots of times I have been without money. I don't spend any money for pleasure, either. All of my money has gone for clothes for my family and something to eat. I have tried to save a little money on what I earn but I can't do it. We have tried to reduce our food bill but with our large family we can't do that. Our food isn't any too good, either, mostly beans, and sometimes just beans. I don't know how it is all going to come out. Do you think times will ever be any better? Sometimes I think they never will. It has been like this for a long time now. And what about the Government relief? I guess it might stop sometime."

Still, one hears the credulous argue that these people will come for miles if there is any possibility of their being certified for work. Such a statement gives no consideration to the fact that little other opportunity exists for them to sell their services. It is not a matter of choice, for there is no alternative. Those who are criticized for unwillingness to take private employment, once they are working on a project, are censured without consideration of what such an exchange would imply. Their hesitation to accept seasonal work from private sources comes only from the fear of delay in being reemployed on the WPA project. In a hand-to-mouth type of existence few feel justified in taking the risk. Experience has taught them the advantage of remaining eligible for this type of relief.

There is general appreciation of what the Agricultural Conservation Program and the Department of Public Welfare are doing. Any improvement of the land or any technique for conserving it is considered important. It is realized that such programs contribute to present and future welfare. Most of the people would favor their continuance on a much broader scope. Aid to old people, to those otherwise incapacitated, and to dependents are duly appreciated. The villagers realize that such aids are alleviating the problems of a group in which the well and able bodied are struggling desperately to survive. This has been a peculiar problem to the native people who have always felt a keen responsibility to care for aged and dependent relatives.

Although these people are accepting Governmental aid and subsidy with a sense of stoic fatalism, they universally recognize the fact that little is being done toward permanent stabilization. In case the present subsidy should suddenly cease they would be in no better position to live than when such aid began to come in. Their greatest comfort seems to lie in the hope that present aid will continue. They are determined to do all in their power to see that this is done, which means, essentially, to keep in power those who are in favor of maintaining the status quo.

What the people would actually prefer is a return to their old status of self-sufficiency and independence. How this might be done none seem to know or to be able to offer an opinion, except those who timorously suggest that the Government buy outlying sections of land. Even the boldest suggest no more than that the land be made available to them, with ownership remaining in the hands of the Government.

In this way one of the villagers gives voice to the general dissatisfaction with remaining dependent upon the generosity of the Governmental agencies. "The trouble here is lack of resources. If we could only get some of our land back. I have heard people say that the only thing to do is to leave us on the land and send us a certain amount of money each month. I wouldn't like that. I don't want things given to me. That ruins a man when things are given to him." Many claim that all initiative of the people is being destroyed. There is a feeling that the young people are particularly affected. One of the older residents of El Cerrito remarked that; "The young people here do not have the drive they once had. The young men used to look forward to having a fairly good home and a flock of sheep, gotten by their own efforts and initiative. This does not seem to be true any more. Instead he looks forward to a WPA job in town where he can depend upon the Government and the county politicians to support him."

It is relatively seldom, however, that a native voices open criticism of the functioning of a Government agency. There is a general feeling that humble acceptance and expressed appreciation is expected of any recipient. Any criticism of a program was usually given with the expressed desire that it should not reach the ears of persons administering the programs. The people have become too dependent upon such agencies as the WPA to afford the risk of being removed. This attitude has likely been responsible for the general belief that the native is perfectly satisfied if in some way, he is aided by relief or subsidy. Actually it is accepted as the sole means for surviving, the only source of obtaining today's, and possibly tomorrow's, bread.

THE COMMUNITY

Spatial Distribution

There is little feeling of interdependence between El Cerrito and its neighboring villages. Villanueva, 16 miles distant by automobile or 3 miles up river on foot, is almost the sole village ever visited and this is largely because of the services it has to offer. The Post Office is there and the people must go for their mail. Limited trading is done there also but far less than is done in Las Vegas. There is mutual attendance at dances which is a comparatively rare thing in this vicinity. Kinship ties have been a strong factor in bringing the two villages into closer harmony.

But the present tendency is not entirely one of moving toward greater harmony. Other and equally strong forces apparently are pulling in the opposite direction. The inhibitions to greater coordination are rooted in a feeling of envy and jealousy toward the larger and more prosperous Villanueva. In turn the people of Villanueva regard those of El Cerrito as rustic and backward. These attitudes have obviously done much in the last few years to bring about a greater unity among the El Cerrito people than ever before existed. This attitude toward the Villanueva people is a general one and is definitely passed on to the offspring. Children are seldom permitted to go to the larger village and then only after special warning.

The remark is often heard that the people of Villanueva are unfriendly and quarrelsome. "They are always fighting among themselves for no other reason than that they like that sort of thing. All their dances have to be patrolled by the local peace officers. This never happens in El Cerrito. There hasn't been a fight here since I can remember." Statements such as these are heard often and clearly indicate how distinctly the local villages are separated.

There is more cooperation in politics between the villages than in any other form of organized effort. The recently formed political clubs of young people in one party have done much to bring this about. During the last few years these clubs have gone so far as to have joint meetings. Candidates for county and State offices are often decided upon and given the joint support of the two villages. But perfect unison is far short of achievement in these clubs. The club in El Cerrito is still fearful that the larger representation from Villanueva will dominate it and thus injure its political strength.

Patterns of Informal Association

The physical structure of this community greatly facilitates cooperation and mutual aid. All houses in the village are within a stone's throw of one another

Fig. 12

LOCATION OF HOUSES AND BUILDINGS, EL CERRITO, NEW MEXICO, 1940

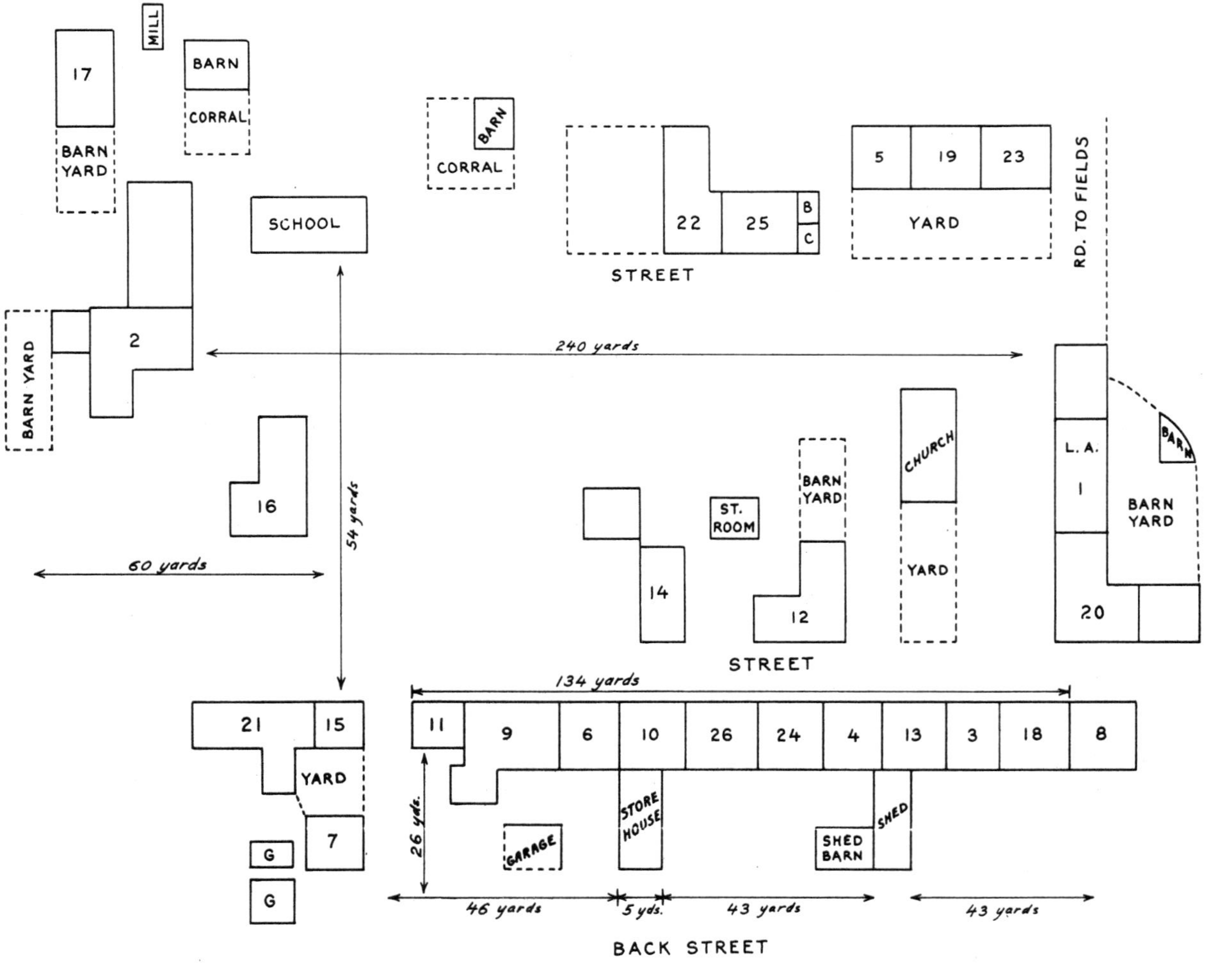

U. S. DEPARTMENT OF AGRICULTURE

NEG. 38805 BUREAU OF AGRICULTURAL ECONOMICS

(fig. 12). Through years of interdependence, the people are conditioned to call upon neighbors and relatives for many types of assistance and, in turn, are expected to reciprocate when the need arises. Any task that requires greater strength or physical effort than a single family has at hand is solved by calling in a neighbor. Such service is freely asked for and given. In case of sickness or similar misfortune the efforts and resources of the entire village may be utilized in order to bring the family through the crisis.

Informal visiting far exceeds any other mode of contact between the villagers. The latchstring is "always on the outside" for any neighbor or relative who may have the time and inclination to call. In a single afternoon 14 different visitors were counted coming to one household, some of them returning as many as three and four times. This was not a peculiar case. Other homes in the village probably had as many. Such visits are expected. If a housewife fails to make a call in the afternoon it is taken for granted that she is ill or has company.

Although visiting is general in El Cerrito, the degree of blood relationship is the chief factor affecting their frequency. The house of the parents of several married sons and daughters is the nucleus for the different visiting groups. The wives and children of such families may come to the central house a dozen or more times in a day. They come to distribute a piece of news or to borrow a little something for the next meal. The children are continuously running into and out of each others' houses. They are together so much that it is difficult to learn to which house they belong.

It is not difficult to understand what these informal visits mean to a woman in these villages. Tied to a drab routine of household duties and child care she is allowed few means of self expression. Social censure prevents any activity outside the village or even in the organized social life within the village with the exception of attendance at church. Even conversation with the opposite sex, other than members of her immediate family, is denied her. Thus visiting among her own sex and status offers the most important means of expression open to her.

Although the visiting of the women far exceeds that of the men, each day affords them also a number of opportunities for conversation. After a day in the field is over they are likely to meet for a short time around the house or in going to and from the corrals. Also for the men there are other outlets, such as the field work, the local meetings, and the trips to town.

All the visiting done within the village is informal. It would be unusual for a visitor to announce his coming or even for the entire family to visit at one time. Only the most general invitations are given. A person is expected to feel welcome whenever he has the desire and the time to come.

In an attempt to describe this visiting a number of charts have been made. Figure 13 is a map of the village with circles indicating approximately the location of the houses and the visiting which goes on between the families. In this chart only the visiting of one parent and at least one other member of his or her family is indicated. This restriction was made to make possible a study of family visiting, thus eliminating the continuous flow of individuals, particularly children, who almost constantly pass in and out of the house.

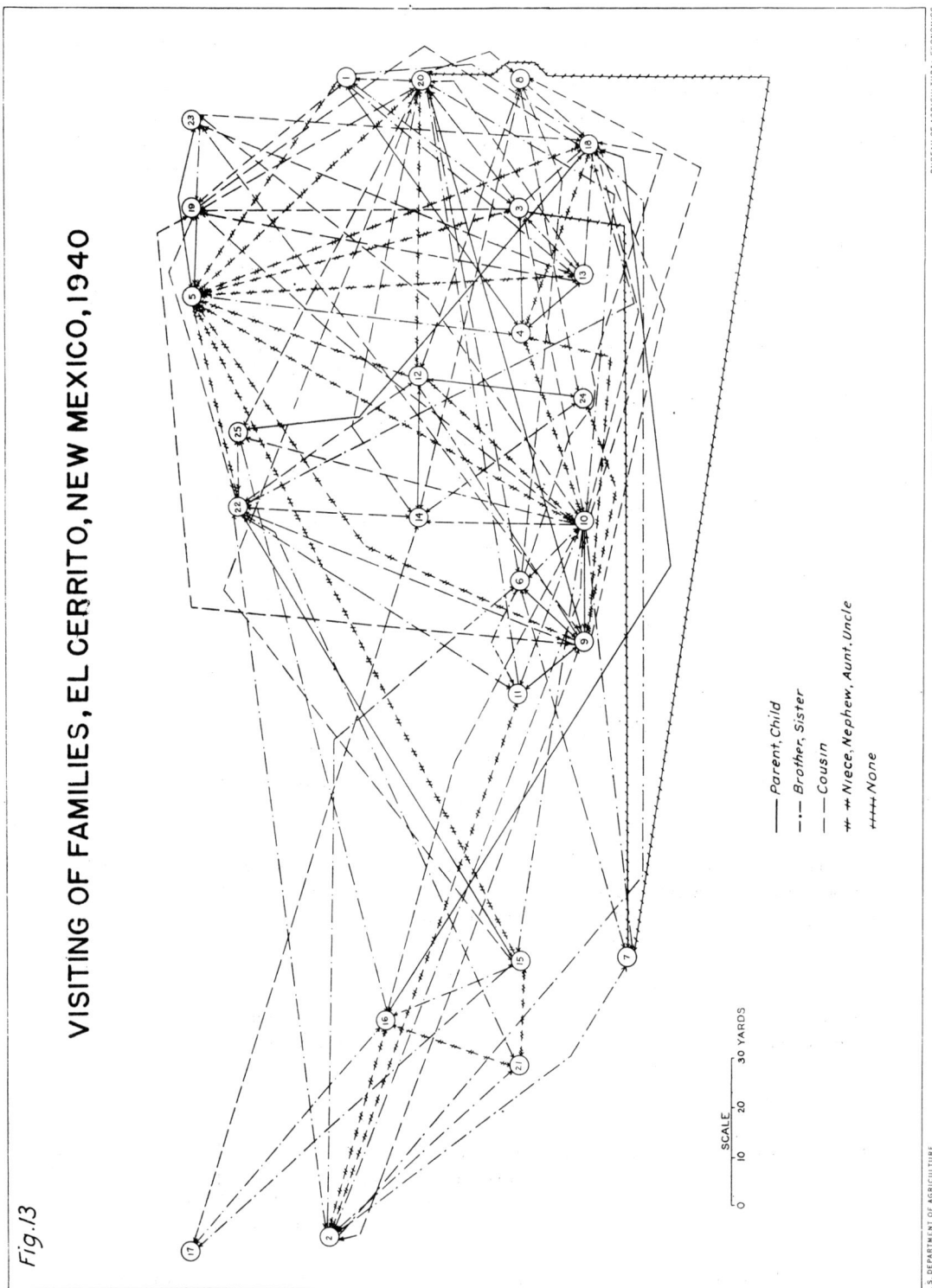

Fig. 13

An observer would be impressed by the fact that only 2 of the 108 lines between the circles representing the families do not designate some degree of consanguinity. This is not surprising when one realizes that practically everyone in the village is related to someone else, and that almost all degrees of consanguinity are represented. The closest degree, that of parent-child, occurs less frequently than the others simply because there are fewer parents than there are persons who can claim other degrees of consanguinity. Thirteen percent of the lines indicate visiting between parents and their children; 31 percent between brothers and sisters; 36 between cousins; 18 percent between nieces and nephews and their aunts or uncles. From this figure the conclusion might be reached that the degree of consanguinity was not important and that visiting was carried on more frequently between cousins than between parents and children. This would be a false impression made because the frequency of the visits is not represented in this figure.

In the remaining figures the families are represented by circles placed on the map with more regard to frequency of visitation and to degree of consanguinity than to original geographical location. Geographical location is completely disregarded in figures 14 through 18. Also, the degree of consanguinity is indicated by a symbol inserted in the middle of the line describing the frequency of the relationship. Figure 14 differs in construction from figure 13 in that figure 14 stresses the frequency of visitation, whereas figure 13 stresses only the degree of consanguinity and indicates by arrows the direction of the visiting, that is, whether or not visiting is mutual.

In figure 14 the important bonds in the village stand out. It is apparent that frequent visiting on a family basis is carried on chiefly between parents and children or brothers and sisters. Other relatives visit a great deal but the frequency is directly proportional to the degree of consanguinity. The figure also shows how the families respond to misfortune. The husband in the family represented by circle 18 is a blind man, 64 years of age. Few people in the village are visited by as many other families as is he, even though he is unable to return visits except to the families of his own three children. This is why so many dotted lines which indicate lack of reciprocation extend away from circle 18. As elsewhere, the personal element enters into the urge to visit. The head of the household designated by circle 5 is the oldest man in the village and also one of the most jovial. Many visit him because they enjoy his company and wit. All marvel at the vivacity of this dapper old man of 85 years.

The world over the taking of meals at the table of another s family signifies familiarity. This is true in El Cerrito. Those families which in the course of their visits, as represented in figure 15, stayed for meals at the visited family's home were in most cases closely related. Most meals were taken when visiting relationships were between parents and children or brothers and sisters. In fact, the families who took more than five meals together during the year and were of more distant kinship than father and child or brother and sister were negligible. Sharing food frequently at the same table during visits is an act which signifies close blood ties in El Cerrito and the frequency of the act is positively correlated with the degree of consanguinity.

The coming and going of children of one family across the hearth of another is also almost a universal indication of close family ties, although it may be less so than the taking of meals during friendly visits. In large cities children may visit one another in homes where their respective parents have never been. In El Cerrito as

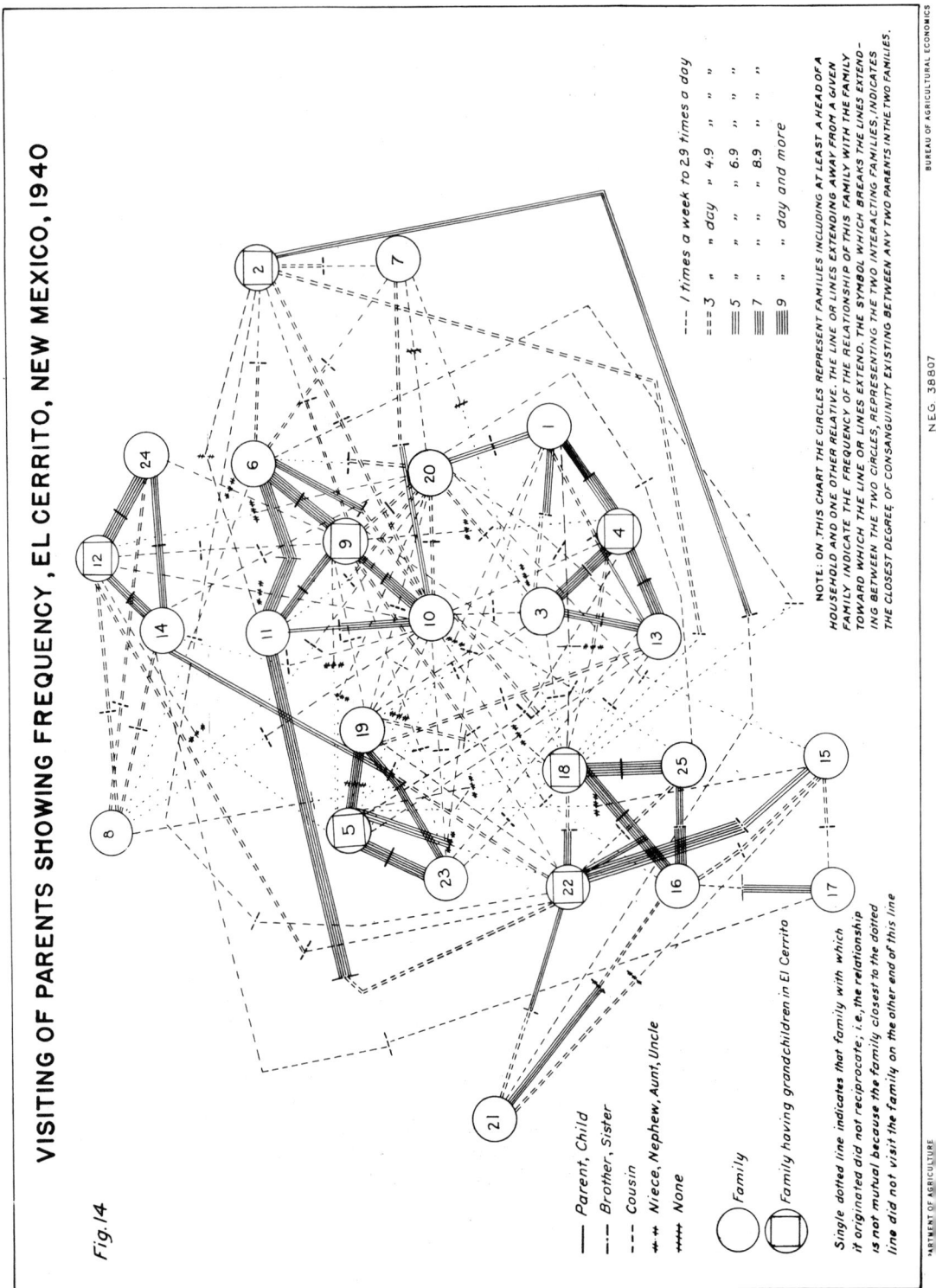

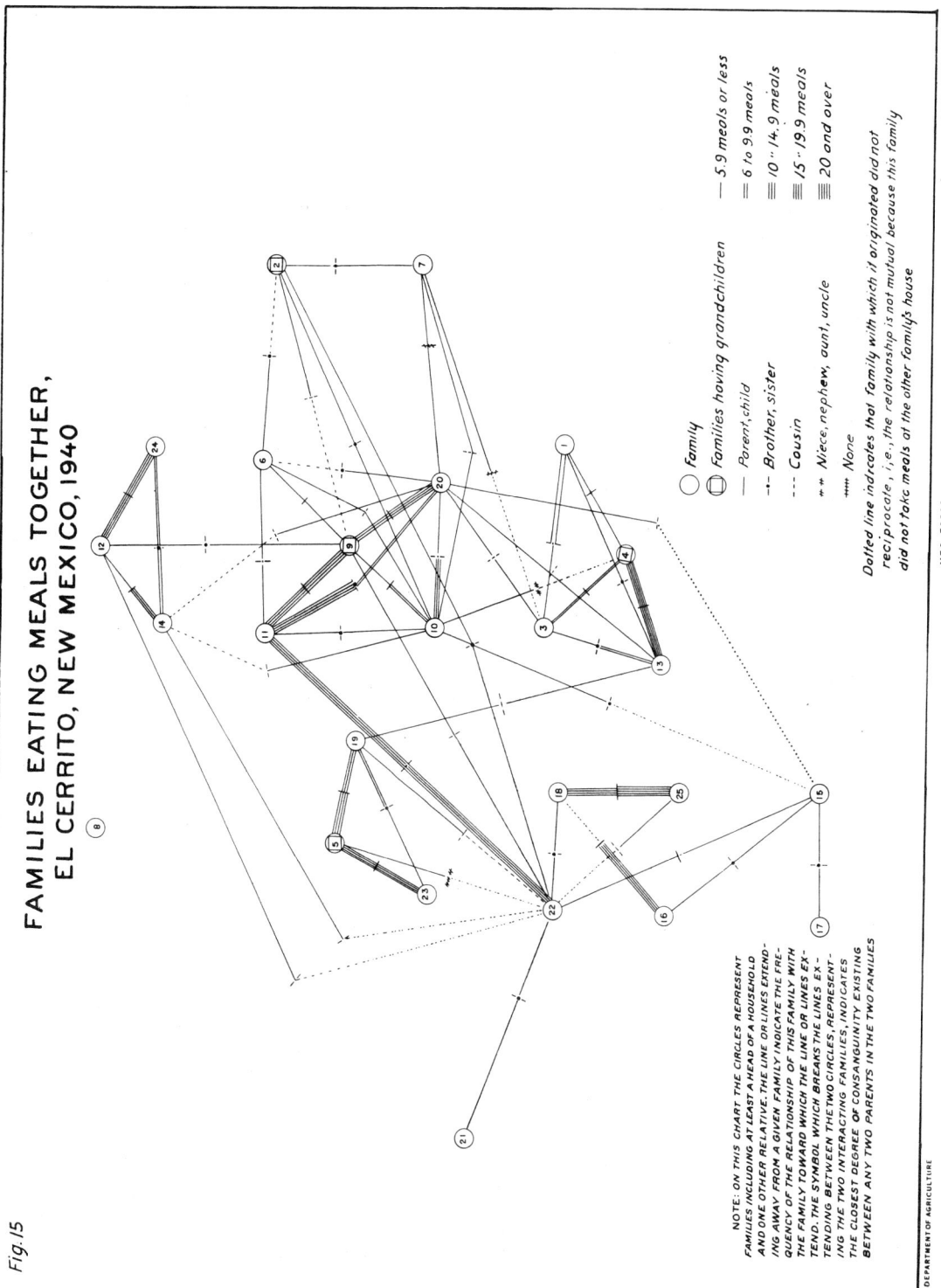

shown by figure 16 the frequency with which children and other separate individuals visit is directly proportional to the closeness of kinship. A study of the chart will show the great frequency of visits of children and separate individuals in the homes of the grandparents of children. Several of the grandparents have grandchildren the sons and daughters of unfortunate parents living with them These grandchildren may return the visits of other grandchildren from other families. Some families are shown as almost isolated on figure 16. They are young childless families such as numbers 11 and 25. If the high frequencies of visitation of children as shown in figure 16 seem surprising one should live with one of the families and attempt to learn which children belong to this family Without asking or remaining for some time, it would be a real task. Nothing could be more informal than the visiting of the children but the frequency of the visitations are for the most part governed by kinship. However geographical distance also plays a part. The children of cousins who live next door other things being equal will probably visit more frequently than the cousins whose families live 200 yards apart.

Little visiting is done outside the village. This is especially true of the women. who seldom see a woman from the outside. The majority do not leave their own village more than once or twice a year.

Visits outside the village are usually to the homes of relatives in Las Vegas. Such a trip to town serves three purposes a chance to remain in town for a few days, a chance to make periodic purchases and a visit with friends and relatives. This visit to Las Vegas may last for as much as a week. That these visits are seldom repaid does not matter. Such hospitality is accepted by both parties as a responsibility the town people owe to their country relatives.

Isolation from the city markets and stores has made it necessary for these families to resort to considerable borrowing and lending. This applies particularly to items of food In case a family should use its supply of flour or lard before a ride to town can be arranged for it is obliged to borrow These loans are strictly if informally kept account of. Such courtesies could not be lightly regarded. They are repaid promptly after the first trip to town

Borrowing and lending among the villagers is not limited to items of food. Farming tools and equipment are loaned freely. Brothers may buy tools together or they may buy different tools for the purpose of exchange. It is not uncommon for several distinct families to own jointly or severally only a single set of farm tools.

Figure 17 describes the frequency of the loaning of farm implements. Kinship ties stand out Harvests are usually family affairs the division of which is quite informal. For instance in the case of families 3 4 and 13 the father owns practically all the equipment All work is done in common There is a common wood pile common barns and common storage of crops and food. The son in law who owns most of his own equipment (family 1) and family 10 deal with this larger family chiefly through the head (number 4) However family 19 deals directly with one of the sons (number 13) who owns some equipment in his own right. Other larger groups are more complicated. There is both common and pooled property. In the larger family, including the smaller families 9 6 20 10 and 11 the smaller families own so much equipment individually that no larger ring is drawn about them. There is much borrowing individually from the brothers even though the mother No. 9, owns most of the land and

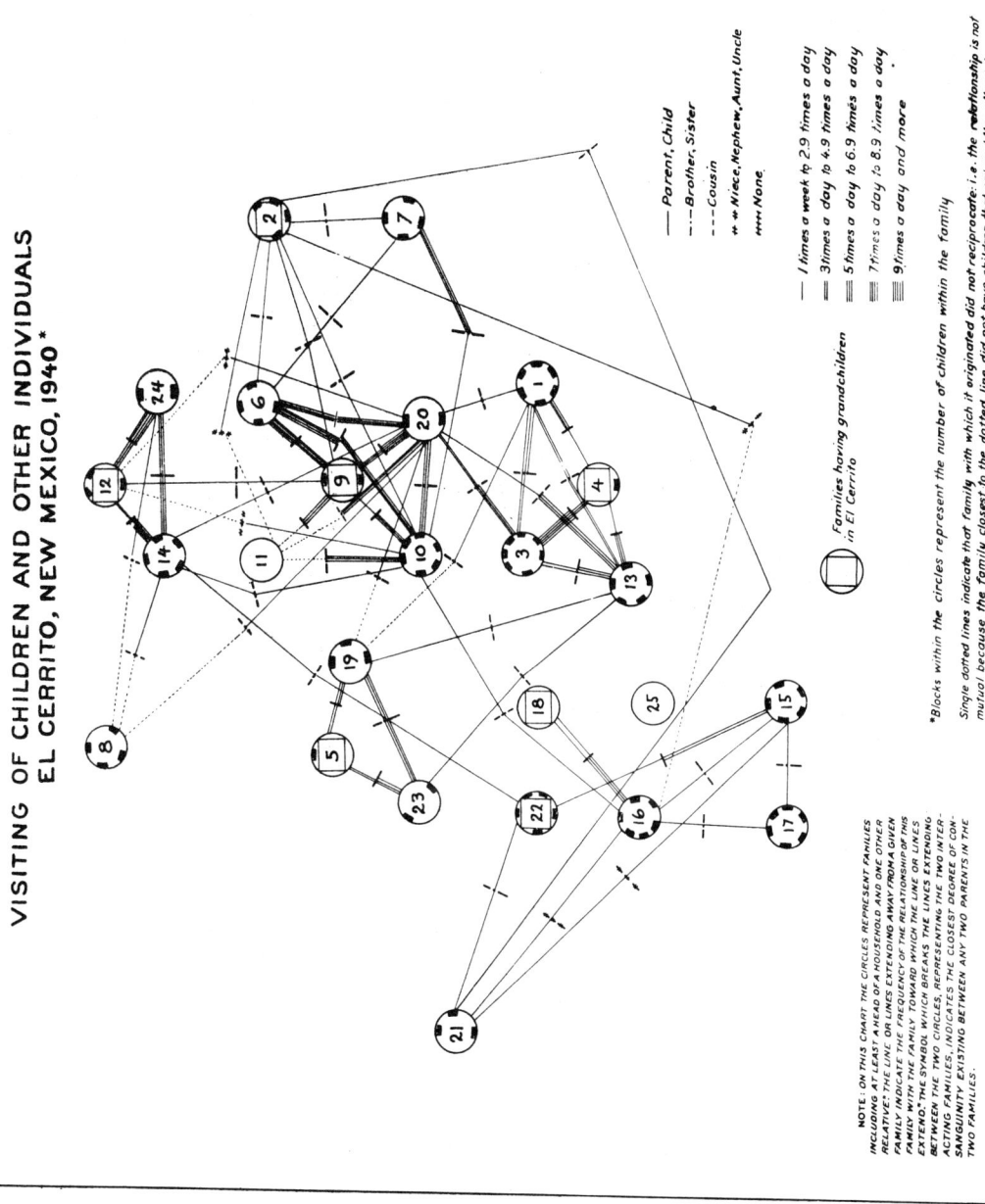

resources. Groups A, C, and D function in a more communal manner, although in each of these groups there is considerable ownership of and exchanging of implements by separate families.

Figure 18 describes the frequency of exchanging farm work, which also follows family lines. Some families do not participate because of the great age of the head, as is the case of Nos. 4 and 5, or because of infirmity as in the case of the blind man represented by circle 18, or because the male head is dead, as in the cases of circles 9 and 16

All of these heads are functional units in larger units which are outlined in the larger circles A, B, C, D, and E. They either direct operations or own most of the equipment with which the work is done. These large circles omit some families who function as parts of the larger families in other respects. For instance, the son-in-law (circle 1) of the head (circle 3) of the larger group (B) deals individually with his brothers-in-law 3 and 13 who do most of their work in common. The families in large circle D are practically mutually exclusive so far as exchanging work with outsiders is concerned, but the brothers 23 and 19 do not do all of their work in common.

Circle E is a much more complicated mixture of common and mutual labor. No. 20 is the school teacher, and No. 6, the son-in-law of the female head (No. 9) exchanges work independently with two brothers-in-law (Nos. 10 and 11) and his own two brothers (Nos. 2 and 7). But even with these variations the importance of kinship in these cooperative activities is manifold. This is true even though the village has also the lone-wolf type of family such as No. 8.

Figures 14 through 18 bear witness to the importance of familism in El Cerrito. The importance of these informal kinship groupings cannot be overestimated in any program designed to assist these people whether it is in their present village or elsewhere. As is emphasized later in this report the mundane leadership of the village is in the hands of the older men, the heads of the larger families. It is to them that those who wish to initiate new programs involving the village should go.

Resettlement of people from these villages where the land resources are too meager has been proposed. One family in El Cerrito is attempting to resettle itself, with great misgiving. It owns a ranch some 30 miles from the village, and the families of four sons are working and saving to restock the ranch so that the whole family can move.

For Governmental resettlement or rehabilitation schemes the fact must be borne in mind that it is the larger family of grandparents, children, and grandchildren with which the schemes should deal. This is clearly demonstrated by the preceding charts. To remove a single smaller family would frequently create hardships and in addition would increase expenditure for frequent visits back to the village. Smaller families than those which include the grandparents and the families of the sons should seldom be considered for resettlement in a new location. If the daughters' families, uncles, aunts, nephews, and nieces, and in some cases, cousins could be part of the group to be removed so much the better. In many cases the parental family would not even consider leaving the family of the daughter. Small familial rehabilitation cooperatives composed of several related families have been successful in their effort to rehabilitate in peace. Thus it is important that action agencies know the importance of familism in this culture.

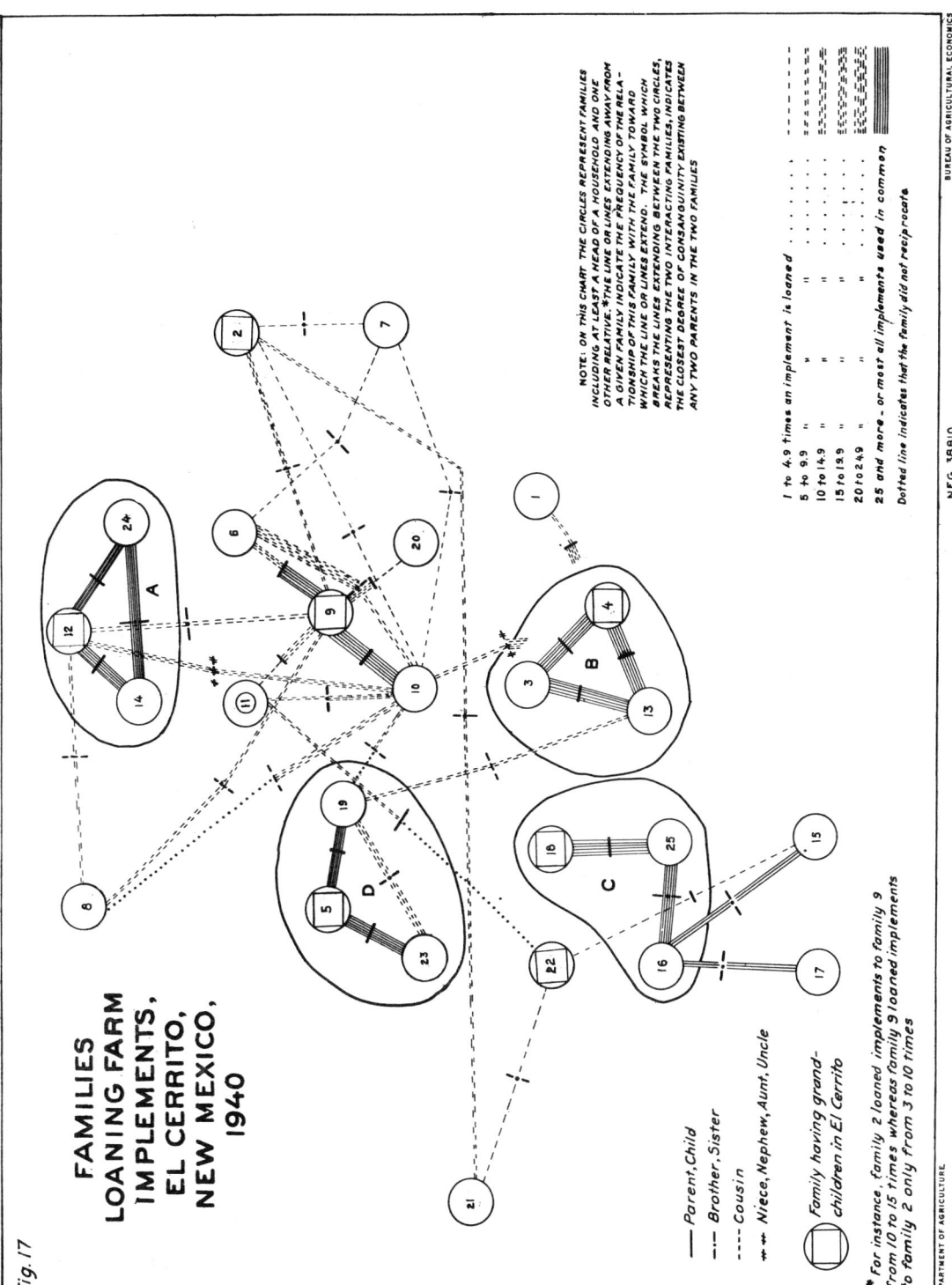

Fig. 17 — FAMILIES LOANING FARM IMPLEMENTS, EL CERRITO, NEW MEXICO, 1940

Fig. 18 — FAMILIES EXCHANGING WORK, EL CERRITO, NEW MEXICO, 1940

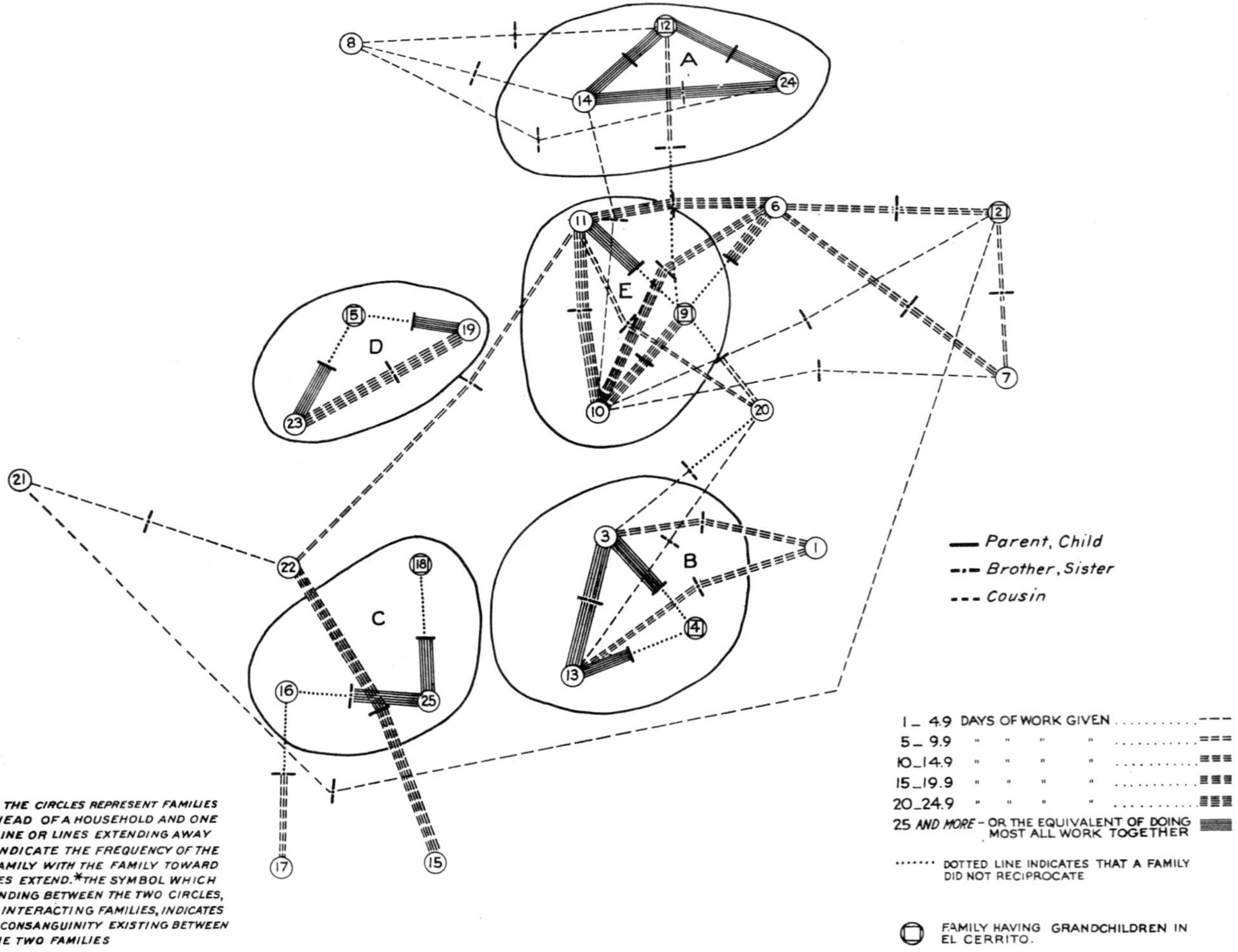

Recreation

Recreation in El Cerrito is limited to those forms that may be participated in for little or no cash. Money is neither available nor thought necessary for recreation or amusement. Activities that predominantly serve the purpose of recreation are local, devised by the residents of the village and for them. Most of them are old, both in type and the way in which they are conducted. The most common types are dances, going to town, attending political rallies, and fishing, listed somewhat in the order of their importance to the people.

The most popular form of group recreation is dancing. Each Saturday night a community dance is held in the local two-room school building. If a special event occurs such as a wedding, one or more may be held during the same week. They are held most often during the winter season when the people are least busy and a good attendance is most assured.

The standard cost of such dances is 25 cents. This money goes to the local Justice of the Peace for issuing the permit. The school building is given free of charge and the music, for the most part, is furnished by local talent. The usual instruments are a violin, guitar, and perhaps an accordion. The musicians play with evident enjoyment, as long as the dancers feel like continuing, which is often well into the morning hours.

Old and young alike attend. All the young people dance while the older ones sit back and keep time to the music with their feet. Although the music is usually fast and rest periods infrequent, each new tune brings the couples back for more.

The dance tunes are old Spanish folk music interspersed at infrequent intervals with selections of modern jazz. All prefer the old tunes. The dance steps are old Spanish such as the raspa, the polka, and the cuadrillo. The younger people are learning some of the more modern steps but still prefer the older ones. The older people do not attempt to dance, other than the Spanish steps and to Spanish music.

These Saturday night dances afford the young boys and girls their only opportunity of talking together. For this reason most of the dances are sponsored by some young man outside the village who has a girl friend in the village. It is the only sanctioned opportunity he has of speaking to her.

The boys are never allowed to take their girl friends to these dances. Instead the girls must come with a parent or an older married brother or sister. Even should the parents allow it, a young girl would not dare face the social censure of coming alone She dares not even sit with a boy at the dance. All girls are expected to occupy one side of the hall and the boys another during the time they are not actually dancing.

For the older members of the group these dances serve still another purpose. They serve as a medium for airing any political view or conducting any business that concerns the group. It is generally recognized and never questioned that such a person has a right to stop the dance when he wishes and talk as long as he likes. If the wine is adequate and the audience at all appreciative he may stop the dance several times during the course of the evening for such speeches.

Going to town is one of the most popular forms of recreation. Next to the dances on Saturday night the men enjoy going to town on Saturday afternoon. Often they have no business motive, only to see and talk with friends in town. Even though business may take them to town there is no hurry to return home once it is done Going to town is a full day's affair.

Participation in political movements or rallies is another popular recreational activity. Any candidate for political office in this county is expected to be liberal in entertaining his constituents. Any candidate who refuses to sponsor a few free dances and to treat his followers to a beer or glass of wine has little hope of winning. These generous affairs are extremely popular and residents of the most isolated villages are sure to come in for their share. Even though the campaign is conducted for an office that does not directly affect the rural people this is no inhibition to their taking part. The candidate appreciates this for he knows that such people have many relatives whose support he may be able to get through his generosity to their rural friends or kinsmen.

Aside from a little fishing done by a few of the villagers, these are the principal types of recreation. There is neither the means nor the opportunity for participation in movies, sports, and other forms of recreation that cost money apparently little regret on the part of the people that such fields are not open to them Those who are heard to express desires for these things are the young people who have been away in the CCC or NYA camps.

Artificial means for recreation are as lacking for the children as for adults. The school has never been able to provide for such common playground equipment as swings, slides or even a ball. All games are spontaneous or invented through the childrens imaginations. These games are not supervised. The child is free to play at any game or with any group he chooses or, if he prefers, does not play at all.

Patterns of Formal Association

The family is the basic channel through which all organized activities must flow. The success of any organized activity depends largely upon the degree to which it fits into the pattern of the family group. The strength of the church in this area can be explained partly by the degree to which it has recognized the solidarity of the family group and has effectively used this solidarity to crystallize and perpetuate its own tradition. The family is able to practice what the church teaches. Each supports and strengthens the position of the other.

A child's status in the family is taught at a very early age. Children soon know their functions as individuals, their relations to other family members and their duties and responsibilities to the group. At three a child knows that it is his duty to obey older brothers and sisters. Children are especially conscious that age is always to be respected and must occupy the seat of honor at every occasion

The individual is still an integral part of the family group after childhood days are over and he is out from under the parental roof. The difference in his position is that he is now married and has thus taken on a new set of responsibilities He is still expected to give material aid to aged parents or to any dependent brother sister, or their children. He is expected to attend and possibly help support numerous family functions. In case of a family reunion, first communion, marriage, or death, his presence is assured unless distance or personal misfortune is great enough to justify his staying away.

When a child takes first communion all near relatives are expected to attend The father who may be working away from home, will travel a long distance to be present Brothers and sisters of the child's parents may incur a relatively large expense to come. The number of relatives present at such an occasion is recognized as a good index of the family s prestige in the area. To one first communion observed in El Cerrito, relatives came from as far away as Trinidad, Colo. A father of one of the boys taking first communion said that it was his first trip to the village in more than a year. The Communion Service has been worked out with local modifications. One of the unusual features is the march around the church building after the service is over In this march the parents of the children are given the places of honor next to the children, and immediately behind the priest. After the service, which takes place in the morning, visiting relatives sit down to well-prepared dinners.

Marriage is another function which brings the family members together. This is an occasion for fun and merrymaking, and everyone has a good time. Food, drink, and music is furnished by the bridegroom, who has likely been saving his money for the event for the last year or more. The bride's family, too, may spend years accumulating enough money to pay for things that are thought necessary for the wedding, including dresses, large and expensive portraits of the bridal party, and church expenditures. Both bride and groom endeavor to bring as many relatives as possible to the wedding. It is considered quite an honor to have a good representation of relatives at such an affair.

A death in the immediate family will occasion a greater expenditure of money and effort to be present than any other event. Following a death a wake is held for one or more nights to enable all friends and relatives of the deceased to pay their last respects. Any near relatives feel an acute sense of duty to be present to welcome the visitors. In this way they are doing the deceased a last honor It also is interpreted as an expression of sorrow at the passing. The whole village mourns for several weeks, but it is the grandparents, parents brothers sisters, aunts, uncles, nieces and nephews who mourn for the remainder of the year. During this time no music should be played, no dances, or theaters attended.

The School

The school building in El Cerrito is an antiquated, two-room adobe structure that was evidently built with little more than a certain amount of space in mind. The furnishings and equipment are in keeping with the building. The lighting arrangement is very poor and the heating system consists of two wood stoves that burn intermittently

This crude building houses from 20 to 50 pupils in addition to the two teachers Instruction is given in grades one to eight inclusive The school is conducted with little supervision from the county system. Roads are too bad and the distance too great for a supervisor to visit except on very rare occasions. It is much more convenient to visit the larger and better equipped schools near the highway or on more passable roads.

The functions of the El Cerrito school involve no other persons than the teachers and the enrolled children. Parents are neither consulted nor are they willing to offer anything in the way of criticism or support. On two occasions during the year they attend a school function. One is at the end of the school term and the other at Christmas time. On each of these occasions the children produce a short play. El Cerrito has never had a Parent Teachers Association or any other organization purporting to bring about closer harmony between parents and school. The Principal of the school has never attempted to organize any activity that would improve his working relationships in the community. In fact, his training and background would be far from suitable for such an endeavor. He was born in El Cerrito and attended the local grade school. Four years of high school and a summer term of college in Las Vegas completed his training.

Despite its condition the people regard this school as one of the most important institutions of the community. It is felt to be serving the purpose of orientating children to the outside world and to some extent to be bridging the gap that separates the two. Although few parents expect their children to complete more than eight grades of school, this minimum is considered essential. Any less would not give the pupil the necessary working knowledge of English.

Few opinions are expressed as to how or what the schools should teach. Other than English and arithmetic there is little consideration as to what the children are learning. It is keenly felt, however, that the primary function of the schools is to teach English. It is realized that if the native is to compete with the ever increasing number of Anglos, a first essential is to speak good English. This necessity is given great emphasis by the older people, who tell many stories of business deals with the Anglo in which their interests suffered because of an inability to speak English. So, if the schools do a satisfactory job of teaching arithmetic and English the people are satisfied. The remainder of what a child should know can be taught by the church and in the home.

Attendance at school is poor. The girls report a much more regular attendance than the boys, especially in the higher grades. After a boy has reached the age of 12 or 13 he is expected to aid in supporting the family and is often kept out of school to help the father or to hire out to anyone needing his services. For this reason few of the boys complete the eighth grade unless they do so at a very early age. It is not uncommon to see a boy 16 or 17 years old still in the fourth or fifth grade.

Despite the desire of the parents to have their children learn English well it is seldom that a local boy or girl attains any degree of proficiency in it. The girls usually speak it much better than the boys because of their longer and more regular attendance at school.

Poorly trained teaching personnel in these isolated rural schools is another basic reason for the children's meager education. Usually natives themselves the teachers are inadequately prepared and are often unable to speak English correctly. Although a State law requires that nothing but English be spoken in the schools this regulation is not adhered to. Knowledge on the part of the children that the teacher understands Spanish tempts them to speak it. In case they cannot make themselves understood in English they are likely to use their native tongue.

FIG. 19. *English is spoken only in the school, El Cerrito, New Mexico, 1940.*

In addition, teaching techniques and materials are not adapted to the peculiar problems met in the local school situation. The sole means for imparting knowledge is the group of standard textbooks. Any other equipment is devised by the teachers and fashioned out of cans, boxes, and other crude materials at hand. No consideration is given to the fact that the pupils are learning a new language in addition to stock material which they are expected to master. Such subject matter as geography, history, and health is taught in terms that are foreign to them. During the school year 1939-40, the pupils of El Cerrito worked out posters and other projects based on such subjects as transportation in Boston and the importance of navigation in the growth of Chicago. Under such a curriculum as this it is small wonder that pupil interest is at a minimum and that progress is slow.

The Church

The people of El Cerrito are 100 percent Catholic. The church and its teachings play a tremendously important role in the attitudes, practices, and everyday life of these people. It is the earnest desire of every individual to live entirely within the doctrine of the church. The priest of the village is recognized not only as the spiritual leader of the community but as a source of advice and community leadership. He is expected to be interested in and to help map procedure for any economic problem affecting his parish. Religion offers these people hope in a world that has become increasingly difficult and uncertain, and this sanctuary is completely dominated by the local priests.

On a visit to one of the local priests mention was made of the important role the church plays in local rural life. To illustrate his point, the priest brought out a letter he had just written to a local government agent in reference to a salary check a local native had received. The amount of the check was less than the native had expected, and he had asked the priest to write the agent a letter stating his case. Said the priest, "The poor fellow is faced by a situation he does not understand and his only recourse is to the church. One of the mistakes of many of the local agencies is to disregard the influence of the church on these people. If we (church and agency) could only work together on local problems, cooperation from the people would be much easier to secure."

El Cerrito has no resident priest. The village is too small to support one. The usual parish in this area covers from 6 to 10 of the villages, depending upon their size and accessibility. The priest that serves El Cerrito lives in Villanueva. He comes once a month to give the mass and hear confessions. In case of a death or similar emergency he may come more often, but the average year would necessitate no more than two or three extra visits. Absence of the priest, however, does not mean that services are not held. The people meet each Sunday and sometimes as frequently as every day of the week to say the Rosary. These extra services are in charge of a local woman who is selected and paid a small sum of money by the church.

The services are conducted in a very humble spirit. The women seat themselves on the benches and the men kneel on the hard floor in the rear of the church. The attendance is usually good. There are never more than a few who are able to rationalize staying away. All present take part in the service. The hymns and ritual that are part of the service are well learned, even by the small children.

After the services are over the men meet in front of the church for a half-hour or more of conversation. This is as much a part of the service as any of the formalized ritual. Such meetings afford the men their most frequent occasion of getting together in a group. The conversation is directed to the entire group. The topics are local happenings or any news a recent visitor has brought back from town. The group never breaks up until each man who has something to offer has had his say.

The church apparently is lenient as to its financial support. Each family is assessed an equal sum regardless of its size or status. Although contributions are often requested in addition to the set fee, the amounts given are very small. Most of the families estimated their total contributions to the church for a year at approximately $3.

FIG. 20. *At worship — all villagers are devout Catholics, El Cerrito, New Mexico, 1940.*

In addition to the regular services the village holds each year a community function in honor of its Patron Saint. This function is held in December and lasts for 2 days. Elaborate rules and procedures have been worked out to govern the affair. Although the villagers sponsor and conduct the function, the priest is invited to attend as the guest of honor.

Two leaders are elected each year to be responsible for the conduct of the function. It is their duty to invite the priest, to provide the food and drink, to open their homes to accommodate the guests, and to supervise any other details of the affair. It is considered an honor to hold one of these posts, and a man regards himself as fortunate to be elected. The term of office is for a year. One of the first things accomplished by the leaders at the function is the selection of their successors for the coming year. No one man is expected to serve 2 years in succession.

These functions begin on the eve of the Patron Saint's birthday. Food and drink have been prepared in large quantities and spread out in the houses of the two church leaders who were elected at the function the year before. Visitors file in and out of the houses at will, partaking of the feast at their pleasure. This continues until late in the afternoon, when everyone marches to the church for mass. After the mass is over they come back to the houses, where they may again take food and drink if they so desire. The last feature of the evening is the dance, which is conducted in the usual way. The second day is merely a duplicate of the first.

Farm Organizations and Cooperatives

No farm organizations are found in El Cerrito. Such organizations as are common in other sections of the country would hardly be applicable to the small local farm business that exists in this area. Several years ago the County Agent organized a 4-H Club for the boys and girls but it was short-lived. Good livestock proved too difficult to buy and maintain.

The one local cooperative enterprise is an old one. Its function is to clean, repair, control, and maintain the irrigation system. No one knows how old the association is, but it has probably been in existence since the valley was first settled.

It is called simply the "Ditch Association." Each family owning or operating land in the valley is eligible for membership. There are no cash fees or dues; instead, it is maintained through contributions in labor. The officers of the association are a ditch boss or mayordomo and three members of a ditch committee. The duties of these officers are well defined. The ditch boss is expected to inspect the main ditch at regular intervals and to call out the men when repairs or other work need to be done. He supervises the annual cleaning of the ditch, his only compensation being that he does not have to do any of the actual labor himself. The members of the ditch committee make any new rules for the regulation of the association and see that the old ones are enforced. It is their duty to distribute the irrigation water according to supply and need. These officers are elected each year at a meeting of the entire village. In many villages the offices carry considerable prestige but in El Cerrito this is not true despite the responsibility attached to them. They are considered rather a duty and are passed around equitably.

This association functions with a high degree of efficiency. One hundred percent cooperation is demanded and usually given. Severe reprisals are certain in case of failure to cooperate. A violation of the code of the association may mean suspension of water rights or heavy penalties in the form of labor. No one dares remain away when the ditch is being cleaned, unless he is able to send someone to represent him.

Labor is contributed in accordance with the area of land operated. In El Cerrito a man is assessed 1 day's labor for each acre of irrigated land, which is adequate to maintain and clean the ditch in a normal year. In case of any disaster that necessitates additional labor the work is again distributed in accordance with the area of land. As it actually operates, the majority of the men work until the job is completed, the larger land operators compensating the others in some way for work done over their quota.

Local Politics

The term "Government" conveys a variety of meanings to the local people. In the last decade the term has taken on a much broader meaning than before. Previously Government was regarded as something foreign to them and to their interests. It dealt with situations, rights, and privileges that were complex and far removed from their everyday life.

Since that time the term "Government" has taken on new meaning. It has come down into their communities and into their homes, bringing such material substances as food, clothing, and work. It has become a source on which day-by-day they are more increasingly dependent.

As the functions of Government have become so much more important to their existence, interest and participation in politics have been expanding. Although Government may be the source of relief and public works, politics governs the machinery by which these are made available to them. Thus the feeling has grown up that a person's benefit from a Government program will be in direct proportion to his interest and participation in politics. One must be "in" with the "politicos."

As a result of this attitude toward politics a candidate for any office is appraised in terms of "what can he do for us." Political, moral, or religious principles are of secondary importance. His attitude toward National or State issues concerning such factors as business or labor are passed over lightly. Instead he is measured in terms of the number of jobs and the amount of grants and relief he has obtained for his constituents. These are what matter.

Much of the machinery for operating local politics is old. Office holders and new candidates still court and retain the good will of their constituents by means of free dances, free drinks, and now and then a fiesta. Priests still urge their following to vote for candidates whom they think will best follow and promote the interests of the church. To this machinery has recently been added many small clubs through which the people are able more directly to make their strength and needs known

Predominant in this field have been the political clubs with membership drawn from the younger people. These clubs are operating in most of the little villages with their own elected officers and membership. In these meetings the local men are able to discuss their political problems in their own way.

The village of El Cerrito is peculiar in this area in that it has no acute local political problems. The fact that the village has no factions enables the people to work in unison. This is true of only a few communities in San Miguel County. In the typical situation two distinct factions work at cross purposes in every situation. Because of the resulting friction, local political issues are on a par with or of more importance than county or State issues. The broader issue may be forgotten in a desire to thwart the purpose or objective of a rival local group.

Any political meeting or rally in one of these local villages incites a great deal of enthusiasm and draws a good attendance. Each village has its well recognized best speakers who are always present to talk at great length and in flowing terms of their favorite candidates. Such meetings are dynamic affairs thoroughly enjoyed by all present. The political issue or candidate is often completely lost sight of in the light of a passionate and dramatic speech. Such speeches are remembered and discussed more from the standpoint of presentation than from content

Leadership and Class Structure

The old class structure which existed for so long in rural New Mexico has virtually disappeared along with the economic basis that supported it. The dons of the local villages who once owned all the cattle, controlled surrounding land, and employed the other residents, have disappeared along with their holdings. It is only in the most isolated instance that such a situation is still found to exist. The preponderance of class difference that still exists in New Mexico is found in the towns and cities or between the town and rural people.

Although the leveling process involving holdings contributed most to the breakdown of the once vast gap that separated the peon from the dons other factors were at work. Not least important was the degree to which all the families of the village became interrelated through marriage. A son or other member of the don s family frequently selected a mate from the class below. This practice was encouraged among the lower class and was seldom given more than slight consideration by the don. As the status of the wealthy families declined this fusion assumed a more rapid tempo. At present there seems to be little, if any, social distinction between the owners and those who work for them. Prestige and respect in the community has come to be based on an entirely new set of factors. Sons and daughters of the once great Patron of El Cerrito have married into families that once would have been considered far below them.

Little real difference is found in the economic status of the families in the majority of the native villages. Although a family may still have sheep or cattle and follow somewhat the pattern of the old don, his land and livestock may carry a mortgage for its full worth. His material wealth and that of the laborer who works for him differs little.

In many of the larger villages this change has not been so complete. There may still exist in some of them a semblance of the earlier pattern. In such instances it is likely that the wealthier families control not only the sources of labor but the greater part of the commerce and business of the village as well. Thus the old village structure is being supplemented and supported by a new set of factors that were necessary to keep it from crumbling.

Although maintaining some sort of working relationship with the local people such families are likely to be almost as much a part of the neighboring towns. They take active part in politics and mingle socially with the town people. In such cases wealth may be the sole determinant of the family s social status. But as a rule these families are the decendants of the old dons who once were in such complete control.

This class distinction is never carried to an extreme. One of these wealthier families would not dare incur the general opinion that they considered themselves in a higher class than the other villagers. Such a mistake would play havoc with his local business. Almost any native would go to endless trouble and effort to carry his trade away from a family whose members seemed to him to consider themselves superior.

Since the breakdown of the old system, the native villages have been looking more and more to the outside for leadership and guidance. In conjunction with their increasing dependence upon the outer world has come a realization of the inadequacy of leadership in their own. The old sources of leadership are felt to be no longer competent to meet present-day problems. This does not mean that the old pattern of leadership has been entirely discarded. The judgment and influence of certain individuals in the village are respected and recognized. But the influence of such individuals is limited to the local situation. One of the young men stated the situation in terms of his own orientation.

"I don't think there is a real leader in the village. There are some who are older and have more experience than others. I would appreciate their advice more than that of others, but they are not actually leaders. That is part of the trouble with this town today. We need people upon whom we can depend for advice. In this village every one is alike. There is no best farmer or best business man. Everyone is in the same situation. If we want advice about a Government program, about schools, or about farming we go to someone in town. Personally, I go to friends in town for advice about anything important."

In this statement are two indications of the change that is obviously going on. The first, as mentioned above is the feeling of the inadequacy of the old pattern of leadership, that it is no longer effective or meeting present-day problems. The second is a shift toward the town for leadership. This second change is being effected through two different channels. One of these is the ever-increasing dependence upon town friends and relatives for information about available work and relief and the procedure to follow in getting either. Because of broader contacts the town people are recognized as better informed and more qualified to give advice than a resident of one of the rural villages. A second impetus toward the change in the source of leadership for these villages is the power of the county politicians who, rightly or wrongly, are thought to control effectively the sources of public relief and employment. Any job on a public works project is first cleared through these offices. In some measure these men have come to take the place of the dons under the old system.

The old pattern of leadership operates strictly within the village. Such individuals as form the pattern in the community are depended upon for advice and leadership in local situations. These people are seldom dynamic leaders in the sense that they initiate and carry out definite programs. Their influence is much more potent in influencing community sanction or disapproval of what already exists.

Qualities that determine leadership in these communities are comparatively few in number, yet are well recognized. The three dominant ones are age, family, and the ability to express oneself fluently, listed in the order of importance. These factors are not entirely independent. A combination of two or more, such as age and family, would far outweigh age alone.

Age is considered the most important quality in a leader because it is felt that age and experience go together. But more is involved than this. The native culture gives great weight to age alone. One of the most serious violations of local social custom would be to ridicule old age or an elderly person. This is one of the things that definitely is not done. Age occupies the seat of honor on all occasions and ever has the right to be heard. All recognize that age alone gives tremendous weight in any declaration or statement.

Status in a family group gives prestige and hence is important in leadership. Family loyalty impels one to give credence to advice or comment from a member of the family. Age becomes a much more powerful quality in leadership if the individual is a member of the family. Young men who were asked about leaders in the village invariably gave the names of elderly persons in their family group. An aged father who has relinquished his possessions to his sons still remains in charge of the operation of the lands or livestock. His authority is recognized, with little thought of contradiction, either in thinking or in practice. That the parents know best is an often-repeated adage throughout the Spanish-American culture.

The ability to express oneself well before an audience is perhaps the most important personal quality for leadership. Anyone who can speak well before an audience commands a great deal of admiration and respect. This is especially true in politics, where such an individual has frequent occasion to exercise this ability. In discussing the leadership qualities of the local president of one of the political clubs it was always pointed out that he was a good speaker. He keeps well informed about the political situation and he has no trouble in telling an audience about it.

Although other qualities undoubtedly are appreciated in local leaders those mentioned are by far the dominant ones. Although other qualities might well be given weight in the choice of leaders, these are largely ignored by the local people. The one young man who is by far the best informed in the village is definitely not recognized as a leader. He realizes this and admits that it is largely because he has little ability or desire to make his ideas felt and heard.

Youth as the Critical Age Group of the Community

The young people of El Cerrito are becoming increasingly aware of their limited opportunities at home. This is in part due to participation in recently established Government agencies for the young people and in part to the influence of the older peoples' opinions upon them. Both are making themselves felt in ever greater intensity.

One of the local boys who is now in the CCC camp gave a frank summary of his case. "I have been in the CCC camp for almost 3 years. It was the first time I had ever been away from home except one summer when my father and I went to Texas to pick cotton. I like it in the camp very much. I have learned more during my 3 years in the camp than I did in all the years I went to school. These camps are a great help to the local boys. I have learned to speak English fairly well and how to do several kinds of skilled work. When I get out of camp I am not coming back to El Cerrito unless there is no work in town." Two other local boys who have been in the CCC camp are now working outside the village. Both stated a preference for living in town.

The older people are not concerned about the new tendency on the part of a few young men to leave El Cerrito. They regard such a move as advantageous because it alleviates the pressure of population at home and feel that the movement should be encouraged as much as possible. Under present conditions they see no other solution to the overcrowded situation than making jobs available in town for a large number of the local young men.

These opinions are being freely distributed to the young people. The father of two boys, ages 18 and 19 is expecting them to leave El Cerrito in the very near future. "I tell them that there is not any future for them here, that they must go to Las Vegas or some other place where there is at least a chance to get work. I have taught them as much as I could about how to find a job. They know how to do several different kinds of work. So I am sure that they will be able to find a job."

Many of the young people show a surprising amount of confidence concerning their ability to obtain work outside the village. Much of this is obviously due to the influence of the CCC and NYA camps. Those who have gone come back and talk of the ease of learning skilled work and the better pay that goes with it.

Boys who have gone to the CCC camp are definitely the heroes of smaller children of the village. The children are never tired of hearing of their adventures and experiences. They hear of life in a modern world full of new, even strange, wonders. Stories and descriptions that would seem drab and prosaic to most young people are listened to and thought exotic by the native boys. Shower baths, new kinds of food, baseball and other games are topics that never fail to interest a group of listeners. Thus, they are impressed and plan for the days when they, too, may be able to go and live through these experiences.

The moral problems of youth are not of serious concern in these native villages. Changes that have taken place in the environment of youth in other parts of the country have not filtered into the local setting. Modern entertainment and amusement is still far from the reach of local young people. Consequently, one hears little expressed remorse or regret about the changing trends of modern youth which made such popular copy elsewhere. True an opinion regarding the immorality of city youth is frequently heard but the city has long been regarded as more corrupt than the rural areas

All the adults of El Cerrito appreciate the superior environment for their young people, especially for the girls. "This is a good place to rear a girl. She is not exposed to the temptations of the city." Many of the people point to the record of the village in youth delinquency. "We never have any crime problems to deal with here." The general opinion is that such a record is the result of the training received by the children in the home and in the church.

Value System and Its Supporting Sanctions and Attitudes

The entire set of values by which the native people live are woven around the family and the family group. Loyalties, responsibilities, and duties are primarily connected with the meaning of family. The esteem for an individual in the community comes out of contributions or failures in relation to this institution. The primary virtues that give an individual or a family prestige in the community spring out of the need and welfare of the family group. The new values the native has learned from his contacts with the Anglo and other racial groups have been shaped and conditioned to fit into his own way of life. Hard work and thrift, which are such important factors in many cultures, have never found local adoption in puritanical form. The native has never found or sanctioned virtue in such practices. True, he has seen and realized what such practices can do and for that reason has accepted them in his own fashion. Work and thrift are valuable in accumulating material goods but carry no virtue in themselves. A child is taught that hard work and thrift may bring him security and independence but never that they will add to his moral well-being.

To be recognized as a good citizen of El Cerrito, one is expected to support not only his immediate family but to give what aid he can to parents or to any other near relative in need. Failure to do this brings social censure in its most formidable form. Living in accordance with this responsibility brings respect of the highest order. This custom is taken for granted and is probably never mentioned.

Honesty is a virtue in strict accordance with church teaching and family sanction. This trait is greatly enhanced by the isolated and intradependent nature of the village, where cooperation and mutual aid depend heavily on such a quality for efficient functioning. Products and even small sums of money are loaned with never a thought of failure to repay. Local trading and bartering is based upon these same ethics. A man would never dare misrepresent an article in a trade with a friend and neighbor, nor ask more than he thought was worth.

This virtue takes on a somewhat different meaning outside the local village. The code is much less rigid in dealing with town or business people. If a man owes a debt at a store in town repayment is postponed until minor liabilities in the local community have been liquidated. Outside obligations are purely business matters and are entirely devoid of the personal and primary qualities given those in the home community.

El Cerrito has little need for formal social controls. Although there is a local Justice of the Peace, his functions are other than establishing or maintaining peace and order. The county sheriff has never been called upon by the villagers. They mention only two instances in the history of the village when outside officers have had to interfere in the community.

Informal social controls govern life in El Cerrito. Although hidden they are more effective and more feared than a much more severe code administered formally would be. Group approval and sanction become tremendously important in the lives of a people living so completely within themselves.

The role of the women is much more restricted than that of the men. From very early youth a male is allowed considerable freedom. He is permitted freedom of speech and action as long as he remembers his responsibilities and his duties to old age, relatives, and the church. This is not true of the girl, who is early taught that her place is in the household. Her role in the community is definitely outlined. She must be good and associate only with her own sex. She must learn to help her mother with the household duties and eventually she must marry and have children. It is difficult for her to break out of this narrow pattern.

It is the wife who symbolizes virtue and goodness in the family. It is she who has the responsibility of setting the example for the family. She must be pure, religious, and obedient to her husband. Her complete life must be devoted to her home and to her family. All money matters and dealings with the outside world are left to the husband.

Local society is much more liberal with the male. If he supports his family, goes to church occasionally, and fulfills his obligations to the group and its institutions, he is allowed free rein in his personal affairs.

Integration and Conflict

El Cerrito is peculiar in its setting in that relatively little conflict or friction occurs between rival groups in the community. This situation is unique in the area because of the degree to which family groups often aline themselves against each other and exert tremendous effort to boost their own interests and injure others. This was once true of El Cerrito until circumstances removed the conflict from the village. The extent to which the problem was typical in El Cerrito justifies a brief summary of the story. It could easily be duplicated in many of the surrounding villages with the exception that, in the other villages, the conflict is still going on. The story is as a resident told it.

The village of El Cerrito was settled by the M's and my family. They came in almost equal numbers, just about as many M's as Q's. Both families had some money and large herds of sheep and cattle. At first there was no trouble between them. All were friends, although only one marriage ever took place between the two families. The M's used to herd their stock on the north side of the village and my people on the south side. But as the herds kept getting larger the M's began to come into our territory. At first we didn't mind so much. There was plenty of grass and we didn't want to have any trouble with the M's. They were bad people. Always getting drunk and fighting among themselves. Finally we had to tell them that they would have to stay out of our territory. This made them very angry and they began doing things to us. Sometimes they would take our calves and lambs and mark them with their brand. Things got so bad that the families would not speak. Then fights began. Finally one of the M's hit my grandfather over the head with a shovel and almost killed him. My uncle ran for the sheriff but the M's heard about it and ran after him. They finally caught him and almost beat him to death. This made my father very angry. He took his gun and shot one of the M's. He didn't die but he was in bed for a long time. There was a big trial after that which lasted for a long time. It cost both families almost all of their sheep and money. The M's were in such bad shape that they all left, and our people were never able to get back their property.

Obviously this story tells much more than the history of the conflict. It shows plainly what such conflicts have done to undermine the resources of the people, and how they have been rendered easier prey for individuals or concerns willing to take advantage of this weakness. These conflicts persist with amazing tenacity. Once they are begun no compromise seems possible.

Conflicts as they exist are almost invariably between groups rather than between individuals. This is understood only in the light of the solidarity of the group. Infringement upon the rights of the individual necessarily means interference with rights of the group, as the relationship between the group and the individual are mutual. In addition, friction between individuals within a group is made more difficult because of the threat to the interests and solidarity of the group. Undoubtedly this goes far to explain the lack of conflict and friction in the village of El Cerrito since the M families moved away.

In the individual's function in the family, in the church, and in the community are seen his integration into the local setting. It has been pointed out that his loyalties, duties, and responsibilities are much more closely tied in with the local village group than with any other unit of society. Many loyalties and virtues which the individual may practice in his own local village are not practiced in his contacts with the outside world.

This orientation to the native village is a logical outgrowth of the isolation and compactness of these native villages. During a child's formative years he is closely associated with every other child in the village. Seldom does he see the outside world or the people living in it. In case he does he is likely to consider himself and to be considered as a stranger. Until he is old enough and experienced enough to take care of himself he is seldom given the opportunity to go outside the village. He hears his parents and older brothers and sisters talk of the outside world but it is usually something far beyond his experience. Thus his only familiar world is the immediate area around him. He soon becomes accustomed to identifying himself with it.

The result of this early conditioning is carried over into adult life. To the adult who has never been far nor long away from the home village the outside still remains a strange and foreign world filled with people and affairs beyond his comprehension. He is at ease only at home, a setting he both appreciates and understands.

To his more widely traveled brother or cousin the difference in orientation remains one of degree only. His early training is neither disregarded nor forgotten. This is seen in the overt behavior of men who have lived away from the native village for long periods of time. Those who have lived away from El Cerrito for periods of a year or 'longer still think of themselves as belonging there. Their mailing address is never changed and all return home to vote. This attitude is also expressed by residents of the towns where some of the El Cerrito people are at present living. People of Las Vegas are always alert to correct any implication that a family from El Cerrito is now living in Las Vegas. "No, he lives in El Cerrito and always has. He is merely here for the time being working or waiting to be certified."

All the relationships between the people of a native village are of a primary nature. One would never think of asking a neighbor, friend, or relative for more than his word to bind a contract. Money is borrowed and food loaned with no more record than the memories of the parties to the act. A family would feel deeply hurt to know that a neighbor was keeping a written record of their exchanges of food and other materials. To ask for the repayment of such a loan would be an equally bad breach of local etiquette and a blow to pride. Such a request would bring immediate repayment and probably an end to such future reciprocities. It would also bring censure from local womenfolk for so bold an act as to question a neighbor's honesty to the extent of asking for repayment.

As stated previously, the exchange of tools, equipment, and livestock is made on an equally informal basis. A man may borrow a plow for an indefinite length of time with no thought of returning it when the job for which it was borrowed was completed. It matters little who has it or for how long if the owner knows that it is still within the community.

Only one family in El Cerrito does not participate in the interchange of food and tools. This family is the least liked of all in the village. People speak of the members as selfish and peculiar. Children are taught the undesirability of selfishness by using this family as an example.

But this trust and informality does not extend farther than the bounds of the community or group. Dealings with a townsman, unless he is known well, are likely to be extremely formal. For a town businessman to dun a resident of El Cerrito would not be resented in the slightest. There would be none of the personal resentment that would accompany such an act within the village. Nor would the debt be so likely to be repaid. There would be none of the group censure or pressure brought to bear on the individual to pay. Transactions made through such formalized agencies as stores or banks are thought of as purely business, with little principle involved. Such agencies are regarded as existing upon their ability to drive a good bargain. The only way the native knows to cope with this is to get as much as he can and pay what he can afford.

The village of El Cerrito is not only an isolated and compact community; it is also a distinct racial and cultural group. Obviously these differences are recognized by the local people as well as the Anglo, who makes up such a large percentage of the population of all New Mexico towns. The native in San Miguel County constitutes approximately 85 percent of the population. The people in El Cerrito, as a group, have never had open conflict with other cultural groups. Completely surrounded by similar native villages, its contacts have been mainly with its own people. What it knows of the Anglo has been learned from local men who have gone out of the State to work or from stories that have drifted down to them from other parts of the State.

Actually there is considerable appreciation of the Anglo and his culture. An Anglo family that once lived near the village is mentioned frequently and their farm practices have been adopted to a limited extent. Many stated a belief that the local village would possibly benefit from having a few progressive Anglo families near. It would facilitate their use of the English language and they could possibly learn many of the techniques which have made the Anglos so successful in their push into New Mexico. It is admitted, however, that such a situation would be dangerous. Such contacts might finally result in the Anglo getting possession of their lands, a possibility that has become actuality in many other parts of the State.

THE FARMER'S EXPANDING WORLD

Recent opportunities for Government work have brought the rural people of San Miguel County more and more into contact with the city. Yet it is highly problematical that such increased contacts have induced more than slight change. The older people are almost as closely bound to their home village now as before the present increased opportunities for employment in the city existed. It is only the young people who have been temporarily taken completely out of the old environment that exhibit any noticeable shift in their thinking and in their desires.

The ties that bind these people to their home village are strong. Families that move to town for the duration of a period of employment still maintain homes and holdings, and being away "on a project" is considered a temporary thing. The inducements offered by the towns and cities are not sufficiently appreciated by the majority of the families to compensate for the many factors that contribute to satisfactory living in the home community.

The types of contacts and associations in the city, once a rural family has moved there, are not especially conducive to the widening of a gap between such families and their original rural environment. Most native families in Las Vegas are still essentially small villagers. Many are transient in the sense that they have come in for temporary work with little thought of remaining permanently. Thus contacts are still mainly with people who have a definite rural background and the limited perspective that is a concomitant of life in one of the native villages. As a result of this the influence of what might be designated as the urban way of life is of much less real significance than might at first glance be imagined.

The rural people do not feel that the townsmen, as such, are in any way set apart or different from themselves. The reason for this is partly accounted for by the fact that there is actually little difference between their living conditions and those of the majority of the natives of Las Vegas, whose housing, sanitation facilities and household conveniences are in no way superior to those found in rural areas. Another significant factor is the degree of blood relationship existing between rural and urban families. This interrelationship obviously minimizes any feeling of difference between the two groups. By far the greater part of any feeling of difference between the two groups is on the side of the townspeople, who sometimes recognize the rustic side of their rural relatives and friends.

The feeling of difference is apparently in direct proportion to the number of years an urban family has lived in town, as well as the degree of financial success that family has attained in the new environment. Families which have lived in Las Vegas for decade or more usually speak freely of the backwardness and provincialism of the rural villages. Often one may hear the criticism that the rural people are not able to speak English effectively and as a consequence are seriously handicapped in their contacts and business relations in town. The more acculturated ones are sometimes bitter toward the rural people, believing that their backwardness is affecting adversely the entire native population. Such critics often offer the additional opinion that the social distance between rural and town people is increasing. They base their statements on the fact that the town people are making needed adjustments while the rural people are remaining in a more or less static condition. The chief factor operating to widen the gap is the schools. An ever increasing number of the native young people of Las Vegas are attending the High School and the local college thus far outstripping their friends and relatives in the village who grow to adulthood with little more formal education than that which enables them to read and write. But the importance of rural urban differences is easily overemphasized.

Many of the town businessmen are definitely antagonistic to any effort that tends toward further breakdown of village and town differences. The most outspoken of these are the businessmen whose stores are primarily dependent for trade upon the rural people. One of these men was frank enough to say that so long as he had a good country trade he was not particularly interested in a large town clientele. Country trade is conducted upon a personal rather than upon a strictly business basis. The majority of my customers trade here because they like me. I can get and hold the trade of these people even if my prices are higher than at some of the other stores This man is convinced that recent education in consumer buying, distributed by the various Governmental agencies, has already affected the volume of his trade.

It seems fairly evident that town stores catering almost exclusively to rural trade have suffered a definite decline in volume of business done during recent years This trade, as indicated by the storekeeper, is upon a personal basis and has been increasingly difficult to maintain. The native's feeling of obligation to trade at a store is based somewhat upon the courtesy received there which, essentially, means credit. For a store to refuse a certain amount of credit to a customer would mean that no more trade from that source could be expected. To invite overindulgence in credit would be equally disastrous. As the storekeeper quoted above expressed, you must always keep them owing a little bit but never too much. No credit or too large an account will likely mean the loss of a customer." Thus it is always a delicate task to maintain the proper balance. This has been increasingly difficult during the last decade as credit has been needed by the villagers as never before and the likelihood of repayment has decreased at an equal rate. A number of the town business places have had to close their doors because of this pressure for credit purchases and the small volume of business done in cash. Employment on Government projects has enabled such business to return to somewhat near its old volume.

Mail-order houses have taken an ever increasing volume of the town's business Poor means of transportation to and from town has made for increased use of the mails for buying goods that may be had at reasonable prices with little more expenditure of effort than going to the nearby post office. Recent emphasis upon time payment has greatly accelerated the use of the mail-order houses. Farm equipment furniture, and clothing are bought on terms requiring payments of no more than a dollar a month. Such terms are proving popular with people operating on cash incomes that are seldom in times of employment, greater than $40 or $50 a month.

It seems likely, however, that the bulk of the trading will continue to be done in the towns. Better goods at cheaper prices and the inducements that go with extended payments are not enough to outweigh entirely the advantages of trading in town. Although the desire to make certain purchases may be the expressed reason for going to town, there are others. Going to town is, and will continue to be, an activity that is enjoyed apart from the economic function. It is also an opportunity to visit friends and relatives, a chance to keep in touch with what is happening in the outside world.

Communication and Transportation

Modern means of communication and transportation have had little effect upon the number and variety of contacts of these local people with the outside world. There has never been a telephone in the village, and the closest one to the village now is at another village, 16 miles distant by car or 3 miles by foot. The few families who own automobiles are limited in their use by the fact that operating expenses are almost prohibitive and can seldom be afforded unless a group can be gotten together to share them. The automobiles in the village are all antiquated, untrustworthy, and incapable of making more than infrequent trips to town. All repair work is done at home. A lost or broken part is usually replaced by some make-shift or home-made device. After a number of such repair jobs it is almost incredible that some of these cars run at all. One of the local men who had lost his gasoline tank tied a gallon oil can to the side of the hood of the car just high enough to allow the gas to run by means of a small pipe into the carburetor.

Newspapers and periodicals are as foreign to the village of El Cerrito as they were 50 years ago. Three copies of the county paper and two religious newspapers come regularly into the village. These papers are printed in Spanish, and are read for political news and any light that might be thrown upon relief or Governmental programs.

There are no subscriptions to magazines or periodicals None of the people know of farm journals or other printed matter that touches upon the problems of the farmer. The most extensive reading materials are the weekly comic strips that are saved by the townspeople and distributed to their rural friends and relatives when they come to town.

The village has two radios that function when the owners can buy batteries for them. There is little interest in the educational and extension service material that is distributed by this means. Programs coming from Latin American stations are appreciated most because they can be understood more easily One of the families listens to many of the news broadcasts and claims that only a few of the other residents are at all interested in such items. The news items listened to pertain to this country. There is too little knowledge of South American Countries to allow any degree of appreciation and understanding.

Few of the older village people ever attend a motion picture This is not because of lack of interest or because such means of amusement are not deemed good Actually, some of the better-to-do native town residents visit the local movie house and are especially interested in the Spanish pictures shown 2 days each week. Lack of attendance on the part of the villager is simply a matter of cost, an item that only few feel that they can afford. The young people are intensely interested in movies an can talk for days about one if they have had an opportunity to see it. But it is seldom that they can go unless the picture is on Saturday afternoon when the matinee price i reduced to 10 cents.

Value Systems and Attitudes Toward
Wider Economic and Political Problems

The people of El Cerrito have had no first-hand experience with organized labor movements. Their knowledge of such movements is limited to information picked up from random conversation. Only one of the men has ever been involved in a strike. The incident happened in Colorado. A group of sugar beet workers planned a strike against this man's employer. When he heard about the strike he chose to leave rather than become involved in it.

The background and experience of these people precludes any sanction or understanding of labor movements. They have never been members of an active pressure group. There is a clear recognition of the rights of private property and the lack of right of the laborer to interfere with production. It is universally agreed here that it is morally wrong for a worker or group of workers to use such means as strikes to force a higher wage or shorter working hours. The concensus is that labor is strictly a commodity, to be bought at the discretion of the employer and at a price that he feels he is able to pay. Any interference with this right is likely to operate to the disadvantage of both employer and employee.

This attitude has undoubtedly been partly the result of the type of labor engaged in. The villager searches for work where there is a definite demand and after the season or peak period of the work is over he returns home to wait for another similar opportunity. The source of their work has never been constant. During one season of the year they may be in Kansas and in another as far away as Wyoming. Even the type of work has varied from agricultural labor to various types of industrial employment. The laborer is always ready to take almost any work he can get.

For example, Benny Sanchez is 24 years of age. He has spent 3 years in a CCC camp, 3 different summers in Colorado, 1 in Texas and 1 in Wyoming. The types of work he has done in these various States range from firing a boiler in a smelter plant in Colorado to picking cotton in Texas. Unless he is fortunate enough to find a job with some permanency in the meantime, he plans to make a circle of all the surrounding States next year to survey all possible sources of employment for the local people.

Almost the entire life of an individual is lived in one of these rural villages. The influence of experience outside the local area is negligible. The wider world in which many of them have traveled is still foreign because of the way in which they have kept themselves apart from it. National policies and politics, foreign and international trade agreements, even the new defense program, except as the draft affects their own people are felt to be the concern of the outside. Politics and party platforms stimulate little interest or attention until they come into the local scene. Knowledge of candidates and public offices is limited to the local situation, with the exception of the President of the United States. To these people the President is a combination of the Executive, Legislative, and Judicial branches of the Federal Government.

Few events in the rural communities occasion more interest than the election of county officials. Candidates are elected mainly upon the basis of what they may be expected to get in the way of material benefit for the voter. All other qualifications are secondary. Appropriations for programs of work or other benefits to the people are never judged in terms of the Federal Government. Blame for the reduction of funds for work relief or other benefits, is always placed at the feet of local officials. Any reduction in benefits is considered to be the result of the failure of the local officials in their duty to the people.

INTEGRATION AND DISINTEGRATION IN COMMUNITY AND INDIVIDUAL LIFE

It is generally agreed among those people, whose work brings them into contact with rural life, that rural people and rural communities are undergoing change. Techniques and technologies of the last few decades have eradicated many of the barriers that once separated rural and urban people. Rural-urban adjustments vary with the different cultural areas of the Nation. Factors or characteristics that are conducive to change and adjustment or that prove barriers to it present interesting and important data for study.

The village of El Cerrito is a singular example of a group of people that has maintained its individuality in the face of the ever increasing forces that have been brought to bear upon it. Not only has it failed to keep in step with modern technological progress but it has managed to exist in its own way after the greater part of its economic base had been lost. In this respect as well as in many others, it is highly representative of a large number of other native villages that lie in the area of the Pecos watershed. Definitely submarginal to date in its capacity to support the present population it is highly integrated and unified socially, functioning in many instances as a single unit.

At the time of settlement the village was completely surrounded by grass land that was adequate for the support of enough sheep and cattle to afford both owner and laborer an independent livelihood. At that time the community was almost a complete and independent socio-economic unit. Its only dependence upon the outside world was for a market for its wool and to supply certain material items that were not produced or made at home.

The destruction of this pattern has been both recent and rapid. During the last quarter-century surrounding land has been leased bought and homesteaded literally to the doors of the village. But, despite this loss, the population of the village has remained almost constant. Loss of local resources failed to disturb the village or its people while a substantial wage could be earned in outside employment. Many of the sources of work in surrounding States paid a much higher wage than could be earned locally. It was only after this resource, also gave way that continued existence of the old way of life threatened to go with it.

It has been only during the last 10 years or less that the solidarity of the village has shown definite signs of cracking. Not until reserves had been liquidated and many months of unemployment had ensued did the families begin to wonder whether the old way of life had not been doomed.

Work relief programs initiated by the Federal Government are proving influential in breaking down some of the compactness of the local rural communities. The influence of such programs is functioning in two major ways (1) In the influence upon the older members of the community who are depending heavily upon relief work to live; (2) and perhaps most significantly, in the influence upon the younger people who are taken completely away from the village for varying periods of time into the CCC and NYA camps.

Work on relief projects is drawing many natives to the towns. Although the majority move to town with no intention of remaining permanently, there are many inducements for them to stay. When in town they are in close touch with the programs and are readily available for work in case a new project is begun. Many believe that town residents are given preference in certification for work.

The effect of a young person's stay of a few years in the CCC or NYA camp is profound. Such persons have a difficult time of readjustment if they return to their native village. They become accustomed to an entirely new way of life which they consider, in most respects, superior to the old. They become conditioned to better housing facilities, new and varied social contacts, new sources of amusement and recreation. Above all, perhaps, they become accustomed to having a certain amount of cash to spend as they see fit.

But these inducements to move out of the rural villages do not operate without opposition. There are strong inducements to remain. That these counter forces are powerful in the lives of the people is evident. Under a different or weaker set of integrating factors the village would likely have disintegrated long ago.

Perhaps the most instrumental element in holding the community together has been the institution of the family. In the native villages the term "family" has wide yet definite connotations. As indicated graphically in chapter IV, it means considerably more than parents and offspring. Structurally it embraces grandparents, brothers, sisters, uncles aunts, and sometimes many cousins. The units of this group are often located upon a single or upon contiguous tracts of land, with the houses together or adjoining. Although each biological family unit may operate a tract of land somewhat delineated there is still a substantial pooling of labor and division of crops. Such a group receives recognition, both social and economic within and outside the village. Misfortune to an individual may bring support and contributions from all others in the group. Obligations and responsibilities to the family are well defined and universally accepted.

It is obviously difficult for a member to break away from a web of relationships so intricately and strongly woven Abandoning this social and economic unit means mutual loss. The strength of the family is weakened by the loss of a member and the individual is forced to function in an atmosphere of independence that is entirely unfamiliar. Realization of this, on the part of the member, makes it difficult to sacrifice the relationship.

The church is another institution that exerts a strong influence in the integration and stability of the native villages. The native is usually a devout Catholic and is loyal to church and priest. The people take marked interest in all church activities. Most of the services are held in the absence of the priest, who holds mass once each month in the local church These services are held regularly and with good attendance. Few choose to evoke the displeasure of God and fellow for the privilege of remaining away. Thus, the integration of the individual into the church affords another barrier to disintegration. Other churches in other towns or villages are never quite the same. Attendance at church away from the village is never done with the same regularity or an equal degree of fervor.

The church "functions" afford a rare means for social expression. Such functions serve the dual purpose of entertainment for the people and an opportunity to pay homage to the church and its saints. The celebration in honor of the patron saint of the village is an occasion that only the rarest of circumstances will justify missing. Although not as religiously important as Holy Week it offers the additional advantage of combining entertainment with worship In addition to the prospect of a good time each person feels a responsibility and obligation to be present and to participate in this annual event.

In addition to a sense of responsibility to and integration in the family group and the church, the individual is conscious of his role as a member of the community as a whole. The sense of belonging to a community is developed in a native child to the extent that it is difficult ever to feel apart from it. This is seen in the individual's feeling of identity with his community as well as in the attitudes of others. Residents of rural villages are especially aware of an expected loyalty to their village. There is never any confusion as to which village a native belongs, and the interests of the village are as clearly recognized in distinction to those of any other.

Perhaps no factor is more important in binding a native to the home village than the privilege of living and associating with his own people. They are at ease only among their own people, who understand them and with whom they can converse in their own language. This is especially true of those who have little mastery of the English language. Such people are strangers in many areas of their home State where the Anglo-Americans have largely displaced the natives. They are never able to feel a part of the culture of the people of the many areas over which they wander working and in search of work. Appreciation and freedom in the home village has compensated for greater material benefits, even economic stability, that might have been possible elsewhere. Those people in El Cerrito who gave reasons for preferring the village as a place to live invariably mentioned the fact that the local people were similar as to race, customs, and language. Those who expressed a dislike for life elsewhere always mentioned the many discomforts of living outside their own environment.

The families that are now considering a break away from El Cerrito recognize fully the extent of such a sacrifice. One of the men who plans to leave permanently, if there happens to be an opportunity said "It isn't that I want to leave. It's a matter of making a living. I used to go to Colorado each year to work in the beets but I always came back. If I go to Colorado to live I know that my wife and children won't like it. My wife gets homesick for this place if she is away for a week. There is nothing else for me to do. I have been out of work for 4 months. All the income I have is from the rent of a room to the school teacher. That isn't enough to buy our food. So, even if we don't want to leave, we will have to if I ever have a chance at anything like a good job again."

A camera report on
EL CERRITO

a typical Spanish-American community in New Mexico

by IRVING RUSINOW

 Miscellaneous Pub. No. 479, Issued January 1942

BUREAU OF AGRICULTURAL ECONOMICS

UNITED STATES DEPARTMENT OF AGRICULTURE

CONTENTS

	PAGE
Frontispiece in Words	1
The Village	4
The People	20
Making a Living	34
The Church	84
The Home and the Family	100
For Fun	114
The School	122
Yet to Come	128
Negative Numbers of the Pictures	136

NOTE

This camera report on El Cerrito is the first of six to be published by the Bureau of Agricultural Economics. Each deals with a community typical of an area or group in the United States. They are designed to serve as companion books for a series of six technical publications relating to the same six communities, resulting from studies carried on by the Bureau during 1940. The first of these, The Village of El Cerrito, New Mexico, is now available. The other five communities studied are Grafton County, N. H.; Lancaster County, Pa.; Putnam County, Ga.; Haskell County, Kans.; and Shelby County, Iowa.

FRONTISPIECE IN WORDS

El Cerrito is located in San Miguel County, N. Mex., 28 miles south of Las Vegas. It was settled early in the nineteenth century by two families that owned great flocks of sheep and by other families that made their living working for the stockmen. The land was not well suited to farming, for the growing season was short and the rainfall variable and often insufficient; but there was room in the valley for irrigated fields where people could produce the food they needed. Each family owned a little plot of land, a horse or two, a cow, and perhaps a pig.

The principal source of income was livestock. Thousands of acres around the village—part of a huge Spanish land grant—were covered with bunch grass. There was more pasture than could be used. When one part of the area was overgrazed, men simply moved their herds to another part. No one thought very much about conserving the land. There was always more to be had for the taking.

As time passed, a few more families were able to build up herds of their own, but always the majority of the people were dependent on the stockmen. Fortunately, the latter recognized their responsibility and accepted it. Even those who were not regularly on a "patron's" pay roll were given work to do when they needed money. The only really independent pursuit of the people was cultivation of the irrigated land.

The early economy of El Cerrito was one of abundance. Every man had everything he needed, and the patrons grew rich. No one tried to live by farming the land.

Today, these people and their descendants have lost nearly all of their once vast holdings. They still own the small, inadequate, irrigated fields that were never sufficient, alone, to support all the people of the village; but the mesa land, which supported the all-important livestock industry, has passed into other hands. The ownership of much of it, granted by the Spanish and Mexican Governments, has been voided by the courts. Even more land has been sold for taxes.

Though the community began losing its land several decades ago, the full effect of this loss was not felt until recently. The railroads were coming in and people found that they could earn more by cutting ties than by working for the sheepmen. After the tracks were laid, labor scouts came in from the mines, metal works, and beet fields of the north, offering work for everyone. This period of prosperity lasted until the 1920's. Then with th[e] coming of the depression, jobs gre[w] scarce and the people returned t[o] the villages and the land.

It was only then that they rea[l]ized what had happened durin[g] their absence. There was no mo[re] grazing land. Homesteaders ha[d] taken up some of the mesa and ha[d] fenced it so that a man who owne[d] a tract 2 miles away might have [to] go 10 miles to reach it. Big co[n]cerns had obtained control of t[he] grazing and water rights.

The people did what they coul[d]. They farmed the land, grew a lit[tle] food, worked whenever they cou[ld] get work, sold whatever they cou[ld] sell. But all they could do was n[ot] enough to keep them off relief. S[an] Miguel County soon became one [of] the most heavily subsidized in t[he] State.

Now, several years later, con[di]tions in the village are almost u[n]changed. In general, agricultu[ral] programs do not fit the situati[on]

...hat exists here. There can be little ...ope of rehabilitating the people ...n their present holdings, and self-...quidating loans are not feasible.

The communities persist, not be-...use of economic conditions, but ...spite of them. The people, being ...distinct racial and linguistic ...oup, hold fast to customs and ...aditions. They are devoted to ...eir village and they resist change. ...hey must, as individuals, find op-...ortunities for self-expression and ...preciation within their own cul-...re, among their own people. When ...ey leave their villages, they go out ...nong strangers. Their thoughts ...e always of home and when they ...ill return there. They distrust ...tsiders. Everyone knows of peo-...e who have lost land and money ...the hands of shrewd dealing ...Anglos." Because of this, even ...e poorest men rarely sell or even ...ortgage their houses and irrigated ...nd.

There is a great deal of loyalty among the people of the village, loyalty to each other and to the village as a whole. And the fact that almost all the families are related to each other binds them together by blood ties as well as community relationships. Marriage within the group is common.

The Church, too, serves to hold the community together, and its influence on the people is profound. All are devout Catholics; all try to live their lives according to teachings of their Church.

Here, then, is a village until recently pretty much apart from the rest of the world. But resources have so dwindled and opportunities so shrunk that the people are convinced that radical changes must be made in their way of life. And many think that these changes will mean the end of some of the customs and traditions and values that have always been of the first importance—the things, in fact, that have made life worth living.

THE VILLAGE

It is 28 miles from Las Vegas to the village; 16 miles of paved road, 3 of improved dirt road, and the rest a twisting shifting track over the high mesa. The country is rough and broken, spotted with piñon, cedar, and juniper—very dry land without much grass on it.

You come upon the village suddenly. The road cuts sharply to the right, and you find yourself on the edge of a cliff looking down into a little, almost circular valley— a land pocket cut by the Pecos River, which now swings across its floor in a huge double S before vanishing through a cut in the cliffs.

There are 20-odd houses in the village, buff-colored or pinkish, with dark shingle or bright iron roofs. The fruit trees are in luxuriant bloom. The place is like an oasis in the dry mesa land.

It is very quiet. This is a holy day and the people are not in their fields.

Even from close at hand the houses seem neat and well-kept. They are all plastered with adobe, but some of them are made of stone.

Only the oldest have flat roofs and solid adobe walls.

Being here is like being in another lan[d

10 • EL CERRITO

El Cerrito has its own character, . .

. . . very different from that of rural communities in other parts of the country.

The oldest buildings were made of adobe bricks. These soon melt away when people cease to take care of them.

Things have been pretty hard here in the past 10 or 12 years, and you see a few abandoned homes; this in spite of the fact that most of the villagers would rather live here in poverty than elsewhere in reasonable comfort.

There is evidence here of the culture of Spain and that of the Southwestern Indian and a few traces of our own culture.

The village belongs here, fits into this country: And the country is like no other region.

THE PEOPLE

You meet some of the people.

They are friendly . .

. . and interested, . . .

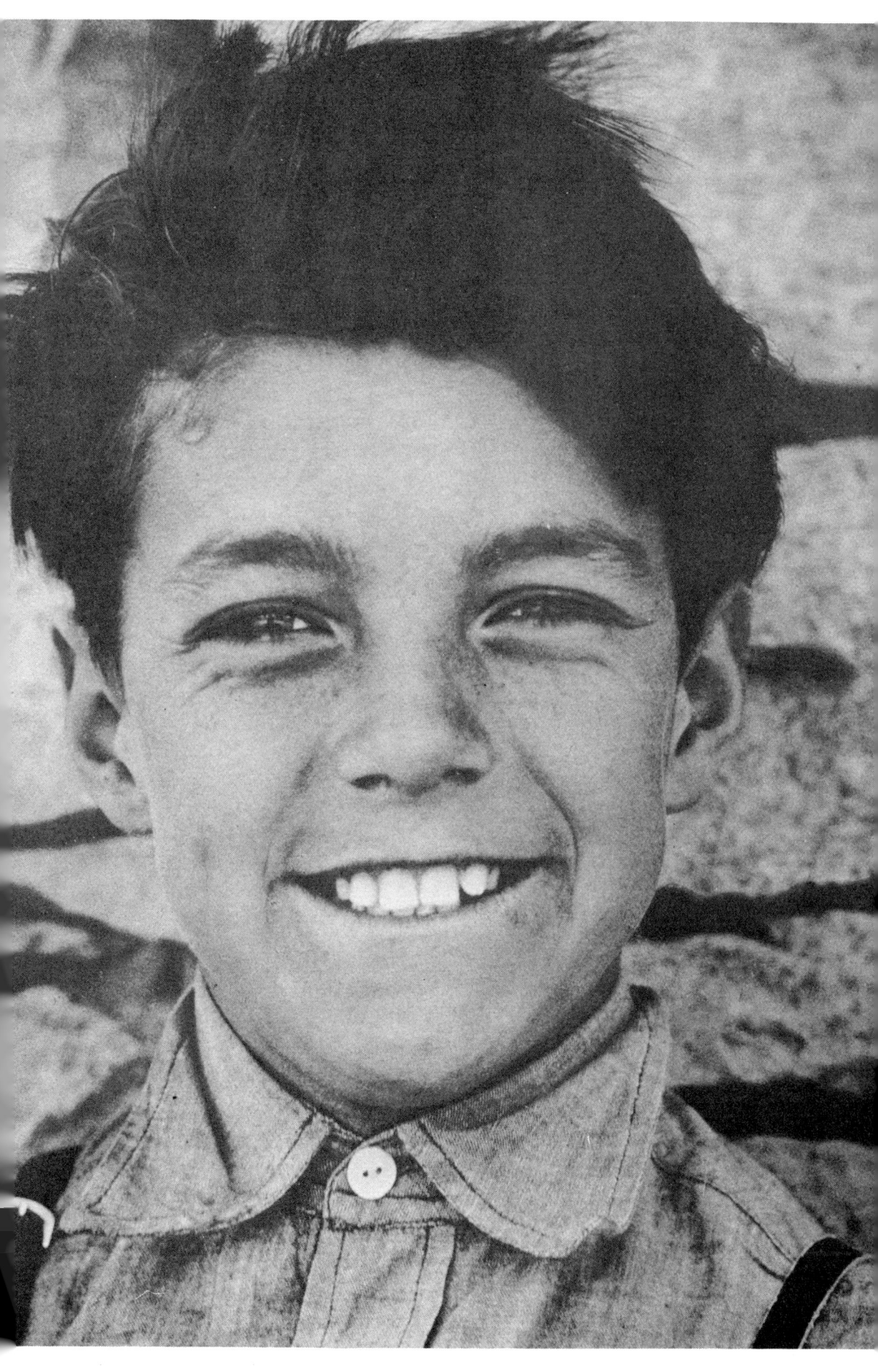

. . . curious . .

. . . and suspicious

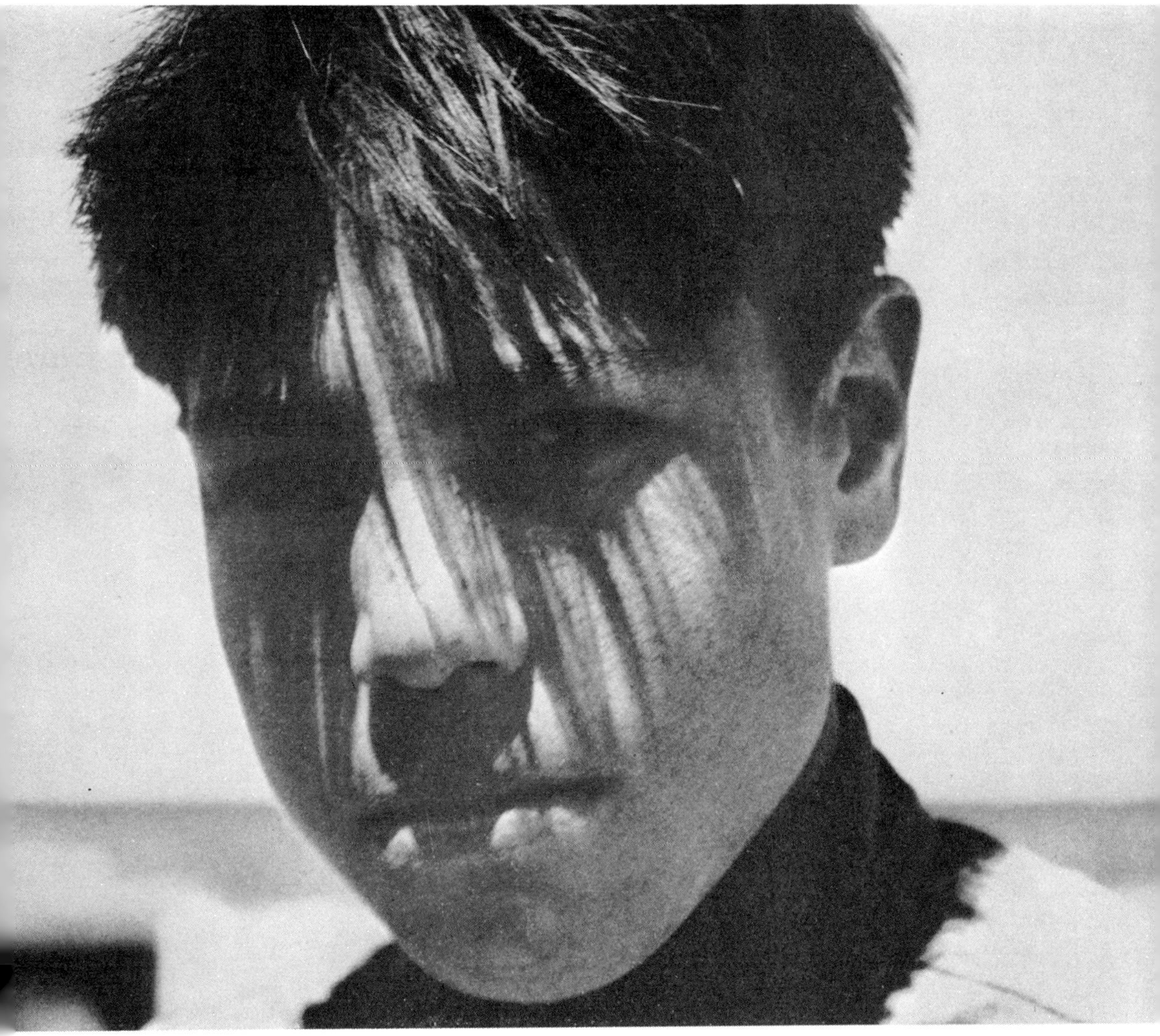

They have little reason to think that an Anglo is sincerely interested in them or concerned about their problems. Strangers have sometimes done them harm, rarely helped them.

Small groups of men and boys talk in the shade. They speak always in Spanish and many of them have no other language.

MAKING A LIVING

Agriculture today is not very differen[t] from what it was 50 years ago here in th[e] valley. As before, almost all crops a[re] grown on the irrigated land. The only re[al] change is that the staple crops are now cor[n,] alfalfa, and beans instead of corn, alfalf[a,] and wheat.

As always, the dam and the main ditch—the "Madre Acequia"—are the basis of a[ll] agriculture in the valley. Without irrig[a]tion there would be no food, no feed, n[o] livestock. Older than the village itself, th[e] dam is a flimsy affair needing constan[t] repairs.

It is 2 miles up the river. Here the ditc[h] branches off from the stream. It fills mor[e] gradually than the river, until, by the tim[e] it reaches the village, it is several feet abov[e] the river level.

Each year the major-domo, or ditch bos[s] enlists the help of every man in the villa[ge] to clean out the Madre Acequia and i[ts] tributaries.

Those who help can take water whenev[er] they need it.

Newly plowed fields are flooded . .

. . . to set out onion

The child's play parallels the father's work

Now, in April,

spring plowing gets under way . .

and men are putting barnyard manure on their land—a custom of long standing.

Two families still own sheep. The flocks graze on the mesa, usually . . .

but this year the pasture was so poor that they grew thin and weak and had to be brought down into the valley where there was a little green grass on the fields that were not yet plowed.

Even so, there are often sights bad to see

The sheds and corrals are in the village. No one owns much livestock, so they need not be large.

Then, too, people here do much of their traveling by wagon and want their horses or mules close at hand.

The sheds are like the sheds of their fore fathers . . .

. . . at once rough and ingenious, . .

. . . others were once homes. Even deserted buildings are put to some use, for usable land is at a premium.

There are always regular daily or weekly chores, subject only to the weather and to the Church. It is bad luck to work in the fields on a holy day.

Little boys chop juniper, cedar, and piñon for their mothers' stoves; . . .

others get water for the house—silt-colored ditch water for both washing and drinking.

There is no spring here, and there is the threat of typhoid.

Women do their washing in tin tubs and hang the clothes in their yards . . .

and make bread in Indian beehive ovens.

Once the village grew its own wheat and milled its own flour. Now people find safer to grow beans and buy their wheat.

There are eggs to be gathered each day. Families have 8 to 10 hens, kept for the eggs they produce.

They are too valuable to kill, except great occasions.

Once in a while a sheep is butchered

Men repair their possessions until there is nothing left to repair.

They make new parts to replace old ones. These are very poor people living themselves; they have neither the money nor the opportunity to hire work done.

But this sort of agriculture, and self-sufficiency, is not enough. The men must earn a little money.

Now, there are only a few ways to bring in cash. Men can load their wagons with fence posts or firewood, drive to Las Vegas come back 2 or 3 days later with some provisions and a dollar or so.

And there are the WPA jobs, lifesaver for many. There are few private jobs for these people, and they have little chance to sell their services. People of the village have almost no land or livestock left, but their needs are greater than ever. They must earn money, and they earn it as best they can.

THE CHURCH

Everyone here is a Catholic and everyone wants to live according to the rules and and teachings of the Church.

Though the village has no priest of its own, services are held regularly.

They have done all they can to make their church beautiful, though they cannot afford to give expensive presents.

On Good Friday the figures on the altar are clothed in black. On the next Sunday there are flowers and the black coverings are removed.

Most men and boys kneel in the back of the church.

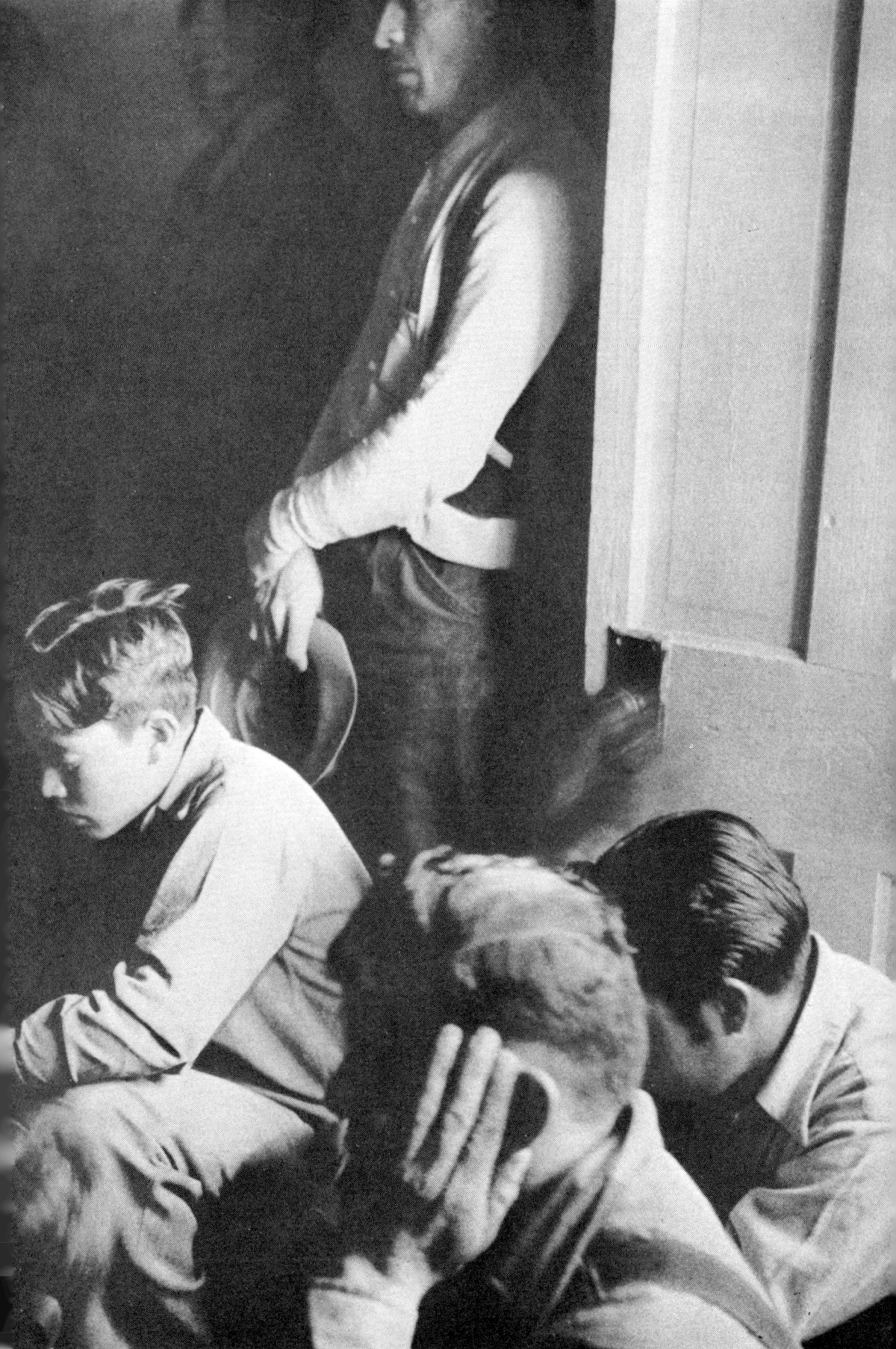

The Christ hangs in the confessional. It is very old. Newer ones, generally store bought, are much more conventional.

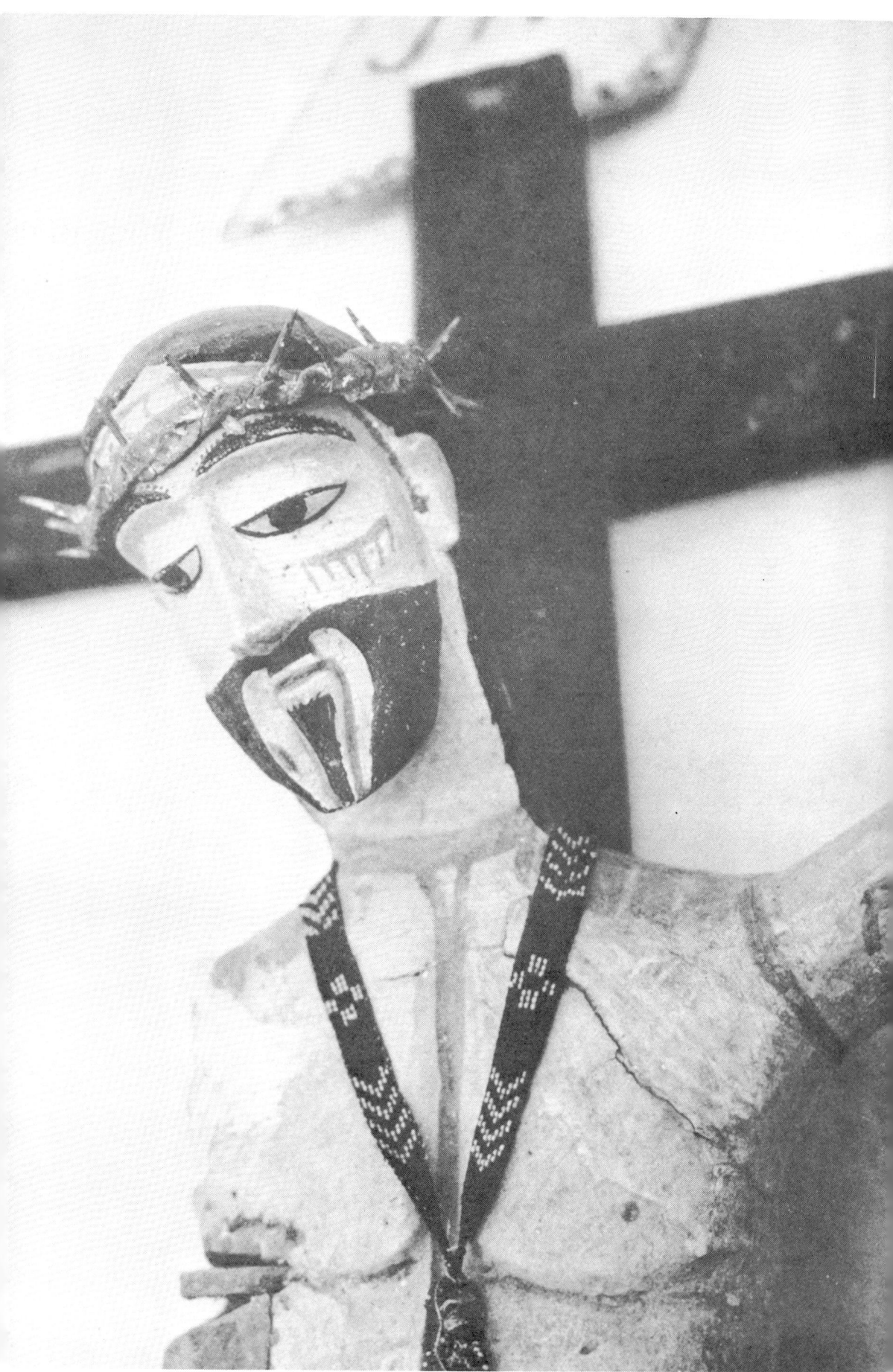

Men get together for a half hour of talk after the service. This is almost as much a part of going to church as the service itself.

Every home has its shrine, though most are less elaborate than this one.

Even the calendars are decorated with religious pictures.

During Holy Week children carry food to their neighbors, receive other kinds of food in return.

The Church binds families together, as well as to itself.

In death as in life,

        they are in the churc

THE HOME AND THE FAMILY

The families who have always lived in the village welcome to their homes those who show good will. They are by nature friendly, courteous people.

A few who have lived for a while in some Anglo town are suspicious.

Most of the pictures in the rooms ar
religious. The rest are usually family por
traits.

Here, the family, including even distant relatives, is almost a sacred institution.

The rooms are clean and simply furnished. Wallpaper is uncommon, though many walls are tinted.

There is nearly always space enough i the homes, especially as some members most families are away working for da wages.

In an old-type house the doors have n
jambs and the roof beams show. The effec
is very simple and very fine.

A wood-burning stove and cheap enamel ware make up about all the equipment the housewives have for their kitchens.

There is no refrigeration, and perishables are cooked in small quantities.

There is usually plenty to eat, but kinds of food are few. Those who can afford them sometimes add canned goods to their usual diet.

FOR FUN

Recreation here is simple and limited. Older people go to town once in a while, but they have no money to spend on such luxuries as movies.

Often there is a dance in the village. When there is, everyone goes to it and has fine time. Then, there is fishing in the river, . . .

and horse racing . .

... and music ..

and the games you see children playing wi[th]
sticks or stones or old tires, games th[ey]
invent themselves.

THE SCHOOL

The school at El Cerrito is very poor an[d] has little equipment. It was built to ser[ve] 30 or 40 pupils.

All of the teaching is supposed to be do[ne] in English; but the children know that the teachers speak Spanish, and so are n[ot] forced to break away from their moth[er] tongue. Many of them have very litt[le] English even after years at school.

The people understand that, despite its isolation, their village is coming to depend on the outside world.

They feel that their school is importan[t] because there the children can begin t[o] learn English and something about th[e] ways of this other society that surroun[ds] them.

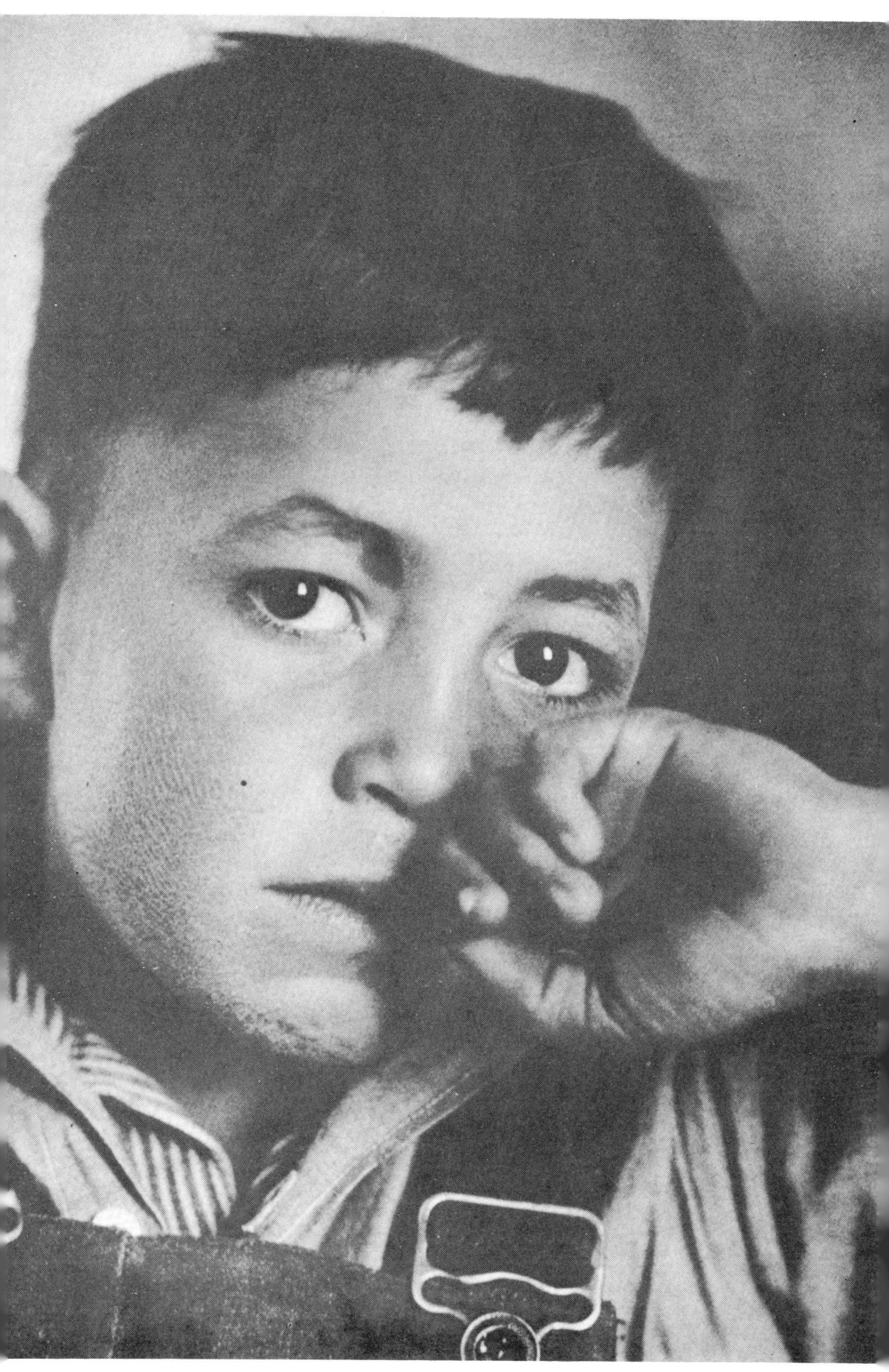

YET TO COME . . .

The future of this boy, and of his family, and of other Spanish-American families everywhere, will depend on their ability to make changes, . . .

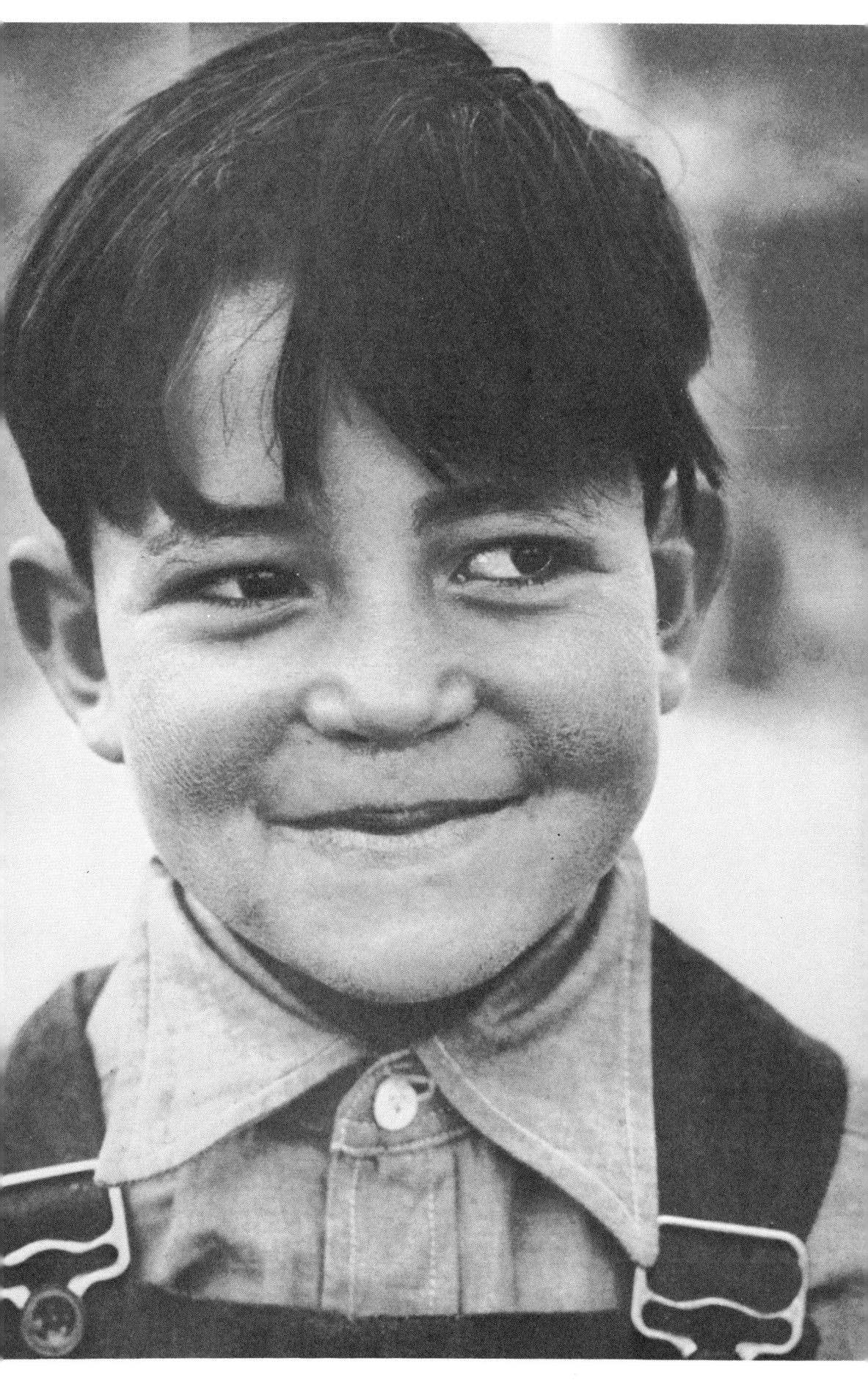

. . . even though these changes may affect their religious life, . . .

. . . their life on the land, . .

... and their life together.

It has taken generations of living to build up the patterns that hold the people of these villages together, but they were built, many of them, on a foundation of natural resources that no longer exist.

Unless the old ways can somehow be made to support the people, they will have to go out into the towns and cities of the Anglos and make for themselves a new life based on, instead of isolated from, the new and changing conditions of the world today.

NEGATIVE NUMBERS OF THE PICTURE

PAGE	NEGATIVE NO.	PAGE	NEGATIVE NO.	PAGE	NEGATIVE N
5	 37793	45	{ upper 37856 / lower 37854	91	 3787
7	{ upper 37795 / lower 37794	47	 37858	93	 3786
9	{ upper 37801 / lower 37804	49	 37861	95	 3783
		51	 37860	97	{ upper 378- / lower 378-
11	{ upper 37797 / lower 37799	53	 37862	99	.... 378.
		55	 37807	101	.... 378.
13	 37805	57	 37812	103	.... 378.
15	{ upper 37798 / lower 37800	59	 37813	105	.... 378.
		61	 37808	107	.... 378.
17	 37810	63	 37839	109	.... 378.
19	 37796	65	{ upper 37840 / lower 37841	111	.... 378.
21	 37815			113	.... 378.
22	 37820	67	 37837	115	.... 378.
24	 37819	69	 37844	117	 378
25	 37817	71	 37838	119	.... 378.
27	 37821	73	 37809	121	 378
29	{ upper 37816 / lower 37823	75	 37863	123	{ upper 378 / lower 378
		77	 37845		
31	 37802	79	 37846	125	 378
33	 37818	81	{ upper 37881 / lower 37882	127	 378
35	 37847			129	 378
37	 37848	83	{ upper 37884 / lower 37883	131	{ upper 378 / lower 378
39	{ upper 37849 / lower 37851				
		85	 37867	133	{ upper 378 / lower 378
41	 37850	87	 37868		
43	 37852	89	 37869	135	 378

136 . EL CERRITO

We Fed Them Cactus

We Fed Them Cactus

by

Fabiola Cabeza de Baca

With Drawings by Dorothy L. Peters

THE UNIVERSITY OF NEW MEXICO PRESS

COPYRIGHT, 1954, BY

UNIVERSITY OF NEW MEXICO PRESS, ALBUQUERQUE

ALL RIGHTS RESERVED

LIBRARY OF CONGRESS CATALOG CARD NUMBER: 54-12881

TO LUIS

PREFACE

THIS IS THE STORY OF THE STRUGGLE of New Mexican Hispanos for existence on the Llano, the Staked Plains.

Through four generations, our family has made a living from this land—from cattle and sheep, and lately by selling curios, soda pop, gasoline and food to tourists traveling over U.S. Highway 66.

The stories of buffalo hunts and other events on the Llano were handed down to us by my grandfather's employees, by neighbors on the land, by our own ranch hands, and mostly by Papá, who spent a lifetime on the Ceja—the Cap Rock, and who traveled over the Llano before the fencing of the land.

In the description of the rodeo, I have used fictitious names, since it would be impossible for me to remember the names of all the people who were mentioned by El Cuate in his tales. It has been many years since he passed on. I was about ten years old when I heard him tell about the rodeos, the buffalo hunt, the mustangs, and other stories which I have tried to tell as nearly as El Cuate told them. Don Manuel Salcedo lived, but in real life he had another name.

All of the chapters present authentic historical facts. For dates which my informants did not have at the tip of the tongue, I consulted New Mexico histories and the Spanish archives of New Mexico. The dates of the founding of the chapels may not be exact, but they are within one or two years of the actual time. These dates I obtained from church records and from people who lived in different areas of the Llano.

On June 10, 1944, I visited Don Paco Baca in Puerto de Luna. He had reached his one-hundredth birthday on April second of that year. From him I secured the history of Puerto de Luna, Las Colonias, Santa Rosa and Antonchico. His health was failing but he had a clear memory—the dates which he gave me corroborated with those which I found in church records. He related many incidents about his trips over the Chihuahua and Santa Fe trails of commerce. Don Paco died on August 24, 1944.

For several years, I had tried to get a real picture of Spanish life on the Texas side of the Llano, and on July 26, 1948, I visited Doña Jesusita García de Chávez at the home of her sister-in-law, Doña Lola Otero de García. Both contributed to this history, and in telling it they relived their youth and early married years on the vast country of the Ceja and the Llano. From them I obtained names of places and people living on the bluffs of the Staked Plains from Texas into New Mexico.

It is fitting that I should dedicate this book to my brother, Luis María Cabeza de Baca IV. This is his book, for without his help, patience, and inspiration in assembling the material, I could not have compiled the Spanish American history of the Llano.

Luis has written a description of the buffalo hunt in his scrapbook:

"I knew many of the men who took part in the buffalo hunt. Among these were: Doroteo Vigil, Concepción Atencio, Santos López, Apolinar Almánzar, Teodoro Gonzáles, Benigno L. Benavídez, Longino Aragón, Luis Tapia, Eulogio Martínez, Juan José Quintana and others.

"My grandfather, the late Don Tomás D. Cabeza de Baca, used to employ a hunter and send, yearly, half a dozen wagons to the hunt. His two older sons, Manuel and Daniel, accompanied these hunting expeditions on two or three occasions in the 70's, merely for the sport. It was from them and others mentioned before that I acquired information for this article.

"I always delighted in listening to those men tell of the buffalo hunt, the fun which they had, the hardships endured—for all was not easy sailing. Blizzards overtook them and on the Llano a blizzard was terrible. There was no shelter and very little fuel available to use in building fires. Yucca roots (palmilla) and buffalo chips were the only materials that could be found suitable for fire building on the Llano proper.

"It was easy to get lost on the Llano, especially in a blinding snowstorm. Men were known to have become lost even on clear days, for on the Llano there were very few landmarks. Before it was settled, it was just an immense expanse of level land and sky.

"The route usually travelled by the *ciboleros* was the present site of Newkirk, the Laguna Colorada at the mouth of Bull Canyon past the south end of the Mesa Redonda and it climbed the Ceja where the present Norton is located. The gap where they climbed the Ceja was called, in those days, El Puerto de los Río-Abajeños."

THE *ricos* in New Mexico, as mentioned in this story, were those who owned land. Many of the Spanish families were given grants of land comprising from several thousand to a million acres each. These families had large herds of sheep and cattle. There were also merchants in the larger towns who owned wagon trains that went into Chihuahua and, later, into the States. These merchants amassed fortunes and they, too, were in the *rico* class.

Many historians and writers have contended that there was no wealth in colonial New Mexico, but there was. It was strictly a feudal system and the wealth was in the hands of the few. The *ricos* of colonial days lived in splendor with many servants and slaves. Their haciendas were similar to the Southern plantations. To those coming from what was then the United States of America, the life of the New Mexican *ricos* was not understood because they kept their private lives secure from outsiders. The latter judged all New Mexicans by the people of the streets, since the families of the wealthy were never seen outside the home and the church. There were family gatherings, but as the families of influence married among themselves, there was not much opportunity for outsiders to learn their ways of living.

There are different ways of reckoning wealth and a set pattern does not exist and may never be found. People who live from the soil have abundant living and, compared with that of the wage earner, it can be classed as wealth. On the Llano, in the days of open range, there were men who ran thousands of head of cattle and sheep. The Baca brothers from Upper Las Vegas—Don José, Don Simón, Don Aniceto and Don Pablo—jointly were running half a million head of sheep in the 1870's.

Fabiola Cabeza de Baca

Santa Fe
June 1, 1950

CONTENTS

I. THE LLANO	1. Loneliness without Despair	1
II. EL CUATE	2. The Night It Rained	9
	3. The Rodeo	17
	4. Fiesta at San Hilario	31
	5. Buffalo Hunters	39
	6. Comancheros	47
III. PLACES & PEOPLE	7. Chapels on the Llano	51
	8. Sheep on a Thousand Hills	68
	9. Las Vegas Grandes	80
IV. BAD MEN & BOLD	10. Vicente Silva, Bandit Leader	89
	11. The Field of Burdocks	111
	12. Incidents	121
V. WITHIN OUR BOUNDARIES	13. Mustangs	126
	14. "Milo Maizes"	138
	15. A Country School	154
	16. The Drought of 1918	171
GLOSSARY		179
INDEX		181

I. THE LLANO

1. Loneliness without Despair

THE LLANO IS A GREAT PLATEAU. Its sixty thousand square miles tip almost imperceptibly from fifty-five hundred feet above sea level in northwest New Mexico, to two thousand feet in northwest Texas.

From the Canadian River, the Llano runs southward some four hundred miles. The Pecos River and the historic New Mexican town of Las Vegas mark its ragged western edge, while two hundred miles to the east lie Palo Duro Canyon—once the goal of Spanish buffalo hunters—and the city of Amarillo, steeped in the traditions of Texas cattle-raising.

Between these boundaries are the settlements, whistlestops, trading posts, chapels, ranch headquarters and homesteader's houses—some new, some old, many abandoned—which tell the story of more than a hundred years of living on the Llano.

Curving along the Llano's high northern and western rim is the Cap Rock, the rough-hewn Ceja, or eyebrow, above the plain.

No other land, perhaps, is more varied in its topography than the Ceja and the Llano country. As one descends Cañon del Agua Hill from Las Vegas, a full view of this great stretch of country greets the sight. There are myriads of hills, peaks, wooded mesas, canyons and valleys. The Montoso, wooded land, extends for miles and miles. In the distance one can see Conchas Mesa, Corazón and Cuervo peaks, the Variadero Tableland, and many other hillocks. Traveling on, descending hills, crossing arroyos, one reaches Cabra Spring. This is an oasis, a spring of sweet water which saved many a traveler from dying of thirst on his way to the buffalo and Comanche country. Later it was a watering place for an overnight stop on the way to the sheep and cattle territory.

It is unbelievable that in a country where rain is scant, there can be so many springs gushing from the earth in the most secluded places. There are lakes all along the land, some made by rains, some fed by springs from the hills. If rains are plentiful, these lakes may be filled the year round; if rains are few, the lakes may dry up from evaporation.

There are deep canyons in the hills, seemingly inaccessible, yet the old-timers knew every canyon, spring and lake from Las Vegas to the Panhandle of Texas.

After passing Cabra Spring, one comes in view of the Luciano and Palomas mesas, Tucumcari Peak, Cuervo Hill and, in the distance, Pintada Mesa. Bull Canyon of the Luciano Mesa presents one of the picturesque panoramas of the area. Its red coloring, from red earth and rocks surrounding it, is typical of the land and a sight comparable, perhaps, to the Grand Canyon of Arizona.

From Cañon del Agua Hill to Luciano Mesa, the vegetation includes juniper, piñon, yucca, mesquite, sagebrush, gramma and buffalo grasses, as well as lemita, prickly pear, and pitahaya. There are wild flowers in abundance, and when the spring comes rainy, the earth abounds in all colors imaginable. The fields of oregano and cactus, when in full bloom, can compete with the loveliest of gardens.

It is a lonely land because of its immensity, but it lacks nothing for those who enjoy Nature in her full grandeur. The colors of the skies, of the hills, the rocks, the birds and the flowers, are soothing to the most troubled heart. It is loneliness without despair. The whole world seems to be there, full of promise and gladness.

Leaving the Luciano and Palomas, the Ceja country, and traveling east and south, one comes upon the great Llano, so extensive that one must see it to realize its vastness. For miles and miles, as far as the eye can see, is the expanse of level land. Here are mesquite, prickly pear, yucca, and grass, grass, grass.

THERE is little similarity between the Llano of today and that of the last century. The Llano, then, was an endless territory of grass and desert plants, with nothing to break the monotony except the horizon and the sky. In the days of the buffalo and the Comanche, the Llano was uninhabited and dangerous. The buffalo hunters knew the waterholes and springs, yet they had to be careful to follow the right trails; otherwise they would perish.

The early Spanish colonists had settled along the rivers in north central New Mexico, using the surrounding land for pasturing their sheep and cattle. They did not extend their grazing because of the aridity of the country south and west of the Rio Grande, and because northern pastures along the smaller rivers lie in the cold belt where rigorous winters make it more difficult for stock to survive. The frequent raids of the Navajos were another deterrent to increasing the herds.

While the colonists had received all protection available against warring Indian tribes during Spanish rule, when Mexico gained its independence from Spain in 1821, the New Mexicans were left to survive by their own resourcefulness. They found it prohibitive to augment their livestock. Indians came down on the settlements, killing herders and driving off sheep, cattle and horses. Between 1821 and 1840, flocks and herds had to be reduced to numbers small enough to be tended close to the settlements. At night all livestock had to be corralled in the *placitas,* the squares within the walls of houses.

THE New Mexican home of the *rico,* or landowner, as I heard my grandmother describe it, was a fortress in itself. It was built around a square, with living quarters on one side. Another side comprised storerooms, granaries and workshops. On the third side was constructed the *cochera* for the family coach, *carretas,* and wagons. The fourth end, which completed the square, was a high wall with one entrance—a massive gate of hand-hewn timbers. Through this gate, the horses, mules, cattle, sheep, goats, and pigs were driven at night. The outer walls of the flat-roofed adobe houses were built high and pierced with *troneras,* loopholes for fighting Indians.

Livestock had to be kept close to the settlements and under close surveillance of the herders. Consequently, the range near the towns and villages became denuded of the natural browse, which for years had pastured the stock. Traditionally, meat had been the main fare on New Mexican tables, but with the decrease in livestock, the supply became more and more scarce.

THE Llano and Ceja country were well known to the New Mexicans who ventured forth as Indian fighters and to hunt the buffalo. They brought back tales of the good pastures and the extensive territory beyond the mountains.

The sheep and cattle owners traveled eastward, and on the Ceja and the Llano found the Promised Land. There, where the mountains end and the plains begin, they found grama and buffalo grass growing as tall as the cattle.

The best pastures were on the Ceja, the Cap Rock area at the top of the Staked Plains. As one descends south and east from Las Vegas, all the country is known as the Llano, and it is the history of this section, of its people and their lives, which this book tells. To one living on the American plains of the Middle West, so level and flat, the land on the bluffs of the Staked Plains, with its rocky hills, juniper, mesquite, and piñon, may not seem a llano, but to New Mexicans, because of the drop of two or three thousand feet from the peaks, it is not the Sierras, and they have called it the Llano—the wide open spaces.

IN 1840, the sheep owners started sending herders with their flocks into the Ceja and the Llano, and the Hispanos continued to prosper in the sheep industry for more than half a century.

In those days a man had to be courageous to face the many dangers confronting lonely living far from the populated areas, yet there seems to have been no lack of men who were willing to follow the herds for the employers, the *patrones*. In feudal times, there were many poor people who became indebted to the *ricos*, and the rich were never at a loss to find men to be sent with flocks of sheep. Then, of course, herding was one of the few kinds of employment available in New Mexico. If a man became indebted to a *rico*, he was in bond slavery to repay. Those in debt had a deep feeling of honesty, and they did not bother to question whether the system was right or wrong. Entire families often served a *patrón* for generations to meet their obligations.

If the flock of the *patrón* ran into thousands, he employed a *mayordomo*, or manager, and several overseers, called *caporales*. The *caporal* was in charge of the herders, and had to see that the sheep were provided proper quarters in the different seasons. He furnished the sheep camps with provisions, and it was his duty to make sure that water was available for the *partidas* under the care of each herder. A *partida* usually consisted of a thousand head of sheep. The *caporales* worked under the *mayordomo*, or directly under the *patrón* if no manager were employed.

I can remember my paternal grandfather's sheep camps and the men who worked for him. They were loyal people, and as close to us as our own family. They were, every one of them, grandfather's *compadres*, for he and grandmother had stood as sponsors in baptism or marriage to many of their children.

Lambing season was a trying one, since the range was extensive. This happened in the early spring, and the weather on the Llano can be as changeable as the colors of the rainbow. If the season was rainy, it went hard with the sheep and many lambs were lost. If there had been a dry spell the year before, the ewes came out poorly and it was difficult for the mothers bringing in young lambs. Sheep raising was always a gamble until the day when feed became plentiful with the change in transportation facilities.

In order to save ewes and lambs during a cold spell, the herders built fires around the herds. The fires were kept burning day and night until better weather came to the rescue. Quite often the *patrones* and their sons, who might have just come back from Eastern colleges, helped during lambing.

Shearing the sheep was done in the summer and there were professional shearers who went from camp to camp each year. This was a bright spot in the life of the herders, for then they had a touch of the outside world. Among the shearers and herders there were always musicians and poets, and I heard Papá tell of pleasant evenings spent singing and storytelling, and of *corridos* composed to relate events which had taken place. These poets and singers were like the troubadours of old. The *corridos* dealt with the life of the people in the communities and ranches; they told of unrequited love, of death, of tragedies and events such as one reads about in the newspapers today.

The sheepherder watched his flock by day, traveling many miles while the sheep grazed on the range. As his flock pastured, he sat on a rock or on his coat; he whittled some object or composed songs or poetry until it was time to move the flock to water or better pasture. Many of the *corridos* are an inheritance from the unlettered sheepherder. At night he moved his flock to camp, a solitary tent where he prepared his food and where he slept. If there were several camps close to each other, the herders gathered at one tent for companionship.

In winter the sheepherder's life was dreary. Coming into his old tent at night, he had to prepare for possible storms. The wood for his fire might be wet, and with scarcely any matches, perhaps only a flint stone to light it, his hands would be numb before he had any warmth. He might not even have wood, for in many parts of the Llano there is no wood, and cowchips had to serve as fuel.

He went to sleep early to the sound of the coyote's plaintive cry, wondering how many lambs the wolves or coyotes might carry away during the night. The early call of the turtle dove and the bleating of lambs were his daily alarm clock, and he arose to face another day of snow, rain, or wind. Yet he always took care of his sheep, and I have never known any mishap due to the carelessness of the herder. The *caporales* traveled on horseback from camp to camp in all kinds of weather to make sure that all was well with the herders and the flocks.

I knew an old man who worked for my maternal grandmother for many years. Often I accompanied my grandmother to the sheep camp on the Salado, and I always came back with a feeling of loneliness. Yet, at camp, the old man always seemed happy. If he was not at camp when we arrived, we found him by listening for his whistling or singing in the distance. When I think about the herders on the endless Llano, I know that they are the unsung heroes of an industry which was our livelihood for generations.

II. EL CUATE

2. The Night It Rained

W<small>E HAD JUST FINISHED BRANDING</small> at the Spear Bar Ranch. For a whole week we had been rounding up cattle and branding each bunch as they were brought in from the different pastures.

As we sat out on the patio of our ranch home, I watched Papá leaning back in his chair against the wall of the house. He always did that when he was happy. The coolness of the evening brought relief from the heat and dust in the noisy corrals during the day.

The hard dirt floor of the patio always had a certain coolness about it. Just a few nights before, the boys had been in the mood to renovate it. They brought a load of dirt, which we sprinkled with water and spread over with burlap sacks. We had such fun tramping it down. We made it a game by jumping on it until the soil was packed hard. This was repeated until we had a solid, even patio floor. Around it the boys built a supporting wall of rock filled in with mud

Our home was a rambling structure without plan. It was built of the red rock from the hills around us, put together with mud. The walls were two feet thick. Viewed from front, the house had an L shape, but from the back, it appeared as a continuous sequence of rooms.

We had pine floors in the front room and dining room and

the other rooms had hard-packed dirt floors. The *despensa* occupied a space of twelve hundred square feet. This room served as a storeroom, summer kitchen, and sleeping quarters when stray cowboys dropped in on a snowy or rainy night. The windows had wooden bars and so had the door.

The *cochera* adjacent to the *despensa* was a relic of the days of carriages and horses. When automobiles came into use, it became a garage, but we always called it the *cochera*. The front had two large doors which opened wide for the carriage to be brought out, and the hole for the carriage tongue always remained on the doors to remind us of horse and buggy days.

The roof on our house was also of hard-packed mud. Many years later, it boasted a tin roof. The dirt roof had been supported by thick rectangular *vigas,* or beams, which remained even after we had the tin roof.

All the rooms were spacious and our home had a feeling of hospitality. We had only the most necessary pieces of furniture. We had Papá's big desk in the front room and dozens of chairs with wide arms. Over the mantel of the corner fireplace, in the dining room, hung a large antique mirror. Grandmother's wedding trunk, brought over the Chihuahua Trail, stood against a wall. It was made of leather, trimmed with solid brass studs. We had no clothes closets, but there were plenty of trunks in every room. Mamá's wedding trunk, made of brass, tin and wood, was the shape of a coffer. Papá's trunk was very similar. We all had trunks.

The most necessary pieces of furniture were the beds. Of these, we had plenty, but many a night three of us slept in one bed, and if we were inconvenienced we were recompensed. Our sudden guests came from different *ranchos,* and they always had wonderful tales and news to relate.

TONIGHT we had no guests. We were a happy family enjoying the evening breeze with hopes for rain. The cowboys did not need chairs; they were stretched out on the ground with their hands clasped behind their heads as a protection from the hard dirt floor of the patio—a typical relaxation from the day's labors.

I can never remember when Papá was not humming a tune, unless his pipe was in his mouth. Tonight he was just looking up at the sky. As the clouds began to gather towards the east, he said, "We may have some rain before morning. Those are promising clouds. If rain does not come before the end of the month, we will not have grass for winter grazing. Our pastures are about burnt up."

From the time I was three years old—when I went out to the Llano for the first time—I began to understand that without rain our subsistence would be endangered. I never went to bed without praying for rain. I have never been inclined to ask for favors from heaven, but for rain, I always pleaded with every saint and the Blessed Mother. My friends in the city would be upset when rain spoiled a day's outing, but I always was glad to see it come. In the years of drought, Papá's blue eyes were sad, but when the rains poured down, his eyes danced like the stars in the heavens on a cloudless night. All of us were happy then. We could ask for the moon and he would bring it down.

Good years meant fat cattle and no losses, and that, we knew would bring more money. We had never been poor, because those who live from the land are never really poor, but at times Papá's cash on hand must have been pretty low.

If that ever happened, we did not know it. Money in our lives was not important; rain was important. We never counted our money; we counted the weeks and months between rains. I could always tell anyone exactly to the day and hour since the last rain, and I knew how many snowfalls we had in winter and how many rains in spring. We would remember an unusually wet year for a lifetime; we enjoyed recalling it during dry spells.

Rain for us made history. It brought to our minds days of plenty, of happiness and security, and in recalling past events, if they fell on rainy years, we never failed to stress that fact. The droughts were as impressed on our souls as the rains. When we spoke of the Armistice of World War I, we always said, "The drought of 1918 when the Armistice was signed."

We knew that the east wind brought rain, but if the winds persisted from other directions we knew we were doomed. The northwest wind brought summer showers.

From childhood, we were brought up to watch for signs of rain. In the New Year, we started studying the *Cabañuelas*. Each day of January, beginning with the first day, corresponded to each month of the year. Thus, the first of January indicated what kind of weather we would have during the first month. The second day told us the weather for February and the third for March. When we reached the thirteenth of January, we started again. This day would tell us the weather for December. After twenty-four days, we knew for sure whether the *Cabañuelas* would work for us or not. If the days representing the months backward and forward coincided, we could safely tell anyone whether to expect rain in April or in May. The *Cabañuelas* are an inheritance from our Spanish ancestors and are still observed in Spain and Latin America.

From the Indians we learned to observe the number of snowfalls of the season. If the first snow fell on the tenth of any month, there would be ten falls that year. If it fell on the twentieth, we would be more fortunate: there would be twenty snowfalls during the cold months.

We faithfully watched the moon for rain. During the rainy season, the moon had control of the time the rains would fall. April is the rainy month on the Llano, and if no rain fell by the end of April, those versed in astrology would tell us that we could still expect rain in May if the April moon was delayed. There were years when the moons came behind schedule.

Whether these signs worked or not, we believed in them thoroughly. To us, looking for rain, they meant hope, faith, and a trust in the Great Power that takes care of humanity.

Science has made great strides. Inventions are myriad. But no one has yet invented or discovered a method to bring rain when wanted or needed. As a child, prayer was the only solution

to the magic of rain. As I grew older and I began to read of the discoveries of science, I knew that someday the Llano would have rain at its bidding. On reaching middle age, I am still praying for rain.

My mind still holds memories of torrential rains. Papá would walk from room to room in the house watching the rain from every window and open door. I would follow like a shadow. My heart would flutter with joy to see Papá so radiant with happiness.

Often before the rain was over, we would be out on the patio. I would exclaim, "We are getting wet, Papá!" "No, no," he would say. He wanted to feel the rain, to know that it was really there. How important it was in our lives!

After the rain subsided, off came my shoes and I was out enjoying the wetness, the rivulets. The arroyo flood would be coming down like a mad roaring bull. Papá and I would stand entranced watching the angry red waters come down. The arroyo, usually dry and harmless, would come into its own defying all living things, enjoying a few hours of triumph. A normally dry arroyo is treacherous when it rains.

If the rain came at night, we were cheated of the pleasure of enjoying the sight. Yet there was a feeling of restfulness as we listened to the rain on the roof. The raindrops on the windows showed like pearls, and to us they were more valuable than the precious stones themselves.

A few rains and then sun, and the grass would be as tall as the bellies of the cows grazing upon it. And Papá was happy.

A storm on the Llano is beautiful. The lightning comes down like arrows of fire and buries itself on the ground. At the pealing of thunder, the bellowing of cattle fills the heart of the listeners with music. A feeling of gladness comes over one as the heavens open in downpour to bathe Mother Earth. Only those ever watching and waiting for rain can feel the rapture it brings.

Papá never saw the lightning. He was too busy watching for the raindrops.

On the Llano, although rains come seldom, the cowboy is always prepared with his yellow slicker tied on the back of the saddle, always hopeful and waiting for rain. The straps on the back of a saddle were put there to hold the rider's raincoat.

As we sat on the patio that evening, the wind suddenly changed and the odor of rain reached our nostrils.

El Cuate, the Twin, who was the ranch cook, spat out a wad of tobacco as he said, "I knew it would rain before the end of the month. The moon had all signs of rain when it started. The signs never fail."

We were always glad when El Cuate spat out his tobacco. We knew he was in the mood for storytelling. What stories he could tell! There were stories of buffalo hunts, Indian attacks, about Comanche trade, of rodeos and fiestas.

El Cuate was an old man, and he had a history behind him. He was a real western character reared on the Llano. To me, he seemed to have sprung from the earth. He was so much a part of the land of the Llanos that he might have just grown from the soil as the grass and the rocks and the hills.

Looks, he had none. He was short in stature, blind in one eye, with an aquiline nose and sensuous mouth guarded by a long tapering red mustache. His skin was tanned by the sun of the prairies and the wrinkles on it portrayed the endurance and hardships of his life. His hair was gray with signs of sandiness in it. His hands were rough and wrinkled, showing that his life had not been idle. He used his hands for talking as well as for working, so they were always in evidence; they were interesting hands.

My brother, Luis, rose from the ground and started to leave saying, "I am going to hit the hay. Today has been a day. I am too tired even to listen to you tonight, Cuate."

El Cuate laughingly answered, "You young fellows are soft, you can't take it. Take your Papá there, although he is still a young man, he and I have seen some tough times. Branding today is play. You should have been part of the rodeos I experienced."

I could never let an opportunity pass of hearing his adventures when he showed signs of talking.

Before he had time to take another chew of tobacco, I said, "Please tell us about life on the Llano, Cuate."

"*Pues,* señores," he started. This was the introductory phrase which always turned into a tale by El Cuate.

We knew we must make ourselves comfortable, for it might be months or years before he would be in a storytelling mood. Even Luis forgot he was tired and resumed his resting position.

Papá was a man of few words. The only time he became talkative was after a rain and then he would compete with El Cuate.

Tonight Papá was happy. The clouds were gathering in the east. This was a sure sign of rain before morning, so he made himself comfortable by leaning his chair against the wall. I knew then that he meant to stay up with us until the first raindrops came. Listening to El Cuate would help pass away the time.

I watched El Cuate take a chew of tobacco as I heard Papá start him off. "I believe it was in this spot or just where the east windmill stands that I was initiated into my first rodeo. I was fifteen years old and fresh from school."

"Yes, sir," replied El Cuate, reminiscing. "I remember that rodeo," and as if prompted, began a tale of a lifetime.

3. The Rodeo

"It was here on the Carrizito that we held the rodeo that year," El Cuate began. "It was in 1886 and we had had an unusually dry spring. We held the rodeo in July."

"Don Manuel Salcedo, (may he rest in peace), was the promoter of the rodeo. He was an aristocrat if there ever was one, and he was wealthy. His herds roamed from the Salado to the Llano Estacado, although by 1886 he was being pushed back by the XIT Syndicate which had moved in the year before.

"There were two rodeos during the year. One was held in early summer and the other just before the fall, unless it was a dry year, and then there would be only one. A rodeo, in those days truly meant a roundup, not a public exhibition.

"Señor Antonio Almanzar was the cook and I was his assistant, with Santiago Estrada as the chore boy. Señor Antonio, who was as stern as he was jovial, was Don Manuel's handyman and a better man he could not have picked; honesty and loyalty towards his *patrón* were his best qualities.

"I can still hear his voice. Before daybreak, we awakened to his cry:

"'Juan, Santiago, Felipe, it is almost daylight, and you lie there as if you were gentlemen of leisure! You have no consciences to warn you that you are stealing precious time from your *patrón*. Get up, and to your duties. Juan, get the *remuda*. Santiago, start the fire for the coffee. Felipe, roll up the beds and get the saddles ready.'

"After sleeping on the hard ground, you would think that we were glad to get up, but we liked our sleep as well as you youngsters do," he said to me and Luis, winking with his white eye and looking at Papá. Papá was not an early riser but his children and the cowboys were up at dawn.

El Cuate, smiling, continued, "Santiago was bold and he answered Señor Antonio, 'If you were not so conscientious, Don Manuel would not be swimming in wealth while we drink black bitter coffee and eat black bread.'

"Felipe just turned over and growled, but when Señor Antonio's voice sounded like thunder, weakly one by one, we got up and started the morning chores, rubbing our eyes as if that would help us see in the dark.

"Juan had been gone almost an hour for the *remuda,* the string of horses.

"We had few matches in those days, but we carried candles which we lighted by striking two flint stones with a piece of cured cloth between them. Santiago lighted a small candle beside his bed, put on his boots and he was dressed. He then lighted the sticks which Señor Antonio had been gathering all the while, and soon a big bonfire was crackling and lighting the surrounding sleepers, who like white specters were seen rising from their beds as if to the sound of an alarm clock.

"The morning was as still as death, with only the hobbling of the horses heard in the distance or an occasional howl of a coyote which to the human ear sounded like a whole pack. The sound of the coffee mill furnished the music to the late risers, and not until the smell of the boiling coffee from the black can on the coals reached their nostrils, did they jump up from their happy dreams to a long day—rounding up cattle for the annual rodeo.

"Before all the men were around the breakfast circle, Juan's whistling was heard as he was approaching with the horses. *Yip! Yip!* went out from the cowboys, meaning 'Good morning and thanks for letting us sleep that extra hour.' Our breakfast was of beans, prunes, sourdough bread, jerky or fresh meat, and black coffee.

"Every cattleman who owned a thousand head of cattle or more made up a rodeo with his hired hands and as many stray men as wanted to go along. A stray man was usually the hired hand of a small cattle owner, or he might be the owner himself.

"Every rodeo had a *mayordomo,* and for this one we had Don Andrés Garduño, Don Manuel Salcedo's head man. We all respected Don Andrés, a sturdy upright fellow, who knew how to give orders. When he gave them I always thought he should have been a general. I feared him more than I did Colonel Canby at Valverde during the Civil War."

El Cuate brushed away a tear as he continued:

"There were many fearless men in those days. They had to be or they would not have followed the rodeos.

"Don Andrés always mounted his horse when he gave orders, and as he started to give the command that day, he half leaned on the saddle:

"'Manuel García and Teles Urbán, follow the trail to Paloma; Andrés Guzmán and Juan Arellano, round up the cattle on the Laguna Colorada; Felipe Tafoya and Carmen Sierra, follow the old trail into San Lorenzo; Felipe Mora and Juan Peralta, your journey will be towards the Mesa Rica; Narciso Paez, Juanito Trujillo, and Rafael Baca, scour the Monte de Pajarito for cattle; Fidel Tapia and Mauricio Lucero, will go to Don Tomás Cabeza de Baca's sheep camp and tell Señor Ramón, the *caporal,* to send me five fat lambs. Ride until you find the sheep, for we must feed our men well or their *patrones* will take me for a miser.'

"As the men on horseback took to different directions, Señor Antonio and I watched them until the last man disappeared over the horizon. It was our job to feed the men, so back we went to our camp. Santiago had been cleaning beans by the campfire and we were always glad to see daylight for that meant fewer pebbles in our beans. As he cleaned the beans, he kept up a weird monotonous song until Señor Antonio, out of patience, called to him in rather strong language, 'Santiago, change your tune or I shall be singing it myself.'

"Santiago was a good worker, but he was born to try men's patience. He seldom changed expression, so we never knew when he was serious or when he was trying to mortify us. He changed the tune of his song but he started another one so mournful that he drove me to desperation. To pass away the time, the cowboys would come to terms only by selling what annoyed their companions. I had to do something to stop Santiago's mournful tune, so I said, 'Sell me your tune and remember after it is paid for, it belongs to me and you cannot use it without my permission.' Santiago thought for a moment, then he replied, 'I'll sell it to you for that new quirt that you brought from Revuelto.'

"The quirt was a priceless possession, but I had to respond to the challenge so I said, 'The quirt is yours and the tune is mine.' While we waited for the return of the *vaqueros,* the cowboys, with the herds, we had to keep up our spirits with jokes and songs or tales.

"At the first sound of the *Yip! Yip!* I put wood into the fire to start the coffee boiling in the same black can which I had used at so many rodeos.

"It was toward midafternoon before all the men returned to camp with hundreds of cattle to be branded. The quiet air of the camp was soon broken by the bawling of cattle and the country became a Sodom of noise and dust from all directions with the *vaqueros* yelling and the cattle tramping.

"The men who remained at camp had eaten their noon meal. They saddled their horses and started out to meet the approaching herds in order to relieve these *vaqueros* who were bringing in the cattle.

"I can still see each man as he galloped into camp, sweaty and dusty. Santiago, our mascot, had the chore of unsaddling sweaty horses as the men dismounted. We watered the horses and then he turned them over to the *caballerango* in charge of them.

"The men were always hungry and I felt great pride because they praised my cooking.

"While the men were eating, the branding irons were being heated to start the marking of cattle.

"Herd after herd approached the camp, until we had about a thousand head of cattle. I saw rodeos where two and three thousand head were gathered for one day's branding. Sí señores, there was almost one cow to each blade of grass in those days." (This, of course, entitled El Cuate to a fresh chew of tobacco.)

"When all was ready, Don Andrés mounted his cutting horse and, with four of his best hands, started separating the cattle with Don Manuel's brand."

"The cutting horse was swift and had plenty of sense, and when its rider spied a cow with his brand, the horse knew which cow or steer he had to follow, and he would plunge after the ani-

mal, driving it out of its herd and into the day herd with a quick rush. The cattle which had to be branded were separated, as I said, and this bunch was called the day herd.

"We had no corrals in those days, but the men on horseback made the enclosure which held the cattle together and, believe me, those longhorns were vicious-looking animals. But since they were used to being rounded up, they were no trouble, unless there were stampedes.

"I remember rodeos when it took days and days to round up the cattle. But by 1886, rodeos had taken smaller proportions as there was less territory to cover. In my youth, the rodeo boundaries were the sierras to the north, the Texas line to the east, what is now Roswell on the south and the Manzano mountains on the west.

"On that first day of the Carrizito rodeo, we only branded one hundred head of heifers and steers with Don Manuel's brand.

"The cowboys all were expert riders and ropers, but we had professionals. Teles Urbán and Carmen Sierra never missed an animal from the first throw of the lasso, and in every rodeo in which they took part they were the roping hands.

"The branding was no different from what you did today, only it seems to me that the men were more hardened and fearless than you boys.

"It seems only yesterday that we were branding, and that I saw Carmen Sierra ride through the herd, throw the rope over the calves' heads or hind feet and drag them toward the branding irons where the ground crew waited. There was Tito Lucero, ready to grab the calf and he threw the animal down. In the wink of an eye, Laureano García had taken hold of it by the front, grabbed the foreleg, and pinned the neck down with his knee while Juan Arellano (in a sitting posture) pulled the hind leg towards him—and the animal was ready for the brand and other operations. The boys on the ground crew knew whose calf it was, and the roper always announced whose brand the calf's mother bore, so there were no mistakes.

"There were professional branders like your Papá is today. He always followed the branding iron—but that's education for you, for those who could not read might have put the letters upside down.

"The burning hot iron was put on the proper place and the brand imprinted. Another man did the earmarking and another the castrating. The only difference from today is that in order to get through with the many herds, more men did the different chores which a small crew performs now.

"Cattle with various brands roamed all over the unfenced Llano, and the cowboys from each outfit were constantly on the watch for their stock as they rode the range all through the year. The spaciousness of the land did not permit them to know exactly how many head of each brand grazed on the plains, but the rodeos brought many surprises.

"The evening meal was the social affair of the day. Señor Antonio and I were very popular with the boys—they called us mamá, sweetheart, or honey. We fed not only the rodeo outfit, but many of the cattle owners who dropped in for meals if the rodeo grounds were within riding distance to their ranches.

"Besides the lambs which we got from nearby camps, we also butchered one or two mavericks, calves which had escaped the branding iron the previous year and belonged to the first cowboy who caught them and put his brand on them. Señor Antonio and I always picked the fattest ones to feed our men and it took a lot for a bunch of cowboys. Their work was hard and the hours were long between meals.

"After supper the boys not on night duty would gather around the campfires and sing ballads and *corridos*. Juan Arellano was a good singer, but there were many others, and we had poets, too. Our poet and storyteller on that rodeo was Fidel Tapia, and he certainly had imagination and good memory. His father and I had been *Comancheros*—Indian "traders"—and buffalo hunters together. As the darkness fell upon us, the music from the different groups around the campfire came softly, bringing cheer to the men tired from the day's labors.

"The first night, the men retired early and before the last embers died the boys were resting on their hard beds on the ground. Each man used his saddle for a pillow, wrapped himself with a blanket and took chances on lying on safe soil for the night.

"The bellowing of cattle, the bawling of calves, the sounds of hoofs stirring up dust, and the hobbling of horses were the nightly lullabies which brought sound sleep to us, for we were accustomed to it.

"The herds had to be guarded at night because it had taken almost the whole day to round up the cattle and all of them had not been separated.

"There were four shifts, with two or three men to the shift. Each shift was called a *cuarto*. The first shift was the coveted one and it usually went to the foreman's favorites, but the cowboys were good sports and, although they grumbled, they took it like men. Yet in the old days before 1886, there were even killings on account of the shifts. Nowadays the men, like the cattle, have become more tame. I felt sorry for the boys, for they had chosen a hard vocation and it was their cross to bear.

"The cattle bedded down at night and the night riders rode around and around the herd whistling or singing. The music kept the cattle aware of the riders and prevented stampedes.

"I MUST tell you about the stampedes. They were terrible. They could be started by a sudden peal of thunder, a large dry weed blown towards the herd, a coyote's yelp, or often a cause unknown.

"The cattle would dash together, as if driven, and run as fast as their hoofs could carry them. Woe to the man caught in their path! If his horse stumbled or if he were thrown from his seat, it was sure death.

"The stampede which remains vivid in my memory happened in 1880, just as we reached Plaza Larga with the rodeo.

"By the time we had finished supper and the first shift started, the sky had clouded and we knew the storm would reach our camp before morning. Flashes of lightning were visible even while we were eating. We knew we were in for a good soaking, but what worried the boys was the possibility of a stampede.

"There would be no sleep that night and all the boys had to be on hand if needed.

"The clouds moved faster and faster, and with them came flashes of lightning and heavy thunder. The lightning which struck in every direction made the cattle restless and the boys were on the alert.

"The storm reached its peak and down came the rain in heavy sheets. The whole camp was in confusion and all at once lightning struck close to the herd. The stampede started. The boys tried to head it off, but the wind was against them. They had to be careful that they would not be knocked down. The lightning flashes made everything visible, but just as quickly the darkness seemed more intense.

"The boys kept whistling and singing but the cattle paid no heed. They were on the run. The boys were all trying to hold them down at the risk of their lives; they whistled; they rode hard—but the cattle were beyond control.

"Señor Antonio and I had stayed in the wagon and all we could do was pray, for hardened as we were, we remembered God and we prayed. We knew there might not be one of the men left if the cattle struck their paths. In a stampede the cattle stay together; they become blinded as they run. And the cattle that night were not only blind, they were mad.

"I do not know how many miles the cattle had traveled, but at dawn, one by one the boys came back to camp exhausted. The rain had stopped and the cattle were under control, and although not a man was hurt, they were a sorry bunch. The cattle had to be guarded, so there was little rest for any of them.

"During the day's work, the *vaqueros* changed mounts as

many as four times because their riding was hard. The cowmen held a high regard for their horses and would not exhaust them by riding them too long.

"There was always a *caballerango,* and for this rodeo Gabriel Anaya had the job. His duties were to drive the horses to the improvised corral which was enclosed by *reatas,* ropes. The horses were well trained, and it was seldom, if ever, that a horse tried to jump over the rope.

"Rafael Sánchez and Polo López had charge of the horses and when new mounts were wanted they roped the horses and the owner stood ready with the bridle in hand to put it on his horse. Each *vaquero* rode the horses which he claimed as his own and he usually had from seven to ten for *remuda,* change of mount. He may not have owned one, but a horse was as much a part of him as the pistol and holster which he never took off; his favorite was the cutting horse and his next best was his night horse.

"In order to have breakfast ready early, we had to start it the night before, so we buried a pot of beans and put our meat to barbecue. In the morning, we set Dutch ovens to heat while we made the dough for bread and started the coffee. We always had black coffee, as Santiago had remarked that morning.

"Some Easterner coming to New Mexico for the first time observed, 'In New Mexico there are more rivers and less water, and more cows and less milk than in any other country,' and he was right. We raise cows for beef; we cannot starve the calves in order to drink the milk.

"Before going to bed, I banked the fire and I hardly had gone to sleep when Señor Antonio's usual morning greeting started.

"THE second day of the rodeo followed the same pattern as the first. Señor Antonio made his daily speech and the men under him swore at him with greater strength, only to do his bidding in the same humble way once they had their boots on.

"A few of the men went out to scour the country for any stray cattle, but the other men kept on with the branding as we did not finish that day or the next. It took a whole week to brand all the calves.

"That evening as we listened to the guitars and to the discussions of the men, Don Andrés turned to the men and asked, 'Why did we have such few calves to brand for Don Manuel today? I thought we sighted a large bunch of cows with his brand on the Mesa Rica as we came along two days ago.'

"Juan Arellano replied, 'We found the cows, *patrón,* but they were without calves; their udders were bursting with milk, so we know they had calves.'

" 'Thieves again,' murmured Don Andrés. 'We must look for tracks tomorrow and see if we cannot find the marauders.'

"He stood up and called, 'I want all of Don Manuel Salcedo's cowboys to come forward.'

"The word was passed on around the camp and all the men not on night duty stood before their *caporal.*

" 'Boys,' he said, 'Tomorrow you are not helping with the branding, you are going hunting for cattle rustlers. They cannot be very far and since unbranded calves are their loot, you cannot miss. All of you start at Mesa Rica, divide in pairs and follow all tracks leading to the four directions.'

" 'Be careful boys, I do not want any accidents, and do not shoot, unless it is in self-defense, for if the law is to be applied let it be done by the proper authorities.'

"Mauricio Sena came forward, 'I am to be *vigil,* on guard, at midnight, señor, could you send someone in my place?'

" 'I shall take your place as night rider tonight. Now all of you go and get your rest, for you must be on your way before daybreak.'

"A sad bunch were Don Andrés' men as they started on a mission, which all the cowboys knew might end in tragedy, and, as they left that morning, all the men wished them good luck and Godspeed.

"Six days elapsed and the men were ready to move camp to the Rio Colorado country. Many of the cowboys had gone ahead to announce the coming of the rodeo so that other men might join the outfit.

"The camp moved slowly, traveling about twenty miles each day, for remember there were no roads and the wagons moved with difficulty over the rough beargrass (yucca) country.

"The rodeo camp consisted of two wagons and about a hundred head of horses. The chuck wagon, which Señor Antonio and I drove, carried the food and the few cooking utensils. The hoodlum's wagon, which was driven by a flunky, carried the bedrolls, branding irons, ammunition and guns.

"When the men of each outfit finished branding its herds, they left the rodeo group and departed for their headquarters.

"The last night in each place was spent in bidding adieu to friends and making promises of meeting at a fiesta, *baile* (dance), or the next rodeo, so there was a great deal of merry-making to make up for the time when work put them to bed early.

"As I said before, there were plenty of musicians and singers to make the evening gay. The storytellers were always popular and when the men tired of music, they surrounded the story-telling group.

"Tales of buffalo hunts were very popular by those having followed the trail into the Ceja and the Llano. Usually the storytellers were old men who no longer rode the range but served as cooks, *caballerangos,* or guides.

"Señor Antonio soon called to the men, 'If we can make good time, tomorrow we can reach San Hilario in time for the evening preparation for the fiesta.' '*Sí* señores,' Alejo sighed. 'The lovely señoritas there are worth a day's hard ride.' 'To bed and let's dream about them,' chimed in several voices.

"Long before daybreak, Señor Antonio had the camp moving. We reached the Gallegos ranch by sunup and the men stopped there long enough to eat breakfast and to be joined by Don Jesús María's cowboys.

"To our surprise, we were met by four of Don Andrés' men who had left us four days before. One of the men had his arm in a sling, and his head bandaged.

"Señor Andrés came forward and asked, 'Did you catch up with the thieves?'

" 'Yes, sir,' answered Juan Arellano. 'We followed their trail into the Mesa Rica where we surprised them at their camp on the Venado Spring. It was a hard fight, for they were well prepared, but by strategy we caught every one of them. Manuel Quintana was slightly wounded. We would have taken the law in our hands and the thieves would be hanging by their necks, but we decided that they would suffer more if we tied them up and took them on to Puerto de Luna to be tried. Rafael and Juanito are taking care of them and the other boys are driving the calves, which they had not killed, back to their mothers.'

" 'Did you brand the calves?' asked Señor Andrés.

" 'Yes, we did, we stopped at San Lorenzo for help.'

"The caravan continued on its way, being joined by different outfits all along the way to San Hilario."

4. Fiesta at San Hilario

THE FIRST PEAL OF THUNDER made us aware of the approaching rain, but the storm was still thirty miles away.

El Cuate seemed not to have heard. He was far away in the days of Spanish fiestas and as the lightning brightened the *ambiente* around us, he continued with his tale:

"In San Hilario, they were expecting the rodeo. We had made good time and arrived there on Santiago's eve, and as the last bell was ringing for Vespers in the Chapel of San Hilario, our group reached the outskirts of the village.

"This chapel was built by Don Hilario Gonzáles, who had long since passed away. Don Hilario, in his day, ran more cattle on the Llano than we had gathered in our rodeo at Carrizito; his wagons traveling from the plains to Las Vegas were counted by the hundreds. May he rest in peace!

"In San Hilario on that day ruled another *patrón*, and I reckon there must have been at least twenty families there. The *patrón* with his sons and daughters, their children and the *empleados*, employees, with their families, made up the settlement, the latter being as much a part of the family as the children of the *patrón*.

"Every man, woman, and child in the village, as well as families from the surrounding plazas, had gathered in the church for Vesper service. Bonfires were burning around the church.

"The sound of singing reached our camp and the boys who were more devout, or those who had reached the age when salvation seemed important, joined the procession which was already forming.

"While Señor Antonio and I started the meal, the boys were making preparations for the *baile* which followed Vespers. We knew there would be few boys there to eat but it was a matter of habit to prepare food.

"On stacks of bedrolls, there were men getting haircuts and shaves, for we had boys who were pretty good barbers; some were shaving themselves beside the wagon and others had gone to get a dip in the village ditch. Clean shirts, socks and underwear came out of knapsacks and *pronto,* the men were ready for the ball.

"I was not too old to enjoy whirling the pretty señoritas, and in those days, as today on the ranches, no one ever got too old to dance.

"You should have seen your papá then. It was his first dance as well as his first rodeo." (Papá only smiled as he puffed hard on his pipe. He was more interested in the rain just then.)

"By eight o'clock, the dance hall was filled and the *baile* had started.

"First came the march in which everyone took part, husbands, wives, brothers and sisters, and some daring young fellows with their sweethearts danced together.

"The musicians with their violins, guitars and accordions were seated on a platform. Ramón Atencio, Francisco Anaya, Juan Romero, Agustín Sena and Manuel Ortega had come from San Lorenzo to play for the dance.

"After the march, the *bastonero,* the master of ceremonies, took charge, and only those whom he called could get a partner for the dances that followed. As a sign of courtesy to visitors, one of our men, Felipe Tafoya, was chosen as the *bastonero*. He was partial to your papá, and were the señoritas glad! For his first dance, your papá certainly danced like a professional.

"It was the custom, when anyone danced for the first time, to take the person and carry him in arms around the hall. This was called the *amarre*. Before he was allowed to go, someone close in friendship or relationship had to redeem him. This redemption was the *desempeño*. The *desempeño* usually was a promise of a dance at a fixed date. Juan María Quintana, your grandfather's *caporal,* came to your papá's rescue by promising a dance on San Lorenzo's day, the tenth of August, as we had hoped to reach San Lorenzo with the rodeo on that date.

"There were many beautiful señoritas at the dance and good dancers as well. The girls were well chaperoned and it was not easy for lovers to have much opportunity for love-making, yet they managed, and after one of these *bailes,* the families of many prospective grooms went in search of brides for their sons. It was still the custom for the parents to make matches, but American influence was becoming more and more evident as the years rolled on, and the young folks were more at liberty to choose their mates.

"The dance was a beautiful sight. The señoritas in voluminous skirts, tight waists and elegant jewelry, were swung around by the cowboys of two languages, in fancy boots, bright shirts and bandannas. The tiny feet of the women were lost in the fast rhythm of the polkas, schottisches, waltzes and varsovianas, and only the boots could be seen and heard.

"The boys from our camp and others who were joining the rodeo at this point, kept assembling for the merrymaking. They were greeted and welcomed by the men of the village as they came in, with the usual greeting of how are your parents and your family, or your *patrón,* heard with every new arrival. The ever-important questions of have you had much rain down your way and how was the calf crop this year, were asked of each one.

"As the dance continued, the conversation was kept up by the older men with an occasional drink. They discussed the weather, cattle bogged down in the creeks and water holes, cattle rustling, packs of wolves attacking the stock, marriages, deaths. Such were the stories exchanged by people hungry for outside social contact in those days of limited communication.

"During the dance those who had prestige with the *bastonero,* would choose the piece to their liking and soon the *músicos* were striking a polka or waltz and putting as much fervor in it as the dancers on the floor.

"As the musicians struck the first waltz, the audience looked around to see who had requested it. The first couple on the floor was the answer: Narciso Paez had Rosa Salcedo in his arms. Every eye was upon them. The couple seemed to have been made for each other and as they waltzed and waltzed, they seemed to be in a world all of their own, quite oblivious of the crowd around them.

"Doña María Inez de Salcedo drew her rebozo to her face as if to hide for her daughter the gaze of the crowd.

"Everyone for miles around the country, knew that Narciso and Rosa were in love with each other, but the match did not please Don Manuel Salcedo, only because Narciso's father was a poor man according to Don Manuel's way of reckoning wealth. The Paezes had less money, but better blood than the Salcedos.

"This has nothing to do with my story, but I cannot help but mention it, as I can never recall that rodeo without thinking of the tragedy which happened as we wound up in Revuelto in September.

"When the dance was over, one by one the boys came back to camp to rest from the long day's travel and a night of pleasure. I watched Narciso as he lay on his bed; he had that far away look which had seemed to accompany him since he became of a marriageable age.

"In those days, dances broke up at daylight for those who came long distances had to wait for daylight to travel home. It became a custom, even when people were remaining for the feast the following day.

"By ten o'clock next morning the bells were ringing to call the people to hear Mass in honor of Santiago, and every home was open to guests and prepared to feed anyone who would share its hospitality.

"Señor Antonio and I knew there was no use preparing a meal, so we joined the crowds in the village and partook of Don Juan Peña's hospitality, for there were no social lines drawn as to who should sit at the hosts' tables. Everyone was treated alike. The men were fed first; I do not know when the women ate.

"In the afternoon we had horse races, bronco riding, and the cock race.

"The boys saddled their most vicious horses and gave performances of their skill, for there were the señoritas, each watching to see how brave was the man of her heart. Often a cowboy lost his seat and landed on *tierra firme,* provoking a great deal of mirth.

"The cock race was the main event, because San Hilario and San Lorenzo were competing for the *corrida,* or run. This sport, like all sports, was colorful as well as cruel. Six live roosters had been buried head down in the ground midway between the two villages. The opposite teams, on horses trained for the game, were ready to start. A shot was fired to send off the cock racers. They dug their spurs into their horses and off they went. The leader of San Hilario contestants was off before the spectators had time to focus their eyes on him. The San Lorenzo contestants pursued him and at every quarter of a mile a *mampuesto,* or guard, was ready to take the *gallo* away from him. The successful rider with horse foaming at its mouth and covered with beady sweat, reached the plaza while the other contenders were struggling with the *mampuestos* all along the way. As I remember, the San Hilario team took four roosters and was declared winners.

"The excited people cheered and shouted. The men and even the women had large wagers on the *corrida,* and it was a long while before the enthusiasm broke down.

"After a night and day of merrymaking, we were ready to retire, but not a boy was fit to do any work on the morrow. The rodeo must continue and again next morning we listened to Señor Antonio's daily sermon.

"We spent ten days in San Hilario and then moved on to San Lorenzo. San Lorenzo had been the home of the López family. Don Francisco López had the most beautiful daughters I have ever seen. Those of my class could only look at them, but there were pretty girls in my class too, only we always like to touch forbidden objects to see if they are real. Don Francisco had long been dead and his family scattered throughout New Mexico, but in the village their influence still could be felt.

"This was to be your papá's dance of *desempeño* and Juan María Quintana was not one to be outdone. He had sent a messenger to Las Vegas to bring the best of musicians and they were there when we arrived in San Lorenzo, but your papá can tell you about that dance."

Papá did not show any interest, as he never discussed his love affairs or youthful sprees before his children.

THE first drops of rain began to be felt, so the audience quickly moved into the house, much to my chagrin. It might be years before El Cuate would be in the mood for storytelling again.

But no, El Cuate seemed to have his mind on the story which he had been telling, for as we sat in the house he remarked:

"Who would now believe that there had been gay and happy plazas on the Llano?"

I took advantage of his word, and to start him off again I asked, "What was the tragedy in Revuelto about which you spoke as you told about the *baile*?"

It was like winding a clock, and El Cuate started with greater interest.

"By September the rodeo reach Revuelto ready to wind up the season.

"We had made San Rafael, Saladito, Plaza Larga. Each of these had their chapels, but we missed the patron saints' feasts of San Rafael, Nuestro Padre Jesús, and Santo Niño. Nevertheless in each place the rodeo crowd was welcomed with a dance.

"The boys were retiring after the *baile*. I had been in bed for several hours, and although when I went to bed, I missed Narciso Paez' mount, I gave it no thought, for he had been at the dance early in the evening.

"The boys were whispering among themselves as they lay on their beds, but I thought they were telling about their conquests at the *baile*.

"In the morning before Señor Antonio's voice started, I heard galloping hoofs approaching. Tito Lucero came towards my bed. I could not see him, but I knew every boy by instinct. Because he dismounted, I knew something was not well, so I asked: 'What happened, Tito?' He and Narciso were inseparable. He could not talk, he only lay his head on my shoulder and wept. This relieved him and he spoke. 'Narciso is dead. He was shot by Don Manuel. He and Rosa were eloping.'

"I made some coffee as quickly as was possible over a campfire. The boys did not have to be awakened by Señor Antonio, for all had heard Tito's horse. Before the coffee boiled, they were getting the details from him.

"Felipe Tafoya, who was always strong tempered, cried, 'We shall lynch that old tyrant,' and he meant it. Señor Andrés came forward and said, 'Be careful boys, I know how you feel. We all loved Narciso but we cannot bring him back to life by revenge or any other means, and I know he would not have wanted any of you boys to stain your hands with blood. The law will take its course.'

" 'The rodeo is breaking up, and those of you who wish to pay respects to the Paez family can move to San Rafael.'

"The whole rodeo traveled to San Rafael; we were all there to bury our pal."

"What became of Rosa?" I asked.

El Cuate, brushing a tear, replied, "Don Manuel took her home and forbade her to leave the house, but the servants said that he need not have done that, because life for Rosa was buried in the San Rafael graveyard. On the south side of the chapel a cross marks Narciso's grave. The people there told that, after dark, a ghost appeared each year on the eve of San Rafael, while the merrymakers were reveling at the *baile*. Some said it was not a ghost, but Señorita Rosa who would ride from San Hilario to cry at her lover's grave. She and Narciso had danced together for this feast since they were children.

"Don Manuel was a broken man after that, but since he was a powerful man, only his daughter knew for sure who had murdered her lover."

5. Buffalo Hunters

THE RAIN KEPT COMING DOWN IN TORRENTS, as it often does on the Llano. We pray for rain and when it comes we get full value for our prayers; then we wish it would be portioned over a period of months instead of one night. But we are happy to see it come when it does.

Listening to El Cuate tell of early life on the Llano brought memories of my childhood and of stories which I had heard when I was so young that I already had forgotten. I remembered we had a dried buffalo hide on which Señor Ramón pounded the wool of our matresses each housecleaning season. I had grown up with the hide as a possession in our home, but what history it might have concealed had never bothered me. Tonight I became curious to learn about the buffaloes that once had roamed even where our ranch house stood.

El Cuate being so generous tonight, I knew we could stay up until Papá went to bed, and that would not happen until he had seen the last drop drained from the clouds.

"Cuate," I said, "You mentioned that you and Alejo Padilla had been *ciboleros*. Did you hunt for buffalo here on the Carrizito?"

"I cannot say that it happened right here, but often when we passed the Pajarito Creek, we saw some stragglers. We were always glad to sight them, for after the long trip from Las Vegas, which took several days, we were hungry for fresh meat. We never let one animal get away from us and we killed these stragglers to feed our caravans.

"The *cíbolos,* buffaloes, were migratory. In the spring they would graze north as far as the Canadian border and in the late summer and fall would wander south as far as the big bend of the Rio Grande where it dashes to its mouth on the Gulf of Mexico. In the latter part of October the herds, which numbered thousands and thousands, would be seen crossing the Canadian river, and in the vicinity of Los Barrancos Amarillos (Amarillo, Texas) the animals would tarry until the weather turned so cold that the blizzards drove them further south.

"After the harvest in the settlements along the Rio Grande and Pecos rivers were finished, the *ciboleros,* the buffalo hunters, started their march towards the Llano. Each village had a *cibolero* and a trained horse, or perhaps two, for the hunt. These horses were guarded with care and never used for any other purpose but the buffalo hunt.

"I do not remember the day of the *carretas,* but my father went to the *cíbolos* when only *carretas* were used for loading the meat. In my day, we had wagons which were pulled by oxen.

"Caravans of ten to thirty wagons were formed from the different villages; each wagon pulled by four or five yokes of oxen. It was a beautiful sight to see these processions on the march. There were burros and mules, and these belonged to the men who went along as *agregados,* assistants. Being poor, I went along as an *agregado.* Our job was to help skin the animals and to cut the meat into strips to make *tasajo,* jerky. We were too poor to organize a caravan of our own, so we were glad to be allowed to join as helpers and in that way secure meat for our families. Our share we loaded on our burros or mules to carry home.

"When the caravan was organized, one man was made *mayordomo* or *comandante,* and he had full control of the outfit. His word was law.

"We traveled very slowly, for the roads were bad and the oxen moved at a turtle's pace. It took about two weeks to make the trip from Las Vegas to Palo Duro Canyon and the Quitaque Country.

"As we traveled along, we met other caravans on the way, and when we reached the bluffs of the Llano Estacado, the Staked Plains, we were many companies. Some were already there and it became a small world, this big land of New Mexico.

"On reaching the buffalo country, the caravans pitched camp. The hunt would not start at midday, if we happened to reach the hunting grounds at that time. We made preparations by getting the horses and hunters ready. At daybreak the hunters from the different outfits gathered together, mounted their prancing steeds and off they went towards the herd. The hunters used no saddle, only a pad on the horse's back. This protected the rider from tangling in the stirrups if he fell off the horse. The hunters used lances five or six feet long made of the finest steel.

"The hunters formed a group before dashing into the herd, bowed their heads in prayer and invoked Santiago, the patron saint of Spain, to help them and guide them in the hunt. After making the sign of the cross, into the herd they rode, jabbing their lances inside the left ribs of choice fat animals, directly into the heart. A run, or *corrida,* usually would be three miles, during which each hunter killed from fifteen to twenty-five animals. This number was sufficient for one day, as they had to be skinned and the meat cut up for jerky. It was a full day's work, and I know, for when dusk came we were ready for rest. The *agregados* and the *carreros,* wagon drivers, followed the hunters into the herd to pick up the carcasses and bring them into camp. We had one man in each crew who was an expert in bleeding the animals, and he always was ahead of the crew."

"Why didn't you use guns for hunting, Cuate?" I asked.

"In the early days, the firearms of the Spaniard were of the musket type and they were not very effective. The early Spanish hunters learned from the Indian that the lance was the swiftest method, and being fond of excitement, they found that hunting with a lance was real sport and that it took much valor to pursue it.

"We enjoyed hunting the buffalo, and had not the *Americanos* come in with their guns, we might still be enjoying the sport, but it did not take them long with their rifles to clear the Llano of buffaloes.

"In the camps there was great activity—the meat had to be cared for quickly or it would spoil. The *agregados* cut the meat into strips. Some of the hides were cut into strips to be used as lines on which to hang the meat for drying. When the meat was dry, it was placed on the wagon beds and tramped down so that the wagon could be loaded to full capacity. It took four yokes of oxen to pull one of the heavy wagons. The fat was rendered into tallow to be used for cooking and for making candles.

"We had many uses for the hides. Some were made into *reatas,* ropes, and others were tanned with the hair left on them for robes or rugs.

I knew, then, the hide we used for pounding the mattress wool must have been a discarded robe or rug, but I did not interrupt El Cuate, for the story was becoming more and more fascinating.

He continued, "We plucked the wool from the buffaloes' shoulders and necks; this was used for filling mattresses and it also was spun into cloth.

"We remained in the buffalo country for a long time and when we were ready to leave, it was cold enough so that we could carry fresh meat in our wagons to supply our tables during cold weather.

"With wagons and pack animals loaded, we were a happy bunch of *ciboleros,* saying *adios, hasta el año venidero.* We headed west to our homes along the rivers and to our mountain habitations to spend a good winter well supplied with meat. We said, *hasta luego*—but there came a day when we did not return because the wonderful sport had vanished. We have only the tales to remind us of when the Llano belonged to the Indian and to the New Mexicans of Spanish descent. Ballads are still sung in the villages about the *cíbolos* and the *ciboleros,* but never again will the colorful processions be seen where the Hispanos and the Comanches met in friendly terms.

"I have heard you children sing the *corrido* about Manuel Maes. Manuel was one of the best buffalo hunters, for a young man, that I ever knew, but it was his fate to die while pursuing his beloved sport. It was in 1863 the tragedy occurred, and those of us who witnessed it shall never forget. Manuel was riding a horse which was not yet broken for the chase. As Maes went to thrust his lance into a buffalo cow, his horse shied from another buffalo and plunged towards the animal he was about to kill. The lance slipped from Manuel's hand, turning completely around with the butt end hitting against the buffalo he was aiming toward. The impact and the horse plunging toward the animal caused the lance to pierce Manuel's body. We were hunting where the city of Amarillo stands today. Manuel was buried there on the Llano, and today his grave remains unknown and unmarked, with perhaps a wheatfield waving over it.

"I have told you about the hunting of the buffalo, but I must not pass up telling you something about the animals.

"The animals were huge; they stood about six feet high and they had a ferocious look on their hairy faces. When we sighted a herd, they appeared like a black cloud in the distance.

"As a rule, the buffalo was a very stupid animal and not only men helped to destroy him, but, just as our cattle perished from droughts, prairie fires and snows, likewise the buffaloes died.

"The wolf was the buffalo's deadly enemy. The bulls were the protectors of the herd, but it did not take much to frighten them, and one would have cows and calves in one's power.

"Some of the horses were deathly afraid of the bulls, especially if they had experienced a stampede. A buffalo stampede was much more to be dreaded than one of cattle. I once saw a herd stampede over a cliff and every head was killed as they fell into a deep canyon. I was so impressed by the tragedy, that, for a day, I could not join the *agregados* in skinning the animals and getting my share of the meat.

"Sometimes we lingered on the Llano until winter, for the hides were worth more when they were covered thickly with hair. Hunting in winter was almost sure death for some of the hunters. The snows and winds on the Llano chill a man clear into his intestines. The Llano furnished no protection for man or beast. Alejo Padilla used to tell about a hunter who was lost in a snowstorm. They had been hunting all day when the storm set in. The hunter removed the entrails from a buffalo which he had killed. He crawled inside the carcass for protection and during the night the carcass froze solid, making the hunter a captive. Alejo and some of his companions went to search for him, and, luckily for him, they heard his cries. After much work they thawed out the carcass but the man himself had to be thawed out too. He fared pretty well, for considering the plight in which he had been, he only lost one arm and was forever more known as 'El Manco.'

"In the days of the buffalo, the lobos, the prairie wolves, followed the herds. Once in a while they killed a straggler, but mostly they lived on carrion, the dead buffaloes left by the hunters who killed the animals for the skins. After the buffaloes were exterminated, the lobos moved into the Ceja.

"They followed herds of sheep and looked for a chance to kill. A lobo was never contented unless he killed wholesale. A lobo would not start eating until it had killed and stripped from twenty-five to fifty head.

"About 1880, some cowboys from the S-T lassoed a lobo pup

on the Mesa Redonda. They put a bell on it and turned it loose. The sheepherders hearing the bell would think it was a *corta,* a stray bunch of sheep, and many a day they spent looking for sheep and sometimes sighted the lobo. The lobo traveled over the Llano country, he was now seen on Mesa Rica, on Luciano Mesa, or around the Alamogordo country. It was a menace to the herds, killing many sheep. The sheep were not afraid of it because of the bell—they were accustomed to the sound of bells on sheep. As the years rolled on, the lobo became a subject of superstition among the herders, and no one would dare kill it. Many heroic feats were attributed to the lobo with the bell over the Llano land. After about six years of roaming and killing, the animal was killed by Don Juan José Quintana on the Chirisco, and thus ended a cowboy prank created to scare the sheepherders and try to end the sheep industry in the feud between cattlemen and sheepmen.

"*Sí,* señores, those were the days. There were no cattle rustlers because meat was plentiful, but it took courage to face the dangers of the Llano."

6. Comancheros

WE ALL STAYED UP THAT NIGHT until the rain started to come down gently. We heard Carrizito Creek roaring like a mad bull, so we were sure that we had been blessed with a good downpour and we knew that when the downpour ceased and a gentle rain set in, we would have a two or three day drencher.

El Cuate told us he was tired, but promised to tell us about the Comanches on the morrow, for he was sure we would have to stay in the house. And, just as we thought, the next day was drizzly. The boys, with slickers on, went out as a matter of habit but soon returned to the family circle by the kitchen fire.

El Cuate started to reminisce about torrential and drizzly rains which he had experienced and somehow wandered to his Comanche tales:

"The Comanche Indians had been friendly with the *ciboleros* for more than a century. As we traveled into the Ceja and the Llano to hunt for buffalo, we carried with us bread, *panocha*—sprouted wheat pudding, whiskey, guns, cotton fabrics, beads, knives, and other articles. These we traded with our friends, the Comanches.

"The Comanches resented the moving of the Texans and other stockmen with their cattle into their land. Stealing cattle was the means of revenge which the Indians used against the cattle owners. The Comanches would meet us at our camps along the buffalo country. There we exchanged our goods for cattle and horses that the Indians had driven from the unfenced land of the cattle kings. We gained very little from the trade, as the Americans to whom we sold the cattle paid us low prices for them. It was merely getting rid of them for whatever we could get. The leading New Mexican *patrones,* who sent their wagons for the buffalo hunt, did not approve of our dealings with the Comanches. They looked upon us *Comancheros* as common cattle thieves.

"Our secret meeting places and dealings were unknown to those for whom we worked.

"Don Hilario Romero, who was sheriff of San Miguel county in the days of illicit trade, was instrumental in stopping a great deal of the Comanche traffic; he aided the *Tejanos,* the Texans, in recovering many of their cattle and at the same time kept them from driving stock that did not belong to them—for when they came to recover their cattle, they would drive every cow which was in their path.

"The *Americanos* around us were the real racketeers in the business. They did the buying from us, then they would drive the loot to Colorado, Kansas, Nebraska, or to California where they sold it at great profit. Very few of the stolen cattle ever were kept in New Mexico.

"I knew an American trader whose ranch was located at Aguilar, a settlement between Chaperito and Antonchico. He did a big business with the *Comancheros.* The cattle owners, from over the line, found out about him and soon were on his trail. He was always alert to strangers seen in his pasture, and this was lucky for him, for when he got wind of being trailed, he took to the hills and kept in hiding in Chupaina Mesa. The *Tejanos* recovered about fifteen hundred head of cattle with their brands but not without a fight. The cowboys hired by the *Americano* brought out their guns and there was real war. The *Tejanos* were victorious and besides recovering their cattle, they took one of the cowboys of the *Americano* and lynched him. They left him hanging from a pine tree close to the house.

"In trading with the Comanches, we rounded up the cattle at night by the light of the moon and we drove them on a fast run. We made thirty miles by daylight. We left the bulls, weak cows and calves behind, as they could not keep up with the herd. A party of Comanche Indians would stay behind to fight and hold the *Tejanos* back in case of pursuit.

"The American Government kept on the trail of the Comanches, but often the officers who were sent out to stop the illicit trade found it profitable to engage in it themselves and thus delayed the end of it for several years.

"By 1876 the trade began to wane, and the Comanches, who were finally rounded up by the military government, were put on reservations. So ended a colorful business which remains only as a happy memory of our meeting with our friends the Comanches in Palo Duro Canyon, Canyon de Tule, Tierra Blanca, Río de Las Lenguas, and the Valle de Lágrimas.

"AFTER the Indians no longer roamed the Llano and the Comanche trade died out, I went to work for John Chisum, a big cattle owner in the lower Pecos valley. I made trips to Bosque Redondo, where the Navajos had been put on a reservation, to deliver meat to the government for my *patrón*. There I served as interpreter between the American officers and the Indians. Juan Anaya, father of Chee Dodge, spoke Navajo and Spanish. I spoke English and Spanish. Juan Anaya, who was of Hispano extraction, had been captured by the Navajos when he was a child and he grew up among them as one of the tribe. His son, Chee Dodge, a great man among his people, became well known and highly respected for his wisdom. Juan Anaya, in his time, was also a great leader.

"Gradually the buffalo disappeared, and on the Llano land the grass grew without disturbance. The Indians no longer roamed the country to endanger the lives of those who saw promise for good grazing on the Comanche domain. Cattle companies began to push forward and the New Mexican sheepman and small cattleman, who was usually a lone owner, could not hold out against the powerful syndicates. The war was on between two contenders, neither of whom had a deed to the land.

"The early livestock man had not needed fences, but the incoming cattle companies started building them. The New Mexicans were ready to fight for the land which traditionally had been theirs, and out of this grew up an organization of influential New Mexicans for protection against the usurpers. These citizens banded together and, by cutting down a few fences, discouraged fence building by those who had no titles for the land. Perhaps the building of fences had not been the main reason for the New Mexicans becoming irate. The cowboys of the cattle companies drove and killed sheep right and left, whipped the sheepherders and made plenty of trouble in other ways.

"Your grandfather, who was then running sheep in the Plaza Larga country, brought to trial a bunch of cowboys who had killed several hundred of his sheep. The cowboys were prosecuted, but the country was too vast for all the sheepmen to catch up with the marauders."

III. PLACES & PEOPLE

7. Chapels on the Llano

As a child, I lived with my paternal grandparents on their hacienda across the Gallinas river from the village of La Liendre, eighteen miles southeast of Las Vegas. This, our ancestral home, was the stopping place for all who made trips into the Ceja and the Llano to oversee their large sheep and cattle holdings. In this environment, the history of the country was imprinted on my mind from early childhood.

My grandfather, Don Tomás Cabeza de Baca, with the help of the Chaperito and La Liendre villagers and his *empleados,* financed the building of a toll road over Vega Hill into Las Vegas in the early 1870's. The climb over this hill had been a treacherous one for travelers. Las Vegas was the trading center for all the country from West Texas, Puerto de Luna and Fort Sumner to the lower Pecos territory. The wagons were a continuous caravan over this road, and it was a good day when they could travel over a graded hill, although it was still a pretty steep ascent. The road was kept up by one man who lived at the foot of the climb and who collected the toll fee of twenty-five cents for each vehicle.

No better-known character than Señor Mariano Urioste will be remembered as the tollkeeper. This lonely soul could tell more stories of Indian raids, cattle thieves, and buffalo hunts than any other man of his time. Every wagon had to rest its horses or mules before starting the hard climb, and Señor Mariano was happy to play host to all the travelers. In his tiny hut, in the open fireplace, was an everlasting pot of boiling coffee.

Each traveler, Señor Mariano would make welcome by saying, "Come my children, drink a cup of coffee, merely the boiled grounds, but my heart goes with it. I can do without it, but you are traveling." The voyager would, naturally, accept the hospitality offered him, and in return would give him coffee and other provisions. Señor Mariano always had a full larder. No traveler ever left without hearing who had gone ahead and what stories had been picked up by Señor Mariano. He was the radio and newspaper from the 1880's until as late as 1912, when the state started road building and the traffic was routed over Cañon del Agua Hill.

Our home at La Liendre was a modern two-story structure. Every room had a fireplace with ornate black moulding. The house was built on a hill and below it were the orchard, the well which supplied us with domestic water, a large cottonwood and poplar park, with the Gallinas river running close by. The village was across the river and most of the men worked for grandfather on the farm and others were on the Ceja with the sheep and cattle.

One of the most pleasant memories I have is of the ruins of the old house which my grandparents had occupied when they first moved to La Liendre from Las Vegas in 1870. It was similar to the ones built by the *ricos* in Santa Fe, Las Vegas and other towns in earlier days.

The people who traveled into the Ceja and Llano and who stopped with us on their way to their ranches or to the plazas, had lived in homes similar to ours, the old and the new, but their homes on the Llano were different.

The towns on the Llano were small, with the families of the *patrón* and his *empleados* making up the scattered settlements. The homes were not like the ones which they left behind; they were simple rock or adobe structures, because materials which were not native to the country had to be hauled from Las Vegas over rough mountain roads or trails—distances varying from fifty to two hundred miles. The chapels were not imposing edifices. They were unpretentious in architecture, built of the best materials available. The women dug deep into their trunks and chests to bring out laces, silk, gold and silver to adorn the interiors. From their ancestral homes, on the lower and upper Rio Grande and on the Pecos river, the colonists brought their favorite *santos*. These *santos,* religious statues and paintings, may have seen their origin in Spain, Mexico, or in the northern New Mexico villages—where local *santeros* may have been the artisans. These families who settled on the Llano were not of the poor classes; they were of the landed gentry, in whose veins ran the noble blood of ancestors who left the mother country, Spain, for the New World. The solid gold or silver chalices, the ornate satin vestments for the priests, and the handmade or hand-painted *santos* were the gifts of the *patrón* and his family to their place of worship.

To the New Mexican of Spanish origin, his religion is his whole being. Everything is entrusted to God, with a faith so sincere and deep-rooted that it is hardly comprehensible to those not of the faith. The chapels were prepared with pomp for the coming of the priest. Each chapel or place of worship had a *mayordomo* for the year. Later it became customary to have two families as *mayordomos,* and the custom still persists in the smaller communities. These *mayordomos* were responsible for keeping up the chapel, but for the coming of the priest, everyone joined in whitewashing the inside walls, in plastering the outside, in cleaning the yard, and in decorating the altar. The priest came to say Mass as often as the roads and time permitted—once a year, twice a year. San Miguel, Chaperito, Antonchico, Puerto de Luna in New Mexico and Trinidad in Colorado, the seats of the parishes, were many miles on horseback from the chapels on the Llano under their jurisdiction. Quite often, Mass was said in a room prepared for the occasion, for not every settlement had a chapel.

I can still remember, just after the coming of the railroad over the plains (1905), going many miles to hear Mass in private chapels of the *ricos*. It had never been my privilege to own a silk dress, and to see girls my age dressed in satins and taffetas, seemed like the fairly tales of princesses which I had read. Everyone was attired more elegantly than anyone I had ever seen in Las Vegas. It was truly a great event. Some of the families came one or two days before the priest's arrival, and all who came were the guests of the *patrón* and his family.

Before the Mass started and while the priest heard confessions, the people gathered outside the church and exchanged news which concerned their daily lives. Rain was always a popular subject and I cannot remember a time when ranchers did not discuss how dry or wet the season was at the time of their meeting.

The priest performed marriages, baptisms, and blessed religious objects. When Mass was over, then came the feast, and a feast it was, for each *patrón* would not let it be said that he was not a generous host. Food was plentiful and it would have been an insult to the host's hospitality for anyone to leave without partaking of his fare.

No fiesta of today can compare with the one when the priest

came to say his annual, quarterly and—later—monthly Mass. In the early days on the Llano, there were families who traveled two or more days by wagon or carriage covering from fifty to one hundred miles to their nearest place of worship.

Messages announcing the Mass, which might have been the celebration of the patron saint's feast, were sent by the *patrón* to the surrounding ranches and villages. Men on horseback were the bearers of the news, because for many years, Las Vegas was the only post office serving the Llano for hundreds of miles. Later, in the '70's, mail could be received at Liberty, a wild West town which disappeared after the coming of the railroad. It was not a town in the true sense of the word, but with its one store, several saloons and a few scattered houses, it served as a gathering point for news, if the families on the Llano cared to have mail addressed to them there. Liberty stood about five miles from the present site of Tucumcari. Mail was so uncertain that if something of great urgency had to be transacted, a man on horseback served the purpose better. He changed mounts at different ranches and picked up his own on the return trip.

Perhaps no other influence was as instrumental in the preservation of the faith as was the Order of Brothers of Our Father Jesus of Nazareth, commonly called "Penitentes." This society is believed to have come from the Third Order of Saint Francis of Assisi, called the Order of Penance by the Saint. Whatever its origin, it certainly has held an important part in the religion of the New Mexican people of Spanish extraction, who, as late as 1850 were being served from Durango, Mexico. At that time there were only ten priests administering the vast territory. It is evident that something must have held the people to the faith and in studying Penitente rules as written in their constitution, one cannot help but feel that the order had a hand in preserving religious rites when priests were scarce. These Brothers spread throughout New Mexico and their influence on the Llano settlers cannot be ignored, for they were far from the parish seats, yet the Catholic religion retained its strength.

Under the articles of incorporation of the Society, they are organized to protect their order from ignorance, prejudice and persecution. The aims of the Society are: To obey Our Lord Jesus Christ; to profess, practice and spread the Roman Catholic faith under the guidance of the Pope, the local bishop and the pastors; to form a religious society that can own property, sue and be sued against; to resist defamation by word of mouth and in writing.

The preamble states that their constitution is intended to promote justice, peace, union and assistance to members. The first seven articles comment on the last words of Jesus on the Cross. They are members of the Mystical Body of Christ; they must ever be disposed to forgive their enemies; Mary is their Mother; prayer should be their support in time of affliction; they must thirst for justice and charity; envy, hatred and ill will must give place to justice and charity; they shall all be united in the charity of Christ.

If the organization has deteriorated in some of its phases, it is because cunning politicians have tried to use its strength for their personal gain. The true, simple Christian faith is still evident and one who participates with them in their nonsecret rites, cannot but feel inspired by the strong reverence which they have for their religion.

There has been a transition in their practices and this has been due to outside influences. Nevertheless, it is a fact that the strong adherents of the order have been responsible for law and order and the spiritual well-being in isolated, remote areas.

As I recall, some of the people who were guests at our home were trying hard to hold the land on which had grazed their sheep and cattle, but they were losing it fast to the homesteaders. Before my day, the large cattle companies had pushed them in and only a few were left over the Texas line.

Those who had large herds of cattle and sheep in the '70's and '80's had helped many a family in the Ceja and Llano to build up their flocks and herds through the *partido* contract.

Many of the smaller ranchers who lived along the Río Colorado and in Oldham County, Texas, had been *partidarios* of the López and Gonzáles families. *Partidarios* were ranchers who took either cattle or sheep on the shares. The customary deal was to take a certain number of animals of certain ages and at the end of five years return double the number of stock of the same ages as those taken on the shares.

I remember clearly my grandfather's *partidarios*. As security, the *partidario* had a responsible person sign the contract with him and the stock was always a part of the security.

Later—in my day—my father had *partidarios,* but it was a different system. In place of returning double the stock at the end of five years, the stock was taken for any number of years agreed by the parties. The *partidario* paid the owner each year twenty percent in calf crop of the number of cattle taken on the shares. This is not correctly called *partido,* or share, but it has never changed nomenclature, a holdover from the early system.

Until a few years ago, the few cattle which I had were held on the twenty percent basis, first by my brother-in-law, Albert Branch, later by my brother, Luis.

Before the coming of the large herds from Texas and other eastern points, and prior to 1880, sizable fortunes were made by the Hispanos on the Ceja and the Llano by taking sheep and cattle on *partido* contracts. The range, then, was free; grass and water were plentiful and the stock raisers had all the land they needed or desired for grazing.

There was abundant living on the Ceja and Llano from 1870 to the beginning of the twentieth century. The calves, lambs, wool, hides and pelts were brought to Las Vegas to exchange for food, clothing, household equipment and money. Over the Vega Hill came the wagonloads of produce from the ranches below the mountains and happy men returned to their families with their wagons loaded with their barter.

THE women on the Llano and Ceja played a great part in the history of the land. It was a difficult life for a woman, but she had made her choice when in the marriage ceremony she had promised to obey and to follow her husband. It may not have been her choice, since parents may have decided for her. It was the Spanish custom to make matches for the children. Whether through choice or tradition, the women had to be a hardy lot in order to survive the long trips by wagon or carriage and the separation from their families, if their families were not among those who were settling on the Llano.

The women had to be versed in the curative powers of plants and in midwifery, for there were no doctors within a radius of two hundred miles or more.

The knowledge of plant medicine is an inheritance from the Moors and brought to New Mexico by the first Spanish colonizers. From childhood, we are taught the names of herbs, weeds and plants that have curative potency; even today when we have doctors at our immediate call, we still have great faith in plant medicine. Certainly this knowledge of home remedies was a source of comfort to the women who went out to the Llano, yet their faith in God helped more than anything in the survival.

Every village had its *curandera* or *médica* and the ranchers rode many miles to bring the medicine woman or the midwife from a distant village or neighboring ranch.

Quite often, the wife of the *patrón* was well versed in plant medicine. I know that my grandmother, Doña Estéfana Delgado de Baca, although not given the name of *médica,* because it was not considered proper in her social class, was called every day by some family in the village, or by their *empleados,* to treat a child or some other person in the family. In the fall of the year, she went out to the hills and valleys to gather her supply of healing herbs. When she went to live in La Liendre, there were terrible outbreaks of smallpox and she had difficulty convincing the villagers that vaccination was a solution. Not until she had a godchild in every family was she able to control the dreaded disease. In Spanish tradition, a godmother takes the responsibility of a real mother, and in that way grandmother conquered many superstitions which the people had. At least she had the power to decide what should be done for her godchildren.

From El Paso, Texas, she secured vaccines from her cousin, Doctor Samaniego. She vaccinated her children, grandchildren and godchildren against the disease. She vaccinated me when I was three years old and the vaccination has passed many doctors' inspections.

As did my grandmother, so all the wives of the *patrones* held a very important place in the villages and ranches on the Llano. The *patrón* ruled the *rancho,* but his wife looked after the spiritual and physical welfare of the *empleados* and their families. She was the first one called when there was death, illness, misfortune or good tidings in a family. She was a great social force in the community—more so than her husband. She held the purse strings, and thus she was able to do as she pleased in her charitable enterprises and to help those who might seek her assistance.

There may have been class distinction in the larger towns, but the families on the Llano had none; the *empleados* and their families were as much a part of the family of the *patrón* as his own children. It was a very democratic way of life.

The women in these isolated areas had to be resourceful in every way. They were their own doctors, dressmakers, tailors and advisers.

The settlements were far apart and New Mexico was a poor

territory trying to adapt itself to a new rule. The Llano people had no opportunity for public schools, before statehood, but there were men and women who held classes for the children of the *patrones* in private homes. They taught reading in Spanish and sometimes in English. Those who had means sent their children to school in Las Vegas, Santa Fe, or Eastern states. If no teachers were available, the mothers taught their own children to read and many of the wealthy ranchers had private teachers for their children until they were old enough to go away to boarding schools.

Doña Luisa Gallegos de Baca, who herself had been educated in a convent in the Middle West, served as teacher to many of the children on the Llano territory.

Without the guidance and comfort of the wives and mothers, life on the Llano would have been unbearable, and a great debt is owed to the brave, pioneer women who ventured into the cruel life of the plains, far from contact with the outside world. Most of them have gone to their eternal rest and God must have saved a very special place for them to recompense them for their contribution to colonization and religion in an almost savage country.

The few who remain have interesting stories to relate of their life on the endless Llano and over the Cap Rock. During a visit with Doña Jesusita García de Chávez and her sister-in-law Doña Lola Otero de García in Albuquerque, I heard many stories of the old days.

IN 1898, Don Antonio Chávez was running sheep at Plaza Larga. Mrs. Chávez tells of her experiences on the Llano, and although now past eighty, she still remembers many incidents of her earlier days. Liberty, originally Tierra Blanca, was then a wild West frontier town, serving as a mail center to the Llano settlers.

There are many mentions in Western books of Black Jack Ketchum, the bandit who terrorized eastern New Mexico. Mrs. Chávez tells that in the summer of 1898, Black Jack and another companion held up and robbed the store at Liberty. The outlaws were masked and at the points of their guns made the proprietor of the store, Levi Herstein, and the bystanders in the store face the wall. While one man held his gun on them, the other committed the raid.

Black Jack and his companion left Liberty and took a southerly course. A posse of four men led by Herstein started on the trail of the bandits. The three other members of the squad were Juan Apodaca, Plácido Gurulé, and Merejildo Gallegos. After trailing the bandits for about thirty miles, the posse overtook them on the banks of Plaza Larga Creek, eight miles west of the present Quay, New Mexico, and a quarter of a mile from the Antonio Chávez ranch.

The bandits watered their horses at the Chávez well and Mrs. Chávez remembers that their horses were shod with rawhide shoes. They had several horses which carried the loot from the Herstein store.

While the outlaws were eating their lunch under a cottonwood tree, the posse made the mistake of not opening fire on the thieves while at a safe distance. Instead, they tried to take them alive.

The desperados, expert at defense, opened fire on their pursuers. Gallegos was killed in the first volley; Herstein fell from his horse wounded and was shot through the heart while begging for mercy. Juan Apodaca made a dash for the Chávez ranch amid a shower of bullets and managed to escape unhurt. Plácido Gurulé, who fell from his horse when the shooting started, played possum, and did such a good job of it, that the bandits shot at him once after he was down to make sure that he was dead. He was shot in the hip, but self preservation gave him courage not to stir, making believe he was a corpse. Gurulé lived to be an old man and humorously delighted in telling of his experience. He often stopped at our *rancho*.

Black Jack met his doom soon after. He was shot by the conductor on the Denver and Fort Worth Railroad after two successful holdups of the same train by his brother Sam. The bandit was hanged in Clayton after a brief trial in April, 1901.

Recalling the incidents of her early married life and her youth on the Llano, Mrs. Chávez said:

"It was in Las Salinas where we lived that the climax of the feud between the Hispanos and the Texans was reached. The Texans were pushing in with their cattle—the New Mexicans resented this. The animosity was a holdover from the Mexican war of 1846. One night, at a dance, a drunken Texan killed an Hispano. The dance became a battle for all. The Hispanos killed the Texan and from then on, the war was on between the two nationalities—until, one by one, the Hispanos crossed into New Mexico to be pushed farther on, or completely out, as the homesteaders began to take up the land." She did not remember the names of those involved.

CONCERNING stories of Indian raids, which I heard as a child, Don Miguel Benavídez, who lived his later years on the Llano country, had firsthand knowledge of Indian life. In 1849, when he was about seven years of age, he and an older brother were herding goats at Los Esteritos, near Dilia. A band of warring Indians dropped in on them at their camp and took them captive. His brother managed to escape, but Miguel was taken by the Indians to the Dakotas, where he lived for many years.

On a campaign, one of many in which he took part against American soldiers, Miguel managed to be rescued. He was taken to St. Louis, Missouri, where he lived with an officer and his family. There he was treated as one of their kin. Years later he was sent back to New Mexico in one of the wagons coming over the Santa Fe trail. I heard Don Miguel's tales when I lived at his brother's house while teaching my first country school.

As a small child on my grandfather's hacienda, I remember an old man who came regularly for his weekly ration of food and clothing—the *hacendados* in those days took care of the poor by providing them with food and clothing. Many poor people came to our home, but I remember Señor Antonio Trujillo, the old man, better than any of the others. He always rode a donkey and had a little boy walking by his side and a pack of dogs following. The people of the village told that he ate dog meat and that was the reason for his keeping so many dogs. They also said that Señor Antonio had learned to eat dog meat when he lived with the Indians.

One of the stories which Señor Antonio used to relate was about his captivity by the Arapahoes and his life with them. When he was a small child, Antonio lived in Taos. A band of Arapahoes came down upon the village and, after raiding the town, they killed several persons—among them Antonio's parents. They took Antonio with them into Montana. (Señor Antonio did not know what state, but by his descriptions grandfather knew it must be the Montana area). He lived with the Indians until he was a grown man. While he was among the Arapahoes, he married a squaw. One night there was an Indian dance which his wife refused to attend. At a very late hour, after the dance was over, Antonio returned to their tepee, where his wife was soundly sleeping. He saw his chance for escape, and knowing that the tribe had no suspicion but that he was one of them, he decided to take flight. Cautiously, he pulled a *reata* from under his wife's pillow and quietly went out to the enclosure where the horses were corralled. There he picked two of the best horses and started on his journey. He crossed many high sierras and although pursued, he finally succeeded in reaching a French trading post. The trappers were very kind to him and helped to hide him for several days while his pursuers were on the trail. The Frenchmen afforded protection for him in a secret room and when there seemed to be no more danger, Antonio continued to travel. After many months of hardship, he reached Taos, being guided all the way by trappers.

Later he followed the buffalo trails and remained on the Llano, finally settling at La Liendre, where he died at the age of 105 years. He served as a soldier in the Spanish and Mexican armies and later fought for the North in the Civil War.

Few of the chapels remain on the Llano. As one travels on the paved highways, ruins of once colorful villages, of ranch houses and chapels, are there to remind us of fiestas, gay pastoral life, and history which I have tried to gather.

The Hispano has almost vanished from the land and most of the chapels are nonexistent, but the names of hills, rivers, arroyos, canyons and defunct plazas linger as monuments to a people who pioneered into the land of the buffalo and the Comanche. These names have undergone many changes, but are still known and repeated. Very likely many of those who pronounce them daily are unaware that they are of Spanish origin.

Amarillo was named Los Barrancos Amarillos, the yellow cliffs. Arroyo de Trujillo was named after the family who founded the plaza. Atascosa, boggy land, is today called Tascosa. Cabra Spring was named so because travelers sighted wild goats in its vicinity. Cañon de Tule, bulrush canyon, has been abbreviated to Tule and even spelled Tool. Conchas, meaning shells, was so named because shells are found along the river shores.

Corazón Peak took its name because its shape resembles a heart. Cuervo is the Spanish word from crow, and the creek received the name from the abundance of crows in that area. La Liendre was originally settled by a family who were small in stature, whose nickname was *liendre,* meaning nit. Las Salinas were the salt mines. Los Alamitos signifies little cottonwoods. Luciano Mesa was named for a man whose given name was Luciano—he lived close to the mesa. Nara Visa was called Narvaez, after the family of that name. Nueve Millas, nine miles, was that distance from Plaza Larga.

We have Ojo del Carnero, sheep spring, named that because of wild sheep that came to water there; Ojo del Llano was a spring well-known on the Llano; Arroyo de Pajarito, little bird creek, is an old landmark. Palo Duro is hardwood, after the hackberry trees growing in the area. Palomas was the name given to that mesa because of the doves which inhabited it. Pintada Mesa received its name because of the varied colors of the earth; it means painted tableland. Plaza Larga, long town, was called thus because of the many eroded buttes having the semblance of houses; these were in long stretches which gave the country the appearance of a city. Saladito means salty and indicated the saline quality of the creek.

Tierra Blanca, white earth, has been shortened to Blanca. Tucumcari is a Comanche word meaning woman's breast; the peak received its name because of resemblance to a well-rounded breast. Ceja means eyebrow, and it was called that because the woody vegetation formed an eyebrow over the endless Llano. The Canadian River, which the early French trappers called after their own country, had been named Rio Colorado or Rio Almagre by the Spaniards from its red mud coloring. Many other sonorous names remind us of a vanished people. Zanjon, translated deep gully, is today called San Jon, a change which would amuse the early buffalo hunters if they were to travel over the Llano again.

The Llano of today is populated: large towns, villages and ranches dot the country where the endless sea of grass, yucca and mesquite bushes so cruelly greeted the buffalo hunters and Comanche fighters. Cotton, wheat, maize and other grains grow in abundance on the Llano Estacado.

When the cattle companies and the homesteaders arrived, it was the survival of the fittest. Much of the land had reverted to the United States government. It was No Man's Land. The Llano became a cattle and farming country and a few foresighted Hispanos abandoned sheep and took to cattle raising on a small scale.

8. Sheep on a Thousand Hills

AFTER THE INDIANS WERE ROUNDED UP and put into reservations, it became safe for the sheepmen to take their families into the Ceja and Llano country.

Families from Las Vegas, Mora, Antonchico, some from the lower Rio Grande valley and many from settlements along the Pecos river, joined the caravan of settlers into the land of the buffalo and Comanche.

San Hilario, on the Canadian river, was founded by Don Hilario Gonzáles, who ran sheep on a thousand hills, as the old-timers used to say. Don Hilario was a very influential man in his day. Even half a century after he passed on, he was remembered and mentioned as the wealthiest man in the '70's. I knew his two daughters, Doña María Ignacia Baca and Doña Juanita Martinez. In about 1860 he built the San Hilario chapel to which the settlers from the Llano and the Ceja traveled many miles to hear Mass.

Every town which had a chapel, dedicated it to the patron saint of the founder. The scattered ranches did not have chapels, but a room in the home of a prominent rancher was set aside for worship and this also had a patron saint.

The plaza of San Lorenzo was about ten miles from San Hilario and five miles from the present Conchas Dam. Don

Francisco López, whose flocks and herds ran into the thousands, founded the town of San Lorenzo. Don Francisco came from Santa Fe. His son, Don Lorenzo, was one of the best-known and most respected citizens in the territory. The chapel, built by his father about 1860, had San Lorenzo as the patron saint. In 1880 there was a newspaper in San Lorenzo called *The Red River Chronicle,* which ran two editions, one in English and one in Spanish.

In 1824, Don Pablo Montoya from La Cienega, near Santa Fe, was given a land grant extending from the Ceja to the Río Colorado (the Canadian river). Don Pablo was instrumental in organizing the early Llano settlers and leading them against the nomadic Apaches and Navajos.

From the Montoya heirs a part of the Pablo Montoya Grant was purchased by Don Francisco López and Don Hilario Gonzáles.

Don Francisco had several beautiful daughters. Two of the Romero brothers from Las Vegas, Don Trinidad and Don Eugenio, married Valeria and Chonita. In 1890 Don Trinidad and Don Eugenio, who with Don Trinidad's son operated a large mercantile business in Las Vegas, sold their livestock holdings in San Miguel County to the Bell Ranch which also took over the Pablo Montoya Grant and other surrounding land. The deal consisted of twelve thousand head of cows, most of them with calves. Papá, who was a first cousin of the Romeros, helped with the rounding up and delivering of the cattle. It was a big event and one of the largest transactions of that era. The Romeros operated their business under the name of T. Romero Brothers and Son.

The Romero brothers also ran thirty thousand head of sheep at Ojo de la Mula near the Bell Ranch. Román, son of Don Trinidad, and who is now past eighty, related to me that one spring he had come home from a college in St. Louis to spend the Easter holidays. It was a very cold season with snow on the ground. His father sent him to Ojo de la Mula to help with the lambing. In order to save the lambs they had to keep fires burning around the flocks. It was quite an experience for a tenderfoot.

Don Trinidad Romero was delegate to Congress from New Mexico in 1877-79. In 1880 he built a $100,000 mansion at Romeroville, near Las Vegas, where he entertained many notables, among them President and Mrs. Hayes, General Sherman and General Grant.

Many of the smaller ranchers who lived between the Pecos river and Oldham County, Texas, came there through the influence of Don Hilario Gonzáles and Don Francisco López. Some of them were relatives, others *empleados* or friends of the families who took sheep and cattle on the shares from them.

A great number of the Hispanos who settled the Panhandle of Texas went there from San Hilario, San Lorenzo, Las Vegas, Mora and the Pecos River country. They were the first settlers of now-extinct plazas with sonorous Spanish names.

Don Agapito Sandoval and Don Casimiro Romero from Mora were the founders of Atascosa in Oldham County, Texas. Don Agapito left the Llano country in 1888 about the same time Don Casimiro moved to El Médano, about fifteen miles from the town of Endee and close to San Jon. At El Médano, Don Casimiro opened a store after the sheep business became impossible. One night after he had closed his store, he was assaulted by masked bandits, supposedly Texans, who robbed him of almost everything which he possessed in the mercantile business. When Don Casimiro moved to Atascosa, the buffalo were still grazing on the plains. Besides his sheep interests, he freighted goods to and from Dodge City, Kansas. He remained in the Llano country until his death.

Don Mariano Montoya, who was the first county clerk of Oldham County, created in 1881, was still running sheep on the Texas side at the beginning of the twentieth century. He went to Atascosa in 1878. When the homesteaders came, it became harder and harder to find pastures for the sheep and Don Mariano moved to Logan, just inside the New Mexico line.

Arroyo de Trujillo joins the Canadian River at the point where the settlement named for the arroyo stood. A Frenchman ran a store there in the days of the sheepmen, but the *patrón* was Don Jesús María Trujillo. He had many *empleados* and they, with their families and the family of the *patrón,* made up most of the population.

Don Pablo Garcia y Apodaca was living in San Hilario in 1874. Like many others, he took cattle on the shares from Don Hilario Gonzáles and moved to the Plaza Larga country and lived at Ojo del Carnero. His daughter, Jesusita, married Antonio Chávez and they moved to Las Salinas on the Texas side. Las Salinas was an important plaza. Salinas means salt mines, and salt mining was an industry there. Men came from Antonchico, Puerto de Luna, Lincoln, Las Vegas and other points in New Mexico for their salt supplies. Some of the settlers along the Salinas made a living by going into Colorado and New Mexico to sell the salt.

Don Emeterio Gallegos was a merchant in Las Salinas. He moved to Logan when the Texans pushed the New Mexicans over the line.

In Rito Blanco lived Don José and Don Miguel Tafoya. They moved to the Clayton vicinity and some of their descendants are living there today.

Don Higinio Esquibel dwelt at Ojo del Llano. There were many families in this plaza, mostly the *empleados* of the Esquibel family. The chapel built there by Don Higinio in 1880 was dedicated to *El Santo Niño de Atocha,* the Holy Child. The Texas Hispanos came there to hear Mass. This part of the country is known as Revuelto, and it is east of Tucumcari just over the Texas line.

The San Rafael chapel, built in 1875 at Pajarito by Don Gregorio Flores, was the early gathering place of worship for families who lived on ranches between what is now Tucumcari and east to the Texas line, as well as those living as far west as Cuervo. It was six miles from the railroad station of Montoya on the Southern Pacific.

Don Apolinar Vigil was the *patrón* at Saladito. In 1880, a chapel was erected there and dedicated to *Nuestro Padre Jesús*. Associated with the chapel was a *morada* maintained by the Penitentes as a place of worship serving the Society's members over the Ceja and the Llano.

Nueve Millas was the home of Don Sabino and Don Pablo Martínez. In Los Alamitos, Don Lorenzo Otero and Don Filomeno Chávez had their sheep ranches and there also lived Don Pedro and Don Macario Chávez. These men had small herds of sheep, a thousand or two head.

ALL the ranchers had some cattle, but until late in the 1890's the Llano was primarily a sheep country.

My grandfather, Don Tomás D. Cabeza de Baca was running fifteen thousand head of sheep on the Plaza Larga country in 1875. In the Pajarito country, where Newkirk is now, he ran more than two thousand head of cattle. In those days there were no bonding companies. My grandfather was one of the bondsmen of the newly-elected San Miguel County sheriff-clerk-treasurer, which offices were held by one man. At the end of his term, the officer was short in the county funds. Grandfather had to produce $40,000. Ewes were worth one dollar per head, cows seven dollars. He sold all his livestock and to make up the balance, he mortgaged 100,000 acres of his land grant, El Valle Grande in Sandoval county, to Don José Leandro Perea for $10,000.

After that time Grandfather managed to increase his flocks and herds to a few thousand, but he never became wealthy. Until his death, he was part owner of the 100,000 acres of the Baca Location Number Two (now part of the Bell Ranch), which later was paid to lawyers trying to save the other three Baca locations.

Don Cruz Gallegos, from Upper Las Vegas, stopped at our *rancho* on his way to oversee his sheep camps near Endee as late as 1913. At that date there still was a handful of Las Vegas sheepmen trying to hold their grazing land, but one by one they gave up as the homesteaders took up the land.

The Hispanos had almost no titles of ownership, and the few who did were not able to compete with the newcomers. The boundaries had been laid by means of indefinite markers and much of the land was lost even after it was taken up by the courts. The history of the New Mexican land grants would fill volumes, but it is not a part of this story.

Those who settled on the Ceja and the Llano, took it for granted that the land was theirs. No other civilized people had become interested in the country until the New Mexican pioneers had made it safe for colonization.

A few of the Hispanos who had taken advantage of the homestead law of 1862 by taking up 160 acres of land remained on the Ceja along the Pajarito country.

In 1900, Don Benigno Benavídez built a chapel on his ranch six miles west of Montoya. I went to Mass there occasionally on my visits to our *rancho*. The chapel was dedicated to Our Lady of Guadalupe. Don Benigno was one of the few men running sheep in the early 1900's. There was also Don Bruno Martínez who lived at Carrizito. After the homesteaders started to take up the land, both men turned to raising cattle.

La Manga, near the Mesa Rica and adjacent to what is now Conchas Dam, was an important settlement in the 1890's. The population was made up of relatives and *empleados* of Don Francisco López and Don Hilario Gonzáles, who moved over from San Hilario and San Lorenzo. A chapel dedicated to San Luis Gonzaga was built about 1890. Don Felipe and Don Juan Delgado, who married two of Don Francisco López' daughters, also lived at La Manga. Later Don Domingo Maes, Don Benito Encinias and Don Juan López were running cattle in the area; some of their descendants still hold the land and raise cattle. Don Isidoro Gallegos lived at the foot of the Mesa Rica and with his sons, had a good sized cattle ranch.

Don Pedro Romero, Don Luciano López, and the Vigil brothers—Don Francisco, Don Doroteo and Don Manuel—lived at El Valle about ten miles from the present Newkirk. Some of the López and Vigil families still hold a few thousand acres there.

My father, Don Graciano, lived at Carrizito and later moved to Pajarito close by. Some members of our family are still ranching in both areas.

In 1905, a chapel was built in Newkirk and dedicated to the Holy Family. This chapel now serves the few El Valle, Carrizito and Pajarito Hispano families.

CUERVO CREEK has its source at the edge of the Staked Plains, about five miles southwest of the village of Cuervo which derives its name from the creek. It was founded when the railroad came in. A chapel dedicated to St. Anne was built in 1903. This town has lasted because there are still sheep and cattle ranchers in its vicinity who have managed to survive because their lands were on the Spanish and Mexican land grants and not opened to the homesteaders. Cuervo Peak, five miles west of the creek and fifteen miles from the head of the arroyo, is a majestic butte, overlooking the Llano for many miles. This landmark guided the Conquistadores in their early explorations. The Coronado route lies just south, by the foot of the peak and north of the Varejón Ceja. It was the junction of trails to the buffalo country.

The Cuervo country was the grazing land for the sheep and cattle herds of the Rio Grande settlers as early as 1780 and it is still settled by a few of the descendants of the same Spanish families. The first ranch house, built in the vicinity of the present village of Cuervo, was that of Don Eduardo Martínez, who came from Antonchico in 1870. The ruins of the house can be seen a quarter of a mile south of U.S. Highway 66, three miles west of the village of Cuervo.

The chapel at the railroad station of Montoya, dedicated to Joan of Arc, replaced the San Rafael chapel after the coming of the railroad.

Las Colonias, on the Pecos River, was settled by people from Cebolleta and Cubero, in the Lower Rio Grande and one still finds families of pure Castilian extraction living in that town. The handsome chapel there is well preserved.

Santa Rosa, where Don Celso Baca reigned as sheep and cattle king, had a private chapel in 1868. The home on Don Celso's hacienda is one of the few landmarks still preserved, but the chapel is in ruins. Don Celso's mother was Doña Rosa, and he dedicated the chapel to her memory. The town took its name from the patron saint of the church. Until the coming of the railroad, this stretch of country was known as Agua Negra, the name of the Antonio Sandoval Land Grant.

When Don Celso Baca built the Santa Rosa chapel on his hacienda, an old painting of Santa Rosa de Lima, brought over the Chihuahua Trail, adorned the altar. In later years, when the transition came, replacing the old with the new, Don Celso purchased a modern statue of Santa Rosa and this is the one which today is in the church at Santa Rosa.

Before the American occupation and until 1857, San Miguel del Vado was the parish seat for all the country east and south of the Pecos river into Texas. The church in San Miguel del Vado was built about 1806 and the first resident priest, as far as I can determine, was Father José Francisco Leyba.

From family papers, I learned that the town of San Miguel was settled by Tlascalan Indians, the descendants of the Mexican Indian servants the Spaniards brought with them during the Reconquest in 1693. When these Indians became unruly in Santa Fe, the viceroy of Mexico appointed Don Luis María Cabeza de Baca, my great-grandfather, from La Peña Blanca, as overseer

to take them into other territory. San Miguel del Vado, on the banks of the Pecos river, was chosen as the site for colonizing and settling of these *genízaros*. Here, Don Luis María supervised the building of homes, cultivating of the land, construction of dams and the erection of a church.

In later years, after the death of Don Luis María, the *genízaros* emigrated to Antonchico, La Cuesta, Chaperito and other surrounding villages. Hispano colonizers, then, seeking farming lands, populated San Miguel del Vado.

WITH the exception of San Miguel del Vado, no other parish served so large a territory as did Antonchico prior to the founding of the Chaperito and Puerto de Luna parishes. Antonchico served all that is today Guadalupe, Quay, De Baca, parts of Lincoln, eastern and southern San Miguel, Union and Harding counties and scattered settlements all along the Llano including northwest Texas.

In 1857, Father John B. Fayet founded the Antonchico parish, and it was not until then that the people of the plains had access to a church east of the Pecos river.

Antonchico was settled in 1834 by a group of families who were given a tract of land, known as the Antonchico Grant. In the confirmation of the grant, the names of these families appear: Salvador Tapia, Bernardo Ulibarrí, Felipe Valencia, Luis Gonzales, Tomas Martín, Miguel Martín, José Medina, Simón Estrada, Lorenzo Tapia, Diego Antonio Tapia, Mariano Aragón, Francisco Baca, Rafael Durán, Juan Sebastian Durán, José Durán, and Juan Cristobal García. These settlers came from San Miguel del Vado and many of their descendants still live there.

Antonchico, originally named Sangre de Cristo, was a settlement of about six hundred inhabitants in 1842 when the expedition of good will led by General McCleod crossed the Llano on its way to Santa Fe, and about which I heard from Papá.

In 1841, an expedition left Austin, Texas, with the General in command of about thirty-two men as troops. Merchants accompanied the troops, because—according to history—the object of the operation was to establish commercial relations between Texas and New Mexico. The expedition was well armed with artillery.

The Texas Congress had approved a law appropriating all the territory east of the Rio Grande and members of the good will mission were hopeful that the New Mexicans were dissatisfied with their government and would be willing to become a part of Texas.

After suffering untold hardships, the men under General McCleod reached New Mexico, but the ruling element in Santa Fe already knew about the good will excursion on its way to this territory. The Texas men were met by General Armijo's army from Santa Fe at Laguna Colorada (Red Lake) at the mouth of Bull Canyon, just over the Ceja of the Llano. When the McCleod army reached the Staked Plains, they nearly perished from hunger and thirst. They stopped at the sheep camp of Don Tomás Francisco Cabeza de Baca at Laguna Colorada to secure food when they were overtaken by Armijo's army.

One of the sheepherders who was at the camp lived to a very old age and served my grandfather, Don Tomás Dolores Cabeza de Baca, a brother of Don Tomás Francisco. It was he who related to Papá about the McCleod men stopping there for assistance. In this sheep camp, the Texans traded a spring wagon to the herders for meat. General Armijo's men led the McCleod unorganized men into Antonchico and there arrested the vanguard which had preceded the expedition. It was well known that McCleod was seeking the annexation of New Mexico to Texas. Don Pablo Aragón, who later lived at Newkirk as our neighbor, used to relate that he was a boy about seven years old when the McCleod army was brought into Antonchico. He remembered that he and other boys climbed the corn cribs and brought down ears of corn for the hungry Texans.

I KNEW Puerto de Luna when it was a parish seat, with visitas as far away as Tucumcari. Puerto de Luna was founded by colonists from the lower Rio Grande in New Mexico in 1862; it was then a *visita* of Antonchico. The Puerto de Luna church was built in 1881, and became a *parroquia,* parish church, in 1896. Father Simon Alvernhe was the first pastor. In 1920, the parish seat was moved to Santa Rosa.

The first Mass celebrated in Puerto de Luna was for the funeral of Don Juan Patrón, who was murdered by a Texan, an emissary of the Murphy-Dolan faction which figured prominently in the Lincoln County War. It was through Don Juan's generosity that the church had been completed and fate had it that he enter it as corpse.

Before the coming of the railroad, Puerto de Luna was the county seat of Guadalupe County.

My baptismal certificate is in the Chaperito church, a *parroquia* which for more than half a century served hundreds of miles on the Llano. Chaperito became a parish in 1876, with Father Juan B. Galon as its first pastor. He served until 1884. Records show that the Chaperito church once had jurisdiction over all the Llano country. There are baptismal entries in the early 1880's from Atascosa, Trujillo, Ojo de San Juan, Las Salinas and Mobeetie in Texas, and from Revuelto, San Lorenzo, San Rafael and Cuervo, in New Mexico.

9. Las Vegas Grandes

SAN MIGUEL HAS BEEN CALLED THE "EMPIRE COUNTY" of New Mexico. It has an area of 4,749 square miles. Las Vegas, its largest town, has figured most prominently in its history.

In 1821, Don Luis María Cabeza de Baca from La Peña Blanca, petitioned the government for a tract of land in the names of himself and his seventeen male children. The land was called Las Vegas Grandes, and the boundaries as claimed were: On the north, the Sapello river; on the south, San Miguel del Vado; on the west, the Pecos mountain; on the east, El Aguaje de la Yegua and the Antonio Ortiz Grant.

In 1823, Don Luis María was given title to the land. He took possession of the land and lived there for a number of years. He had great dreams of an empire in the name of Cabeza de Baca, but the Indian raids from the north made it impossible for him to continue living on the land which consisted of half a million acres. At the time, he also had a large tract of land known as El Ojo del Espiritu Santo in what is now Sandoval County near his home at La Peña Blanca. The latter grant consisted of about 113,141 acres.

These facts I know from family tradition, for Don Luis María was my great grandfather, and I remember when my grandfather received some money from the sales of some of the land.

I was a very small child, but the name of Don Luis María, for whom my brother was named, was very important in our family. I heard many times that when he was living he held a very prominent part in the government of the province of New Mexico. It is told that when a new governor arrived in New Mexico, Don Luis mounted his mule, and with his bodyguard went to Santa Fe to greet the newcomer. If my great-grandfather liked him, all was well, but if he displeased Don Luis, soon a letter went to the Viceroy of Mexico to replace the governor—and he was replaced.

Don Luis María died in La Peña Blanca in 1833, but his heirs continued to hold to the Las Vegas Land Grant. With the coming of the Santa Fe Trail, Las Vegas began to be populated and soon became an important stop on the trail. The citizens of Las Vegas petitioned that they be given title to the grant, and after reaching an agreement with the heirs of Don Luis María, the land was turned over to the petitioners. In the agreement with the government, the Cabeza de Baca heirs were given five tracts of land known as the Baca locations, each consisting of approximately 100,000 acres. My grandfather inherited Baca Location Number One, known as El Valle Grande, near Los Alamos of atomic renown.

My grandfather, Don Tomás D. Cabeza de Baca, moved to Las Vegas from La Peña Blanca in 1865. He built his home on the east side of the Plaza and there conducted a mercantile business. He also owned wagons which freighted over the Santa Fe Trail. His sheep and cattle grazed on the Ceja.

From my grandparents, I learned much of the early history of Las Vegas. On the plaza lived Don Romualdo Baca, Don Miguel Desmarais, and Don Miguel Romero. The Catholic church was on the west side of the plaza, but in later years, Don Romualdo Baca gave a tract of land for building a new church, which still stands. My grandmother used to tell that when they excavated for the foundation of the new church, the priest asked that the bodies which had been buried in the church cemetery be moved to the new location. Those who had relatives claimed the bodies, and they were placed inside the foundation of the new structure. Don Romualdo, when donating the ground for the church, asked that he be buried inside the church, but when he passed away, another priest had jurisdiction and he was buried in the cemetery, although his family had a signed agreement concerning his burial.

In 1875, the Jesuit Fathers founded *La Revista Catolica,* a newspaper in Spanish, which had great circulation in the Southwest. In 1877, the same priests established the Jesuit College, which was a godsend to New Mexico and surrounding territory. Education had been possible only to those who could afford to send their children to Mexico, to the States or Europe. The priests were mostly Italians, but they must have been excellent teachers because my uncles and Papá, who received all their education there, had a wonderful command of the English language and a vast knowledge of the arts and sciences. My education seems meager compared to theirs.

Later the College was moved to Denver and is now Regis College. *La Revista Católica* remained in Las Vegas until 1918, when it was moved to El Paso, Texas, and still is published there.

The College was no longer in Las Vegas when I went there as a child, but the Jesuits had the newspaper and a chapel where I heard Mass. It was not the official parish, but the Las Vegas Catholics went there in larger numbers than to the parish church. The chapel was beautiful and I shall never forget the May devotions with the lovely Virgin, whose robes of satin were renewed each year. I still remember the beautiful hymns led by Father Alfonso Rossi, who had been professor of literature at the College. He was the director of the choir and he played the organ. One of my older cousins sang in the choir and I accompanied her to practice and to Mass on Sundays. In those days, a girl never went anywhere unless accompanied by her mother or a chaperone, and if an older person could not be on hand, a small child went along. It was my lot to be a companion to my older cousins, and often I was sworn to secrecy about them meeting their sweethearts on the way to church or other places.

I loved Father Rossi, he always had candy for me and refreshments for the girls in his choir. It was he who heard my first confession.

It was a sad day for Las Vegas when the Jesuits left. They had done much for the spiritual and educational needs of the people. I knew Father José Marra, who had been the Dean of the College and later director of the newspaper. He was a very learned man and he served as Superior of the Jesuit order.

The most saintly man I have ever known was Father Enrique Ferrari, who directed the printing of *La Revista Católica*. He came from the nobility of Italy and he was truly noble. From 1877 to 1880, he served as editor of the paper.

Two altar boys helped serve Mass on Sundays at the Jesuit chapel. As a small child, I remember Francisco Delgado and Pablo Hernandez as altar boys, and when Pablo left for Spain, my brother Luis and José Sena, a cousin, took their places.

When my grandfather was on his deathbed, he asked that one of the Jesuit priests hear his last confession. Although it was against the rules of the parish, Father Rossi came as a friend and confessor.

Las Vegas was the shopping center and market for the cattle

and sheepmen from the Llano country. It became the most important town of the territory. I remember we once considered Santa Fe and Albuquerque as mere villages.

THE Sisters of Loretto came to Las Vegas in 1869. I went to their school in the grammar grades. Don Romualdo Baca gave the Sisters their home and three of his nieces joined the order. Girls from Las Vegas and all the surrounding country came to the day and boarding school. The daughters of the wealthy classes would never have been sent to a public school. Those who were poor often worked to earn their tuition, for it was a privilege to attend Loretto Academy. My mother received all her education from the Sisters in Las Vegas.

As I remember Las Vegas in my youth, it was a very democratic town. We lived on the Hot Springs Boulevard in Old Town. There were many beautiful homes in our neighborhood and nationalities were merged into one big family. There was no discrimination as to color or race. One of the best liked families was that of Montgomery Bell. He and his wife were mulattoes and I have never known finer persons. We had German, Jews, Spanish and plain American neighbors, but we all played together as one big family and we all loved the Bells. Mr. and Mrs. Bell were from the South; Montgomery Bell came with the Stephen Elkins family to New Mexico. He was the son of a slave of the Elkins. By thrift, he accumulated a large fortune and he was a friend of the poor people. He was their money lender.

As a child, I was a problem to my grandmother and was forever running away from her. She called me from morning till night trying to locate me. The Bells had a parrot and he learned to call me. Every Christmas Mr. Bell had a present for me from the Parrot. On one occasion he gave me a necklace with a small diamond from the parrot. I am sure that he did the same for all the neighborhood children.

One of the happiest recollections I have of Las Vegas concerns the Fourth of July celebrations. We always got new outfits for the occasion. By nine o'clock in the morning we were gathered on the plaza for the fiesta. The band played on the kiosk in the park all day. Around the park were stands selling ice cream, cold drinks, food and candies. In the afternoon there were races and the climbing of the greased pole and at night, they had fireworks. By nine o'clock the fiesta was over and we were a bunch of tired children full of ice cream and candy, for we had been saving money for the day ever since Christmas. It was the one day that there were no restrictions on the amount of money we spent nor a set hour for us to come home.

I do not remember when the Fourth of July celebration was discontinued, but after I was in my teens, the Cowboys' Reunion took its place. By then, there were too many outsiders and it was not as much fun. My experiences on the ranch did not make a rodeo interesting as I felt that it was not real.

I am sure Don Luis María never thought that the empire of which he dreamed would be the home of some of his descendants and that they would play an important part in its history. My grandfather was county commissioner during the litigation over whether the county seat should be in Old or New Las Vegas. He was instrumental in getting the vote for the old town and there the courthouse was built while he was in office. When the old courthouse was replaced during W.P.A. days, Las Vegas lost one of its most imposing structures. How well I remember, upon climbing the mesa on a return trip from our *rancho,* seeing the tower of the old courthouse and how happy it made me that our journey was ending and I would be in Las Vegas again.

My grandfather is buried in the church cemetery, but by the time grandmother died, a ban had been placed prohibiting burial there. She and her sons all lie in the Catholic cemetery, Monte Calvario, in Las Vegas Grandes, on the ground which had once been their land grant.

THE cemetery lies in view of Hermit's Peak and it brings to my mind the story of the hermit which my grandmother enjoyed relating. A few years ago I was attending a 4-H club meeting in Las Gallinas at the foot of the Peak. The leader of the club was Mrs. Domitilo Martinez and she recognized me as one of the de Bacas who went camping in the Gallinas country many years before. I asked her if she knew any stories about the hermit, and to my surprise she had written the story as told by her father—who had known the hermit. She had written the story in Spanish and asked me if I would translate it for her. Many tourists come to her place and are always eager to hear the story. I did the translation, and in doing it I learned much that would have been lost of the personal side of the tale.

She relates that her grandfather was an adobe maker and had been hired by Don José A. Baca from Upper Las Vegas to do some work for him. He took one of his sons with him and Don José had liked the boy and he hired him as cowherder. One day, while he and other boys were herding the milk cows near Hot Springs, they saw a man walking along with a cane. He came towards them and asked them for a drink. They had no water and told him that they went to drink by the river which was quite a distance. It was a very hot day and they, too, were thirsty. The man told them: "You see those rocks there by the hillside, there is water there." The boys could not believe it as they knew the spot and they had never seen water there. They went to the place and there found a spring of clear water.

The man went on his way and finally reached Las Gallinas. The people were surprised to see a stranger, as in those days very few outsiders came to the village. Several of the villagers invited him to their homes, but he asked for a shed in which to put the things he had in a knapsack. In the evening he preached to the men and in a few days he had become part of the village. After a time, he asked the men to climb the Peak with him. No one had ever ventured the ascent, for the terrain was very craggy and rugged. He showed them the way and soon they were on top. There was no water anywhere and every few days some man went up to take him water. He started encouraging the men to come up to the Peak and there he fed them. He had some cornmeal from which he made gruel. Those who tasted it claimed that it was the most delicious food they had ever eaten, and the strange part of it was that they felt it was not going to be enough to fill them, yet after eating it, they felt satisfied.

One day, the hermit told them that they were going to find water. He led them to a rocky spot and with little effort water was found. The men were happy because the carrying of the water had been a difficult task.

He organized a society which he called the Society of the Holy Cross. They built a Via Crucis, and there they said the Stations of the Cross.

He lived alone on the Peak, but kept in contact with the villagers who lived below. Once in a while on Sundays, he came down and walked to Las Vegas and to hear Mass.

My grandmother used to relate that he was an Italian by the name of Juan Agostini and that he was friend of a relative of theirs who lived in Upper Las Vegas. He brought his clothing there for laundering and his undergarments were stained with blood, showing that he practiced penance. On the feast of the Holy Cross, which is the third of May, he built *luminarias,* little bonfires, on the peak and the people of Las Vegas would watch for them and joined in saying the rosary. When I was a child, he was long gone, but the Gallinas villagers kept up the practice and we joined in praying.

Mrs. Martinez did not seem to know of his departure from the Las Vegas country, but I heard the story from grandmother that he had decided to return to his native Italy. He travelled to Old Mesilla and there stayed with Father José de Jesús Cabeza de Baca, grandfather's brother, who was the resident priest at the time. The hermit went up in the Organ Mountains and there he lived in a cave. One day, he came down bringing his books and other possessions to Father de Baca. He told him that on the next day he was leaving for his journey into Mexico to take the boat and that evening he would light a bonfire and for him and his parishioners to join him in prayer. Father de Baca waited for the signal, but it never came. He waited several days and finally sent up to search for him. He was found murdered, supposedly with intent of robbery.

Mrs. Martinez, in her story, credits him with superhuman powers and tells of miracles performed, and that he could foretell events and even read peoples' minds. She claims that he was a priest, but I have not been able to confirm that fact.

The Gallinas residents at the foot of Hermit's Peak still practice the rites which Don Juan Agostini taught them.

IV. BAD MEN & BOLD

10. Vicente Silva, Bandit Leader

WHILE I GATHERED MATERIAL FOR THIS BOOK, I made visits to men and women who were living in some of the San Miguel County communities at the time of Los Gorras Blancas. Among them was Don Luciano López, who is now past eighty and lives as our neighbor at El Valle.

In 1890, Don Luciano was living at La Concepción, about twenty miles east and south of Las Vegas. He tells that the citizens of the different communities who had sheep on the Ceja and Llano had banded together for protection against the building of fences on their grazing lands and to help each other with crops and farming in the communities. They called the organization Caballeros de Labor, Gentlemen of Labor.

The party served a good purpose, but as there is always some bad element in all organizations, politicians saw where they could gain prestige. In place of protection, this element wanted common pastures and since the cutting of fences on public domain had appealed to them, they carried the practice to the farming lands of the communities. These men called themselves El Partido del Pueblo, the People's Party. It became a secret society. They sent anonymous letters to those not in their party, threatening their lives and telling them that their fences would be cut down, their homes and farm buildings set on fire. They carried out their threats. Don Luciano tells how they tore down his father's gristmill and burned his barns and corrals. I remember my grandmother telling us about their fences being cut down at La Liendre. She heard the bandits when they came and she wanted to go out and fight, but Grandfather knew it would be suicide. Next morning miles and miles of their pasture and farmland fences were cut into fragments.

The respectable citizens could not go out at night without a bodyguard and heavily armed. They did not know who the members of the gang were—in many cases they were the same neighbors who had been Los Caballeros de Labor, as it was learned later.

These marauders wore white hoods over their heads when they were out pillaging and came to be known as Los Gorras Blancas, the White Caps.

For protection, the good citizens formed a new party which they called El Partido de la Unión, the Union Party, composed of members of both major political parties. They held community meetings and for protection they used a password in order to keep out those from the bad element who might seek admittance. Don Luciano served as secretary to El Partido de la Unión in 1891. He tells that there were men whom they never suspected as belonging to El Partido del Pueblo in the new organization and they served as spies for the corrupt politicians. The wife of one of these men once confided to a neighbor about her husband's work. She was found out and was given fifty lashes as punishment.

El Partido de la Unión became strong, but in it were many from the other faction. Often they would get rid of the good citizens by breaking up the meetings with the pretense that it was late and proceed to their own haunts to plan their maraudings.

During this time the Republican Party was down. When it was built up again many who had been Republicans left El Partido de la Unión and joined the Democratic Party.

In going over grandfather's papers, I found a printed notice which explains El Partido de la Union, and which I have translated:

"BE ON THE WATCH
UNION PARTY OF SAN MIGUEL COUNTY!

"Being that a few days ago we have seen some leaflets signed by ————, as president of the Central Committee of the Union party, in which a call is made to the *Republican Unionists,* that they gather in convention on March 17, 1896 with the aim of dissolving the Union which now exists in our county; we wish to make public that said call is without the authority of the Central Committee of said party, which has neither been consulted nor has any Republican Unionist, being merely a wicked treason by means of which the president of the Central Committee of the Union Party desires to seek personal vengeance and for which end he wishes to use the people, who in our concept are not ready to lend themselves as instruments to satisfy personal vengeances for any person whoever he may be.

"Now, since it might happen that the Republican Unionists, who read the communication from said Señor ————, believe that the Union has dissolved and that the adherents of that party will have to follow whatever path they desire, we advise the people in general and our friends in particular that what the *President* exposes is only a trap built by others and signed by him with the aim of breaking up the Union Party, which has been of great service and to form, not a political party, which they boast as the Republican party, but the old Ring so that they may divide among themselves the political offices and to bring to the people displeasure, rivalry, enmity, quarrels and general misery as were prevalent during the rule of some of the officials of a past administration, whose records form a black page in the history of our county.

"Wherefore, those of us who are signed publish the present notice to inform the people in general and to the loyal adherents of the Union Party that today, more than ever, we are ready to remain with the party which we formed of our own free will and with the will of the people, not with the aim of renouncing our political affiliations, but in order to hold back the reins of government from the hands of those who defalcated it, the protectors of all evil and political usurpers and in order to place it in the hands of honest and upright men.

"The reasons which motivated this declaration from us are here exposed and in conclusion we appeal to the patriotism of all the San Miguel County citizens to cooperate with us in upholding the Union Party which has to this day given us endearing results and thereby establishing, as everyone knows, peace and harmony in our county.

Very respectfully,"

There are forty-nine signatures to this paper, among them those of two of my uncles and many of our relatives and friends from both major political parties.

From the Gorras Blancas grew up another menace to the citizens of San Miguel and the surrounding counties and that was Vicente Silva and his forty bandits.

THE story of Vicente Silva made a very vivid impression on my early life. The crimes were committed by his gang before I was born, but I well remember hearing that on the day my brother Luis María was born, a messenger was sent to Las Vegas to notify our maternal grandfather, Don Cirilo Delgado, about the birth of his first grandchild. The messenger was Don Juan Aragón. The date was May 26, 1893. As he was riding along, he noticed a team of burros dragging something. He became curious and led his horse towards them and his words were: "Upon seeing such a horrible spectacle, my hair stood on end." The burros were dragging the bodies of two men who had been murdered by the Silva gang near El Vegoso, six miles east of Las Vegas. Again and again I heard the story and my hair also stood on end. Don Manuel Cabeza de Baca tells about the murder and I quote:

"On the 26th day of May, 1893, the people of Las Vegas were

greatly disturbed. Great excitement and consternation ruled the town upon hearing that two men had been murdered. Benigno Martinez was a sheep grower, who at great sacrifice had been able to accumulate about two thousand head of sheep, which he and his ill-fated companion were herding, unaware of danger when the black hand of Cecilio Lucero, a member of Silva's gang, came to exterminate them.

"Cecilio Lucero, cousin of Benigno Martinez, was married and with his wife lived in Benigno's house, where he was provided with all the considerations and favors of a friend and relative.

"The day before, Cecilio had been in Watrous, where he offered a bunch of sheep for sale—it is not known whether anyone accepted the trade or not. The following day, he went to the sheep camp of his cousin Benigno and there spent the night with him. At daybreak, without reason, he shot Benigno, killing him instantly and then turned and killed Juan Gallegos, who also died immediately. Not content with the bullets which pierced their bodies, he took a rock and smashed their heads; the victims remained unrecognizable except for their clothing and letters which they carried in their pockets and which were found when the investigation was conducted.

"To add to the crime, he tied a rope to a burro's neck and to the other end, he tied Benigno's feet; he did the same with the other victim.

"The asses dragged the bodies all day and all night, until next day when a man by the name of Juan Aragón, who was coming along the road, noticed the burros dragging something. Immediately he sped his horse and took the news into Las Vegas.

"In a short while the officers accompanied by a number of respectable citizens reached the scene of the crime.

"The excitement was general and hundreds of persons viewed the bodies and upon seeing them, they called for vengeance.

"It did not take long to find out who the murderer was. Cecilio Lucero was arrested and in the preliminary investigation, it was proved that he was guilty of the murder of Martinez and Gallegos. About three hundred persons gathered and at eleven o'clock that night they took Lucero out of jail and lynched him on a telephone post."

This was one of the early stories which I remember hearing. We moved to Las Vegas from my grandfather's hacienda of La Liendre in 1901. We lived in the home of my uncle, Don Manuel Cabeza de Baca, who wrote the Silva story. It was a spacious home built around a courtyard. We occupied the south wing of the house, and in summer evenings we sat out in the patio listening to stories and tales of perilous days in San Miguel County. It was in this same patio that, during the Silva terror, Uncle Manuel almost met his death. He and my Uncle Ezequiel, who later became Governor of New Mexico, were on Silva's blacklist. One night, as Uncle Manuel was leaving for an evening meeting, two masked men jumped from behind some lilac bushes. Don Manuel always carried a gun, but as he went to reach for it, the bandits fled. Later on, rumor spread that they had fled because a beautiful lady in white robes was accompanying him. No one was with him.

Uncle Manuel was a handsome man. He was not as tall as his brothers (Papá was six feet tall). He had deep blue eyes and the fairest skin I have ever seen. He dressed meticulously, always. He wore white stiff bosom shirts and a diamond stud under his black bow tie. His suits were grey or black and strictly tailored. On his right hand he wore a diamond ring which was most becoming to his soft white skin. He always carried a cane with a gold head and for special occasions, he dressed in his Prince Albert and stovepipe hat. I remember him well in that garb at my grandmother's funeral in 1912.

He was the oldest of six sons, and as was the custom in Spanish families, his brothers respected him completely. He received his early education at St. Michael's College in Santa Fe and at the Jesuit College in Las Vegas. Later he studied law under his friend, Ralph Emerson Twitchell, and was admitted to the bar in 1880. In 1886, he served as a member of the House in the territorial legislature from San Miguel County and was voted Speaker of the House for that term. In 1899-1901, he was Superintendent of Public Instruction, and in 1904, he again went as representative from Guadalupe County, then Leonard Wood County. He was a stanch Republican, but in 1912 he voted for his brother, who ran for Lieutenant Governor on the Democratic ticket in the first state election.

Besides his law practice, he engaged in cattle raising on the Ceja with Papá. It was he who hired El Cuate as ranch cook.

He was a very proud man, but after his death, we found out that he was quite a humanitarian. His books were filled with cancelled debts of poor people who were unable to pay him for his services as a lawyer. From the time of the coming of the railroad into Las Vegas and until his death, he was lawyer for the Atchison, Topeka and Santa Fe.

In 1896, Don Manuel Cabeza de Baca wrote the story of Vicente Silva and his bandits. It was published by *La Voz del Pueblo,* a newspaper printing office owned by Don Felix Martínez, Don Antonio Lucero and Don Ezequiel Cabeza de Baca in Las Vegas. In its day, *La Voz del Pueblo* was the most influential New Mexican newspaper printed in Spanish. It was a paper leaning decidedly toward the Democratic party.

At the turn of the century, the Vicente Silva story was still vivid in the experience of the Las Vegas inhabitants. I remember passing the Buffalo Saloon on the plaza and seeing some of the characters who still remained of what had been the Silva henchmen. Some had served their sentences, others had been pardoned for having given information about the crimes committed. I knew Julian Trujillo, who drove a coal wagon for many years. El Moro, El Lechuza and El Cachumeno were those who hung around the Buffalo Saloon and the ones who impressed me. As I recall, they looked the part of criminals or perhaps they appeared so to my imagination. They were poorly dressed and they carried a sad look on their faces. I was afraid to meet them, but that was only childish fear.

Although my uncle relates that Jose Chávez y Chávez was sentenced to be hanged, in 1920 my brother Luis met him in Pintada at a political rally. He was very old and blind.

El Cachumeno was herding sheep for one of my brothers-in-law near Las Vegas in 1929. He was very old then. He was a short man and quite bent from age.

Before I was ten years of age, I had read the Silva story written by my uncle—but it was only a review, for I knew every story by tradition. I knew every landmark relating to the items in the story and often I rambled around the terrain.

Don Manuel describes Vicente Silva thus:

"Vicente Silva was born in Bernalillo County, Territory of New Mexico, of poor but respectable parents in the year 1845. He never attended school and was, therefore, illiterate. On first appearance he gave the impression of being an honorable man. He was tall and well-built, and his personality helped to hide his inner self.

"Those who knew him well, liked him and one never

dreamed that such a human had been born to lead a life of crime and that in that handsome body dwelt the most perverse soul. It seems that the Devil had endowed him with all that is vile and corrupt.

"Vicente Silva had lived in Las Vegas for more than fifteen years. Soon after his arrival there, he opened a saloon and gambling house where by 1892 he had a large clientele made up of men and women whom the law brands as outcasts. The saloon was open at all hours and it never lacked wine, women and song.

"Among the notorious women who frequented Silva's place of drink were: One called La Golondrina, the Swallow, and two nicknamed Las Elefantas, the Elephants.

"Silva's house of drink and gambling, was a two-story structure; besides the rooms used for selling liquor and gambling, there were many others where Silva and his accomplices held their crime conferences.

"Silva was married, and his immediate family was composed of his wife, Doña Telesfora Sandoval, her brother, Gabriel Sandoval, and an adopted daughter, whose origin and birth will hold an important part in this story."

Often when I was in church or at a celebration where many people gathered, I wondered if Emma Silva was one of the persons around me. I heard the story about her adoption many times. The infant had been found in a stable run by John Miner. I always heard that she was a beautiful child and perhaps of Nordic extraction. It was only by eavesdropping that I heard the story. Our family did not discuss subjects pertaining to morality in the presence of minors, but we managed to run errands when our grandmother and her guests were conversing and in this way we learned the facts of life and the current gossip—mostly in small doses, but enough to arouse our curiosity. Vicente Silva and his wife Doña Telesfora, were childless, and when the child came up for adoption they were given the preference, and she became Emma Silva. It was said that both Silva and his wife as well as Doña Telesfora's brother, Gabriel, loved the child very much. The sad part of it was that Silva, in order to show off the child, took her to the saloon, yet she had the protection of her foster mother who brought her up with the most patient and moral care that was possible in their surroundings.

Doña Telesfora knew of Silva's shady enterprises, yet she never dreamed that he would harm their adopted daughter. When the girl was old enough to go to school, she was placed in Loretto Academy, where the daughters of the most respectable families in Las Vegas and surrounding territory received their education.

On the morning of January 23, 1893, Emma was sent to school as usual. By noon she always came home for her midday meal. She did not come at the usual time and Doña Telesfora became alarmed. She walked to the Academy and, on the way, she was informed by one of the students that at ten o'clock that morning Emma had climbed into a carriage. Doña Telesfora sounded the alarm of the disappearance. Several days passed and she had had no word of her child. Both she and her brother were grief-stricken.

By this time Silva was becoming obsessed with the idea that his wife and brother-in-law were planning to expose him. He hated them and wished to do something to punish them. His first act was to call a meeting of two of his accomplices, one called El Mellado, Toothless, and the other El Lechuza, the Owl. He told them that Gabriel Sandoval, his brother-in-law, was their enemy and they must get rid of him. Their rendezvous was in

Los Alamos, a village twelve miles northeast of Las Vegas. As soon as their plans for the murder of Gabriel were completed, Silva sent El Lechuza, the most cunning of his companions in crime, to Las Vegas to look over the situation in Doña Telesfora's house. He found that they had guests, so the murder was postponed until the next night.

Silva had a paramour who was his confidant. He went to her home that evening and revealed to her his plans for killing his brother-in-law. The woman, whom Don Manuel called Flor de la Peña, was frightened at the thought of murdering a man whom she considered innocent of attempted betrayal. Flor knew than Doña Telesfora was jealous of her, but felt that she had a right to be, for Silva and Flor had been indiscreet. She was with child by Silva and she begged him not to commit the intended crime. Silva would not listen to her. Flor knew there was nothing she could do but keep quiet.

Besides the services of El Mellado and El Lechuza, Silva had secured the help of three of the city policemen, Chávez y Chávez, Julian Trujillo and a man named Alarid. They were part of his gang, yet no one suspected them as other than honorable law enforcement officers.

The kidnapping of Emma had a great effect on Gabriel Sandoval, and Silva knew well that he would leave no stone unturned until she was found. With the pretense that he knew the whereabouts of Emma, Julian Trujillo lured Gabriel into the trap. He told him that he was taking him to Flor de la Peña's home where Silva was hiding Emma. He also told him that they would have the help of the other two policemen. At eight o'clock that evening, they would meet at the appointed place.

By this time it was known that the abductor of Emma had been El Lechuza. As Gabriel was leaving Trujillo, he met the abductor and was about to strike him, but Trujillo intervened. El Lechuza denied any connection with or knowledge of Emma's disappearance. He then proceeded to de la Peña's home to inform Silva that all was in order for Gabriel's murder.

Gabriel had been asked not to relate anything to his sister about the plan to take Emma from Silva, but he was so happy over his success that he told her all. She promised to wait patiently, and he left full of hope. In front of the Buffalo Saloon he met the policemen; they turned towards the Catholic church on their way to Flor's house. Silva was waiting by the ruins of the old Alcalde house. As they approached, he jumped from behind the walls while Alarid and Chávez held Sandoval. Gabriel then knew that he had been betrayed.

Silva had a dagger in his hand. Gabriel begged for mercy, but Silva had none. The two policemen fired on him and Silva thrust the dagger into Sandoval's heart. Silva and El Lechuza dragged Sandoval toward Moreno Street until they reached an old house directly back of Silva's saloon. They threw the body into a hole which had served as a latrine for the saloon. They covered the body with dirt and trash. Doña Telesfora waited for her brother, but when morning came and he had not returned, she went to Uncle Manuel's office. She related to him the incidents leading to her brother's absence. Don Manuel proceeded to the office of the Police Judge. Here I quote from my uncle's relation of the interview:

"Knowing Silva's reputation, immediate action had to be taken to find out if Sandoval had met with foul play.

"Señora de Silva received encouragement and left with great hopes that soon she would hear from her brother.

"About six o'clock that evening of February 14th, one day after Sandoval's disappearance, the author of this story stepped into the office of the Police Judge, who then was Capt. José L. Galindre, a fearless man.

" 'What brings you, Señor de Baca?' he asked.

" 'I need the Chief of Police to help find a young man who has disappeared!'

" 'That is serious,' he said, 'Quite often persons come here to report lost women, but men—'

" 'The loss of a man is more serious than that of a woman.'

" 'There is a little egotism in your reply,' said the judge.

" 'I shall explain: A woman may be lost because her lover has kidnapped her and her disappearance which may cause her family grief, may cause her joy. When a man disappears he may be in a hospital, a suicide, or in jail, or—'

" 'And do you fear that the man you seek may have met with foul play?'

" 'I am afraid so; he has not been home since nine o'clock last evening. I can assure you that Sandoval, if he were alive, would not have failed to come home to his sister's home to sleep or to eat his meals because he has always been punctual, and therefore, I fear that something has happened to him.'

"The Police Judge left his office and in a few minutes he was back and said he had sent for the police chief who in effect came in a brief while.

" 'What do you wish, Señor Galindre?' he asked.

" 'Mr. de Baca wishes to know the whereabouts of Gabriel Sandoval who has disappeared and I ask you to leave no stone unturned until you find him.'

"He answered, 'All the police force is in charge, for I had already been notified about this disappearance. I have conducted some investigations and I believe he has left town.'

"Mr. de Baca said, 'Knowing his habits, I know he would not

have left without informing his sister, so I fear that he has met with some mishap.'

'Anyway,' said the police judge, 'it is urgent that you bring all your forces together with your bloodhounds and search every corner for the missing man.'

'I shall do so,' said the Chief of Police, and he departed.

"He went towards police headquarters and once there, he called Julian Trujillo, Chávez and Alarid, and told them what he had learned from the police judge. They, of course, promised to start the search at once, and they did. They looked everywhere except in the vile hole in which they had buried him. Finally they reported that they could find no clues except that someone had said that at El Puertecito (now Romeroville), a man had been hanged on a pine tree and it might be Sandoval.

"Doña Telesfora, knowing that Julian Trujillo was to have been with her brother the night before, went to inquire from him, as he had promised to help Gabriel bring Emma back. Trujillo denied everything but promised to help in the search in every way possible. They went to El Puertecito and searched every possible place but found no one hanged as had been reported. They returned satisfied that the rumors of a man having been hanged there were without foundation. Gabriel's disappearance remained a deep mystery."

THE old bridge dividing the towns of East and West Las Vegas is one that I shall never forget. It was one of those huge structures of steel which today have disappeared in most places. The old bridge had a history behind it which made it a landmark. Some of our shopping was done in New Town, as we called East Las Vegas. We lived in Old Town. The Gallinas river divides the two towns, and it was the old bridge we had to cross when I was a child. Every time we crossed, I lived the stories I had heard about murders and criminals hiding under the bridge.

No story stood more vividly in my mind than the murder of Patricio Maes by the Silva bandits. Patricio was one of Silva's confederates. I do not know if it always rained or snowed when crimes were committed, but it seems that all storytellers in my young days made it quite dramatic by describing the weather. Be that as it may, one very cold and snowy night, while Las Vegas citizens slept, Silva and his gang were in conference planning the murder of one Patricio Maes.

For some reason or other, Silva suspected Patricio of betrayal. In the conference, he told his companions that they must do away with Patricio. They held a council among them similar to a court trial. Each member held a position in the court, and the trial continued to a late hour in the night. Most of the men were in favor of giving Patricio a chance; even as criminals, they must have felt that whatever Silva had against Maes, he had been one of them. The defendant was invited to the trial and he denied all the accusations. In those days the politicians in San Miguel county were divided into factions rather than parties.

I have told about the Gentlemen of Labor in another chapter. It seems that Maes had affiliated himself with this faction and it was the one waging war on the evildoers. The first offense of which Silva had been accused was the theft of some horses from Don Refugio Esquibel. Silva suspected Patricio as the informer. Whether Patricio was guilty of treason will never be known, but he was sentenced to die and on the appointed night he was taken to the bridge by the bandits. A rope was tied around his neck, one end was tied to one of the iron railings of the bridge. After he was dead, one of the men pushed the body into the air. As he did so, the noose gave way and Patricio fell into the river, which in those days had water and this night was ice. They pulled the body back and left it hanging by the bridge. Next morning, Silva himself gave the alarm that a body was hanging by the river bridge. The police, who were Silva's accomplices, certainly were no help.

Another story which made the bridge memorable to me was about a man by the name of Carpio Saiz. This poor man had been the treasurer of the Sabinoso school on the Rio Colorado. He had come to Las Vegas to receive some money, $160, which had been apportioned to his school district. He was held up by the bandits as he crossed the bridge, and was murdered in cold blood under the bridge. His body was never found, but in those days many persons disappeared and were never found.

The old bridge was replaced by a concrete structure in 1909. This is the bridge which I crossed every day while I was attending high school and later college at what is today Highlands University. With the old bridge went all the memories, but it had to be that way, for Las Vegas became a different place from the one in which my uncles lived in terror.

In 1929, I was appointed Home Demonstration Agent for Santa Fe County. One of the scenic places which I visited once a month was the San Pedro country on the way to Cedar Grove. Many times as I drove through those piñons and junipers, I thought of this as Silva's paradise. And it is a paradise. This is the place which Vicente Silva selected to hide his loot. His manager was El Romo, Flat Nose, who took care of the horses, sheep and cattle which were taken from the San Miguel, Guadalupe and Mora county people. It was in this place that Don Refugio Esquibel found his horses branded with Silva's mark and which proved his first offense. After that he had to go in hiding, but the crimes continued.

THE Silva terror did not die out for many years, at least not in the memory of the people. I must have been fourteen years of age one summer I spent with a cousin of mine who lived in Los Alamos. This village had been the hideout of Silva and his bandits. That summer I heard many stories about the pillaging and murders. One was the robbery of Mr. William Frank's store. At the time that I was there, Mr. Frank was still running his place of business. He was quite reticent and even though I tried to get the story from him, he did not tell much. Enough to arouse my curiosity. My cousin's father-in-law enjoyed telling stories, and from him I gathered a few details. The condition of the weather was always important.

On a rainy April night, Silva and his accomplices decided not to leave out Mr. Frank from their number of victims. In order to find out where the merchant kept his money, Silva sent one of his men by the name of Medrán to buy some liquor. He gave him a twenty dollar gold piece so that Mr. Frank would have to make change. Mr. Frank was not one to distrust his customers, and without any suspicion he went to his safe and got the change and gave it to Medrán. Medrán watched carefully and to his way of figuring, it appeared that there must have been three hundred dollars in the safe. This he reported to Silva.

They waited for Mr. Frank to retire, and to make sure that the villagers were not venturing out in the torrential rain. They put on their masks and then proceeded to the store which they entered by breaking the front door. The safe was a large one, weighing about a ton. In some way, the six men assigned to the robbery, who were El Mellado (Toothless), El Moro (the Moor), El Patas de Mico (Monkey Feet), Dionicio Sisneros, Medrán, and Silva carried the safe to a wagon which they had left outdoors waiting. One saddled horse pulled the wagon.

They were not satisfied by taking the safe, which to their chagrin contained only forty dollars, but they took the books in which Mr. Frank kept his records of debts and other important papers which he kept in the safe. They built a fire and burned everything—papers only of value to Mr. Frank. Silva said to his companions, "Let us be charitable to the poor fools who owe money to the rich merchant." It was said that Mr. Frank lost over ten thousand dollars in debts, and possibly more.

Another story common in Los Alamos and which I heard during my visit there, was about the murder of Pedro Romero. This young man lived in Los Alamos. He fell in love with a

woman who had been married to Germán Maestas, a man who, when he was not in jail, had just been released from there. He had been one of Silva's henchmen. His marriage to the woman involved had not been announced or even registered. The woman, whose name was Rosa, took advantage of German's absence during one of his trips to the jail for some robbery which he had committed. She went after Romero and since she was an attractive woman, he married her. The ceremony was performed by El Mellado, who was then Justice of the Peace.

Germán heard about the marriage while he was in jail and he swore he would get revenge. He did not wait to finish his sentence. He was a trusty of the jailer, who was so accustomed to having him as a guest that he did not bother to watch him. With a companion he picked up, and a couple of horses which he roped in someone's pasture, he proceeded to Los Alamos. They found Rosa with Romero. After insulting him and beating him up, Germán took Rosa back to her home, which was about twenty miles distant. She did not remain there long; as soon as Germán had gone on one of his horse-stealing trips, she walked back to Los Alamos and joined Pedro, who had been left tied to a chair.

Germán was enraged with Rosa. That same day, he went in search of Jesús Vialpando, one of Silva's men, and in his company started a search for Rosa. Before arriving at Los Alamos, they spied a sheep camp. Being hungry they decided to stop and get breakfast. They had spent the night in search and had not had any food. Arriving at the camp, the dogs came after them. Maestas shot at them. The yelping of the wounded dogs reached the camp tent and who should come out but Pedro Romero, who was the overseer of the sheep. One can imagine his terror at seeing Maestas and Vialpando. They ordered him to prepare breakfast, which he did. Once the meal was over Maestas began insulting Romero. Romero had a gun, but before he could reach for it, Maestas and Vialpando fired and Romero fell dead into the embers of the fire he had built for the preparation of the meal. A small boy, who served as sheepherder, was the only witness of the crime. Maestas proposed to kill him, but Vialpando opposed it.

Soon after the bandits were out of sight, the thirteen-year-old boy removed Romero's body from the fire and started for Los Alamos to report the murder.

WRITING about Vialpando brings to mind another murder in which he was implicated. He and two other companions were on their way to San Pedro, in Santa Fe County, to sell some horses which they had stolen. After remaining a few days there, they were returning to Las Vegas. They stopped at the ranch of a man by the name of Tomás Martínez. There they killed a cow belonging to Martínez. About the time that they were cooking some of the meat, Tomás arrived on the scene. The bandits knew that the animal was one of his herd. Immediately, they planned to murder him. Tomás was accompanied by his dog. He reached the fire which the bandits had built and talking to them, he drew near to warm himself. The winter had been snowy and there was about eighteen inches of snow on the ground.

He noticed the cowhide near by, and as it was customary for cattle owners, he proceeded to examine it. While his back was turned, Vialpando fired two shots which killed Martinez. He and his companions took the body and placed it on the fire, adding more wood to make sure of its burning completely. One of them fired at the dog. The dog ran towards the house where Martinez lived, which was about six miles away. The Martinez family at first did not pay any attention to the dog; they thought Tomás would come along presently. The dog kept barking and howling, and finally aroused the family to suspect that all was not well. Some of the members started out, guided by the dog until they reached the place where the fire had burned. There was nothing but ashes and their thought was that Tomás might be frozen somewhere, and the dog was trying to tell them. The dog would not leave the spot. Finally one of the men noticed that the dog was digging in the ashes and succeeded in finding one of Tomás' legs which still had the shoe on. They scattered the ashes and there found the bones of their kinsman.

The ranch where the murder took place is on what is now called Glorieta Mesa, not far from the railroad station of Rowe, in San Miguel County. Feliciano Chávez had been Vialpando's partner in crime. My uncle, Daniel Cabeza de Baca, was Deputy Sheriff under his cousin, Don Hilario Romero, at the time, and it was they who arrested Vialpando and Chávez at Los Valles de San Agustín, near La Liendre.

The Martínez family were prominent citizens of Santa Fe County and my home in Santa Fe is built on the land which was originally theirs. I have heard the story from them on different occasions.

11. The Field of Burdocks

FOR THREE YEARS, SAN MIGUEL COUNTY LIVED IN FEAR. Not a day passed when the citizens could have respite from the many crimes committed. It might be robbery, arson, rape or murder. A man by the name of Abraham Aboulafia, who had come from Turkey and who had a small business, was murdered and no one ever knew who killed him. He was the first victim found. After that, it was a daily occurrence. The purpose was robbery. Later the body of a tailor by the name of Jacob Stutzman was found in one of the arroyos near Las Vegas. His murder came out in the confession of the Silva bandits at their trial.

Vicente Silva became a fiend. Shortly after the murder of his brother-in-law, he sent a letter to his wife signed by her brother asking her to come to Los Alamos to join the brother, Silva and Emma. Doña Telesfora, who loved Silva, thought that perhaps he had repented and immediately made preparations for her departure. El Cachumeno, the Twisted One, was sent to take her to Los Alamos and with him he had a letter from Silva. I quote from the de Baca version:

>   "Los Alamos, New Mexico
>   May 18, 1893
>
> "My dear Doña Telesfora:
>
> "I hope this finds you in good health. Gabriel, Emma and I are well, thanks to God.
>
> "The bearer of this letter has taken a wagon and he has his orders to bring all your furniture and other belongings, and he will take them to El Coyote where we shall establish our residence.
>
> "I hope you will comply with my request to send your household things and tonight El Cachumeno will call for you. I shall meet you at Cañada Pastosa and as soon as we reach Los Alamos, I shall see that you join Emma and Gabriel.
>
> "Make sure that your departure from Las Vegas will be as secret as possible. Wishing to see you, and with all my love,
>
>   Vicente Silva"

Doña Telesfora was extremely happy and she made plans for her husband's conversion into a respectable citizen. By nightfall, she had everything ready. She left for Los Alamos by an unfrequented road. At Cañada Pastosa she was met by Silva and El Lechuza.

In Los Alamos, five of his men were waiting for them. These were his best henchmen and for some time they had been dissatisfied with the way Silva was treating them. He gave them part of the loot, but they felt that they should have had more of it. On this night, they were known to be plotting against him. They had helped Silva to amass a fortune, and this time they planned to bring him to a compromise or else. Don Manuel Cabeza de Baca tells of the conversation in these words:

"One of the members of the gang who possessed more courage, spoke to them saying,

" 'Let us be frank with one another; between friends there is no need to deny that while we remain under Silva's domination, we cannot get very far; we are in constant danger of falling into the hands of the law, and it is time that we sever our relations with him and divide the money which he has in keeping among our group. Tonight he will join his wife into eternity. He has gotten us into all these crimes and we have had enough. It is time that he pay his debts to Lucifer!

" 'You are right,' answered all in one voice. 'Let us end it all tonight.'

" 'If Silva kills his wife, I swear that I will get rid of him when he least expects it,' said one of the bandits, an obese man, frog-legged and one who was capable of disposing of Silva.

"The bandits agreed on their scheme and only awaited the proper moment.

"A few hours later after the men had made their plans, Silva arrived with his wife whom he had met at the appointed place. He sent El Lechuza back to Las Vegas to observe the reaction which Doña Telesfora's departure had upon the town's citizens."

SILVA arrived in Los Alamos with his wife on the night of May 19, 1893. He took her to the house where his henchmen were waiting. He ordered them to leave as he wanted to be alone with her.

As soon as they were alone he began to tell her that he must get away from the Las Vegas country and that he planned to take her to Taos with Gabriel and Emma who were now in El Coyote, near Mora.

The author of the Vicente Silva story who helped in getting

the confession at the trial of the bandits describes the scene as related to him by those who overheard it:

"'I have arranged in Fernando de Taos to establish our home there. In a few days you and the family will start for that place; I shall go to Las Vegas and settle some business that I have there, then I will join you.

"'I wish you would let me have whatever money you may have with you in case I should need it, because the little money I had, I left in Taos to be delivered to you upon arrival there.'

"Doña Telesfora thought it strange that Silva would want to take her money and at first she refused to part with it, but finally turned over two hundred dollars to him. After taking the money, Silva said, 'I would now like to have your jewels.'

"Doña Telesfora, who was an intelligent woman, immediately sensed that something was amiss. 'Why would you want my jewels?' she asked. 'Perhaps to give them to your paramour.'

"Silva, at the mention of his mistress became furious and angrily said, 'Do not dare talk like that. Seal your wretched lips.'

"'The truth hurts you, does it not?'

"'It is true that I love Flor more than I do you.'

"'Then you are not only a criminal but a despicable person.'

"'And you accuse me of being a criminal, you the only being on earth who might overlook it?'

"'I overlook your crimes! No one knows better than I why you have dedicated your days to a wicked life and no one could despise you more deeply. You have been unfaithful to me; you have branded yourself with the most infamous deeds; you have become a monster and you are not content with what already you have done to me, you have taken my money and now you wish to deprive me of my jewels. What do you mean to do, Don Vicente?'

"'To take advantage of this supreme moment and punish you as you deserve,' Silva answered in a defiant tone.

"Doña Telesfora arose and made for the door but it was locked. She knew she was trapped. In anguish, she asked, 'What are you planning to do?'

"'Sit down,' he said.

"'Don Vicente, Don Vicente!'

"'You know me well enough and I shall take advantage of this moment to make you pay for your faults, Doña Telesfora.'

"'Holy heavens, what are you going to do?'

"'Punish you as I told you.'

"'Have pity, Don Vicente. Have pity!' she begged as she fell on her knees.

"'There is no pity.'

"'What have I done?'

"'Arise and read.'

"Don Vicente took a letter from his pocket and handed it to her. Doña Telesfora could hardly read; her whole body was trembling and the words became blurs. She felt death so near that she could not control even her hands. Coming close to a lamp, she read:

MY DEAR DON VICENTE:

> Your wife, Doña Telesfora, is about to turn us into the depths of the law. She has made public all the secrets which she had about our corrupt lives and there is going to be a devil of reckoning for all of us. If you wish to avoid this you better dispose of that woman. If she remains here any longer, it will be too late for the rest of us.
>
> Your friend,
E. A.

" 'And why should you credit this letter? There is no truth in it. I have never even thought of doing such a thing. Do you believe that if I had intended to act in that way, I would have come to you here tonight? I came because I love you in spite of your faults and because you are my husband.'

" 'You do not love me, you are a wicked, devilish woman.'

" 'What words to use on a defenseless woman. Do not torment me, for the love of God! Do you intend to kill your wife?'

" 'Not my wife, my dishonor. Read the words in that letter and hide in shame for your deeds.'

" 'I have nothing to hide. I have done nothing for which to be ashamed. If it is a crime to follow you, if it is a crime to prove my love, if this is unforgivable, then kill me but do not use fiction. I can see that you intend to get rid of me so that you can be free to unite yourself to Flor; I am an obstacle to your plans.'

"Everytime Doña Telesfora pronounced Flor's name, Silva's eyes flashed like those of any angry beast. At this moment, he took a dagger from his belt.

"Doña Telesfora seeing herself attacked, felt a cold chill through her body. She could not move but her lips invoked God's help, 'Heavenly Father, have mercy on me, save me, soften his heart!'

"Silva, filled with anger, took his wife by the arm and shook her violently.

"Doña Telesfora, trembling, half dead, her heart beating fast, saw death approaching at the hands of the beast who had once given her his pledge of love.

" 'I read in your eyes what your soul feels,' he said. 'You did not expect to pay for your betrayal in this manner; the surprise is disagreeable!' And the assassin laughed. The laugh sounded in Doña Telesfora's heart as the echo of approaching death.

"'Well, let us finish this. I do not want to be cruel, it is more generous to kill promptly,' and saying this, he pierced her between the breasts with the dagger. A sea of blood spurted and slowly Doña Telesfora fell on the hard floor.

"Silva watched his victim as the last signs of life disappeared. The face of the martyred woman paled, her eyes closed and her lips half opened gave a deep sigh and in a moment she had ceased to exist.

"Silva was satisfied, he had added another black page to his life of crime.

"'All is ended,' he said. 'If the dead could be grateful for the privilege of dying, this unhappy woman would thank me and forgive me for the favor I have done her. She would sooner or later have betrayed me. Now, I am safe.' And he joined the men in the next room.

"'What is our program for tonight?' questioned El Patas de Rana, Froglegs.

"'I don't know,' answered Silva, 'but I have done away with this woman and now I need help to dispose of her body. We must give her decent burial as it is fitting to a group like ours.'

"The bandits entered the room where Doña Telesfora's body lay and El Mellado, after looking at it for a moment said, 'How well our chief handles the dagger.'

"'Yes,' said another, 'he is an expert in the art. If Captain Esquibel should cross his path!'

"'I would make him dance a jig,' answered Silva, who had not forgotten that he had turned him in for the theft of Refugio's horses.

"Silva opened a belt which he had tied around his waist, took out some money and handed each man a ten dollar bill, saying, 'prepare to give burial to that unhappy woman.'

"He ordered them to wrap her in some blankets and a shawl and then to follow him. He led them to the Campo de Los Cadillos, field of burdocks, which is about a quarter of a league from Los Alamos.

"The Campo de Los Cadillos has a plain runoff, but at a short distance there is a fall of about a thousand yards in width with myriads of narrow arroyos, some with a depth of about twelve feet. Silva, upon arrival, chose the one which he thought would best conceal the body of his wife and there he ordered the body to be lowered. After they pushed the earth from the sides of the arroyo, the body was well covered.

"The burial of his wife finished, Silva ordered his men back to the house. They had gone hardly thirty paces. El Patas de Rana, who was walking beside Silva to his left, upon a given signal, pointed his gun and discharged it at Silva's left temple. Silva fell to the ground like lightning, never to rise again.

"The bandits went through Silva's pockets and belt, and after having taken the money and jewels which he had, they pushed his body without ceremony into an arroyo close by the one in which they had buried his wife. They pushed the sides of the earth upon it and there left him. All was finished; the infamous bandit who had terrorized the citizens of San Miguel and other counties received his well deserved punishment from the hands of the family of devils which he had created and so ably trained.

"After dividing the loot, the criminals dispersed in different directions. El Rana arrived in El Coyote by daybreak; Medrán and Sandoval in Las Vegas, El Moro and El Mellado in their respective homes in Los Alamos. Dionicio Sisneros went to Watrous. The next day, Sisneros borrowed a team and wagon with the pretext of taking his family to Ute Creek, but a few days later he was in Winslow, Arizona."

Silva's death did not end the terror from the bandits and it was not until the governor of the territory sent out a proclamation offering pardon to the accomplice or accomplices who would be willing to tell all and a reward of $500 for each of those arrested.

During the second week in April, 1894, the Court started its session and among the trials was that of El Mellado, who had been arrested for robbery. He knew there was no escape and his best chance was to make a complete confession of all the crimes and gain his liberty. He told everything from the beginning of the organization, which was named La Sociedad de Bandidos de Nuevo Mexico, to the current crimes committed at the time of his trial. He testified before the interpreter of the Court, who at the time was Don Rafael Romero from Mora, the district attorney, and my uncle, Don Manuel Cabeza de Baca, who was present.

The confession of the crimes by El Mellado aroused the interest of my uncle Manuel in finding out the details of other events in the work of the bandits. From Medrán he obtained an account of Silva's end and the murder of Doña Telesfora. He proceeded to the place where Medrán told that the victims had been buried. The bodies were found in an arroyo by a field of burdocks near Los Alamos.

The Silva bandits had nicknames or aliases, yet it does not necessarily mean that these names were given to them because of their alliance with crime. The New Mexicans of Spanish extraction are quite fond of giving nicknames to everybody around them. Sometimes they may be pet names, but more often they are given in ridicule.

My first trip to Los Alamos was for the wedding of Uncle Manuel's son, Florencio. It was in 1905 and we were riding in the same carriage as Don Manuel. As we went by the arroyo, he pointed it out to us saying that it was there Silva and Doña Telesfora had been buried. The evil doings of the bandit were always a topic of interest to our family, for it was an era never to be forgotten by the respectable citizens of Las Vegas and surrounding country. As I remember, only those who lived in the perilous days could appreciate peaceful living which came with the turn of the new century. By 1900, the men who had been at the head of the political parties that tolerated corruption had passed on or had lost prestige, yet it seems that honest men were always in the minority in San Miguel County. I grew up in an atmosphere of political chaos to the point that even though I try to be liberal in my political views, my childhood experiences will not allow me to even consider voting a certain political party and I will not vote a turncoat either.

Don Manuel Cabeza de Baca was very influential politically in his early life. In his late years and after writing the Silva story he lost ground. In 1901, he moved his voting rights to Guadalupe County where he spent at least three months during the year and most of his law practice was in that county. He wrote the Silva story in English also, but for some reason or other, he never published it. His daughter, Eloisa Cabeza de Baca de Gallegos, has it in her possession and I have had access to it.

Don Manuel died in 1915, a disillusioned man. The men he helped to climb in politics betrayed him and were responsible for his downfall.

12. Incidents

BILLY THE KID HAS BEEN GLAMORIZED in song and story. In the eyes of respectable persons, he was never a hero. As I remember, he and Vicente Silva were hardly mentioned except as criminals by members of my family. As a matter of fact they were hardly worthy of mentioning at all. I am sure that a great deal of history has been lost due to the hatred our family had for criminals or even politicians who were supposedly respectable but had dual personalities—and there were many of them. This I have learned after leaving the shelter of our ancestral home.

One story about the time of Billy the Kid, I heard from a woman who had been a servant in my grandmother's sister's home. She was our next door neighbor and she was like one of our own. Her grandfather had been a bond slave in my grandmother's home and her whole family had to serve out the bondage. Once they were free, they still worked for the family in some capacity or other.

This woman, I shall call her Remedios, delighted in telling how one day she was washing clothes by the acequia for her mistress. An American rode by and said to her, "Go with me?" "Yes," she said, and off she rode with him. He took her to Fort Sumner and there she lived with him. I do not know if she was married to him, but she had children by him. He was one of Billy the Kid's partners and she was in Fort Sumner at the time that Billy was killed by Sheriff Garrett. She was one of the chief mourners, as she used to tell us. When she started her tale of adventure, grandmother sent us to bed and later would say, "If Remedios had any decency about her, she would not tell the story of her life. I do not want you children to listen to her." She was a marvelous storyteller and full of humor, but our puritanical rearing made it almost impossible to delight in her tales.

Another story of Billy the Kid, I heard from a man whom I shall call Ramón and who worked on the ranch. When Ramón was a small boy, he and his brother used to freight goods to the Indians at Bosque Redondo, now Fort Sumner. One night he was sent to the store to buy candles. Billy the Kid was there and when Ramón finished his purchase, Billy approached him and asked, "Where is the poker game?" "In our camp," he replied. Billy said, "Tell your brother that I will be there to win all his money." He went to the camp and after playing all night, he lost heavily, but took it good naturedly. As he remembered, Billy always had someone outside watching while he was in a game or in some hall, bar or house. Another impressive account which Ramón gave was that Billy found it too dangerous to sleep inside a house. He and his henchmen slept always out in the brush with their guns across their bodies.

GEORGE ECHOLS lived in the Trementina country, not far from Las Vegas. Very few people, if any, knew him intimately. He lived as a recluse, and his neighbors scarcely ever saw him.

In the late summer of 1914, the notorious Carter brothers went to his ranch with the excuse of buying cattle from him. Echols took them out on the range to show them what cattle he had for sale. After the trio rode about a mile from his ranch, one of the Carters pulled a gun on Echols and the other brother handcuffed him. They then rode on for fifty miles until they came to Luciano Mesa at the head of Bull Cañon, which is part of the Ceja of the Llano. That part of the country is rough and rugged, and broken trails are few. At that time, only cowboys in search of strays penetrated the Bull Cañon country.

Echols was taken to a lonely half-dugout on the rim of Luciano Mesa overlooking the cañon. At that place the mesa is about a thousand feet high and very steep. One of the Carters tied Echols to the beam which supported the roof of the cabin, with a trace chain padlocked to one of his legs. The other Carter headed for the Echols ranch where he hired three cowboys with shady reputations and rounded up the cattle—Echols' entire herd. The cattle were driven to Montoya, a town not far from where Echols was held prisoner, while one of the Carters watched him.

The other brother shipped the cattle to Kansas City, Missouri, after they were inspected by an inspector with no scruples. Upon the brother's return with plenty of money in his pocket, the two Carters departed for Mexico.

In the meantime, Echols was left alone and he managed to slip the chain off the beam to which it had been tied. The chain was still locked to his ankle, but he was able to make it into Montoya after having been captive for two weeks. On the day he arrived in Montoya, my brother, Luis, happened to be doing our monthly marketing and buying. He heard the story from Echols who had stopped at a ranch house, where he had the chain sawed off.

Two or three days after Echols had come to Montoya, H. L. Thurman, a citizen of the town, received a letter from the Carters in which they enclosed the key to the padlock and instructions as to where they had left George Echols. They enclosed a ten dollar bill to pay Thurman for his trouble.

Echols lived in fear that the Carters would return and finish him off, but they soon got into trouble in Mexico. They crossed into Luna County in New Mexico, where they were arrested and turned over to the San Miguel County Sheriff, Lorenzo Delgado. They were tried and sent to the penitentiary in Santa Fe.

Cattle rustling had been quite a game in the early days and continued for many years. By 1914, the laws had become more strict and the Carter-Echols incident caused quite a sensation. The fencing of the land did away with the stealing of livestock, although once in a while one heard of some rancher losing a few head. After the land was taken up by the homesteaders, the cattle rustlers were more cautious. It was not easy to drive cattle without being seen, as they had to go through someone's pasture or gate and the landowners were forever watching for trespassers.

Don José María Baca was Don Paco Baca's father. He was born in La Cienega in Santa Fe county, but had moved to Chihuahua where Don Paco was born. In his middle age he came back to New Mexico and then lived in Las Colonias. He was a great buffalo hunter and during these expeditions he met a Comanche chief who was known as El Puertas. They became steadfast friends. On one occasion, El Puertas was going to Las Colonias to bring back a horse Don José María had given him. He was also taking an Indian girl as present for the Baca family. She was a captive from an enemy tribe. About a mile from the railroad station of Newkirk and what was then the sheep and cattle ranch of Don Antonio José Gallegos, El Puertas encountered a group of Indians from Bosque Redondo who were on their way to their former hunting grounds on the Llano. The Indians killed and scalped him and took the Indian girl with them, for she was one of their tribe. They hung the scalp to a juniper stump as they traveled east, and many an old-timer used to point out the stump as the one on which El Puertas' scalp hung. Santiago Vigil from El Valle, one of our neighbors, showed the stump to my brother and he pointed it out to me.

Soon after the murder, Don Paco and a group of buffalo hunters, came by on their way to the hunting grounds. They buried the body in an arroyo called Arroyo de las Cuevas.

In the 1920's a grandson-in-law of Don Paco found the skeleton, which had been uncovered by the erosion of the soil on the arroyo banks. Don Paco, who then lived in Puerto de Luna, came to view the skeletal remains and he was sure they were those of El Puertas.

V. WITHIN OUR BOUNDARIES

13. Mustangs

AFTER THE LAND WAS FENCED, a new page was turned in cattle history. Papá became aware that quality rather than quantity would be the salvation of the cattlemen.

The cattle in the days of the unfenced range were descendants of the cattle brought in from Mexico by the Spaniards. In the early sixteenth century, Spanish cattle had been brought into Mexico from the island of Santo Domingo. These were the longhorns, a breed which by necessity had become hardy. They could resist all types of climates and during droughts, if far from watering places, they could go several days without water. If the grass were scarce, they could subsist on hardy desert plants. These cattle were ferocious-looking animals, of great stature, bony and thin flanked. Their long horns, gave them their title as a breed, but in color, they had no particular identification; there were brindle cattle, dun colored ones, white, spotted and black animals. The longhorns being natural rustlers, the cowmen did not have to upset themselves about the welfare of their stock; the cattle managed to survive all sorts of difficulties.

They were not heavy, and, in order to bring good prices, the steers were left on the range to grow to maturity before they were driven to market or sold to the buyers. To derive a comfortable income, the cattle owners had to run hundreds of animals, but that was not difficult when the range was free and extensive.

I do not know if these longhorn steers were vicious, but they had a wicked look and many a time I climbed the windmill tower when a bunch of them came to water.

The boys derived a great deal of fun from seeing me sitting up on the tower, for I always wished to be considered brave. I lived in the land of storytelling and I wanted to be like the pioneer women who settled the sparsely inhabited sheep and cattle country.

I remember one morning a herd of steers had kept me up in the windmill ladder for almost two hours. I came into the house, meekly trying to avoid the sneers of the boys, but El Cuate took my side.

"It would not be so funny," he said, "if those steers had trampled you and turned you into dust. They cannot be trusted; it is lucky that you had a place to escape to."

Papá joined him in his sympathy as he said to the boys,

"I have been thinking it is time we were improving our cattle. These animals have to be kept in the pasture too many years to be worth anything.

"A great many of the cattlemen have already started breeding their cows to Hereford bulls and the cross is a good one. If our herds are improved, we can diminish their numbers and derive as much or more profit as we did when we did not have to limit the numbers."

Luis replied to Papá's discourse by adding:

"We have to face the fact, also, that our grass will feed only a limited number, so the sooner we improve our stock the better it will be for our land. Our pasture is already overgrazed."

Some of the boys thought it was just a notion Papá and Luis had absorbed from reading, but El Cuate agreed with them. He had worked on ranches where they raised thoroughbred cattle and he gave Papá the names of men who had bulls for sale. It was not long before Spear Bar Ranch boasted of registered bulls.

Each morning, the boys rode out in the pastures to make sure the cows had not jumped the fences. Fences were substantially built with posts cut from junipers on Papá's land. Three or four wires were stretched from post to post; each post was placed fifteen or twenty feet apart with *entremedios* to keep the wire from sagging. Even though the fences were strong, there was danger of the cattle jumping over, as they were not used to being held within one pasture.

In the late summer, Papá went out with the boys to cut hay on the meadows. If we had good rains, the grass would grow tall enough to make hay. It was necessary to feed the cattle in the middle of the winter, at least those who might come out poorly. Cottonseed cake was coming into use, but the hay helped to supplement the ration, and it was easier on Papá's pocketbook.

The land was divided into winter and summer pastures, and in this way grass was available at all times unless there was a drought.

In the days of unfenced range, the cattle watered in the arroyos, springs or water holes. Now, Papá had to drill wells, put up windmills and build tanks to provide water for the stock; there was not an idle moment on the ranch.

WE had many horses, and they had been bred from the early Spanish mustangs into different types. But the best cow ponies were those in whose blood was that of the early horses of the plains. A good cow pony must be swift, and the imported horses were heavy and needed training to learn to head off cattle. We had palominos, paints, duns, bays and many others. The boys had their favorite horses and were closer to them than to their best human friends. Each boy on Papá's ranch had from ten to twelve horses as *remuda*. I had my own horses, too, but they were gentle ponies. True to my aristocratic rearing, I had to lead a ladylike life and should not resemble that of our uncouth neighbors whose women were able to do men's work. I always envied any woman who could ride a bronco, but in my society it was not done. How skillfully they saddled a horse! I often watched them catch a pony out in the pasture, just as the men did on our range, but it never was my privilege to have to do it. When I arose each morning, my horse was already saddled and tied to a hitching post waiting for me if I cared to ride.

The horses which were not used as *remuda* or for ranch chores, roamed wild in our pastures. When new horses were needed, they had to be broken. I remember José Gonzáles of statewide fame, who came to our rancho to break horses for Papá. On one occasion, José broke ten horses for us. He kept the ten horses on *persoga,* that is, tied to a pole. The horses were tied with horsehair *reatas* because hemp or rawhide ropes shrank when they got wet. (Often, I helped Papá make hobbles and *reatas* from horsehair by turning the *tarabilla,* a sort of spindle, for him.) Each day José *cabalgaba,* mounted, each of the ten horses, but only one horse went through the tactics of horse breaking.

José Gonzáles went from ranch to ranch breaking horses for the different owners. By 1899, before my time, his fame had become quite widespread. In that year, at Las Vegas, he gave an exhibition of his skill as "bronco buster" at the Rough Riders' Reunion when Colonel Theodore Roosevelt was guest of honor.

Since that day the event has become an annual affair, called the Las Vegas Cowboys' Reunion.

Cattle inside of fences take care of themselves, but there was always work for the owner and his men. Fences had to be kept in repair to prevent the stock from wandering into other pastures; gates had to be kept shut, and we had many gates in all parts of our land; the windmills had to be oiled and repaired constantly. There were arroyos to endanger the cows. These were not a great menace when cattle were fat, but if cattle were poor and they became bogged down, they might perish if the boys did not find them in time. The range had to be ridden daily; the boys watched for missing cattle. One single cow could cause several boys to ride for a week in her search.

It never failed to amaze me to hear the boys discuss the cattle as they came in each evening after the day's ride. They had a name for each cow, or some way to identify her, and there were several hundred. To me, they were all white-faced and dun-colored, but to the boys, each had an individuality. If one single cow was not grazing in its accustomed place, they searched for her until she was found. Often the cow had strayed with another bunch, but if she were not found, the boys reported it at headquarters and the next day all the men kept on the lookout for the missing animal. With the fencing of the land, there was not much cattle rustling, but the cattle owner took no chances.

HOUSEKEEPING on the rancho fascinated me when I was very young. There was not very much of it. Breakfast was the most important meal and that was a real one consisting of cereal, eggs —lots of them, stacks of hot cakes, piles of bacon, fried potatoes and plenty of coffee. The cooking utensils were all black on the outside. Meals had to be prepared in a hurry for a hungry lot of cowboys and the pots and pans had to be placed next to the wood fire.

On our part of the Llano, there was plenty of firewood, for we lived just over the Ceja from the real Llano land. We had juniper and piñon trees and it was a matter of a few hours to supply the rancho with a week's or month's supply of dry wood.

El Cuate was the ranch cook, but his duties were not confined to cooking alone; anyone was cook when he arrived and no food was ready. All the boys could cook. I am sure Papá was a good cook, too, but he had turned this job over to the men who helped with the ranch work.

There were no regular hours for meals. One never knew when the men would cover the vast territory over which the cattle roamed, although, by the time the sun came up, they were well started on their daily roundup. It might be three, four or five o'clock in the afternoon before anyone returned. Beans were a common fare and anyone remaining at the ranch house kept the pot boiling until the others came home. We had beans with plenty of salt pork in them. This was a summer dish, for in the winter, beef was eaten at all meals.

As each boy left his bed in the morning, he rolled it and put it away for the day. Papá and my brother had bedsteads, of course, but their beds were made only when they were changed. Usually after they arose, they pulled the covers over the pillows, and the beds were ready for the next time they were to be used.

The men on the rancho were careful about sweeping the house once a week, whether it needed it or not, as they often remarked. They washed dishes after meals and Papá was a fanatic, as the boys thought, about scalding the dishes. He did not see a need for washing them on all sides, but they must be scalded.

Our mother had died when we were babies and our Spanish grandmother had reared us in the most fastidious manner conceivable. If she had known how well adapted I was to carefree housekeeping existence, she would never have permitted my summer vacationing on the rancho. But as I grew older, my former rearing became evident and I made new rules, which the men resented but accepted meekly.

BRANDING time was the most delightful experience, for then Papá allowed me to ride with him after cattle. I shall never forget my first ride on a real cow pony. I was so proud of having graduated to that degree, and, as we were bringing a bunch of cattle for branding, an animal strayed from the bunch and my horse made a rush for it, as all cow ponies always do. Not prepared for the quick sway, I came down on *tierra firme*. Papá kept the secret for a long time, but when it escaped him, I had to hide myself, until the men had their attention turned to more serious matters.

It took several days to round up the cattle for one day's branding. These were put into the big corral and kept there overnight. The bawling of calves and the bellowing of cattle, from the time they were driven into the enclosure until they were turned out, when the branding was finished, resounded in the air, with only an occasional coyote yelp to change the tone of the noise. On a quiet night, it was wonderful to be lulled to sleep by the bellowing music.

Branding was a social gathering as well as a necessary task. It took many men to perform all the usual jobs of driving the herds, separating them, roping, throwing the animal down, branding, earmarking and castrating. We had neighbors who still had small herds and they came to help. Sometimes the women came along, too, to help with the cooking. I remember times when twenty or thirty persons were gathered at our rancho. It was quite an event, for in the evenings, although the men were tired, there was an exchange of gossip, stories of early "cow punching," killings, cattle rustling and pioneering in the prairies.

UNTIL 1915, there were still a few sheep owners who had their flocks east of us, and who came from Las Vegas to visit their holdings. Our home was a stopping place for the night, and, to me, this was a page from a fairy tale. They were sad people, these men, for their days on the Llano were numbered. Papá and El Cuate would converse about them after they were gone and I knew that one day they would not be coming through.

The priest from Puerto de Luna came occasionally to say Mass in the few chapels of that day, at El Valle, Benavídez,

Newkirk, Cuervo, and at the Pedro Romero Ranch. These were built in a late era to provide a place of worship for families who took up land in the early twentieth century. Sometimes, Papá would take me to one of these places to hear Mass and it was an event never to be forgotten. Families came in carriages, wagons or automobiles, men came on horseback for the festivity. The *patrón,* or owner of the chapel, was host to all visitors. Food was served after the Mass, and the old custom of feeding the men first still prevailed. I always sat by Papá and the women and girls eyed me with curiosity.

My summer vacations seemed so short, and before I realized, I had to go back to school and leave the land that I loved.

The trip of about one hundred miles to Las Vegas, by carriage, took two to three days, depending on the horses and, of course, the weather. We had to prepare for the journey such food as could not be cooked over a campfire. Coffee had to be ground and bread baked for our three meals each day.

The trip was delightful. We were up at dawn in order to take advantage of the hours of coolness, and naturally we had to cover as many miles as possible during the day. Thirty miles in one day was average travel, but fast horses might make forty. Papá loved his horses too well to drive them fast.

The horses had to be watered and rested, so Papá, or whoever was driving the team, always planned the trip so as to stop where there was water. It might have been a water hole in the open spaces or a rancho on the trail. While we ate our noon meal, we rested the horses for at least an hour. The horses, after being watered, were turned into the grass for a snack.

Our stopping place for the night was determined by the availability of water and pasturage for the horses. If rain overtook us, we had to seek shelter in a house. I liked it better when we stopped under the sky for a roof. Sleeping with the stars above was more interesting and cooler, also. How peaceful it was outdoors! The horses were hobbled, so that they might not wander too far, and often a cowbell was tied to the neck of one of the horses. The sound of the bell and the hobbled horses is the sweetest lullaby I have ever heard. A distant, or sometimes near, howling of the coyotes was the only other sound which might break the silence of the great outdoors.

Morning seemed to come too soon, and yet, one could hardly say it was morning, for when Papá called us, the stars were still in the heavens. How cold the mornings are on the Llano, even though the temperature may rise to one hundred degrees in the daytime!

The people along the trail were friendly and hospitable. They welcomed us with open arms, for they seemed hungry for outside intercourse. On the road there were still many large ranchos, since the homesteaders had not invaded that part of the country. Their land was on the Spanish and Mexican land grants. They were far from the railroad centers and those seeking land had not discovered the routes to those hidden spots.

ON this road, we encountered chapels which served the ranchos for many miles. In El Chirisco lived Don José Gonzáles, father of the famous *mesteñero,* wild horse hunter, Don Teodoro Gonzáles. At the time that I knew Don José, he was blind, but he ruled his household and *empleados* as a king rules his realm. A room set aside for the purpose of worship on the Gonzáles hacienda, stood as a monument to the faith of the early settlers. Surrounded by the homes of Don José's sons and *empleados,* the Gonzáles hacienda was a village in itself. Don José ran thousands of cattle on his domain. I remember hearing during conversation that in 1906 he had branded one thousand colts. These colts must have been the descendants of the *mesteños,* the wild horses, which had roamed the Llano country in vast hordes over the unfenced land.

I can still recollect when wild burros were hunted and killed for soap making on our rancho and, as a small girl, I often heard the boys tell of horses inhabiting remote canyons close to our land. From them and Papá, I learned the stories of these *mesteños.*

As the buffalo hunters went into the Comanche country, they sighted droves of *mesteños.* They took word back to the settlements and when horses were needed, expeditions were formed to go into the Llano to capture wild horses.

The expeditions usually were made in the spring of the year, since at that time the horses were poor and easy to run down. The men hunting for *mesteños* brought fat, swift horses, making the chase not as difficult as it might seem. With a good horse, the victims soon were overtaken. They were roped with *reatas,* lariats, and once roped, they were easy to get down. They were then hobbled with strong horsehair ropes. There was a special way of hobbling, quite unlike the usual way used for tame horses. The rope was tied from the horse's tail between its hind legs and to one of its front feet above the hoof. This was called *gavilla.* This type of hobbling kept the horses from running away. Sometimes the *mesteño* was tied neck-to-neck with a burro. The sturdy ass was a good match for the wild horse, and rarely, if ever, did a horse get away when guarded in this manner.

Mesteños on the run were a magnificent sight to behold, those who followed the sport related. Every bunch of mares was led by a stallion, and that animal showed its importance as the leader of the herd. He was hard to follow; he was superb as he defended his *manada,* his herd. Once caught, the horses were not as beautiful as they appeared when running. There were all colors of horses, but the dun predominated.

These horses seemed by instinct to know when they were being hunted. The leader of the band seemed at times to have given his *manada* a warning, for so swiftly did they disappear that the hunters were not sure of their prey.

There were some famous *mesteñeros* who could drive a whole herd of wild horses with little trouble. They claimed that once away from their habitat the horses became shy and easy to handle.

No greater *mesteñero* ever lived, perhaps, than Don Teodoro Gonzáles. It is said that he made those around him feel that it was an easy sport. At the first throw of the *reata,* he had his horse, and as swiftly, he was off his horse and down came the *mesteño.* His own horse, of course, was a superior one, but it took great skill.

As the land became fenced, the wild horses were a menace, for one horse out-eats two or three cows, and the cowmen had to conserve grass. Many wild horses were killed, and another Llano sport passed into history.

There were many other ranchos on our way to Las Vegas, but the Gonzáles hacienda stands more vividly in my memory than the others. Perhaps because Don José was such a courteous, hospitable person.

14. "Milo Maizes"

THE RAIN CEASED AFTER THREE DAYS of good drenching and the land took on a new aspect. In a week, the grass seemed to have grown inches and the cattle were happily grazing and putting on slick covers on their bodies. Ours was a happy household!

The ground became dry enough for the boys to resume their daily labors and Papá at breakfast was making plans with El Cuate and the boys for the day's work.

"We shall start fencing on the Pajarito today," he said to the boys. "Cuate, you and Luis will go with me to survey the land, while Pedro and Nereo haul the wire and posts. It will be several days before we will be ready for them, but you can start digging the post holes."

I was delighted, for I would ride out and explore new country. Contrary to Spanish custom, Papá always allowed me to go wherever he or Luis went. The men were always kind and I ruled the rancho like a queen during my summer vacations. There was so much unwritten history of the Llano, and as I rode out in the pastures, ruins of houses and chapels made me wish they could speak so that they might tell of the life of the inhabitants who had dwelt within. But they were silent and I had to create in my mind imaginary characters living in these lonely ranchos. Yet they may not have been lonely; there may have been much gaiety and real living with nothing to disturb their tranquillity.

The country not only held in secret the lives of the Spanish colonists, but of the Indians who thousands of years before had inhabited the land. There were the petroglyphs depicting human figures, animals and other signs. What did they mean? In my mind, I would decipher the figures to give directions towards where the enemy were encamped or where there was a spring of clear water for the nomads—or were they nomads? I would often picture villages of happy primitive people living abundantly from the soil with no destructive civilization to mar their joyful lives. I lived in the past as I roamed the range and studied the petroglyphs. These may have been relatively recent, for in the rocks were deep grooves where the women ground the maize into meal.

My brother and I hunted for arrowheads and other artifacts and these we found in profusion. Luis has a fine collection of arrowheads, scrapers, awls, points, axes and grindstones, and all these were found in our pastures or within a radius of fifty miles.

While the men were fencing, I was free to wander into secluded canyons and caves and to acquaint myself with the wonders of country new to me. Yet those before us certainly had known it well but had left few records for posterity.

We had to fence our lands, for the country was being settled, and where once the boundaries over which our cattle grazed had been the earth's horizon, now we were being pushed in and in, until it became necessary to build fences.

In the pre-Hispanic era, the Llano Indians walked—with the Spaniards came horses and the life of the Indians changed. Then came *Ciboleros* using *carretas* pulled by oxen to go into the Llano for their meat supply, and later wagons with horses began to wind their way over the Llano's rough roads.

The railroad came through Las Vegas in 1879, and the Santa Fe trail, with its caravans of ox wagons, passed into history. The plains Indians were on reservations and life became tame for the New Mexicans who had traveled over the trail. Las Vegas became an important railroad center, but it also continued to be the market for sheep, cattle, wool and hides from the Llano country.

Over the Vega Hill, where Señor Mariano daily played host to travelers, came hundreds of wagons to trade in the Meadow City, yet many of the sheep and cattle from the Llano were driven to Liberal, Kansas, where the Rock Island Railroad had its terminal. From Liberal the stock was shipped to Kansas City, St. Joseph and Chicago.

In 1900 the Rock Island was being built across the Llano country, and by 1901 it had reached Santa Rosa, where it connected with the El Paso and Southwestern to El Paso, Texas.

The land of the Comanches and the *Ciboleros* underwent great changes in the years 1900 and 1901. The Rock Island gave contracts for the building of its lines. Camps dotted the Llano country from Kansas into New Mexico. These camps were a bedlam of foreigners, where many tongues were spoken. There were Italians, Austrians, Greeks, Slavs, Chinese, Negroes, Mexicans, and of course, Americans.

Men were killed by rocks from blasting, and it is rumored that many a man lies buried in the fills of the roadbeds.

On the Pajarito ranch of Don Nicasio Cabeza de Baca, my late uncle, one of these camps was located. There was a commissary in each camp, but there were many articles which were not carried in their stock. My uncle took advantage of the opportunity and set up a store in which he carried clothing and food.

The Italian workers had great confidence in him and when payday came, they turned their money to him. He took it into Las Vegas for deposit in the bank, and a great deal of it he sent to the families of the workers. My aunt, Doña Isabel Stephens, Don Nicasio's wife, tells that when the money started rolling in, she feared a holdup, since there were many bad men among the workers. Until Don Nicasio was ready for the one-hundred-mile trip to Las Vegas, she kept the money in her baby's carriage under the mattress. They did not have a safe and she felt that no one would think of disturbing the baby if someone came to rob them.

There were two really bad characters in the camp, and these were a Filipino and a Mexican. One morning, as Don Nicasio started on his monthly journey to Las Vegas, he saw two men standing on either side of the road, a mile or so from the camp. It was still dark, but he recognized them as the Filipino and the Mexican of bad repute. Don Nicasio always carried a gun by his side, and before the desperados had a chance to point their guns, he had his in his hand. He ordered them to move on. Don Nicasio was not alone in his carriage, a niece was riding with him to Las Vegas. Perhaps the criminals did not recognize in the darkness that the person was a woman, for they quickly disappeared.

Many incidents happened in the year that the camp was located on the de Baca ranch, but considering the many hundreds of laborers and no officers of the law, it was quite peaceful.

A young man from St. Louis, Missouri, who came from a wealthy and influential family, strayed into the camp as a laborer. He was refined and highly educated and why he was there, no one knew. One day, while working, the foreman of the crew became angry at him because he did not work as fast as the other laborers. The foreman used a horsewhip on him. The boy swore that he would have revenge. That night he decided to avenge his wrong, and knowing where the foreman was lodged, he approached the tent. It happened that, for one reason or another, the foreman had changed tents and the boy shot the wrong man, an Italian worker. The boy hid in some caves in the near by hills and there his buddies supplied him with food and water. There was a search for him, but he remained safe in his hiding place until the first flat cars rolled over the tracks. One evening, one of his buddies came to pick up the boy's baggage at the de Baca home, where he always kept it. No one ever heard about the mysterious boy again. Mrs. de Baca says that the boy's luggage was of the most expensive type of its day and often, when the boy came to the house to get clothing, she noticed that his clothes were such as only the wealthy could afford.

The workers lived in tents and the camp manager with his family lived in a dugout which he built for their abode. The Italian workers were very economical and usually saved all of their wages. They lived on bread, rabbits and tea made from snake brush (*gutierreza teunis*). They used milk in their tea for extra nourishment. Ruins of the mud ovens which the Italians built for baking bread can still be seen on the old de Baca homestead.

The land on the Llano is not for the tenderfoot, and an incident which happened at the camp proves it: A young easterner came as office secretary and on the first night of his arrival, a thunderstorm, such as can be experienced only on the Llano, struck the area. Lightning and thunder, followed by a cloudburst, kept him awake in his tent all night. In the morning, as he was rolling up his bed, two rattlesnakes were coiled under it. He took the next stagecoach for other terrain.

At the time the railroad was in process of construction, the Mesa Redonda (Round Mesa) Brothers, notorious bandits, were making stops at the camps all along the way robbing and pillaging. On one occasion, two of them stopped at the de Baca store, where they bought lunch goods. No one could have picked them out as lawbreakers, for they had pleasing personalities. They wore elegant clothes and their fingers shone with diamonds. They must have been bold to make their appearance in broad daylight where they planned to make a holdup. They were heavily armed. That evening they held up a Mr. Buckley, who had charge of the camp commissary, and got away with more than three thousand dollars. To the de Baca's they were friendly and left them unmolested, although there they could have found more money than in the railroad commissary.

These bandits lived on Mesa Redonda, just over the bluffs of the Staked Plains. The flat top of the mesa is extensive, comprising ten thousand acres or perhaps more. There the bandits kept stolen cattle, horses and other loot. It is very rugged with only one or two accessible places and these the brothers kept carefully guarded. They lived there from 1901 until 1907, when the homesteaders began to populate the country. On top of the mesa, there are several natural lakes and *aguajes,* water holes, which made it very convenient for the robbers to live unmolested.

AFTER the coming of the railroad, many towns sprang up along the way over the Ceja and across the Llano. Tucumcari, today one of New Mexico's larger cities, came into being because of the railroad. Santa Rosa was, because of its location, the logical point for the railroad shops—and they were built there. But, unfortunately, the hard water of the Pecos river at this point was not usable for the desired purpose and Tucumcari profited from Santa Rosa's misfortune.

Santa Rosa and Tucumcari grew into towns and many small towns benefited by the coming of the Nesters, at least for the duration of the influx of the homesteaders. Montoya, named after the Pablo Montoya Grant and situated within its bound-

aries, was an important trading center for some twenty years. The few cattle and sheep owners, the homesteaders and railroad section hands living on the Ceja, traded in Montoya. There was a large general store, several smaller ones, a drug store, two hotels, a three-room public school, a newspaper, a land office, a country doctor, one or two Protestant churches, and the one Roman

Catholic chapel—which still exists and is a *visita* of the Tucumcari parish. Montoya was a busy place while the money of the homesteaders lasted and until the droughts put the stockmen out of business. Today, Montoya is a ghost town and survives only because of U. S. Highway 66 and the few railroad section hands who make up its population.

Cuervo, another railroad station, is the trading center for the ranchers from Garita, Cuervo Creek and others who are running sheep and cattle in the surrounding country.

The people of the vast Conchas country—which lies northeast of Cuervo Creek—formerly traded in Las Vegas. After the coming of the railroad over the Llano they turned to Cuervo and Santa Rosa for the shipping of their wool, sheep and cattle.

The decision of the courts about land grants, the coming of the homesteaders, the railroad over the Llano and the building of highways, caused a transition in the history of the Ceja and the Llano. Amarillo and Tucumcari grew into cities and Las Vegas remained static, contented with one main highway and the crossing of the Santa Fe railroad through its boundaries. Many of its inhabitants little know that once it was the largest trading center in the vast State of New Mexico.

With the coming of the railroad over the Llano, immigration started. Caravans of covered wagons dotted the country over the buffalo and Comanche trails. Another people came to settle where once the New Mexicans of Spanish extraction had lived, where they had found the promised land for their flocks and herds. Gone were the sheep and only a few cattle ranches remained.

PAPÁ was unhappy as he saw the shacks of the newcomers rise on the acres which had been his pastures.

Papá was in good humor when we started out one day, but as we reached the place where they were going to start surveying, his mood changed, for just a quarter of a mile from his boundary line, a wooden cabin had gone up overnight and then Papá was infuriated.

Angrily, he alighted from the wagon and turned to El Cuate, saying:

"If those 'Milo Maizes' have put their house on my land, they shall rue the day they came here. They will ruin the land for grazing and they will starve to death; this is not farming land."

"Calm down, Papá," I said. "Wait until you find your boundaries and then get angry. These people have a right to file on the land. You have always owned land, thousands of acres; they are entitled to their half section."

"No one has a right to ruin pasture land and those idiots in Washington, who require that they break eighty acres for farming, are to blame for these poor fools destroying the land. It is a crime for these misguided people to try to make a living in a country that does not have enough rain for growing crops," papá answered.

I felt sorry for the homesteaders. Young as I was, I realized that they could not make the land provide them with even a meager living. I had grown up with a ranch background, where sheep and cattle furnished our livelihood, and I knew the hard times Papá and Grandfather had endured in order to survive. Then, we had control of the land, and only that had saved us from destruction. I knew that, along with the "Nesters," we were due for a transition. They could not exist from farming and we could not increase our herds in the land that was left for grazing. Papá had been resourceful and had acquired all the patented land available, school sections and what he could file for a homestead, but this was not enough. We had to think of droughts and when they occurred we had no lands toward which the cattle could be moved. On the Llano, unless it is very unusual, droughts are not general; there are always spots where it rains when others are dry. In one's pastures there are rainy and dry spots, and the pioneer sheep and cattlemen knew them.

In 1901, after the coming of the railroad, the Rock Island line promoted colonization into the land it traversed over the Cap Rock. Chartered immigrant cars brought a big colony of Iowa farmers. In the cars came draft horses, farming implements, dairy cows and household furnishings. These people were good farmers, but the Llano country was not farming land. The horses did not become accustomed to the country and neither did the dairy cattle. The Iowans built good substantial homes, but their endurance soon gave out and in order to prove up on the land, they commuted for $1.25 per acre. In three or four years, all but a handful moved to other states or went back to their homeland. Papá liked these Iowans and counted them among his best friends. He bought a great many acres from them upon their departure.

When the Enlarged Homestead Act was passed, families from Texas, Oklahoma, Arkansas and other Southern states began to look towards New Mexico as the land of promise. These families had been sharecroppers or tenant farmers in their own states and to own the land was their most cherished dream. By saving and skimping, they accumulated two or three hundred dollars in cash. With a wagon, a team of horses, chickens, possibly a milk cow and their household goods, they joined other caravans and the march started toward the Utopia of their dreams.

Our rock house may not have been elegant, but it was a

mansion compared to the lowly shacks which the newcomers built. These were merely roofs over their heads and sometimes they did not have even protection from the scant New Mexico rains. There were a few who built substantial houses, because they had brought a little more cash, but they, likewise, soon spent their savings.

They were kindly, simple folks, these homesteaders. Their hospitality was boundless, and Miss Fabiola and Mr. Luis were idolized by young and old. My brother, Luis, and I loved them, but El Cuate and Papá kept aloof, never quite understanding what Luis and I saw in those uncouth people.

A few of the colonists were of the better educated class. Their standards of living were above the average, and Papá did not fail to pick them out as he had the Iowans from the others whom he called "Milo Maizes." This name he gave to those he disliked, because, milo maize was a hardy crop they planted for feed. It was introduced by them into New Mexico.

I do not know why Papá and El Cuate were intolerant towards these humble people, for both Papá and El Cuate were two of the most tenderhearted, sympathetic, understanding and courteous persons I have ever known. May they rest in peace, as El Cuate would say.

Soon after Papá started surveying that morning, an amiable, big husky man dressed in blue denim clothes came toward Papá. He greeted him, saying, "Are you Mr. de Baca of the Spear Bar Ranch?"

Papá was not cordial as he answered,

"Yes, what do you want?"

"I thought you were a white man when I saw you."

Papá, using strong language, replied:

"Of course I am a white man—and an educated one, too."

Papá was tall and very fair skinned. His eyes were the blue of sapphire and his hair was reddish brown. He could not have been mistaken by anyone as not being white, yet these people who came to settle in our midst were ignorant of history. To them, the only white people were those who spoke the English language as their mother tongue.

The man half apologized, not quite grasping his mistake, but I came to his rescue. In Spanish, I spoke to Papá.

"Please, Papá do not hold it against him. He does not know any better; I am sure he meant no disrespect. We have to live among them and we might as well live peacefully."

Papá replied to me, "You can live among them. I intend to fence my land and stay within it."

I knew he could not mean what he said, it was all said in anger. But years after, I knew he meant it, for he never mingled with them—yet he did not forbid us from making friends with our new neighbors.

The man tried to be friendly and addressed Papá again,

"Mr. de Baca, I would like to borrow a milk cow from you. You have so many of them and I can take good care of one. And I would like to haul water from you-all's well in this pasture."

"Do you have children?" papá asked.

"We have five young 'uns, Mr. de Baca," answered the man.

"Come to the ranch house tomorrow and I shall have a cow for you. If you haul water from my place, be sure you close the gates," Papá replied in a resentful voice.

To us he said in Spanish, "I am doing it for his children."

There were many families already hauling water from our wells and many were milking Papá's cows. We did not have dairy cows, but some of the range cows were good milkers and they provided milk for us and the newcomers.

Fence after fence went up and soon all our land was enclosed within our own boundaries.

In spite of the hardships, which to the homesteader may not have been such, these people were happy and easy-going. The women worked right along with the men in the fields; they milked the cows and tended the poultry. Their housekeeping was poor, for they had miserable houses with which to contend, but they were excellent cooks, considering the scant variety of food which they had. They knew how to utilize their milk products in many ways and all other food they managed to make

palatable. With all my home economics training, I could not compete with them, perhaps because El Cuate took care of our daily diet.

If today I can fry chicken, make sour milk biscuits and cornbread, I owe it to the friends of my youth on the Llano.

These people did not build chapels, as my people had done, yet some were very religious. As in any settlement, there were various types of families. There were the churchgoers and those not affiliated with any church; there were those who danced and those who positively considered dancing sinful.

But whether they danced or not, life for all seemed blissful. I never heard them complain about the heat or the drought or hard work. The churchgoers met in the schoolhouse for prayer meetings and Sunday school. This was not only a religious ceremony, but also a social gathering. The women brought food, and after services the families spread out their victuals and all ate together. The congregation then separated into neighborly groups, exchanged gossip and then went home to get ready for another week of toil.

In the summer, there were "Singings" among the religious groups. Neighbors would gather in some house any day of the week. The young folks played games and sang songs early in the evening; later, young and old joined together and sang hymns. About midnight, refreshments were served and then the guests departed.

The "Singings" reminded me of our *velorios,* when we gather to pray and sing on the eve of some saint or to ask special favors. Ours is more formal and quite solemn, but it is very much a social gathering. At midnight, we serve supper, after much praying and singing of hymns.

The dancing groups met together at the schoolhouse or some

house for a night of swing. The dance started as soon as it became dark. The ranches were six to fifteen miles distant and the dancers came by wagon, carriage or horseback. We had to leave home before dark, for although horses have good sense, it was not safe to venture in the dark. We danced until daylight, for we needed to see the road to avoid accidents, or perhaps, we liked to dance so well that a few hours did not suffice. At midnight, the men made coffee by a campfire; the women brought cakes and we certainly had a feast.

On Sundays, the non-church families took turns in going to some home to spend the day. The women always helped with the preparation of the noon meal; the men played cards and sometimes the visits lasted until midnight.

My brother and I divided our time with all groups and although there was animosity among them, Mr. Luis and Miss Fabiola were heartily welcomed whether to a prayer meeting, singing, or dance.

In the summer, we had enjoyable picnics, celebrating the Fourth of July or just for a Sunday outing. Sometimes there were as many as twenty families together.

Although I did not live in the days of the Spanish fiestas on the Llano, I have happy recollections of the days of the homesteaders. My brother and I belonged to a different age from El Cuate and Papá. Both eras were colorful and both contributed much to the history in the land of the buffalo and the Comanche.

Hardly a day went by but some new family arrived, until nearly every inch of ground was taken.

There came droughts and the settlers found it harder and harder to exist. The little money which they brought with them was soon exhausted, and the merchants in the small railroad towns started to give credit to the farmers, with the hope of getting the land in return, and it did not take long for them to acquire it at a low price.

The few cattle and sheep men who were left and who had not been foresighted, had to diminish their herds and they also had to live on credit from the country store. One by one, they also disappeared and Papá would say:

"Someday the land will be washed away, for there is no grass nor shrubbery to protect it. I may not live to see it, but you young folks will realize why I have been so perturbed over this colonization by the Nesters." But he did live to see it, for when the "Dust Bowl" became a menace, he was here to see his predictions become a reality.

The homesteaders were a persistent folk; they plowed and planted and lost their seed, but they stayed on three or four years, or at least until they made final proofs on their claims. A handful remained, but others, although late, realized that their Utopia was a cruel land ready to suck the last trace of hope from them.

One by one they departed, and Papá bought or leased acres and acres of land from the disillusioned colonists and his pastures increased to good proportions, but it was bad land. So much of it had been plowed it would be years before grass would grow. The merchants in the railroad towns became the cattle kings, although some of them had started in the mercantile business with less money than one Nester had brought to see him through. By sagacity they had built up fortunes and the land was theirs.

The homesteaders further east were more fortunate, or perhaps more enduring, for today as one travels towards the Texas border, one sees wheat and other grains swaying with the wind. They have seen some hard times, but such is the lot of those who live from the soil—yet they have taken roots as Papá had on his land.

15. A Country School

MY SCHOOL DAYS WERE OVER and I had come to the rancho to stay. It was a changed place. El Cuate had passed on to a better land and new faces greeted me as I arrived.

Automobiles had come into use, but the roads were in poor condition and only the Model T Ford could make the high centers which were still prevalent—reminders of horse and buggy days. The Ozark Trail traversed our land, but there were no automobile roads to travel over into the neighboring ranches.

It had never occurred to me that schools in rural areas were different from those which I had attended.

I had not been home very long when I began to learn that the children around us had from five to seven months of school and that many of the teachers in the county did not have even an eighth grade education. Education in our family had always been mandatory; that other children did not have the same opportunity as I, did not seem fair to me. When one of the school directors came to solicit me to teach school in our school district, I felt privileged. Papá was not so sure that it was the proper thing for me to do and it took a great deal of pleading to gain his consent. In giving it, he stressed that if I signed a contract I had to live up to it and, whether I liked it or not, I had to stay the full seven months. He was certain that after I found out what the environment held for me I would repent, but I was determined to keep my word.

The schoolhouse was six miles from our ranch, but six miles was a great distance on horseback, and I could not ride back and forth each day. It meant that I had to find a boarding place.

One family lived close to the school—they were simple folk, but very gracious. They arranged to give me room, board and laundry for twelve dollars. My salary was seventy dollars a month, paid in warrants which could be cashed at ten percent discount at the bank in Santa Rosa. Since Papá was able to pay my bills, I kept the warrants for several years—until the county had enough funds to pay.

The school was governed by three school directors and one of these resented my appointment as the teacher for his school. What my qualifications might have been did not concern him, since he had a *compadre* who had taught the school, and schools were given to teachers not for merit, but because they might be relatives or belong to the right political party. I did not understand all this and little did I care. The joy of teaching and helping those around us, although I had hardly realized what it meant except in ideal surroundings, was my ambition for the moment.

I had a huge room with a bed in one corner, a small table, an improvised washstand, possibly two chairs and a niche with a beautiful *bulto* of San Miguel. The floor was of hard-packed mud with not a rug to relieve the bleakness of it. I might have longed for my room at home—my cozy bedroom which I had decorated in the latest style—yet if I wished for it, I did not admit it even to myself. I was going home every Friday. Why it did not occur to me to take furnishings from home, I do not know, but perhaps the reason was that, even as a youngster, I could not bear to hurt anyone, particularly those who were poorer than I.

The one-room school stood in a lonely spot among the junipers and piñons with Mesa Rica as a background. It was built of rock with four narrow windows, two on each side. The room was so devoid of furniture that a weaker heart might have been disillusioned, but I remembered my promise and papá's warning.

There was a desk for the teacher and a chair which was held together with bailing wire. The desks for the pupils were all the same size and each held three to four children who had to share it together.

The children came to school from ranches—two, three, five and six miles distant; a few drove in buggies or rode horseback, but the majority walked.

Our first chore was to clean the schoolhouse, and the children were as eager as I to tackle the job. We scrubbed the pine floor, washed the desks, cleaned windows and swept the yard. While sweeping the yard, we had the fright of our lives—close to the door was coiled a six-foot rattlesnake. When I heard the rattles, I flew into the schoolhouse, but soon the children had it under control—with a blow from the hoe the snake was decapitated. The weeds had grown up to the door after the summer rains, yet carefully, the larger boys cleared the growth making sure that no more snakes were there to scare the teacher. Some of the boys must have been nearer to my age, but they were as obedient as the younger ones.

It was a mixed school. There were the children of the homesteaders, the children of parents of Spanish extraction and children with Indian blood but of Spanish tongue.

When the room was in order, I started to seat the children

according to grades. Luckily, only six grades were represented, as in those days few of the pupils stayed to finish the eight grades.

This was a new experience, but by the end of the week I was as settled in my work as if I had been teaching a lifetime. The children were very docile and, in general, very adaptive.

Notwithstanding the distances the children had to travel to come to school, they were there early to help the teacher bring water, sweep and dust the school room. In the winter there were fires to be built in the wood stove.

We opened the morning and afternoon sessions by singing and the children loved it. The Spanish children knew folk songs and the Anglos, cowboy ballads and hillbilly songs. As a reward for good lessons, we sang these, but I also taught them songs which are sung in school nowadays. *The Star-Spangled Banner* resounded on the Mesa Rica each school morning. We had a small flag, but we had not yet heard of the Pledge to the Flag.

There were few diversions at these scattered ranches. Therefore, school programs were well patronized; I soon learned this from the children and we began to plan for a Thanksgiving function. Our school had started in October so that the children would have finished helping with the harvest.

At first I had fifteen children enrolled, but when the word spread that I was the teacher in the Benavídez district, pupils from other districts started to come. I had a Normal School education and that was more than very few, if any, had in the whole county. And as I said before, the majority of the country school teachers had not even completed grammar school. Much was expected of me, but I was having fun.

I soon became acquainted with the children, and by the second week of school I was receiving invitations from different ones to go and spend the night with them. I certainly appreciated that, although it meant walking several miles and getting up before daylight in order to get to school in time to sweep, dust, and haul water before nine o'clock. It was adventure and I was getting plenty of it.

During some weeks I did not sleep in my boarding place more than one night. But when I did, I enjoyed it; I could then have a sponge bath. I read, corrected papers, or sewed by lamplight, and the family with whom I boarded dropped in to talk to me. Every individual is different and one can learn something from each one. I am sure that I underwent one of the best educations anyone could receive. I learned the customs, food habits, religions, languages, and folkways of different national groups. They were all simple, wholesome people living from the soil. They certainly were a hardy lot, for otherwise they could not have survived the cruelty of the wind, the droughts and the poverty which surrounded most of them. They asked my advice on many subjects but I never felt capable of giving it to them. My education was from books; theirs came the hard way. It was superior to mine.

I taught reading, spelling, history, grammar, arithmetic, physiology, penmanship and geography.

In my Normal School education, I had been trained to teach reading by the phonetic method, but I had nothing like a phonetic chart. From my practice teaching notes, I improvised some charts and had a difficult time with the few beginners as their parents knew that the alphabet method was the only way to learn reading. They may have been right, but I taught phonetics and the children were able to read in a few months.

The classes had to be combined whenever possible, as there were too many grades for one teacher to handle. Spelling and reading were combined in all the grades, all the primary pupils in one and the intermediate in another class. The sixth graders had all their classes separate from the others.

American history was an important subject from the fifth grade up but the textbooks stressed American colonial history, and since that is the way in which I had learned it, I made a good teacher. One sentence or perhaps a paragraph told about the Indians and the Spaniards in the Southwest. The children learned about the Delawares, the Iroquois and the Mohawks, but learned little about the Comanches, Apaches, Navajos or the Pueblo Indians—and the teacher knew not much more, except by absorption through family conversations and fireside story-telling in her home.

The geography lessons were strict in the fifth and sixth grades; the pupils had to learn the name of every state and territory and their capitals. Each one knew the industries and products of the states as well as all the large rivers, lakes, oceans and principal mountains of their country. European and Asiatic geography were not neglected. The pupils could name every country and its capital. They knew where the Dead, the Red and the Mediterranean seas were and what races populated each country. I am sure that those sixth graders knew more about Mexico, Central and South America than the average high school graduate knows today.

I know they knew more grammar than many college entrants do now. I say this from actual teaching experience in later years.

The pupils learned about germs from their physiology lessons and every sixth grader had to learn the names of all the bones in the body from the cranium to the phalanges.

Reading was interesting in all the grades. The textbooks had stories with morals in them and many were quite dramatic. The children cried over many of the stories. As a reward for good lessons, I allowed the children to dramatize "Little Red Riding Hood," "The Three Bears," and others from their readers.

Poetry must have been one of my favorite interests as it is today, for I made every child learn one poem each week, from the first grade to the sixth. These were later used for school programs.

We had no books for supplementary reading, as they do today, but we managed quite a library by buying the "Progressive School Classics" at a penny apiece. The children brought their pennies, I ordered the books, and we contrived quite a collection. I have today in my library copies of many of these booklets and tears come to my eyes as I remember my first country school. In a "Child's Garden of Verses" are marked the names of the children who had to learn a certain poem in it. We learned to sing many of Robert Louis Stevenson's verses.

In our collection we had the stories of the great men in history, and as I look back, the teacher and the pupils had a well-rounded general education.

For a blackboard, we used pieces of black oilcloth which had become so badly cracked that I wonder how writing on it was possible.

The pupils had to be very careful with their paper and pencils. It was almost a day's journey to Montoya and most of them had to count their pennies. Each day before school was dismissed, I collected all the tablets and pencils and each morning a pupil was assigned to pass them out. We had no automatic pencil sharpeners, but the larger boys performed the chore of sharpening them with their pocket knives.

For drinking water, we had a bucket which a monitor was responsible for keeping filled. As well as I can remember, there was a common drinking cup for all, including the teacher. Physiology failed there, but the parents would have resented it if I had used my own cup.

A can of water was kept on top of the stove which heated the room. This was used to scrub the hands of the pupils who had failed to do so at home. In general, all the children were meticulously clean but occasionally one escaped his mother's notice upon leaving home.

I remember one child biting me once when I was scrubbing his hands. They were chapped badly and it must have hurt him. His brothers told it at home and next day the father came to apologize and to ask me to punish him before all the pupils. It was not necessary, and I did not believe in corporal punishment. There was not a bad child in the school. Discipline is obtained with love and I had plenty of it for each and every pupil.

There was no privy for the school and when I told Papá about it, he went to one of the school directors and told him to have one constructed. The director told Papá that it was not necessary—there were plenty of junipers around the schoolhouse.

The weekly spelling match was something toward which the children looked forward on Friday mornings. The contest was conducted between boys and girls from the fourth grade up. How they studied for it!

Morning and afternoon recesses were great events. We played baseball, singing games, Hide and Go-Seek, Run Sheep Run, the Farmer in the Dell, London Bridge Is Falling Down, and many others which I have forgotten. Every pupil took part in all the games. We had several baseball teams, as I remember.

We had bi-lingual readers for the primary grades. These were the adopted texts of that day. In this way, the English-speaking children learned Spanish and the Spanish-speaking learned English.

The best method for teaching reading was for the pupils to read aloud. This was done in order to teach correct pronunciation of the languages. The Spanish-speaking pupils in all the grades had had very poor training in pronunciation, and the beginners knew not one word of English. It is amazing how well both groups learned each other's language in just seven months of school.

The *th* in a word was difficult for the Spanish-speaking children to pronounce. Hours were spent with them pronouncing *this, that, with, those, them* and similar combinations.

I taught addition and subtraction by the number table combination method which was similar to the multiplication tables that all the children had to memorize beginning in the fourth grade.

Grammar was very important, with sentence analysis, parsing and conjugation of verbs. How I remember trying to break the children of the homesteaders from using a singular verb with a plural noun, and to say "Guy and I," instead of "me and Guy!" How very important it was to me that they speak correctly!

I had to improvise the busy work for the children. Those who have followed teaching as a profession well know that children must be kept busy all the time or trouble will brew for the teacher. I brought magazines from home. *The Ladies' Home Journal, The Mentor,* and others with pictures. The third graders made geography books from the pictures and from them learned about people in other lands.

When the small children became tired, I let them go outdoors to play until time for their lessons. Outdoors, they gathered pretty rocks to represent cattle and horses, and we had a big rock corral built to put them in. We also built a rock ranch house which kept them busy building and tearing down. The house had barns and corrals and even a mud oven. We had plenty of shrubs to select from for the landscaping and the children were never idle.

THIS was an election year, and I mention it because the school was the center of it. My uncle was running for governor of the State. I had lived in an atmosphere of political influence, yet I never had witnessed an election nor thought much about it, except as something which excited the populace.

Some member of my family had always been a candidate for office, but politics belonged to the men. This was the second election since statehood, and my uncle was the incumbent vice-governor. I believe I was his favorite niece, at least he trusted me with some of his most important business affairs. I kept books for him, signed checks and measured type in his newspaper establishment when I was fourteen years old and only in high school. Later I was his private secretary on Saturdays and after school hours. He was a slave to the cause of the poor people and no one, perhaps, knew it as I did. In those days, being a member of the political party to which my uncle belonged in San Miguel County was indeed martyrdom. But we had many great men who were martyrs to the cause and my uncle was one. It took courage year after year, to run or support that party, yet when New Mexico became a state, my uncle was one of the men selected for one of the high offices and he was victorious.

Elections were held in the schoolhouses in the country places, and the eve of election was celebrated by a big dance by both major parties. Our school was chosen for the *baile,* and the voting was to be held in the neighboring school of the precinct.

Just before the dance broke up, a party of politicians arrived to announce that the voting place had been changed to our schoolhouse and Papá was furious. The ranches were far apart and only those attending the dance would know of the change and many votes would be lost. It had been a trick of the *politicos* of the opposing party, for they had already notified their people.

There was one automobile within a radius of twenty miles, but luckily the owner, Don Vidal Ortega, was on our side. There were all those people who lived on top of the mesa and the church people who did not dance. The roads were so bad that fewer families could be reached by automobile than by horse, but we had many horses.

It must have been three o'clock in the morning when we planned our itinerary. Papá was the *patrón* and we were all ready to obey his orders. My horse was saddled and I was sent to take word to those on the mesa five or six miles distant. It was not a pleasant journey at that time of day and less so when I had not had experience in opening gates. On my way back, I was told to stop at the Ortega ranch to pick up a beef which they would have ready on my return from the *ranchos* assigned to me. With no sleep that night, only the excitement of my mission could have kept me awake.

By eight o'clock, I was back at the Benavidez ranch and ready to help with the cooking, for we had to feed all who came to vote. Although women did not have the ballot, whole families drove to the voting places. It was an important event in their lives, and one of the few social gatherings in which everyone would concur.

Whiskey flowed freely and the men were feeling quite happy. It took several drinks for some of them to decide which way they would vote. The voting place was not far from us, but a hill made it impossible to see just what was happening. However, we were kept informed of events, as the *politicos* had a private room for conferences in the house.

At noon we fed every man, woman and child who had gathered at the voting place: Republicans, Democrats, Anglos, Hispanos and others.

In my scrapbook, I keep a ballot, which thirty years ago I marked for a souvenir, and it shows that one hundred twenty-three ballots were cast, and of those, my uncle received seventy-six. The precinct was definitely on the opposite side from the ticket on which my uncle was running, but the homesteaders stood by us one hundred percent. I know that some of our *empleados* and the young man to whom I was betrothed did not vote for my uncle.

In the evening, while the election judges were counting votes, the atmosphere around the polls became hotter than a one hundred degree sun. Men with plenty of drink became quarrelsome. It is unbelievable that men who in daily living seemed so calm and peaceful could become as fierce as beasts over an election. But it was so, as I remember that election in 1916. Certainly these men could have had nothing against a man who had devoted his life to the cause of the underprivileged, but such is the way of the populace.

OUR first school program was successful. The mothers gave generously of their time to help. We improvised a stage in the front part of the room by curtaining it off with sheets which the children brought from their homes. Local musicians gladly furnished music for us. Some of the boys played the harmonica and that everyone enjoyed.

I believe my brother took more interest in the school than I did. He would tell me what to do on all occasions, for he knew

the country better than I. For our programs, he was master of ceremonies, and a good one.

After Thanksgiving we started to practice for the Christmas exercises. That, of course, was to be a greater event than Thanksgiving.

On Christmas eve, men on horseback, families in wagons and carriages came and soon the school room was filled to capacity. Lanterns, hung from the ceiling, furnished the stage lights. I wonder, today, how I managed in the small space left for the performance, but everything went on smoothly. In one corner we had a dressing room covered with sheets to hide the actors. Sheets also served as the stage curtain.

How I had the courage to put on a two-act Christmas pantomime is something beyond comprehension, but I had city ideas, and the limitations of a country school did not trouble me.

My brother was Santa Claus and he had a bag with candy, nuts and a big orange for every pupil and child who came to the entertainment. No child was left at home, although it meant a long ride home after midnight. It was customary to make the program as long as possible so that the audience would be repaid for their trip.

Papá financed the Christmas treat, for surely I had no money. It would have been cheaper for Papá to have paid my salary and have kept me at home. In those days there were no funds for materials, books or equipment. The teacher either bought them out of her own pocket or did without. Having been trained in a teachers' Normal School, I had high ideals, and Papá's pocketbook was the victim.

The County School Superintendent came once to visit our school. I learned from him that we were using books that were out-of-date or as they said in those days—"not the adopted texts." The children were learning from them and I did not bother to change. The children in general could not have afforded it.

We had pictures of Woodrow Wilson on the wall and the superintendent was upset until he discovered that Abraham Lincoln's picture hung in a prominent place.

But there were Fridays and I went home. Sometimes Papá came in the carriage to fetch me, or if I had brought my horse I would ride home alone. I loved those lonely rides. I would live over the days of buffalo hunting and all the history El Cuate had described so beautifully. I would picture rodeos encamped on spots which I thought might have been ideal.

Soon I was home and my dreams were forgotten. Reality faced me with so many things that had to be done since I was taking my housekeeping duties seriously. The house had to be cleaned, cream had to be churned and there was baking to do.

I had to catch up with my reading between darning and patching, but when Sunday afternoon came, the house was in order and I was ready to go back to my teaching.

The children brought their lunch to school and every mother remembered the teacher. There was always an extra sandwich, a cookie, a piece of cake or perhaps only a biscuit with fried salt pork for me. I managed to eat all that food and I did not put on a pound. My weight remained amazingly at one hundred pounds.

Mass was an important event and on that day there was no school. The majority of the children were non-Catholic, but the directors still followed the rule which prevailed before the day of the homesteader.

The chapel had been built and furnished by the Benavídez family and was dedicated to Our Lady of Guadalupe. The Benavídez family had one room especially built for the priest, who always stayed for the night. He came from Puerto de Luna—a good fifty miles. No one ever went into the priest's room, which was the best furnished room in the house. I got my first glimpse of it when the priest came. Besides the host, I was the only one asked to sit at the table for meals when the priest was served.

Not only did I teach the three R's, but I taught the girls sewing and needlecraft, and the boys drawing and outdoor sports.

On a Friday afternoon, on the day devoted to needlecraft, one of the girls sat on a crochet hook and it stuck in her thigh. I was panicky for we were many miles from a doctor and no means of conveyance except a wagon and team of burros which some of the children drove to school.

There was no privacy in the schoolroom and a snowstorm raged outdoors. I managed to hide the girl from the boys by having the girls make a close circle around her. I worked on the crochet hook but it seemed to go in deeper. As I walked out of the circle to get hot water from the stove to clean the blood, the boys were all eyes and wondering what was happening. One of the boys came up to me with an opened pocket knife and said,

"Let me cut her flesh, the hook can only be removed that way."

I almost fainted at the thought, but the boy was serious. I had often watched the boys pick out thorns and yucca points from their hands and feet with pocketknives and to them it was natural.

There was no need for a surgical operation, for by the time I went back to the girl, the hook had worked out and I regained my composure. I would have dismissed school for the day, yet I did not dare for one could not see ten feet ahead. The snow had been falling since noon and now it was sure to continue through the night. Would the parents worry if the children did not go home, or if I sent them on and they lost their way, would I be guilty if any of them perished in the storm? I almost wished I had not compromised myself to schoolteaching, but wishing did not relieve me of the responsibility. Fortunately, we had plenty of wood to last several days. I took a vote from the pupils and it was unanimous that we stay in the schoolhouse for the night.

We had no lamps or candles but the light from the wood stove served us for the night. Our wraps served as beds and covers. I tried to stay awake in order to keep up the fire but I was not alone; the older boys took it as seriously as I did and the fire did not die down. The stove roared all night.

By morning the storm had subsided and the world around was covered by a foot of snow. We were a dismal and hungry bunch. The boys were used to hardships, and as soon as there was enough daylight, they cleared a path to my boarding place.

The family there were prepared for our call and soon we had food and water. Snow on the Ceja and Llano does not last long if the sun makes its appearance at all. Soon men on horseback from different directions came to our rescue with food and clothing. They knew we would be safe and I was thankful that they had placed that much confidence in me. Everyday I became closer to the parents and to the children.

The school directors asked me to close for Holy Week. I had not planned to go home and here I had a whole week to spend as I pleased. On Monday evening I went with some of the children who lived five miles east from the school, planning to come back to my room next morning. On my return I found the house deserted and every door locked. I walked to the next rancho, three miles distant, but there I found all doors latched. I was so tired I did not know what to do but I had to keep on traveling. April days are hot on the Ceja and on the path which I followed there was not even a tree to provide shade or shelter. After walking three more miles, I found folks at home and there I stopped but I was already too homesick to wish to stay. I borrowed a horse and rode on to our rancho.

We had only one more week of school after Easter and it was with deep regret that I bade goodbye to the children. As I look back to my first year of teaching, I know I have never been happier and I have never been among people who were more hospitable, genuine and wholesome than those who lived on the Ceja.

16. The Drought of 1918

THE LAND AROUND US WAS BEING ABANDONED. The homesteaders, one by one, had given up trying to make a living from farming and had departed to other regions. The ground which had been plowed became hills of sand and nothing grew but tumbleweeds.

The wind seemed to blow harder than ever, but this may have been because there was nothing to hold the dirt from blowing.

I knew Papá had been right when he said that the plowing of the land would destroy it for pasturage.

The spring of 1918 had come and gone and no rain. There was no grass and the cattle were in poor condition. The two previous years had been dry and, although Papá had fed his stock and rented pastures for them, they had come out poorly.

With the war the cost of living had risen, and flour and sugar were rationed. We had to buy cornmeal to stretch our wheat flour allowance. It was a hard year for the Ceja in every way.

When it is dry, the sun seems to burn up what little vegetation there is. The cactus and mesquite had always grown in abundance, but now only the cactus survived. Papá and the boys were up at daybreak cutting it and burning off the prickles before feeding it to the cattle.

The men never complained about the work or the heat, but when they came in at noon for a snack, burnt brown by the sun, they were exhausted. My brother would say, "This is God's cursed country and we shall perish expecting to live from the land."

Papá would answer, "We shall pull through somehow. We can always start again when the rains come and the grass takes root. I have lived through many droughts. Cattle have died but I have built up my herd again and again."

The drought spread from New Mexico into Texas, Oklahoma and Kansas, but in the northeastern part of New Mexico on the Ute Creek country, Luis was received by Don Nestor Cabeza de Baca, who, then, owned two townships. There was grass there and Don Nestor offered pasturage for our herd, small compared to his two-thousand head of cattle.

We had to round up the cattle and it took several days to bring them all together for the train ride. Papá ordered the cars for shipping them and they had to be ready on the day the railroad officials said the cars could be picked up.

Papá had already reduced his ranch help, so I had to help with the roundup. It was another experience in my life, as before I had only ridden the range for pleasure or as an adventure. Now it was real work.

It took every hand on the place to drive the cattle, but the hard work began when the animals had to be loaded on the railroad cars. It was a new event for the cows and calves and they rebelled. All day the men had been driving them through the chutes and into the cars. It was very hard labor and when the sun sank behind the horizon they were still loading cattle. Some of the cows almost had to be carried into the cars. These animals refused to move as they reached the chute leading into the box car and it took two or three men to push them through.

After the last cow was safe in its overnight shelter, there were the horses to load in the car provided for them. There were several opinions as to how the horses should travel, whether with saddles on or off. I believe the saddles were put on and taken off at least four times before everyone was satisfied. The horses rode with saddles on. The cattle had to be driven fifty-five miles after they reached Logan, the railroad station.

When the train pulled out and five of our boys were riding the caboose, I broke down and cried. I do not know why, but I felt sorry for the cattle riding so close together in those cars. I knew they would be back, but parting to me has always been hard. Papá was standing beside me and tears rolled down his cheeks when he saw me weeping. We did not speak, but we each knew what was in our hearts. One is never lonely on a ranch while cattle roam in the pastures, but it can become a very forlorn place when one does not see them grazing as one rides the range. I knew what Papá was thinking.

The cows that were too weak to make the trip were left behind and those had to be fed every day. It kept Papá and one other man busy burning cactus prickles and putting out cake for even that small bunch. The other boys would not be back for several weeks.

Our cash must have been very low, but we were concerned only in saving our cattle. We all had to work together to save every penny possible. My sisters, Guadalupe and Virginia, were home on vacation from boarding school and the three of us did work we had never dreamed we could do. But we had to help papá and it was enjoyable. We fussed a great deal as to who had to do what, but we got the job done. Getting up early in the morning was possibly the hardest task for us, but washing, ironing, baking, cheese- and butter-making, and all the other housekeeping along with them, took a great deal of energy, yet they were good lessons in homemaking for us. It was hard on Virginia's beautiful piano hands. She was the family musician. I was the ugly duckling, so it did not matter what housework did to my hands.

Papá was forever watching the sky for signs of rain but there were none in evidence. The few summer showers that came seemed to make the earth drier and hotter. It was a long summer.

The cattle were coming home in the fall and Papá decided to drive them back instead of shipping them by rail. It may have been because Papá had to save money that he made this decision.

My brother had stayed with the cattle and now Papá and the boys who were working for him started on the 150-mile journey to bring back the herd. It took them ten days to drive the cattle back. When they reached the Canadian River, about three miles from the present site of Conchas Dam, the river was up and they could not cross. They had to wait three days before they could venture the swollen stream. On the third day, they took a chance and I have always enjoyed my brother's description of the hundreds of cattle swimming across the red waters, driven by our boys and Papá.

Papá shipped most of the cattle to Kansas City to market that fall, as he knew that not many could survive the winter, and it was well that he did, for in December the snows came. The snow fell and fell until two feet covered the ground. The snow stood on the ground ninety days. There were no cattle left and very few horses lived through the severe winter. And Papá had to start again.

Many cattle and sheep men went out of business in 1918 and few were ever again able to build up their herds. The land began to fall into the hands of men who had made money with the war just passed.

WHEN New Mexico became a state, millions of acres became available for sale as state land, but it was a political graft and only those belonging to the right political party were privileged to buy or rent. Papá was on the wrong side, and although he was approached by the political leaders in power to change his party affiliations in order to secure state land, he did not care to do so, and so he lost a chance for becoming a big cattle king with thousands of acres at five cents per acre rental.

Papá had acquired considerable acreage from the homesteaders, but the land had undergone too much erosion and it would be many years before all the plowed and overgrazed land would go back to grass.

With the drought of 1918, even the mesquite had died and the cactus had been depleted by using it for feed. Papá would have to reduce his herd unless he could acquire better land. Underground water was abundant on our pastures and men who had purchased or acquired large tracts of land and had no water, were forever interested if Papá would care to sell.

And Papá did sell; but he had taken deep roots on the Ceja, roots deeper than the piñon and the juniper on his land. He had endured hardships and had stayed on when others had given up in despair. It was not easy for him to become accustomed to another terrain.

He had his children, but they never could be as close to him as the hills, the grass, the yucca and mesquite and the peace enjoyed from the land. He loved solitude and the noise of the cities was not in accord with his life.

Before Papá had finished closing the deal with his buyer, he was buying other land, but small compared to what he had controlled. This was not strange land, for before the coming of the Nesters, it had been part of his grazing acres on the Monte de

Pajarito. He would not be far from the hills which had surrounded his former pastures. The same arroyo that had crossed his land, traversed the country into which he was moving. It was as if he had moved over inside another one of his fences. Yet, this must have been hard on Papá, for I remember when we built a new home a mile from the old ranch, he lingered in the old homestead until the last piece of furniture had been removed.

Although our ancestors were adventurers who left their mother country in quest of new lands, yet those of us descended from them are of a stable nature. It takes more than droughts and other hardships to move us. The loss of our lands has been the only cause for abandoning our pastures and farming land, and that has been because we were unprepared to defend our rights when outsiders pushed in.

When General Kearny talked to the citizens of Las Vegas on August 15, 1846, he promised protection for the New Mexicans and their property and the United States in agreement with Mexico. He also promised that the Spanish and Mexican land grants would be respected. But New Mexico, isolated for so many centuries, did not have enough lawyers to plead the cause for its people. The owners of the grants and other lands were unable to pay for the surveying and gradually most of the land became public domain. Unaccustomed to technicalities, the native New Mexicans later lost even their homesteads because of ignorance of the homestead laws, but all this belongs to a subject too vast to discuss in this history of the Llano.

The rains and snows after 1918 did not bring back the grass —there had been too much overgrazing and plowing for Nature to compete with the scant moisture. Papá built up his herd according to the capacity of his land, but droughts came again in 1933. There was no rain from the fall of 1932 until the third of

May, 1935 and the drought was not broken until that winter, when a foot of snow covered the Ceja and the Llano.

The land, between the years 1932 and 1935, became a dust bowl. The droughts, erosion of the land, the unprotected soil and overgrazing of pastures had no power over the winds. The winds blew and the land became desolate and abandoned. Gradually the grass and other vegetation disappeared and the stock began to perish. There was not a day of respite from the wind. The houses were no protection against it. In the mornings upon rising from bed, one's body was imprinted on the sheets which were covered with sand. One no longer breathed pure air, and continuous coughing indicated that one's lungs were permeated with the fine sand. One forgot how it felt to touch a smooth surface or a clean dish; how food without grit tasted, and how clear water may have appeared. The whole world around us was a thick cloud of dust. The sun was invisible and one would scarcely venture into the outdoors for fear of breathing the foul grit.

The winds blew all day and they blew all night, until every plant which had survived was covered by hills of sand.

Papá kept on feeding his cattle, but the day came when his purse became empty and he could no longer buy feed. He became disillusioned and as quickly lost the strength to fight.

The government started buying the cattle and killing off those which were too poor to move. Papá's cattle were in good condition, but he did not know how long they could survive, so along with other cattlemen he had to sell. He could not take it and he became ill of an illness from which he never recovered. For the cows that were killed, he was paid twelve dollars per head; for those that were in good shape he received eighteen and the calves brought six dollars.

Papá was past sixty and he knew it would be many years before the land would come back; he knew he could not start again.

The land which he loved had sucked the last bit of strength which so long had kept him enduring failures and sometimes successes but never of one tenor. Life so cruel and at times so sweet is a continuous struggle for existence—yet one so uncertain of what is beyond fights and fights for survival. One has not lived who has not experienced reverses. Papá had a full life.

He is gone, but the land which he loved is there. It has come back. The grass is growing again and those living on his land are wiser. They are following practices of soil and water conservation which were not available to Papá. But each generation must profit by the trials and errors of those before them; otherwise everything would perish.

GLOSSARY

Agregado. Assistant, helper.
Baile. A ball or dance.
Bastonero. One in charge of selecting couples during a dance; the director of a ball.
Bulto. A religious statue.
Caballerango. A man in charge of horses during a rodeo.
Caporal. An overseer on a sheep or cattle ranch.
Carrero. Wagon driver.
Ceja. The Cap Rock country.
Cibolero. Buffalo hunter.
Cíbolo. Buffalo.
Comanchero. A man engaged in trade, often illegal, with Comanche Indians.
Corrida. A "run" or "try" on horseback.
Corridos. Folk verses or songs recounting local events.
Cuarto. A quarter of the day; a shift or watch.
Despensa. Storeroom for food.
Empleado. Employee, servant.
Gallo. A rooster.
Gavilla. A method of hobbling a horse; see page 136.

Hacendado. The owner of a ranch or an estate.
Llano or Llano Estacado. The Staked Plains of New Mexico and Texas.
Los Gorras Blancas. An organization so named because its members wore white masks or hoods.
Manada. A herd of horses.
Mayordomo. The manager of a ranch.
Mesteñero. A mustang hunter.
Mesteño. Mustang, wild horse.
Milo maize. *Sesuto maile,* a sorghum grown as grain and forage for stock.
Morada. A Penitente chapel.
Panocha. Sprouted wheat pudding.
Parroquia. Parish church.
Partidas. Flocks of sheep. Each *partida* usually consisted of one thousand head.
Partido. A head of stock taken on shares.
Partidarios. Ranchers who took stock on a share basis.
Patrón. A landowner, employer, or "boss."
Penitentes. A religious group; see page 55.
Politico. Politician.
Reata. Rope, lariat.
Remuda. A string of horses.
Rico. A member of the wealthy class.
Rodeo. A cattle roundup.
Santeros. Makers of religious art.
Santos. Statues and paintings representing the saints.
Tasajo. Dried meat, jerky.
Tejano. Texan.
Vaquero. Cowboy, horseman.
Visita. A rural church without a resident priest.

INDEX

A

Aboulafia, Abraham, 111
Agostini, Juan, 86-88
Aguilar, N. M., 48
Alarid, 100, 103
Albuquerque, N. M., 84
Alvernhe, Father Simon, 79
Amarillo, Tex., 1, 40, 44, 66, 145
Anaya, Juan, 49
Antonchico, N. M., viii, 48, 54, 68, 71, 75, 77, 78, 79
Antonchico Grant, 77
Antonio Ortiz Grant, 80
Antonio Sandoval Land Grant, 76
Apodaca, Juan, 62
Aragón, Juan, 94
Aragón, Pablo, 79
Arapaho Indians, 65
Arroyo de Trujillo, Tex., 66, 71, 79
Atascosa, Tex., 66, 70, 71, 79

B

Baca. *See also* Cabeza de Baca
Baca, Aniceto, x
Baca, Celso, 75-76
Baca, José, x
Baca, José A., 86
Baca, José María, 124
Baca Location Number One, 81
Baca Location Number Two, 73
Baca, Doña María Ignacia, 68
Baca, Pablo, x
Baca, Paco, viii, 124, 125
Baca, Romualdo, 81-82, 84
Baca, Simón, x
Bell, Montgomery, 84-85
Bell Ranch, 69, 73
Benavídez, N. M., 133, 157
Benavídez, Miguel, 63-64
Billy the Kid, 121-22
Blanca, N. M., 67. *See also* Liberty, Tierra Blanca
Bosque Redondo, 49, 122, 194. *See also* Fort Sumner
Branch, Albert, 57
Buffalo, vii, viii-ix, 1, 2, 3, 24, 39-46, 47, 48, 50, 66, 67, 140, 145, 152
Bull Canyon, ix, 2, 78, 123

C

Caballeros de Labor, 89-90, 104
Carter brothers, 122-24
Cabañuelas, 12
Cabeza de Baca. *See also* Baca
Cabeza de Baca, Daniel, ix, 110

Cabeza de Baca, Gov. Ezequiel, 95, 96
Cabeza de Baca, Florencio, 119
Cabeza de Baca, Graciano (Papá), 7, 9, 10, 11, 14, 15, 16, 18, 23, 32-33, 36, 39, 57, 69, 74, 78, 95, 96, 126, 127, 128, 129, 131, 132, 133, 134, 136, 138, 145-49, 153, 154-55, 156, 161, 164, 167, 171-78
Cabeza de Baca, Father José de Jesús, 88
Cabeza de Baca, Don Luis María, 76-77, 80-81
Cabeza de Baca, Luis María IV, viii, 16, 18, 57, 81, 83, 93, 97, 123, 127-28, 132, 138, 139, 148, 152, 165, 167, 172, 174
Cabeza de Baca, Manuel, ix, 93, 95-96, 97, 100, 101, 102, 119, 120
Cabeza de Baca, Nestor, 172
Cabeza de Baca, Nicasio, 140-41
Cabeza de Baca, Tomás D., ix, 6, 20, 51, 72-73, 76-77, 78, 81, 83
Cabeza de Baca, Tomás Francisco, 78
Cabeza de Baca de Gallegos, Eloisa, 120
Cabra Spring, 2, 66
El Cachumeno, 97, 111, 112
Cañada Pastosa, N. M., 112
Canyon de Tule, Tex., 49, 66
Cedar Grove, N. M., 105
Chapels, 31, 39, 42, 53-55, 66, 68, 72, 74-76, 79, 81-83, 133-34, 145, 151, 168
Chaperito, N. M., 48, 51, 54
Chávez, Antonio, 61, 71
Chávez, Feliciano, 110
Chávez, Filomeno, 72

Chávez, Macario, 72
Chávez, Pedro, 72
Chávez y Chávez, José, 97, 100
Chihuahua Trail, viii, 10, 76
Chisum, John, 49
Chupaina Mesa, 49
Churches, *see* Chapels
Clayton, N. M., 63, 71
Comanche Indians, 3-4, 44, 47-50, 67, 124, 140, 152, 159
Conchas, N. M., 66, 145
Conchas Dam, 68, 74, 174
Corridos, 7, 24, 44
Cuervo, N. M., 66, 72, 75, 134, 145

D

Delgado, Cirilo, 93
Delgado, Felipe, 74
Delgado, Francisco, 83
Delgado, Juan, 74
Delgado, Lorenzo, 124
Delgado de Baca, Doña Estéfana, 59
Democratic Party, 91, 96, 165
Desmarais, Miguel, 81
Dilia, N. M., 63

E

Echols, George, 122-24
El Chirisco, N. M., 135
El Coyote, N. M., 112, 118
Elkins, Stephen, 84
El Paso, Tex., 60, 82, 140
El Valle, N. M., 74, 89, 125, 133
El Vegoso, N. M., 93
Encinias, Benito, 74
Endee, N. M., 70, 73

Esquibel, Higinio, 72
Esquibel, Refugio, 104, 117

F

Fayet, Father John B., 77
Ferrari, Father Enrique, 83
Flor de la Peña, 100, 101, 114, 116
Flores, Gregorio, 72
Fort Sumner, N. M., 121, 122. *See also* Bosque Redondo
Frank, William, 106-07

G

Galindre, Capt. José L., 102
Gallegos, Antonio José, 124
Gallegos, Cruz, 73
Gallegos, Emeterio, 71
Gallegos, Isidoro, 74
Gallegos, Juan, 94, 95
Gallegos, Merejildo, 62
Gallegos de Baca, Doña Luisa, 61
Galon, Father Juan B., 79
García de Chávez, Doña Jesusita, 61, 71
García y Apodaca, Don Pablo, 71
Garita, N. M., 145
Garrett, Pat, 122
Gentlemen of Labor, 89-90, 104
Glorieta Mesa, 110
Gonzáles, Don José, 135, 137
Gonzáles, José, 129
Gonzáles, Hilario, 31, 57, 68, 69, 70, 71, 74
Gonzáles, Teodoro, 135, 137
Los Gorras Blancas, 89, 90, 92
Grant, General Ulysses S., 70
Gurulé, Plácido, 62

H

Hayes, President Rutherford B., 70
Hermit's Peak, 86, 87, 88
Hernández, Pablo, 83
Herstein, Levi, 62
Homestead Act, Enlarged, 147, 176

J

Jesuit College, 82, 96
Jesuit Fathers, 82, 83

K

Kansas City, Mo., 123, 140, 174
Kearny, General Stephen W., 176
Ketchum, Black Jack, 62-63

L

La Cienega, N. M., 69, 124
La Concepción, N. M., 89
La Cuesta, N. M., 77
La Liendre, N. M., 51, 52, 60, 65, 69, 90, 95, 110
La Manga, N. M., 74
Land grants, 69, 73, 76, 77, 80, 81, 86, 135, 144, 145, 176
La Peña Blanca, N. M., 76, 80, 81
Las Colonias, N. M., 75, 124
Las Gallinas, N. M., 86, 87, 88
Las Salinas, Tex., 63, 66, 71, 79
Las Vegas, N. M., 1, 2, 5, 36, 39, 41, 51, 52, 53, 54, 55, 58, 61, 68, 69, 70, 71, 73, 80-88, 89, 93, 94, 95, 96, 97, 98, 99, 100, 103, 104, 105, 109, 111, 113, 114, 118, 120, 122, 129, 133, 134, 137, 140, 141, 176

Las Vegas Land Grant, 81, 86
El Lechuza, 97, 99, 100, 101, 113
Leyba, Father José Francisco, 76
Liberal, Kan., 140
Liberty, N. M., 55, 61, 62. *See also* Blanca, Tierra Blanca
Lincoln, N. M., 71
Lincoln County War, 79
Logan, N. M., 71, 173
López, Francisco, 69, 70, 74
López, Juan, 74
López, Lorenzo, 69
López, Luciano, 74, 89, 90
Loretto Academy, 99
Loretto, Sisters of, 84
Los Alamitos, N. M., 66, 72
Los Alamos, San Miguel Cty., N. M., 100, 106, 107, 108, 109, 111, 112, 113, 118, 119
Los Alamos, Los Alamos Cty., N. M., 81
Los Esteritos, N. M., 63
Los Valles de San Agustín, 110
Lucero, Antonio, 96
Lucero, Cecilio, 94-95
Luciano Mesa, 2, 3, 46, 66, 123

M

Maes, Manuel, 44
Maes, Patricio, 104
Maestas, Germán, 108, 109
Maestas, Rosa, 108
Marra, Father José, 83
Martínez, Benigno, 94-95
Martínez, Bruno, 74
Martínez, Mrs. Domitilo, 86, 88
Martínez, Eduardo, 75
Martínez, Felix, 96
Martínez, Pablo, 72
Martínez, Sabino, 72
Martínez, Tomás, 109-10
McCleod, General, 78-79
Medrán, 106, 119
El Mellado, 99, 106, 108, 118
Mesa Redonda, ix, 46, 143
Mesa Redonda Brothers, 143
Mesa Rica, 19, 28, 30, 46, 74, 156, 157
Montoya, N. M., 72, 74, 75, 123, 144-45, 160
Montoya, Mariano, 71
Montoya, Pablo, 69
Mora, N. M., 68, 70, 113, 119
El Moro, 97, 106, 118

N

Nara Visa, N. M., 66
Newkirk, N. M., ix, 72, 74, 124, 134
New Mexico Highlands University, 105
Norton, N. M., ix
Nueve Millas, N. M., 66, 72

O

Ojo de la Mula, 69, 70
Ojo del Carnero, 66, 71
El Ojo del Espiritu Santo, 80
Ojo del Llano, N. M., 66, 72
Old Mesilla, N. M., 88
Ortega, Vidal, 164
Otero, Lorenzo, 72
Otero de García, Doña Lola, viii, 61
Ozark Trail, 154

P

Pablo Montoya Grant, 69, 144
Paez, Narciso, 19, 34, 35, 37
Palomas Mesa, 2, 3, 70
Palo Duro Canyon, 1, 41, 49, 67
El Partido de la Unión, 90-92
El Partido del Pueblo, 89
El Patas de Mico, 106
El Patas de Rana, 117, 118
Patrón, Juan, 79
Peña Blanca, 76, 80, 81
Penitentes, 55-56, 72
People's Party, 89
Plaza Larga, N. M., 25, 37, 50, 61, 66, 67, 71, 72
Perea, Don José Leandro, 73
El Puertas, 124-25
Puerto de Luna, N. M., 30, 51, 54, 71, 79, 125, 133, 168

Q

Quay, N. M., 62
Quintana, Juan José, 46
Quintana, Juan María, 33, 36

R

Railroads, 54, 55, 75, 96, 140-45, 147, 173
Red River Chronicle, The, 69
Regis College, 82
Republican Party, 91, 165
La Revista Católica, 82, 83
Revuelto, N. M., 20, 34, 37, 72, 79
Rito Blanco, Tex., 71
Romero, Casimiro, 70
Romero, Eugenio, 69
Romero, Hilario, 48, 110
Romero, Miguel, 81
Romero, Don Pedro, 74
Romero, Pedro, 108-09
Romero, Rafael, 119
Romero, Román, 69
Romero, Trinidad, 69-70
Romeroville, N. M., 70, 103
El Romo, 105
Roosevelt, Col. Theodore, 129
Rossi, Father Alfonso, 83

S

St. Michael's College, 96
Saiz, Carpio, 105
Saladito, N. M., 37, 67, 72
Salcedo, Manuel, vii, 17, 18, 19, 21, 22, 28, 34, 38
Salcedo, Rosa, 34, 38
Sandoval, Agapito, 70
Sandoval, Gabriel, 98, 99, 100, 101, 102, 103, 113
San Hilario, N. M., 30, 31, 35, 36, 38, 68, 70, 71, 74
San Jon, N. M., 67
San Lorenzo, N. M., 19, 30, 32, 35, 36, 68, 69, 70, 74, 79
San Miguel, N. M., 54, 76
San Miguel del Vado, N. M., 77, 80
Santa Fe, N. M., 52, 61, 69, 78, 81, 84, 96, 110, 124
Santa Rosa, N. M., 76, 79, 140, 143-44, 145, 155
Sena, José, 83
Sherman, Gen. William, 70
Silva, Emma, 98-101, 103, 111-13

Silva, Doña Telesfora Sandoval y. *See* Vicente Silva
Silva, Vicente, 92-108, 111-120
Sisneros, Dionicio, 106
La Sociedad de Bandidos de Nuevo Mexico, 119
Spear Bar Ranch, 9, 128, 148
Stutzman, Jacob, 111

T

Tafoya, Felipe, 33
Tafoya, José, 71
Tafoya, Miguel, 71
Taos, N. M., 65, 113, 114
Tascosa, Tex., 66, 70, 71, 79
Thurman, H. L., 123-24
Tierra Blanca, N. M., 49, 61, 67. *See also* Liberty, Blanca
Tlascalan Indians, 76
Trinidad, Colo., 54
Trujillo, Antonio, 64-65
Trujillo, Jesús María, 71
Trujillo, Julian, 97, 100
Tucumcari, N. M., 2, 55, 67, 72, 79, 144, 145
Tule, Tex., 49, 66
Twitchell, Ralph Emerson, 96

U

Union Party, 90-91
Urioste, Mariano, 51-52, 140

V

Valle de Lágrimas, 49
Valle Grande, 73, 81
Vialpando, Jesús, 108-09, 110
Vigil, Apolinar, 72
Vigil, Doroteo, 74
Vigil, Francisco, 74
Vigil, Manuel, 74
Vigil, Santiago, 125
La Voz del Pueblo, 96

W

Watrous, N. M., 94, 118

X

XIT Syndicate, 17

The Mexican American

An Arno Press Collection

Castañeda, Alfredo, et al, eds. **Mexican Americans and Educational Change.** 1974
Church Views of the Mexican American. 1974
Clinchy, Everett Ross, Jr. **Equality of Opportunity for Latin-Americans in Texas.** 1974
Crichton, Kyle S. **Law and Order Ltd.** 1928
Education and the Mexican American. 1974
Fincher, E. B. **Spanish-Americans as a Political Factor in New Mexico, 1912-1950.** 1974
Greenwood, Robert. **The California Outlaw:** Tiburcio Vasquez. 1960
Juan N. Cortina: Two Interpretations. 1974
Kibbe, Pauline R. **Latin Americans in Texas.** 1946
The Mexican American and the Law. 1974
Mexican American Bibliographies. 1974
Mexican Labor in the United States. 1974
The New Mexican Hispano. 1974
Otero, Miguel Antonio. **Otero:** An Autobiographical Trilogy. 1935/39/40
The Penitentes of New Mexico. 1974
Perales, Alonso S. **Are We Good Neighbors?** 1948
Perspectives on Mexican-American Life. 1974
Simmons, Ozzie G. **Anglo-Americans and Mexican Americans in South Texas.** 1974
Spanish and Mexican Land Grants. 1974
Tuck, Ruth D. **Not With the Fist.** 1946
Zeleny, Carolyn. **Relations Between the Spanish-Americans and Anglo-Americans in New Mexico.** 1974